UNDERSTANDING SARKAR

INTERNATIONAL COMPARATIVE SOCIAL STUDIES

VOLUME III

UNDERSTANDING SARKAR

The Indian Episteme, Macrohistory and Transformative Knowledge

BY

SOHAIL INAYATULLAH

BRILL
LEIDEN · BOSTON · KÖLN
2002

This book is printed on acid-free paper.

Die Deutsche Bibliothek – CIP-Einheitsaufnahme

Understanding Sarkar : the Indian episteme, macrohistory and transforma-
tive knowledge/ by Sohail Inayatullah. – Leiden ; Boston; Köln :
Brill, 2002
   (International comparative social studies ; Vol. 3)
   ISBN 90–04–12193–5

Library of Congress Cataloging-in-Publication Data

Library of Congress Cataloging-in-Publication Data is also available

ISSN   1568-4474
ISBN   90 04 12193 5

TABLE OF CONTENTS

ACKNOWLEDGEMENTS

The writing of this book spans three decades. The initial chapters were first written in the late 1980s in Hawaii, the final writing and editing in this millennium in Brisbane and Mooloolaba, Australia. My gratitude to the many who helped me with this project is surpassed by the extent of their aid. In the initial phases, Gregory Sugimoto, Joy Labez, Anna Wilson-Yue, Phil McNally, James Monma, Mitch Yamasaki, Louise Ohara-Bninski and Many Ann Teshima, provided personal warmth and support, as well as interesting discussions. Moreover, they patiently listened to me talk endlessly of Sarkar and poststructuralism. Darlene Yamauchi provided support—conversation and dinners—when it was most needed. Julie Schoen graciously edited the entire first draft of this book. Young Hee Lee provided care during the endless edits in Hawaii.

Of course, a deeper intellectual debt goes to my father, Inayatullah who guided us early on during youth with lectures on international relations. My mother, Zubeda, through her sufi mysticism provided the spiritual context. Naeem Inayatullah read this book proposal during his honeymoon in Kauai and was instrumental in reconfiguring it. Dada Maheshvarananda read an earlier version word for word and provided valuable criticisms and Dada Daneshananda constantly reminded me that beyond discourse are not other discourses, but real human suffering. Shalini Bhatnagar helped me understand Indian history.

Professors at the University of Hawaii, where this project first grew were all kind and brilliant, a wonderful mixture. James Dator, Michael Shapiro, Peter Manicas, Bob Stauffer, Robert Bobilin, and, of course, Johan Galtung. Without any of the above, this book would not have been possible. But it was Galtung who challenged me to place Sarkar on the global intellectual map; he encouraged me to pursue Sarkar's project when I had doubts and he provided great criticism and personal support. My gratitude to the above can never end, only grow.

In the 1990s, I am in debt to colleagues and staff at the Communication Center, Queensland University of Technology. In particular, Tony Stevenson, Jenny Worthington, Susan Leggett and Lyn Simpson.

Architect Daniela Minerba provided tables depicting sadvipra evolution. The final act of transformation—in 2001—goes to David L. Wright, who painstakingly edited the entire manuscript once again.

Joed Elich has been a wonderful publisher.

On a final personal note, my wife, Ivana Milojevic, was incredibly supportive in the endless rewrites, and my children, Saim and Mariyam, as long as they received dessert and computer time to play their cd-roms, were helpful as well.

I remain in debt to all those who helped, but especially to "the mysterious traveler," who has provided the microvita that has made all this possible.

CHAPTER ONE

INTRODUCING SARKAR

We are proceeding towards effulgence from darkness, from imperfection along the golden steps to perfection. No obstacle on the way will be able to stop our advancement. Pushing aside and smashing all obstacles and impediments we will move along our destined path. Our ideological rationality is our valuable asset, the blissful glow of macrocosmic effulgence is our goal and the inherent desire to bring well-being to all living creatures is our way. Moving ahead is the very wont of life. Wasting valuable time in lethargy is nothing but inertness; hence we must keep moving. The chant of our forward movement will be the very expression of our vocality, the very pulsation of our life.

P.R. Sarkar, *Full Moon of May Message*, 1989[1]

The Rational is the Real

Embedded in the words of Prabhat Rainjan Sarkar's message is a notion of linear time, a notion that tomorrow can be better than today. His message is meant to inspire individuals to imagine a new future and to move towards it. It is not incidental that the message is given on the full moon of May, for Sarkar also lived in the cyclical time of antiquity, not solely in the quantitative linear time of modernity. The full moon is not simply another day for Sarkar, rather, it is a day that evokes and recovers historical meanings. The full moon is of the cycle—of the rise and fall, of the waxing and waning of life, of civilization. Yet there is a linearity, a movement from darkness to light, from ignorance to knowledge, from imbalance to balance, to *prama*.

This notion of opposites is central to Sarkar's metaphysics. Like other dialectical thinkers, Sarkar asserts that obstacles lead to individual and societal growth. They are a necessity. Challenges lead to

---

[1] Prabhat Rainjan Sarkar is also known as Shri Shri Anandamurti, his spiritual name, which means in whose presence one realizes bliss. He uses this name for his spiritual talks. Sarkar gave a biannual message, one the first of the year and one his birthday celebration in May. In general, Ananda Marga Publications presents his spiritual texts with his spiritual name and his social and political texts with his family name. As much as possible, we follow this division in our bibliography.

responses: to the resolution of conflicts, for what is, is essentially ripe
with opposites, with complimentary contradictions.

This move from darkness to light is not solely a mystical move,
it is not the traditional dichotomy of the sun as the rational and the
moon as the irrational, the sun as the conscious surface and the
moon as the unconscious deep. Rather, Sarkar's project is not to
leave the rationality of scientific modernity for the irrationality of
the religious, rather, it is the creation of a new rationality that
attempts to reconcile traditional dilemmas between spiritual and
material, scientific and mystical, individual and collective, structure
and agency. His rationality is centered not only on humans though,
an integral part of the rational is pure, undefined and unbounded
Consciousness. Finally, his rationality is not one that excludes the
environment of animate and inanimate beings normally thought of
as *un*living, rather, it includes all living creatures.

His rationality is grounded in a universal humanism, what Sarkar
calls neo-humanism, a new humanism that has as its goal a consciousness that cannot be described, but which can be personally
experienced as blissful, as beyond pleasure and pain. The grammar
of the "blissful" is central in Sarkar's cosmology, for it is that state
of mind that is the end all of existence. It is not the accumulation of
wealth, beauty, knowledge or wisdom, rather it is a state of unity
wherein distinctions between subject-object no longer exist, where
the mind moves in a continuous flow of unconditional love. The
location of the preferred or the good in the blissful also ties Sarkar
into the Indian spiritual and philosophical tradition. In this tradition,
the goal of life is not the attainment of a specific quality—virtue,
beauty, patience or goodness—but the location of self in a state of
no-qualities, what, then, positively has been called, *ananda* or bliss.

This state of bliss is not the social utopia associated with the
European Enlightenment, rather it is the eupsychia of the individual. For instance, for Hegel the ideal state is that of Being realizing
itself through the vehicle of the nation. For Sarkar, the vehicle is
the individual. A good society is one that manages to represent harmoniously the spiritual needs of its individuals (Carspecken, 1987, 29).

From the traditional Tantric shamanistic perspective, the problem
with the construction of the good has been the problem of what
William Irwin Thompson (1976) calls misplaced concreteness. The
real cannot be translated into institutions such as "God," "nation,"
or "society." Thus, the tantrica has consciously remained on the
fringe, unintelligible to all—silent, naked, and disruptive. However,

Sarkar as a mystic does not seek unintelligibility. Unlike the left branch of Tantra, he does not seek to disrupt all pieties. Sarkar is unlike the Tantric yogi who lives naked, unconcerned with body, food, manners, gender, government and economy. Nor does Sarkar advocate that one sleep with one's mother, defile one's sister, and rest one's feet on the head of one's guru (Garrison, 1983). Rather he breaks with this perspective and argues that his philosophy and the movements he has begun are consciously and eminently rational.

The rational is the real, it is that which leads to the spiritual, to the maximization of individual and collective "happiness" and a minimization of pain. The irrational is not the right brain and the "intuitive" of the New Age spiritual movement, it is not counterposed to the rationality of modernity. Rather to Sarkar, modernity is the irrational for it exists within a grid of the geopolitical. That is, it exists within a network of nations, religions and ideologies that have as a goal the finite, the limited and thus the dogmatic. Modernity exists within a grid of discursive identity that necessitates an opposite. For example, identity in one nation means non-identity in another; identity in one religion means non-identity in another; and, identity in one gender means non-identity in another. For Sarkar, the rational must be an identity that is all embracing, the ultimate real. Being itself. His philosophical point of departure, Tantra, then is the struggle to break out of all boundaries, to dialectically transcend the limits of what is, and to move to a location where one exists in the presence of the spirit, not the nation, or as Sarkar states it, any "ism."

At the same time, Sarkar participates in the traditional religious discourse that claims a more profound revelation of truth that is not irrational nor arational. Rather, it is the truth and thus, a priori rational and, of course, natural. Unfortunately, the frames of meaning of modernity have hidden or distorted these alternative spiritual frames of meaning as escapes from the real, refusals of the sensate world, or as pre-historical and pre-scientific (Nandy, 1987). But this is to be expected, as for Sarkar, everything that exists, moves in cyclical and pulsating patterns. The banishment of the spiritual from modern life is part of *his* reason of being. His mission was to recover these vanquished meanings and at the same time to reinterpret them to create a new tomorrow.

It is through this reinterpretation that Sarkar separates himself from conventional constructions of Hinduism or the Indian condition or indeed the religious. Like the Protestant ethic of the West

and Bushido of Japan, Sarkar has articulated a code of behavior
that is amenable to economic growth, to a dynamism, to an innovative based distribution discourse that acknowledges the value of
differences between individuals. For him, economic equity is a goal,
the intellectual and existential sameness of totalitarianism is not. Yet
Sarkar does not neglect the distribution formula of the democratic
socialists. Through his theory of political-economy, he argues for a
limit to wealth accumulation and a progressive distribution of wealth.
Central to his alternative political economy is his location of the spiritual and the intellectual in the language of resources. They are assets
that contribute to the good society; most of humanity's present
predicaments are caused by their misuse and under-use. At the same
time, Sarkar distances himself from conventional New Age utopian
spiritual thinking.

Sarkar believes that individuals make a critical mistake by arguing that the transpersonal is similar to the pre-ego state (Wilber,
1998), the archetype for Jung, myth for Joseph Campbell (Towsey,
1986). The transpersonal is not a return to the Freudian id: it is not
that type of unrestricted and undisciplined primitive freedom. For
Sarkar, there is a dialectical progression from the crude mind (located
in the senses) to the ego mind (located in the intellect) and the
transpersonal causal mind (located outside of brain in the collective
mind). The solution to modernity is not the return to the primitive,
the shamanistic, or a return of the ancient gods. It is the building
of a new spiritual rationality. Consciousness has already emerged
with the breakdown of the bicameral mind, one cannot return to
pre-consciousness, to an inability to distinguish personal thoughts
with the voices of Gods (Jaynes, 1982). For Sarkar, the movement
now is to a deeper layer of mind that is increasingly abstract and
grounded in bliss, the body and intellect are mere tools for this level
of mind.

In addition, unlike the historical Indian, "hindu" conception, he
does not simply place the attainment of bliss—of the eternal—as the
sole goal of life. Rather, by calling for movement in individual and
community life, in calling for change, he questions philosophies that
are solely other-worldly oriented. But like the ancients, this movement
is a chant still, a word that represents the real, the ultimate Real
and its realization by symbolic participation in it. For unlike other
philosophers, Sarkar is also located in the guru discourse. The world
is known not solely through the intellect, but it is also divinely
revealed through spiritual practices and through devotion to the Other,

the Supreme. Moreover, he is perceived by the faithful as omni-scient, one who can give boons to the true. He can as well bestow healing and powers upon individuals through his power—a power that comes from the touch, the sight, the presence and the word—and more importantly can lead others to enlightenment, to *moksa*.

Sarkar then should not be read only as an intellectual nor should he be seen only as a mystic. Indeed, there are many sites in which we can place him. Unfortunately, most of our situating practices come from Western categories. What language does one have for someone who is guru, mystic, political philosopher, linguist, histo-rian, social movement leader, to mention a few categories. Genius, of course, would simply be a description that privileges the intellec-tual construction of the real, guru privileges the spiritual dimension, and movement leader, the activist, praxis dimension. Much of this book is an attempt to find a location for Sarkar inside and outside his own Indian tradition. In addition to comparative analysis, we ask whom does he speak to? While he often remains in the devotional discourse, he also speaks to the intellectual, the revolutionary, and the movement organizer. But ultimately, the audience for Sarkar's discourse is humanity as whole for his mission is to create a new culture, a new discourse, a new cosmology.

Sarkar's Organizing Concepts

To do so, a new map of knowledge is required that frames self, soci-ety, Other, nature and the transcendental. One way to think about this is to imagine Sarkar's scheme as if it were a library. Instead of floors on government documents, the humanities, social sciences and science (as in conventional libraries), he redesigns the real around the following orderings of knowledge, floors, if you will: *Tantra* (Intuitional Science); *Brahmacakra* (cosmology, the evolutionary link between matter and mind); Bio-Psychology (the individual body and mind); PROUT (specifically, the social cycle, economic growth and just/rational distribution, and the *sadvipra*, or spiritual leadership); Coordinated Cooperation (gender in history and the future); Neo-Humanism; and, Microvita (the new sciences and health). Certainly a library as constituted by Sarkar's categories would be dramatically different from current libraries. Thus it is not only that Sarkar adds specific data, information, and knowledge to current fields of dis-course, but he offers a new rendering of what constitutes reality.

Understanding Sarkar then is not merely a technical concern of asking what are Sarkar's specific additions to contemporary discourse but asking what are the categories Sarkar himself uses to see the world. Issues of validity therefore must be seen in a dialogical framework, using current categories to understand Sarkar's truth claims but understanding as well how Sarkar transcends the current knowledge of humanity and gives rise to new orderings of knowledge. In this book, we hope to accomplish this ordering by understanding the epistemic context of his work, from the Indian episteme and from other civilizational epistemes.

Generally, Sarkar's intent was and is (his organizations continue his work) to create a global spiritual socialist/cooperative revolution, a new renaissance in thought, language, music, arts, economics and culture. His goal was, and still is, to infuse individuals with a spiritual presence, the necessary first step in changing the way that we know and order our world. Sarkar differs from the socialists of the past who merely sought to capture state power—forgetting that the economy was global and thus in the long run strengthening the world capitalist system. He also differs from utopian idealists who merely wished for perfect moral places that could not practically exist as well as from spiritualists who only sought individual transformation at the expense of the collective, of humanity. He has a far more comprehensive view of transformation. His model of change is spiritual yet concerned with issues of economic growth, global yet committed to local and regional diversity, and, socialistic yet based on cooperative economic democracy.

To create such a future, he has developed multiple strategies of transformation. These include: individual transformation through the Tantric process of meditation; the enhancement of individual health through yoga practices that balance one's hormonal system; moral transformation through social service and care for the most vulnerable; economic transformation through the theory of PROUT and *samaj*—or people's movements, as well as through self-reliant master units or ecological centres; political transformation through the articulation of the concept of the *sadvipra*, the spiritual-moral leader, and the creation of such leaders through struggle with the materialistic capitalistic system and immoral national/local leaders; cultural transformation through the creation of new holidays and celebrations that contest traditional nationalistic sacred time-space places (such as Childrens' Day) and through the recovery of the world's spiritual cultures as well as through the establishment of Third World social movements that contest the organisational hegemony of Western organisations; language transformation through the elucidation of a new encyclopedia of the Bengali language and through working for linguistic rights for the world's minorities; religious transformation through upholding the spiritual reality that unites us all while contesting patriarchal and dogmatic dimensions of the world's religions; scientific transformation by rethinking science as noetic science as well as laying bare the materialistic and instrumentalist prejudices of conventional science; and temporal transformation by envisioning long range futures and designing strategies for centuries and future generations to come.

Obviously such a broad range of transformative strategies must be both deep and shallow. As writer Roar Bjonnes argues in *Transcending Boundaries: P.R. Sarkar's Theories of Individual and Social Transformation* (Inayatullah and Fitzgerald, 1999: 121–130), such a transformation must offer a new story of who we are and who we can be that is more satisfying than conventional institutionalized religions or the ideologies of capitalism and communism offer. But a new mythology must also tell us about the details of living day to day. Sarkar does this through his practice of 'sixteen points' that address issues of cleanliness, inner balance, spiritual direction and service to others.

But while Sarkar's movements challenge the modern project of humanism and scientific rationality, his re-enchantment of the world does not place us anchorless in a world of unbridled diversity. As Maori activist Ramana Williams argues (Inayatullah and Fitzgerald, 1999: 155–166), Sarkar remains ever situated in the rational, however, he does redefine the rational as that which reduces human suffering, not the rational *qua* instrumentality. Even as Sarkar expands our communicative community by including microvita, the divine, animals, plants as well as those outside the imperium of power— that is he unleashes diversity—he does not create a totally horizontal world where there are no levels or dimensions. There is a hierarchy of consciousness in Sarkar's thought, the layers of mind or *kosas*. Thus, as ethicist Jennifer Fitzgerald argues, Sarkar is not a postmodernist (Inayatullah and Fitzgerald, 1999: 61–78). Sarkar has an ethical base, the yogic principles of *yama* and *niyama*. These principles of morality provide the base for Sarkar's worldview. They include such principles as non-stealing, non-violence, seeing the divine in everything, truth for benevolence, simple/modest living, inner contentment, service to others, study of spiritual texts for the deeper meaning of the real, and moving towards the supreme. These principles help purify one's actions so that spiritual practice is possible.

In addition to the ethical as his base, Sarkar gives us the following concepts that are essential to his alternative paradigm: Tantra, Neo-Humanism, PROUT, Coordinated Cooperation, and Microvita.

Tantra is the ontological position that Sarkar takes. It is the spiritual foundation underneath his social and political theory. Based on India's indigenous culture, Tantra means to liberate oneself from crudeness. Unlike other spiritual approaches, Tantra involves individual and social struggle—it is not a passive spirituality. In addition, Tantra stresses the practical experience of inner transformation as opposed to the religious textualism associated with the Vedas, India's other spiritual tradition.

The social expression of the mystical cosmology of Tantra is Neo-Humanism. Sarkar's theory of Neo-Humanism aims to relocate the self from ego (and the pursuit of individual maximization), from family (and the pride of genealogy), from geo-sentiments (attachments to land and nation), from socio-sentiments (attachments to class, race and community), from humanism (the human being as the centre of the universe) to Neo-Humanism (love and devotion for all, inanimate and animate, beings of the universe). As the intellect is liberated from these bondages of ego and other identities, there arises: (1) higher and higher degrees of empathy and compassion; (2) increased commitment to social equality instead of ego-pleasure; (3) increased levels of unity with the Other, and (4) a re-identification of the self with the Cosmos.

Paramount is the construction of self in an ecology of reverence for life not a modern/secular politics of cynicism. Spiritual devotion to the universe is ultimately the greatest treasure that humans have. It is this treasure that must be excavated and shared by all living beings.

Pictorial 1: Sarkar's Neo-Humanism—The Liberation of the Intellect

The central framework for his Neo-Humanistic perspective is his Progressive Utilization Theory. PROUT encompasses Sarkar's theory of history and social change, his theory of leadership and the vanguard of the new world he envisions, as well as his alternative political economy. Sarkar's theoretical framework is not only spiritual or only concerned with the material world, rather his perspective argues that the real is physical, mental and spiritual. Concomitantly, the motives for historical change are struggle with the environment (the move from the *shudra*/worker era to the *ksattriya*/warrior era),

Pictorial 1: Sarkar's Neo-Humanism

neo-humanism
(love and respect for all beings, animate and inanimate, in the universe)

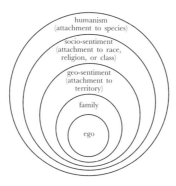

struggle with ideas (the move from the warrior to the *vipra*/intellectual), struggle with the environment and ideas (the move from the intellectual era to the *vaeshya*/capitalist eras) and the spiritual attraction of the Great, the call of the infinite. Thus physical, mental and spiritual challenges create change. The structure of historical change is the four stages of history: the Shudra era, the Ksattriya era, the Vipra era, and the Vaeshyan era. At the end of the acquisitive era of the Vaeshyans, there is a transition to the new Shudra era, either by revolution or evolution.

Table 1

The Stages of the Social Cycle		
Shudra	Worker	Dominated by Environment
Ksattriya	Warrior	Struggles with and dominates Environment
Vipra	Intellectual	Struggles with and dominates Ideas
Vaeshya	Capitalist	Struggles with and dominates Environment/ Ideas

Sarkar thus gives a cyclical view of history. However, through the ideal form of leadership, *sadvipra leadership*—one that is inclusive of the economic (exchange), the cultural (ideas), the warrior, and is populist—the exploitive, degenerating, dimensions of the cycle can be eliminated, thus creating a spiral. Thus Sarkar intends a good society that retains its contradictions, not a perfect society wherein diversity is eliminated. Sarkar gives us an elegant theory of history and future in which neither the linearity of progress nor the fatalism of history dominate.

Pictorial 2: Historical Social Cycle and Ideal-Future Social Cycle

Central to creating a good society then is the creation of individuals with balanced and complete mind. For Sarkar, crucial to comprehensiveness, of regaining dynamism, is for women to regain their voice. "How can a bird fly with one wing?" he asks. This process of regaining one's authenticity, however, is not merely social, but also hormonal and spiritual. As poet Ananda Gaorii Avadhutika argues, "Both females and males need to be liberated from the [limits of their gender] in order for there to be true equality between the sexes in society in terms of mutual respect of gender differences, and [an] egalitarian outlook in terms of social roles" (Inayatullah and Fitzgerald, 1999: 49–60). Women's liberation is thus not only about political and economic power but also about transcending imposed biological gender limitations. The challenge of the future, however, is to work together to create a socially just spiritual society, what Sarkar calls coordinated cooperation.

Equally important to the social, is the personal. For Sarkar, social transformation comes first from adopting a different metaphor of *who* we are—he suggests the family on a caravan, where members take care of each other and there is clear movement towards a given direction. As important is for individuals to change themselves. Sarkar offers meditation and yoga as suggested paths. Bio-psychology, the science of emotions, the glands and the *chakras*, is Sarkar's theorizing of individuals' physical, emotional and spiritual health.

While Sarkar gives us social and spiritual theory, the goal of his work is a new universalism, a cosmic universalism. History for Sarkar is partly the attraction of the Great, the move to higher and higher levels of organization. But the move to the universal, to world government does not mean a loss of the local. Indeed, Sarkar intends to localize and democratize economies, allowing as much decentralization as possible. But local cultures and economies often suffer from a fear of the Other, especially when they become coopted in national politics. Neighbourhood love becomes violence to the 'Other'. Thus for Sarkar, universalism means local bioregional economic zones based on the ideas that we are world citizens.

Pictorial 2: Historical and Ideal-Future

HISTORICAL

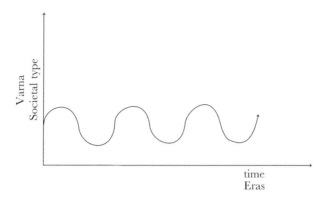

IDEAL-FUTURE

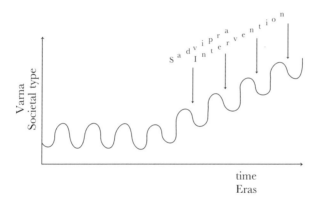

Microvita is the organizing concept that provides a link between the spiritual and the physical. Microvita are the software of consciousness just as atoms are the hardware, argues Andrew Diver (Inayatullah and Fitzgerald, 1999: 209–222). They are both ideas and the material, what many have called spiritual vibration in colloquial language. Positive microvita enhance one's own health and can create the conditions for a better society. They are related to one's thoughts but are also external, that is, microvita move around the universe shaping ideas and the material world. Microvita are not dead but alive, and can be used for spiritual betterment. Microvita provide a link between ideational and materialistic worldviews. They help explain the placebo effect in medicine (through attracting positive microvita) as well as psychic healing (the transfer of microvita from one person to another). However, the existence of microvita is still hypothetical. Even as they potentially advance the goal of scientific understanding (challenging the materialistic paradigm) they must yet be empirically verified.

Of course, there are other important concepts in Sarkar's thought. Noteworthy are his theories of pedagogy, particularly children's education, and the establishment of the modernized Indian Gurukul system (a schooling system that can enhance a child's physical, emotional, mental, leadership, moral and spiritual development). For Sarkar, morality, spirituality, humanity and a blending of extroverted science and introverted philosophy constitute the very foundation of his system of education.

Even though Sarkar has contributed to nearly every human field of knowledge, it was the spiritual that was central to him. It is the recovery and rearticulation of the spiritual that is Sarkar's greatest contribution to humanity. It is this devotion, the love of self, Other, nature, universe and the divine that is the centre of his project. Ultimately then, even as Sarkar gives us new theories of individuals and social transformation, he himself seeks to transcend these boundaries. Our challenge in this book is to understand, contextualize, and situate these theoretical moves.

Biography and Cosmology

In attempting to understand Sarkar's cosmology, we must first survey his life story, as he tells it. While born in Bihar, India on May 1921 (and died in Calcutta, October, 1990), fortunately or unfortunately, his response when asked by his students and followers as to the meaning of his life, was cryptic. His much-quoted response is: "I was a mystery, I am a mystery, I will remain a mystery" (Kalynesvarananda Avadhuta, 1986, 11). Understanding this statement is problematic. It may be a spiritual statement, that great souls cannot be captured by earthly discourses. Alternatively, it may be a textual strategy to keep the self elusive, not being captured by discourse. Or it may be an effort to state that the truth of Being cannot be intellectually explained or understood for the will to under-standing leads to a distortion of being and truth itself. Specifically, this assertion places him outside of conventional discourses and allows for the creation of a new mythology.

The other way to extract the problem of identity is to see whom Sarkar aligns himself with. In his writings we find him speaking to those who are central to the Indian philosophical discourse such as, Shankaracharya, Sidhartha Guatama, Maharishi Kapil, Caetanya Mahaprabhu, Rabindranath Tagore, Subash Chandra Bose, and Mahatama Ghandi, among others. But specifically he speaks of two figures: Shiva and Krishna. To him, both were extra-historical figures. They existed empirically, but they played a grand and mythological role in righting the balance of the world. Like other philosophers who speak from the ancient, classical episteme, the rise and fall of *Dharma*, the truth or the way, is among the central theoretical con-structs of history.

According to Sarkar, both Shiva and Krishna were figures who brought about a cultural renaissance in their time and, more sig-nificantly, fought against evil and for righteousness. Both endured incredible trials and traumas and both were eventually victorious in their battles. While Sarkar does not compare himself to these two historical figures, it is noteworthy that Sarkar as well initiated numer-ous renaissance movements and also asserts that the most critical task is that of bringing truth in to the world. He too has been a controversial figure in India. He spent seven years in prison. His organizations were all banned by Prime Minister Indira Ghandi in 1975; all his schools and other projects closed; monks and nuns bru-talized; and numerous nations refused him entry. Followers believe this was because of his spiritual activism and moral courage and crit-ics believe that he was refused entry because of violent acts allegedly committed by some of his followers during the Indian Emergency (Schneider, 1983).

For Sarkar, Shiva was exemplary in that he aided in the epochal transition from humans as animals qua survival of the fittest, to humans as family qua social responsibility. In addition, he system-atized spiritual activities (for example, the stages of meditation), invented dance and composed music.

Krishna had two main roles. The first was to bring about a spir-itual transformation through the *bhakti* cult. This was the notion that the good could be realized through the heart, through the worship of the symbol of the transcendental: Krishna as godhead. Krishna placed the devotional system first, ahead of the yogic system of enlightenment. The yogic system was based on discipline and austerities as well as gaining enlightenment through intellectual questioning, that is, the view that one arrives at the real through negation, *neti, neti* (not this, not this). This system, according to Sarkar's interpretation of Krishna, resulted in an escapist, ideational society. In contrast, Krishna in the *Bhagavad Gita* reminded Arjuna of his duty to fight, to struggle. One could interpret this historic and myth-laden conversation as a call to fight against the demons of the self, or that Arjuna had to follow through in his duty to unite "India"—even if it meant the death of his beloved (but enemy) cousins. But for Sarkar's purpose, it is a confirmation of the view of struggle, of dialectics, and their resolution, a struggle that is valid at the personal and the societal level. It is as his earlier Full Moon of May message exhorts, a call to move forward, to reject the old and embrace the new.

Thus Shiva is in many ways the father/mother of the family and society, and Krishna the father/mother of the larger India. By placing himself textually in their midst, Sarkar sees his mission as that of providing the means for the unification of humanity. Of course, Sarkar never states this as his role. Gurus are far too wily to make this type of strategic mistake. To maintain legitimacy they must stay outside the ego-identification game, yet at the same time they must locate themselves somewhere concrete to allow the devotional process to occur.

When pressed during his embittered court case by the Prosecution if he was like Shiva and Krishna, a *taraka brahma*—the door between the world of the known and the unknown—Sarkar replied in the negative (Reiter, 1976, 2). And yet in his article "The Transitional Period", he writes how in times of crises, in the transitional eras between epochs, great leaders emerge to bring a new era (Sarkar, 1987, 62–64). These are universal women and men. But in the much longer cycle, the moral cycle of the rise and fall of Dharma, it takes a Taraka brahma to destroy the old and bring in the new. While he does not claim himself to be a Taraka brahma, many of his students certainly do.

Read such, the texts of his numerous movements are attempts to create a mythology that provides legitimacy for his role as redeemer. The critical question then that guides this book is clearly: What is Sarkar's meta-purpose? Our answer is: the creation of a new cosmology, a new discourse, a new way of knowing and thus being and doing. But the deeper question is: Is this possible? Is it possible to create a new way of knowing, an entirely new worldview and yet have it intelligible to those in the present? And if it is entirely intelligible, then in what ways does it re-inscribe the present, and thus cease to be come a new discourse that creates a rupture with the present?

Rethinking Time

Among the strategies available in creating a new discourse is that of rethinking time. The present is seen as a transitional point between a tragic past and a bright future to be. In Sarkar's words, "Human civilization now faces the final moment of a critical juncture. The dawn of a glorious new era is on one side and the worn out skeleton of the past on the other. Humanity has to adopt either one or the other" (Ananda Marga, 1982, 22). At the level of the person, his birth is now interpreted by followers as having special significance, as is the expected date of the beginning of Sarkar's planetary society, in the first few decades of the 21st century. This textual move places him immediately in dramatic time, time that begins with a great event. Resituating time is among the myth creation processes necessary to begin a new discourse. One of the ways to understand him is then to see his work in the context of myth generation, in the context of the genesis of a new cosmology.

Besides his historic birth time, there are other stories that augment the myth creation process. Among those include Sarkar's claim to see the room of his birth from his mother's womb, trying to sit up at birth, and desiring to communicate with others but not having the physical resources to do so (Ananda Marga, 1976, 10–13).[2] Also useful for our interpretive effort is a story Sarkar tells of himself when he was only a few years old. In this story, every night he

---

[2] These are called Baba stories that are passed on among Ananda Marga members orally as well as printed in a variety of movement newsletters and magazines. They create a very specific devotional discourse by placing Sarkar in the mythological discourse. The stories are consistent with the rich guru as god "magical" talk that inhabits India. The range of newsletter are available in the U.S. from Ananda Marga, 97–38 42nd avenue. IF. Corona, NY 11368 and in India from Ananda Marga, VIP Nagar. Tiljila, Calcutta. 700039. All of Sarkar's texts are also available from these two addresses and at www.anandamarga.org as well as www.prout.org. Also see: www.proutworld.org, www.gurukul.edu and www.metafuture.org.

is taken far away across the river Ganges to a wide stretch of sand. There an old man meets him. The old man carries the *trishula*, the trident of Shiva and attempts to teach the child the Shiva mantra. Sarkar is annoyed that his sleep is lost every night. Finally one night, he snatches the trident away and attacks the old man. The man disappears and in his place stands Shiva. Sarkar realizes his past lives and his future destiny (13).

One may read this cynically, arguing it is simply a story to gain believership and credibility. Instead of myth creation and meaning generation, critically read, this mythification, may function as the obscuring of truth for purposes of power. However, according to Joseph Campbell in *The Hero With A Thousand Faces* (1968), avoiding the truth/false of stories problem is far more instructive. Myth is the unconscious, the deeper patterns which give meanings and make understandable the moments and monuments of our daily lives.

Sarkar's stories are the classic stories of the hero. There is a challenge. A battle. A struggle. The hero meets the challenge and is victorious. Great boons are bestowed. Every religion, ancient or modern, is enveloped in this. Equally significant is that the old man is nothing but oneself, for he disappears when young Sarkar attempts to eliminate him. It is Sarkar's own consciousness projected in order to resolve a fundamental conflict.

The next significant story occurred when Sarkar, Prabhat, was four. While with his parents at the Shiva temple, Sarkar recited the Shiva mantra in accurate classic intonation much to the shock of the priest and others. It was the same mantra he had learned from the yogi by the river. Later when he was five years old, his parents and sister criticized him for not studying, for day dreaming, and, indeed, for not even being able to learn the Bengali script. In response, the next morning he wrote his name down in six different scripts. About those early years Sarkar later wrote, "A list of my activities for the future and the method of doing them as well as a rough plan were prepared by me while lying on the bed of that hut in Bamunpara. Whatever you see today is the yield of my thought process at the age of seven years" (Sugatananda Avaduta, 1985, 10).

While these stories establish him in the guru discourse, another story places him in a different perspective. Sarkar narrates this story:

> I was a very young boy then, possibly 8–9 years old, and I used to go to the field at the bottom of Jamalpur Hills every day. Many renowned astrologers had seen my horoscope after my birth, and the

majority of them had declared that I would vanquish all religions and establish my own *dharma*. This revelation about my future personality frightened the fanatic followers of a particular religion. I am deliberately omitting the name of that religion. They thought that if all the religions were vanished, theirs, too, could not survive. Consequently, they decided to end my life so that the very cause of their fear would be eliminated forever. This would have saved all the religions from virtual extinction, which they considered to be a great calamity for humanity. They were always in search of a suitable opportunity to kill me, but they couldn't get one until I started visiting the field regularly. I climbed up the hill; they chased me. When they were sure no one else was present on the spot, they caught hold of me and tied my waist and belly with dry clothes. They sprinkled kerosene oil on the clothes and lit them up. The clothes were burning furiously. I stood motionless. They were watching the scene with anxiety and patience. Because of the heat of the burning flames, my stomach burst forth, throwing out my intestine and other internal organs. I then fell down. Thinking that I was dead, they fled away. But I didn't die, I was in a coma. After I regained consciousness, the clothes were still emitting smoke. With great difficulty I got up, held all the organs (which had since come out) with both my hands, and proceeded towards home. Whosoever saw me in that condition fainted, it was such a horrible scene! I was thereafter admitted to a hospital and was stitched and treated for three months before being discharged (Kumar, 1984, 22).

Along with the hero mythology—the fight against evil—the other significant aspect of this story is that it is a preview of struggles against opposing forces in Sarkar's life.

The next significant story occurred in the early 1950s. It helps lay the foundations for the numerous discourses we wish to analyze. By this time Sarkar had become a mystic with a small following. However he continued to work as an accountant at the railways. In this particular narrative, he had gathered five of his disciples together and told them that each would be allowed one wish that he would fulfill. This is the personal representation of the wishing tree, again so prominent in world mythology. His disciples interestingly enough decided not to wish for power, wealth, beauty, eternal life or any of the other fabled wishes. Instead, they asked that Sarkar remain alive until he could establish a spiritually-oriented society on the planet. Sarkar, then, instead of dying replies, "so be it" (Harigovind Acharya, 1977, 8).

Besides bringing forth the notion of social responsibility, this story clearly shows that the will of Being can emerge in many ways. There is a plan and it can expressed in a myriad of ways that are unknown until after the fact, thus there is structure and agency. Sarkar was ready to leave his body, but the wish of the people bade him to stay. This story also locates him in the Bodhisattva discourse, the one who exists without *samskara*—without personal desires and needs that must be expressed. He exists not for himself, but for the purpose of others.

It is at this point, in 1955, that Sarkar began his spiritual organization Ananda Marga, or The Path of Bliss. A few years later he started other sister organizations, Renaissance Universal and Renaissance Artists and Writers Association as well as the more directly political, PROUTist Universal. While in this book we do not explore in detail the politics of Sarkar's organizations—sufficient to say that Ananda Marga followed a cyclical pattern of rise and fall. By the late 1960s Ananda Marga had grown to a few million followers. The Indira Gandhi government had banned any civil service workers from joining it, arguing that it was a subversive organization.[3] The Ananda Marga version was that its workers and members were morally opposing and directly challenging the massive corruption of Indian government, particularly in the civil service. The Central Government's version was that Ananda Marga had become a defacto political party and that it was thus not a religious organization (which was allowed) but a radical and violent political movement (which was far more contentious) (Schneider, 1983).

In 1971, one of Sarkar's most senior monks defected turning state's evidence. (This follows the mythic pattern of the closest disciple betraying the Master). Sarkar was arrested on over one hundred accounts ranging from murder to homosexuality. The organization was banned during the 1975 Indian Emergency, its schools closed, workers tortured, and its membership decimated. In prison, Ananda Marga and PROUTist Universal managed to work with other banned political groups. They then perceived Ananda Marga in a different

---

[3] Anthony Spaeth quoting T. N. Seshan's *The Degeneration of India* writes that the Emergency Rule of Indira Gandhi was the turning point in the breakdown of the Indian civil service. "Civil servants carried out illegal orders, helped Mrs. Gandhi jail her opponents and," Seshan writes, 'almost gleefully' helped gag the press. "The bureaucracy, for the most part, utterly caved in," he concludes. "Over the years, the practice of corruption has become so endemic that it has acquired a veneer of almost complete legality." Anthony Spaeth, "Heat on Corruption", *Time* (23 September, 1996, 44). It should thus not be a surprise that Ananda Marga with its strident anti-corruption campaign was among the hardest hit by Gandhi's brutal repression.

light than the fanatical marginal image that had been constructed by the Indira government. To protest the tortures and conditions that his workers were placed under, Sarkar endured a five year fast. His only sustenance was a daily fortified cup of milk. Through this sacrifice the hero mythology was kept alive, and the organization operated underground, vital and expanding throughout the world.

The next decline occurred during the late 1970s when he was found guilty by the Courts, although the International Commission of Jurists and other international groups protested that he had not received a fair trial. In defiance, a subgroup of the PROUT movement allegedly threatened government officials, threw blood at diplomats and firebombed numerous Indian embassies. Vimala Schneider in her *The Politics of Prejudice: the Use and Abuse of Power to Suppress the Ananda Marga Movement* chronicles these events and attempts to deal with the issues, albeit from an Ananda Marga partisan view. Schneider concludes that most of the alleged terrorist actions were part of a disinformation campaign, with a few actual incidents committed by overzealous and misguided followers. Sarkar immediately distanced himself from these activities saying they were being committed by the misguided and that he would not gain his release from prison through extra-judicial means.

These illegal activities led to Ananda Marga being named a terrorist organization with Interpol, FBI and CIA actively monitoring certain members' activities. The most famous case was in Australia where three members were convicted of conspiracy to murder the then leader of the National Front in Australia, and suspected bombing of the Sydney Hilton Hotel during the Commonwealth Heads of Government Meeting in 1978. However, as Tim Anderson reports in *Free Alister, Dunn and Anderson*, the case was manufactured by the Australian secret police to gain more funding to stave off possible budget cuts. The three were pardoned and obtained sizeable civil awards from the government for their many years in prison.

The 1970s were difficult to Sarkar and his movements as well. Eight monks and nuns self-immolated in protest of Sarkar's jailing. His health deteriorated in prison where he could hardly see or speak. However after prison his health returned. Following Indira Gandhi's defeat, the Supreme Court released Sarkar declaring him innocent of all charges. However, his travel plans around the world were truncated as the Filipino, American, Japanese, Italian and other governments refused him entry.

In his classic mythic language Sarkar had this to say in his annual message while in prison.

> History bears testimony that whenever persons state the absolute truth in any sphere of life, whether it be spiritual, social, economic or otherwise, sought clarifications of doubts, or protested against injustices, the evil forces forthwith plotted against them, administered poison to the them, and slandered them, jumped on them with rage, misused their authority against them, and mercilessly dealt them blow after blow. But the blows boomeranged and ultimately the evil forces were annihilated by those very blows. Remember, by an unalterable decree of history, the evil forces are destined to meet their doomsday (Ananda Marga, 1982, 36).

This is clearly different from the language of the traditional yogis; in fact, its style is prophetic or revolutionary. Moreover, as with numerous other passages, Sarkar often reverts to the laws of *karma*. They are intended to give hope during periods of grave crisis, reminding believers that in the final analysis that which is true will survive and that which is distorted will die. This metaphor of truth and falsehood is the central metaphor of Indian history, from Shiva, Krishna and onwards to present day.

However, the history of Sarkar's movements can be interpreted in a various ways. One might use the sociological discourse and examine the rise and fall of social movements or one might use the political/national security discourse, or one can use the world systems discourse, thus seeing Ananda Marga and PROUTist Universal as anti-systemic movements.

In Sarkar's own view, movements follow a dialectical path: thesis, antithesis and synthesis. A movement is born, it is suppressed (if it truly challenges the distribution of meanings and resources), then oppressed, and if it survives these challenges it is likely to be victorious. The strength of the movement can be measured by its oppression. If it is truly part of the new, and the present is one of brutality and corruption, then certainly there will be major battles. Costly battles.

Continuing our historical gloss, in 1981, allegations spread through Calcutta that Ananda Marga members were stealing children. A mob formed and eighteen monks and nuns were burnt alive. A dozen, in addition, were severely injured. It has taken over twenty years for the case to be resolved in Ananda Marga's favor.

Interestingly, Mother Theresa, who also has similar projects in Calcutta but at a smaller scale when compared to Ananda Marga's, has received numerous International awards instead of suppression or oppression. Sarkar's response to this would be that Mother Theresa was *a*political, only serving the poor and not questioning the structural basis for poverty. Moreover, she, unlike Sarkar, did not refuse to meet with world leaders. Sarkar, in contrast, refused to meet leaders unless they changed their individual life behavior or received initiation into his meditation practices.

Until his death on October 21, 1990, Sarkar remained active in Calcutta composing over 1000 songs called *Prabhat Samgiit* (songs of the new dawn), giving talks on spiritual life, lecturing in over 120 languages on spiritual and social theory, providing leadership and managing his organizations, and teaching meditation to his numerous disciples, especially his senior monks and nuns, *avadhutas* and *avadhutikas*. His most recent projects were twofold. First, the creation of a vast educational system—from early childhood to the doctoral to life long learning—based on the classical Indian *Gurukul* (the house of the Guru), albeit modernized and influenced by the educational ideals of other civilizations. Second has been the creation of self-reliant ecological communities, or what Sarkar has called Master Units. These communities have been designed with PROUT principles in mind: ecologically sensitive, spiritually vibrant, socially progressive, service-oriented and embedded in the local culture of the area.

Taking a phenomenological approach, the key to understanding Sarkar's life is its mythic nature. Central to understanding Sarkar's history include claims to his omniscience, his incredible struggles followed by equally fantastic victories and a belief by his followers of his saint/godhood, if not his role as world spiritual teacher.

Equally important in understanding Sarkar is the rise and fall and rise of his organization. The movement progressed from only a few initiates in the 1950s, to tens of thousands in the 1960s, to again a few thousand in the 1970s and then growth again in the 1980s. This was followed by a period of reflection following Sarkar's death in 1990. The reflection has been centered on followers themselves desiring to ensure that Sarkar's movements themselves are living the ideals set by Sarkar.

Is the movement likely to expect struggle again? If Sarkar's plan is to create new levels of awareness and success then certainly in the next century might be as trying as the 1970s. Using Sarkar's own typology of physical, mental and spiritual, if the first cycle was political and physical oppression, the next stage would be intellectual scrutiny, a battle of ideologies. If this is survived, then the final stage is perhaps the most difficult, the spiritual struggle of worldly victory—the problem of governance, of the possibility of the victors becoming the new tyrants.

Sarkar's Unique Contributions

Having provided background information on Sarkar's new knowledge base and his personal history as well as the worldview from which he emerges, we ask: how and why Sarkar? To begin with, he has spoken extensively on nearly every field from world history to biology to literature. But as mentioned earlier, it is the new knowledge base of humanity that he offers: an alternative rendering of what it means to be human, the good life, the purpose of the universe, and the future of civilization.

In India, he is considered one of the few "God-men," (this term has currency within the Indian philosophical context, but within western discourses, of course, this category is non-existent) having not only initiated an organization of yogi monks/nuns with the intention of spreading basic Tantra meditation practices, but also for having begun a social service relief organization, Ananda Marga Universal Relief Team.

But what makes him and his various organizations he created unique, is that along with providing social services, he also asks why does hunger exist, why is there poverty, and why is there human suffering at the individual, structural and spiritual levels. His conclusions, unlike others who argue that (1) it is related to self, (that is our *karma* not in the personal sense but in the cultural sense of a people who deserve to be colonized, "we as a people are rotten" as it is so often said in South Asia) or (2) related to military (that is, poverty exists because of lack of organization and discipline), or (3) related to development (the institutions are inappropriate, the religion backward, the people lack greed)—claim that it is India's place in the capitalist system, its colonial legacy and its lack of local political will.

This is a legacy of the mal-distribution of resources, of underdevelopment and over-development, of center and periphery, of rich and poor, of the domination of the few by the many, and the development of local and global economic, political, cultural discourses to legitimize this domination. However, Sarkar does not use the above terms. For him, there is an imbalance between the physical, mental and spiritual domains and between the individual and the collective. For him, it is that India suffers from geo-political sentiment (nationalism) and socio-sentiment (racism and caste-ism). Finally and perhaps most significantly, the leadership is immoral, working on the principle of ego gratification instead of social responsibility.

Sarkar's multiple efforts have been to construct a way out. His alternative is Progressive Utilization Theory. As mentioned earlier, largely this is the self-reliance model but coupled with a new spiritual episteme and an internal global dynamic. However, unlike the Gandhian effort—the Bhudan movement, for example—Sarkar is far more radical in his land reform demands. Simply asking the landlords to give up their land is absurd as the structure is too deep, the discourse privileges the powerful. The key to Sarkar's political economy is the cooperative system. This is contextualized by limits to private ownership and income. This involves a rethinking of resources toward the intellectual and the spiritual (moving toward a true knowledge to a transcendent economy). There is also a move from a materialistic consumption vision to a spiritual needs vision. Obviously to do this, one needs at least normative power, if not military and economic. One needs revolutionary changes. However, this revolution must be far deeper than simply seizing state power for the political victors remain within the world interstate system, or in Sarkar's language in the worldview of the *Vaeshyan*. Moreover, the ideas of the present remain dominant. Thus, one needs a deeper shift, a cultural revitalization, a spiritual revolution of being. Needed is the initiation of populist movements to retrieve hope and vision.

The ontological basis for Sarkar's thinking is primarily Tantra. In Tantra, the ultimate "stuff" of the universe is pure Consciousness, pure Being, a reality beyond the scope of the human mind and the root of all that is. Consciousness, for Sarkar, is pure subjective synthetic proposition.

For Sarkar, the motivation for social movement and individual movement can be described as struggle, movement that is at once is pulsating and cyclical. The goal of existence is the realization of the infinite. Thus, the language of PROUT privileges the spiritual.

Sarkar is also unique because of his theory of history. His PROUT is significantly different from other ideologies and civilizations, whether

Marxism, Buddhism, or Islam, key macrohistorians such as Marx, Sorokin, Toynbee and others.

For Sarkar, society is not based on two classes, the bourgeois and the proletariat. Rather, he sees four classes with leadership ideally vested in those who have attributes of all classes. There are the *shudras*/workers, controlled by the physical environment, wherein the wave of the environment is longer than the wave of the worker. There is the *ksattriya*/warrior, who attempts to control the environment through physical strength, or military technology. The *vipra*/intellectual, who uses theory, intellect and mind to control the environment. Finally there is the *vaeshya*/capitalist, who controls through the acquisition of wealth. To him, their centrality in history is cyclical, such that over the *longue durée* there is a circulation of elites. Thus, we have the era of workers, the era of the warriors, the era of priests and intellectuals, and finally the era of capitalists. It is in the capitalist era that everyone becomes a worker (wage laborer), and all classes become the "boot lickers of the capitalists" (Sarkar, 1987b, 5: 64). At the end of the capitalist era, there is a workers' revolution and the social cycle commences again.

In each era the ruling elite has cycles of ascent then descent. Then the next class comes into power and this continues. Of course, there are counter-revolutions and there are counter-evolutions, as well as revolutions and evolutions. Thus, for example, Russia underwent a workers' revolution (the 1918 Bolshevik Revolution) that was followed by the warrior era (the centralized government of the Soviet Communist Party), and one might predict an age of intellectuals next with increased liberty for all, and perhaps a resurgence of the religious and spiritual.

Of course, all this is problematic. How does one know which era one is in? What are the appropriate units of analysis? And more significantly, what is the social and historical context of this theory. How does it relate to other theories of history that emerge from the Indian context? Is Sarkar's macro-history ever new or a mere restatement of the classic caste division of labor?

As well, Sarkar's social cycle raises numerous problems in terms of unit of analysis: civilizations, regions, nations, or societies, structures or associations. What about, say, Pakistan (and other Third World nations), which has its natural cycle influenced by colonialism and globalization—is it in the beginning of a capitalist expansion of the Muslim era, or is it the typical military, authoritarian, peripheral State? In addition, what is the relationship between class and the world system as a whole? How do we determine the mass psychology to ascertain the particular era of a collectivity?

While empirical questions of testability and falsification are crucial, they are not the focus of this book. Much more important will be questions that arise from the poststructuralist model, that is, what is the basis for this discourse? How has this cyclical notion of theory developed? The obvious link is with the Indian system of *varna* (color), caste. Also relevant for exegesis is the Indian notion of cycles, that the basic pattern of history is repetition. As mentioned earlier, of particular interest will be comparing Sarkar to other macrohistorians. For example, does Toynbee's use of civilizations correspond with Sarkar's basic mentalities? What is the telos of history?

These questions notwithstanding, the contribution, nonetheless, is in seeing history as cyclical, as dialectical, as not rooted in the empirical world, but in the collective psychology, in the episteme that organized prevailing ideas. And it is in that politics does not end, unlike the communist vision, when class struggle ends, and utopia is realized. Struggle between classes continues, in Sarkar's model. Sarkar's mission is to create conditions where the exploiting phase of each class rule is shortened, where one gets the benefits of the new cycles— capitalism, or religion, or a centralized polity—but does not have to spend unnecessary centuries in its deep contradictions. Like Marx, however, Sarkar seeks not merely to write a new theory of history but to transform the future.

In addition, given that Sarkar not only is creating a new cosmology but is shaped by Indian cosmology, we trace his work in Indian philosophy, particularly the six schools of Indian philosophical thought, and recent major reconstruction projects, by Shri Aurobindo, for example. Thus the effort will be to deconstruct Sarkar's cosmology in the context of Indian philosophy as well as other significant macrohistorians, and myth creators. How does Sarkar have to speak to be understandable? What are the epistemic contexts from which and to he speaks?

While PROUT as the social movement will not be the focus of this book, we will nonetheless pay attention to the actual strategies that result from the way his worldview is configured. From the Marxist perspective, and now anti-globalization, the obvious strategy is uniting those that are oppressed and seizing control of the means of oppression, particularly challenging the hegemony of global financial institutions such as the World Bank.

For Sarkar, the strategy that is needed is far more complex and multi-fold. It is obviously (1) partly spiritual, in the sense of promoting awareness-transforming technologies such as meditation; (2) partly cultural, in the sense of regaining one's sense of identity; (3) partly universalistic, in the sense of identifying with the cosmos, the universe, as opposed to one's particular family, tribe, ethnicity, or nation; (4) partly educational, in the sense of changing what we learn and how and when we learn, and, finally (5) partly action-oriented, in the sense of organizing workers, initiating cooperatives and building model communities. Sarkar does not simply desire to create the space for an alternative politics, but also an alternative culture, economics, and spirituality.

Concretely, a central praxis element in PROUT strategy are society movements—based on cultural revolutions—that organize those whose language, culture and employment prospects are being oppressed. The task is to create cultural struggles as well revive indigenous peoples. At the same time, the effort is economic self-reliance, not against free trade per se, but self-reliance leading to economic confederations leading to a truly fair global economy. And, all this in the context of a larger spiritual humanism. Perhaps the best examples are *Amra Bengali* in India and *Kasama* in the Philippines. Kasama is a federation of regional self-reliance PROUT movements. Their demands include—100% employment to local people; creation of local industries based on locally available raw materials, non-export of raw materials; instruction to be in local languages, and then various specific demands, for example, the removal of foreign military bases and land reform.

Sarkar, like Marxist writers, focuses on structure—namely, his social division of worker, warrior, intellectual, and capitalist. However, he is also concerned with not only describing what he believes to be the real, but positing an alternative future as well. For Sarkar, the goal is a society where individual rights such as employment, food, health, education, shelter and clothing are guaranteed as are intellectual rights—self-expression. It is to create a society where people are materially taken care of, and intellectual free to pursue the spiritual quest of one's relationship with the pure Being.

Development then is not modernization since modernity actually makes the spiritual pursuit difficult as cultures are cannibalized, becoming increasingly focused on sensate pleasures. At the personal level, instead of freedom we have anomie, apathy, mental illness. At the structural level, we have unemployment, inflation, and inequity. At the cultural level, we have inferiority, imitation, lack of innovation and creativity, a sense of defeat and fatalism, a sense that one's own ideas are not worthy at the cultural level.

We have under-development and over-development, poverty beside richness.[4] For Sarkar, the key is *prama* or dynamic balance—societal balance, ecological balance and personal balance. Globalization has to transform economic globalization from below and above, for capital, labor and for all the classes otherwise the trends of increased inequality will continue.

Balance at the societal level is unattainable unless there are clear limits to the accumulation of wealth. However this does not imply the confiscation of all personal wealth, rather there remains individual wealth. But by and large the system is one of cooperatives. The State sets the limits—society is run by autonomous boards and cooperatives. While this addresses with the equity portion of the economy problem, what of growth? Sarkar argues that inequality is only allowable as long it leads to the growth of the overall system. As the wealth of the rich increases, the State must endeavor to reduce the ratio of the rich to the poor. This ratio has to be constantly reduced (the minimum guarantees thus constantly increase). The final goal, however, is not full employment, but with each technological advance working hours should decrease. Productivity should benefit labor not just capital (or consumer). The goal then is to go beyond survival, and create a society, where internal development, mental bliss is possible. These are outlined in his various principles of PROUT which call for a (1) limit to wealth accumulation; (2) better, progressive, use of physical, intellectual and spiritual resources at the individual and group level; (3) more rational distribution of resources; (4) balance between the individual and the collective good; and, (5) an understanding that these principles have to applied differently in different places at different times.

The other key difference and relevance of Sarkar's work is the emphasis on the environment. But again this is informed by the

---

[4] For example, the poorest 20% of the world's population only had a share of 1.2% of the global income in 1998. The top 20% of the world's population earned 89% of the global income (International Herald Tribune, May 2, 1999, 6). See also The United Nations Human Development Report.

spiritual philosophical tradition. Plants and animals are living, pos-
sessing some degree of mind. Sarkar argues for a new humanism, a
spiritual ecology that does not put humans at the center of all political economic and cultural discourses. Rather, they are one of many
the inhabitants of Earth, even if currently the only species that can
engage in spiritual practice and the most linguistically evolved.

Just as there must be balance in the social discourse, in personal
life as well there must be a balance between action, thought and
meditation. An overemphasis on any one area causes the individual
to be out of harmony with self.

Along with a theory of the social, Sarkar presents a new cyclical
theory of consciousness that includes material and ideational evolution, in sanskrit *Brahmachakra*. Being as Pure Consciousness becomes
bounded and de-evolves to Cosmic Mind and further breaks into
light and basic particles (Big Bang) until finally there is the solid universe. For Sarkar the real is composed of waves of consciousness.
These waves transform into various forms of energy. The final form
is physical matter. At this stage evolution moves towards Being
through various struggles. Humans stand at a point where they have
reflective consciousness, a sense of duty and the possibility to awaken
in themselves pure being. This model attempts to metaphysically
resolve the evolution-creation problem. Moreover, he theorizes about
new particles—microvita—that bridge the gap between mind/body
and unify the other forces of physics: weak force, strong force, grav-
ity, electromagnetism. Microvita are the basic units (forms of con-
sciousness/matter) of life but exist more as mind than as matter.
They are the missing factors that help explain material processes and
numerous present scientific anomalies. They carry ideas and diseases
throughout the universe and are "the mysterious emanations of the
Cosmic Factor" (Sarkar, 1987a, 8: 23).

More than any other characterization, Sarkar is comprehensive.
He has a new theory of cyclical history. He suggests a new development model, a new development ethics and a global development
strategy. He has also articulated a new model of inner spiritual development. Sarkar has developed new spiritual practices calling them
the science of intuition. He argues that spiritual realization is impossible without a commitment to challenging injustices.

Sarkar intends to create a new planetary civilization. For him, this
entails meeting six criteria: (1) a founding leader; (2) a socio-economic
theory; (3) a universal outlook; (4) a definitive text; (5) a spiritual

theory; and (6) spiritual practices. According to Sarkar, most movements and ideologies as well as cosmologies are lacking in some of these components. For example, Buddhism is weak on socio-economic theory while Marxism is obviously weak on spiritual practices and spiritual theory.

Thus Sarkar's PROUT offers not only has a critique of the present, a theory of change, but a vision for an alternative future as well. Finally, it is a concrete social movement that is attempting to transform this present into its preferred future.

However, our concern largely with Sarkar and comparing the discursive spaces he is creating with those created by other macro-thinkers, and only tangentially with PROUT the social movement. And again, we do not to provide empirical proofs for his assertions. Rather, we compare his thoughts with other key thinkers so as to assess their differences and similarities so as to understand their projects. In addition, we wish to understand how it is that he has constructed this discourse. We place his ideas in a historical context. We wish to take Sarkar out from the heaven of devotion and faith to the real world of implications, inquiry and analysis. We place him within epistemological various sites: the sites of other macro-thinkers and the site of Indian intellectual history. For while Sarkar may be creating a new cosmology, a new discourse, he at the same time is created and contextualized by various discourses. He too is a subject of very particular ways of constructing the real, of the ordering of historical knowledge. It is these connections that will be explored and made transparent.

We also examine the structural implications of Sarkar's writings. What are the underlying structures and attitudes toward structural and personal violence, for example. Does he indeed transcend the mind/body, structure/agency, collective/individual, spirit/matter distinctions as his students' claim, or does he simply restate them from a different philosophical view?

We will also in a cursory manner attempt to critique the world created by Sarkar—to evaluate the good society he seeks to envision. At a broader level, we will explore the discourse of utopias: their contradictions, their structures, the conditions that allow their creation, the languages that create victimhood and oppressor.

Thus while Sarkar claims to be universal and claims that his theory is time invariant, space invariant and perception invariant, he is still rooted in a third world context; one born in Calcutta, in a tradition of poverty, personal and institutional corruption and the utter pervasiveness of death. In this regard, spirituality is the defence against the onslaught of modernity.

While the style will be that of comparison and later critique, the purpose is to develop an inter-civilizational dialog between great macro-thinkers. However, we hope that this critique will make the carriers of new ideologies more reflective of their contradictions, more willing to see the alternatives of one's own discourse, more willing to see the similarities, and more willing to see how various identities are distributed and shaped by the discourse at hand. In the case of PROUT, how, for example, the discourse of hierarchy is embedded in spiritual perspectives. By seeing the spiritual as foundational to the entire enterprise, negatively, feudal hierarchy is reinscribed and democracy threatened, and positively, the vertical gaze of global ethics—brutalized in modernity and lost in postmodernity—is reinstated.

The comparative critique will be multifold. Much of it will center on the problem of ideology. Sarkar claims to lay truth bare. Is such a claim problematic given the history of such grand claims? How are we to situate his truth claims? We will place them in different sites, specifically, the comparative and the poststructural. Initially Jiddhu Krishnamurti is particularly instructive.

> Now is there a means, a system of knowing oneself? Any clever person, any philosopher, can invent a system, a method; but surely following a system will merely produce a result created by the system? . . . by following a system, a method, a means through which to know myself, I shape my thinking, my activities, according to a pattern, but the following of the pattern is not the understanding of oneself (Krishnamurti, 1966, 25).

And:

> In order to transform the world about us, with its misery, wars, unemployment, starvation, class divisions, and utter confusion, there must be a transformation in ourselves . . . but not according to any belief or ideology, because revolution based on an idea, or in conformity to a particular pattern is obviously no revolution at all (27–28).

This evokes the idea that revolutions all create new victors, the deeper structures of oppression rooted in our mind remains untouched, or as Zen master D.T. Suzuki would say, mind remains *unnatural* (Suzuki, 1964). Or as Ashis Nandy has written, "yesterday's dissent is often today's establishment and, unless resisted, becomes tomorrow's terror" (Nandy, 1987, 13). Also relevant with respect to the comprehensiveness of Sarkar's work is William Irwin Thompson's commentary. "As Homer recognized long ago, your unique excellence is also your tragic flaw; your greatness hobbles you" (Thompson, 1976, 80). Comprehensiveness too carries a negative. Instead of future visions, the results are blueprints that close the possibility of a new future and limit new categories of thought. Power is simply delivered to a new broker.

But part of the human condition is that people do start movements, new ideologies are born, and we must examine them, discern their contribution, and determine if they will join the dustbin of ideas, or actually create new languages, structures, and visions.

Chapters that Follow

Chapter one has alternatively read Sarkar's life by sympathetically placing him in the mythological hero narrative and critically placing him in the politics of mythification and movement allegiance discourse. The significance of this book—Sarkar's numerous contributions ranging from social, economic, and cultural theories as well as his concrete political movements—have been articulated.

Chapter two places Sarkar in the context of the Indian episteme. This model of knowledge constructs the real symmetrically, dialectically and hierarchically. The goal of theory is to create a condition where the physical, social and cosmic worlds are in harmony with each other. Sarkar uses the Indian episteme as a point of departure but articulates an alternative economic growth and alternative distribution mechanism. In this sense, he radically transforms Indian thought using perspectives from alternative cosmologies, and indeed, constructs a new discourse, if not a cosmology.

Chapter three contextualizes Sarkar's theory of history within various Indian constructions of time. Sarkar's model consumes these various constructions: the classic rise and fall of dharma perspective; the *yugas* of man (the degeneration of history); the critical Subaltern and Marxist perspectives; the dynastic view; the scholarly narratives; as well as the Orientalist and nationalist constructions. While Sarkar takes the classic cyclical historical viewpoint, he includes within it the possibility of individual and societal spiritual and economic transformation, thus allowing an exit from history. Finally, his reordering of varna is considered alongside with the politics of class and caste.

Chapter four summarizes the prose of his history. We trace his various movements and disjunctions—the Shudran, the Ksattriyan, the Vipran, and the Vaeshyan eras as well as the Shudra revolution and the intended spiritual revolution. His prose is likened to Marxist prose, especially his analysis of the capitalist era.

Chapter five places Sarkar in the context of other macro-historians. Specifically we compare and contrast the following: Foucault, Voegelin, Lazslo, Galtung and Polak in terms of recent efforts. Ssu-Ma Ch'ien and Chang Hsueh-Cheng from Chinese macrohistory and Ibn Khaldun from Islamic macrohistory. From the West we choose Vico, Comte, Hegel, Marx, Gramsci, Pareto, Mosca, Spengler, Toynbee, and we conclude with Sorokin. Sarkar can be better understood in the context of these thinkers for now we understand him not only on his terms but in the language of others.

Chapter six situates Sarkar's social laws. They are critiqued from empirical positions, compared with Marxian laws of dialectics and then placed within a poststructural model of science and the real. For us, Sarkar speaks from an alternative construction of science and of social theory. Representing him in narrow empirical theory merely produces an apolitical reading of the Indian episteme. However, the poststructural perspective in which the real is denaturalized allows us to fruitfully examine the implications of Sarkar's laws, both phenomenologically and politically.

Chapter seven concludes this book asserting that Sarkar's theoretical moves and social movements will most likely be among the most significant in this and coming centuries. We, however, also suggest that the strength of Sarkar—his comprehensiveness and level of generality—is paradoxically his greatest weakness. "Our excellence is our greatest flaw," Homer reminds us. But for Sarkar, the magnitude of the present civilizational crises requires a comprehensive approach, a cosmological transformation. We also ask whether Sarkar's monumental work will create new visions (the renaissance he intends) or limit future visions by becoming hegemonic. We leave the text open, ever awaiting new interpretations and new discourses that speak to us and in return must be spoken to.

CHAPTER TWO

THE EPISTEMIC BOUNDARIES

Sarkar and the Indian Episteme

Women and men who begin new cosmologies evoke the universal and the transcendental, but their grand efforts also spring from the dust and the mud of the particular and the mundane. They are born in particular places, they live in specific homes, and they die in locatable sites. Ibn Khaldun asserts that his sociology is time, space and culture invariant, but the bases for his theory emerged from the specific ground of Islam. His theory of history, his comments on historiography can be located to the current thinking of the time, the 14th century. From knowledge of Bedouins, from personally participating in various coups and assorted palace intrigues, it is not surprising that what emerges is a history of dynastic change, with Bedouin unity derived as the key explanatory variable.

But using the life cycle of an individual to infer the nature of his theory simply personalizes a series of events, while remembering the subjective does not place the subjective in historical economic and language practices that surround that person, the episteme. The personal discourse is useful but there is more than that. To demarcate his work, Khaldun had to speak to previous writings of history. He had to write of those who solely aimed to tell what had happened, to write the daily affairs of the royal. Khaldun, too, existed within the Islamic episteme, a way of knowing that privileged rationality and logic, that believed in the development of knowledge over time, and like Khaldun's theory of the rise and fall of unity, had unity among Muslims as the key axis for the growth of Islam.

Chinese macrohistorian Ssu-Ma Ch'ien had to write within the Confucian episteme before he could change it. There were various problems as to the periodicity of history, as to the causes of the rise and fall of dynasties, which had to be resolved. But, however unique and revolutionary his writing was, it still existed within a particular sea of knowledge. While this is obvious to us when we examine the past, however when we examine our present, we locate it developmentally as the rational and the scientific. The past is constructed as relative and ideological with the future the fulfillment of truth once the last vestiges, the remnants, of the past have been vanquished. Thus, we submit our own present to ourselves as outside of history, outside of a metaphysic. Too, Sarkar's writings and those that attempt to interpret his world locate him outside of history, they claim that Sarkar is outside of his Indian tradition as if his knowledge was not contextual.

But every writer comes from a discourse. Hegel's conception of history was a direct response to the third antimony and Kant's problematic solution to it. "According to Kant, both universal natural necessity and freedom are necessary and also antinomy, since every event must have a prior cause, and yet, unless there is a first and hence free cause, the series will always be incomplete and the law of nature thus never sufficiently grounded. Kant solves this antinomy by showing that the contradiction is not in the world but in consciousness, positing two distinct and independent realms, the phenomenal realm of nature and noumenal realm of freedom" (Gillespie, 1984, xiii). Hegel accepts Kant's antinomy and makes it his dialectic.

Marx too, although he attempted to create a perfect new world realizable through an objective understanding of the real, was responding to a tradition speaking to and from 19th century Europe. His philosophical thought was contextualized by the Enlightenment and its German response, even as he tried to speak to the problem of hierarchy and oppression throughout history.

Our perspective then is that every thinker and every thought exists within boundaries of what is considered intelligible. There is no place where one can speak from objectively, to be able to speak outside of discourse. Epistemological boundaries—languages, structures, and practices—exist and they define the significant and the trivial, the negotiable and immutable. And, these boundaries are also subjects of different discourses. New discourses, ways of knowing, are created. These new discourses are then the historical ruptures that end the old and begin the new. They are periods when the future ceases to be an image, to be a vision, and becomes a present.

Michel Foucault calls these ruptures epistemological acts and thresholds.

> . . . they suspend the continuous accumulation of knowledge, interrupt its slow development, and force it to enter a new time, cut it off from its empirical origin and its original motivation, cleanse it from its imag-

inary complicities; they direct historical analysis away from the search for silent beginnings, and the never-ending tracing-back to the original precursors, towards the search for a new type of rationality and its various effects. They are the displacements and transformations of concepts (Foucault, 1972, 4).

These new discourses break the ground of previous ways of knowing. They reorder knowledge and claim new positivities: they rearrange what is significant and what is trivial; they rearrange the relative placements of self, nature, god; space is turned over; time is reestablished and suddenly the world is anew again. But these new discourses must spring from the soil of other discourses. To function, the ever new must be intelligible to the old and the aging. Without this intelligibility, only those who exist outside of contemporary notions of the natural and the rational can participate in the new discourse. A new discursivity then is not created, rather, the alternative structure remains in the mind of a few, if at all.

Our questions and intentions for this chapter are simple. We begin with the geographical. Sarkar was born in 1921 in India. With the exception of a few trips outside India he has lived there all his life. Our larger question then is how has India influenced him. The obvious level is that of the Indian languages he speaks. But we are not concerned solely with language but with discourse. How have the ways in which Indian thought, history, culture been constructed, handed down to him, influenced the choice of his categories? Does he have an Indian mind?

When he speaks, to whom is he speaking? When he writes, what are his metaphors, his comparisons, his analogies? Simply seeing who and what he writes about and what he chooses not to be write about is one approach in placing him. The other approach is to examine Indian philosophy, Indian history and Indian culture and determine the large movements, the important events, the critical stages, the various constructions and determine what objects and subjects Indian thought itself creates. What language does the Indian episteme give as its resources to present day Indian writers? What are the norms that create the categories in which an Indian thinker, philosopher must speak? To who must Gandhi, Tagore, Aurobindo and other twentieth century activists and writers speak? What ordering of knowledge speaks them? What are the discourses, the worldviews that circumscribe the boundaries of what they can see, feel, hear, conceive, and act upon?

To do this, we first need to deconstruct the Indian episteme, asking what is considered natural? What rational and what irrational? How has the real been divided, how have categories been spaced? A sociological way of saying this is to ask how do Sarkar's various theories and theoretical frames compare with the history of Indian thought, with the history of Indian history, with the history of Indian culture and with the history of great Indian thinkers? Who else has attempted to create new discourses, or does Indian thought present itself with an alternative unity of discourse that is not centered with the author?

Thus in our analysis for this chapter we will proceed dialectically between the assertions, the knowledge claims of Sarkar and an idealized interpretation of Indian thought. Our goal, again, is a particular type of deconstruction. We seek to locate Sarkar himself within the Indian episteme. We seek to find out whether Sarkar is Indian or is his thought beyond its historical limit? Or is he Indian and not-Indian at the same time? Is he creating a rupture in Indian thought by re-conceptualizing its grounds? Does he create a new discourse?

This chapter is an effort to come to terms with the question whether it is possible to produce a new cosmology and maintain intelligibility in the cosmology from which one springs. Our task then is also genealogical in the sense that we seek to place Sarkar in history, not outside of history and culture. As much as he might claim to have access to universal knowledge and claim to have created a theory for the "good and happiness of all", we assert that this "universal" is grounded in a particular.

Our decision to locate Sarkar in Indian thought does not merely arise from his Indian birthplace. His various texts are written in Bengali or Sanskrit. He has specifically written two tracts on Indian historical figures: the first on Shiva and the second on Krishna. In his writings there is repetitious mention of the *Upanishads*, the *Bhagavad Gita*, the teachings of the Buddha, and present day Gandhi and Tagore. Islam and Christianity receive but a few lines although he has certainly been influenced by their more horizontal structures, especially the notion of the brotherhood, the fraternity of Islam. In his article, "The Views of Other Faiths" (Sarkar, 1987b, 3: 31–41) he focuses on the various divisions in Indian thought as well as on Marxism. In his writings on PROUT his emphasis is on a comparison of Marxism and Democracy—his critique is of capitalism. He is signaling to ancient history and to the problems of the present. *The relevance for us here is who does he seek to differentiate himself from.* This "who" is one working definition of the culture from which he springs (with the exception of Islam, Marxism and liberalism, although they too constitute present India).

To begin with let us lay out various points of departure and categories from which we can locate, compare and contrast Sarkar. We will lay the groundwork of Indian thought. How is Indian thought constructed? What are its rules and regulations? What are the conventional readings of Indian-ness, of Hinduism?[1]

How is Indian thought divided up? Are there schools, authors, divisions of time? And how does Sarkar locate himself in these various schools? Is he orthodox or heterodox, or outside of the tradition itself?

Using Galtung's cosmological analysis, that is, the division of cosmologies and the structures embedded within them (Occident and Orient and their interrelationships—as to person, nature, self, structural and direct violence, and growth and distribution) we place the Indian system and then Sarkar within the structure. We will comment generally on the Indian intellectual style and Sarkar's own intellectual style. Finally we will compare Sarkar's perspective to the six major orthodox schools: Nyaya, Vaisheskika, Sankhya, Yoga, Mimamsa, and Vedanta; and the three heterodox schools, Buddhism, Jainism, and Carvaka. The obvious question is will Sarkar's cosmology become a new school and if so, orthodox or heterodox or outside of the Indian doxa? Or will it like Aurobindo's worldview be seen as inspiring, but simply an update of previous thinking?

Sarkar's Self-Location

First of all, how does Sarkar generally locate himself? He writes:

> Many theories have been propounded in the world. Some of them were concerned mainly with the spiritual world; they had no concern for the rationality of the psychic world at all. Unfortunately, most of these theories have been thrown into the garbage heap of history. There were some theories that showed some concern for the psychic

---

[1] This, of course, is a recent category in itself developed by Muslims to differentiate themselves from those who had not yet converted to the true religion. In this sense, while Islam, Marxism and Secularism have become an integral part of the plurality of India, by Indian, in general, we refer to Tantric, Vedic and Buddhist perspectives.

realm as well, but they could not develop the mental equipoise of society and were rejected by the people. Some of these philosophies pertaining to the physical realm sounded very fine indeed, but they were not in perfect tune with the hard realities of the objective world. Those philosophies were quite satisfactory in the dreamland of theory, but they had no connection whatsoever with the practicalities of the earth. Other theories, sounding somewhat pleasing to the ear, have spoken glibly of human equality, but upon application people discovered the ineffectiveness of these theories because the fundamental principles were contrary to the basic realities of the world 'Diversity is the law of nature: uniformity will never occur.' The world is full of diversities— a panorama of variegated forms and colors, diverse varieties and expressions. One must never forget it. Sometimes the superficial display of these theories has dazzled the eyes of the onlooker, but actually they contained no dynamism . . . Many philosophies in the past have rendered this kind of disservice to humanity. In the end they only flung humanity into the quagmire of dogmatism, the breeding ground of innumerable mosquitoes. They did not contribute to the welfare of any human being (Sarkar, 1983, 2–3).

For Sarkar, it is consciousness as desire directed toward the infinite that is the highest and most valuable treasure of humanity—what he calls devotion. The correct theory aids in finding the balance between "the spiritual and material worlds and [is] a perennial source of inspiration for the onward movement of society" (Sarkar, 1983, 4).

In the above quotes, Sarkar speaks to the various philosophies that have made India today. It is a disguised critique of the most dominant strain of Indian thought, Shankaracharya's Advaita Vedanta (overly other-worldly), of Gandhism (impractical) and of Marxism (overemphasis on equality at the expense of individuality). But more importantly is his criterion of a good theory: human welfare. A human welfare based theory must: (1) lead to the meeting of basic human needs for shelter, food, education, health and security; (2) be balanced in its approach to the physical, mental and spiritual realms, and (3) create an intellectual discourse that leads to *bhakti* or the uninterrupted movement of mind toward that which cannot be symbolized—Krsna, Brahman. This then are the criteria Sarkar uses to evaluate theories of reality.

Significant is a lack of claim of the truth in-itself of the theory. It is not that some were ontologically false and others metaphysically real, but it is that the more basic value of human needs—mental, physical, and spiritual—were not met by these theoretical constructs. This is in accord with his position that the phenomenal world is utterly and totally dependent on three variables: time, place (space) and person (the status of the individual observer). It is this relativization of truth that distinguishes the Indian tradition from the Western tradition. For Sarkar, the critical difference is between truth as *rta* or the facts and truth as *satya* or human welfare, that which leads to physical, mental and spiritual growth.

Sarkar and Indian Philosophy

The Indian tradition is first of all a tradition that has therapy as its primary focus, the resolution of a specific problem. The goal is to end pain, to transcend suffering. The realization of this goal is the same as Truth. Truth in-itself that does not lead to the cessation of suffering is merely *rta*. Truth is Bliss,[2] *Sat* is *Ananda*. Thus when we examine Indian philosophical thought (or Sarkar's thought) we must be careful of our own structural biases, of our pre-understandings (of, for example, truth as outside of value or outside of bliss). While it might be over generalizing, it is a useful point of reference that most knowledge claims in Indian philosophy are predicated on the secondary nature of intellectual truth (truth as correspondence to a real world outside of the observer) and the primary nature of truth as bliss. This is not however a utilitarian reading of the text of Indian philosophy; the goal is not the practical. It is not simply that happiness feels better than sadness, rather Indian thinking attempts to move beyond mental-emotional states of pleasure. *Ananda* is beyond the pleasure and pain of the body. It is beyond the desire of the physical world and the mental world. It is located in the site of the everlasting.

This is the second key point. The first is philosophy as therapy, and the second is that the real is outside of time and space and individual perspective. The real is outside of mind and thus self is defined as personality, ego, family, place, region, nation, class, race, religion, and ideology. It is timeless and thereby pre-discursive, prior to language and practice. God is simply a symbol of this reality, however, while this symbol can by used as a point of focus (in so far as the symbol participates in that which it points to), it remains transitory. And that which is transitory is not real except in terms

---

[2] It is not incidental then that Sarkar named his organization Ananda Marga, the path of bliss.

of the relative world. That which is everlasting is real. Thus the distinction is that of permanence and impermanence. True knowledge
leads to the permanent, whereas false knowledge (however valuable
on its terms) leads to the impermanent.

There is thus a real self, called *atman* and a variety of social or
false selves. But this atman is not simply static as commonly described—
it is not a thing—rather it is goal directed. As Sarkar states, "There
is in every living being a thirst for limitlessness" (Sarkar, Ananda
Marga Brochure). Thus, human consciousness once emergent is "goal
directed, giving rise to a set of peculiarly human needs and motivations" (Carspecken, 1987, 28). Human consciousness is primarily
social in nature and "the self is not something ready-formed which
pursues desires and interacts with other ready-formed selves in a
mechanistic way. Instead, all selves are interpenetrated with each
other. Human actions cannot be understood as simply movements
of selves to gratify various desires, [however], rather all action is
better conceived of as human expression which changes the self
either positively (causing growth) or negatively (causing constriction)"
(Carspecken, 1987, 28).

From this most Indian thought derives an objective basis for morality; that which leads closer to the spiritually constructed self. However,
the objective morality does break down for the human who has been
able to distinguish the permanent and the impermanent, who knows
what leads to *dukkha* (sorrow) and what to *ananda*. There is conventional morality and there is extra-morality for the enlightened one.

This essential nature is called Dharma, or duties, laws, obligations,
but essentially it can be read as the basic nature of the self. There
are different dharmas: human dharma is the struggle to discover
ananda. According to Sarkar: "The evolutionary forces have not
stopped. The theatre of action has shifted to the psychic level.
Evolution is now expressing its power in the daily struggle of men
and women everywhere to attain dignity" (Carspecken, 1987, 28).
This last statement is certainly very Gandhian in that political dignity becomes associated with the traditional other-worldly *ananda*.
Sarkar, as did Gandhi, perceives his role as more than spiritual not
only the enlightenment of a few souls, but as planetary, the creation
of a structure for the enlightenment of all.

Understanding the self then is at the center of Indian thought.
Indeed, one could argue that the entire history of India is the history of the regulation of the self: who has the right to control the

self, to give it *mantras* for its freedom, to gain tributes from it, to extract labor from it, to gain its homage, to place it in the body or in the mind, and finally to set it free.

The Karma Discourse

The control and responsibility of the self relates to the next fundamental concept in Indian thinking: *karma*. Karma, in short, is a system of merits and demerits, the baggage that travels with the self, throughout time and space. In more rigorous language it can be spoken of as *sanskara*, or potential desires that must be experienced. The ways out from desire are numerous and these paths of escape cover the space of the landscape of Indian philosophy and history. Indeed, karma and the escape of the self is the subheading of the historical text of India. The traditional way or the mass way is through giving priests—the keepers of the self—food and other donations. Alternatively, one might do good works, as defined by the spirit of the times. This notion of good works remains undeveloped in Indian thought, except as articulated in the *yamas* and the *niyamas*: least-violence, truthfulness, cleanliness, contentment, simplicity, non-attachment and other moral principles. However, good works often lead to good *sanskaras*; thus, various tracts assert that chains remain chains whether they are made of iron or gold.

Another historical alternative has been to do nothing, that is, to avoid all types of action and not create or reap karma. This is the path of renunciation. The notion of simply doing one's duty, however defined, as a way of avoiding undue karma, or iron chains, has been another response. The radical Zen position in response to the karmic problem has been: how can that which is essentially pure—the self—gather dust? The ego is simply unaware of its own inner nature. Thus the Zen master finds ways to break the ego from mind and then to re-identify it with pure self. With this re-identification, there is sudden enlightenment. All karmas fall away. The counter response to that position has been even the enlightened get cancer and other diseases, they just do not identify with the pain since they know it is temporary. They perceive the world from a position of compassionate non-attachment. They cannot escape one's previously implemented desires, one's previous actions.

Sarkar's position again reaffirms his move to balance the spiritual

and the material: the reflective and the dynamic. Individuals must
do their duty, yet at the same time, they must, through the use of
various *mantras* keep their mind identified with *atman* or *paramatman*
(the supreme self), or within the devotional discourse, with Shiva,
or Krsna. Thus one acts but one does not identify with the actions.
This in effect is a reconfirmation of the advice of Krishna to Arjuna
in the *Bhagavad Gita*. The final way out of karma (or sin in the comparative Christian reading) is surrender to the Godhead. While the
privileging of the Godhead has led to the reification of the god-sym-
bol, philosophically, it has coherence in that the mind of the self is
ever thinking of the Other. Thus, as there is no ego-identification,
no new karmas arise. One is free. At the same time, there is the
notion of the savior who can erase and wipe clean the slate of karma.
Here one is also free.

Thus, within the karma discourse there remain numerous debates
over the proper place of karma. In contrast, however, to the Western
notion of sin, karma can be read as linking responsibility with the
individual. It can thus be conservative (do nothing to cause change)
or welfare orientated (help others to cleanse karma). Karma can be
used as a way to blame the victim or as a way to encourage good
works that benefit self, family, and other collective groupings. It can
also be ambiguous as no one (except the Godhead) really knows who
is getting what karma and how.

Typically karma is seen as the deeper cultural problematic that
has kept India from becoming modern and developed—karma as
fatalism and acceptance of one's horrendous conditions. Karma at
the populist level has found meanings and structures quite different
from its various philosophical interpretations. Sheryl Daniel in her
article entitled, "The Tool Box Approach of the Tamil to the Issues
of Moral Responsibility and Human Destiny" tells these stories:

> In another case, a ... boy of about eight years fell seriously ill and
> died. His family could not trace his death to any sin of his own or of
> the known family members, but they confided to me that it must have
> been the result of the bad karma resulting from the sin of an ances-
> tor two or three generations earlier. ... [O]ther types of karma exchange
> are said to occur when a person accepts cooked food from another
> person. It is for this reason that Tamils are eager to accept the cooked
> food and even leftovers of the gods, Brahmins and holy men: they
> believe that they are acquiring some of their good karma and will gain
> greater prosperity as a result. For the same reason, they are selective
> about accepting food from undesirables such as thieves and prostitutes

who will transfer a measure of their bad karma in the food which they cook. . . . Fear of karma transfers from mere physical proximity makes villagers cautious about whom they allow to enter their homes. A holy man . . . is, of course, always, welcome . . . the same cannot be said of widows or barren women (Daniel, 1983, 29).

Good and bad karma can be passed on from the family and to the family. The enlightenment of one individual creates enough good karma to guarantee the enlightenment of an entire clan. While a more critical reading would examine the role of the priestly class in providing this enlightenment vehicle, significant is the complexity of rules and logic that accompany karmic transfer.

On a modern level, articles in the journal *Vedic and Modern Science* (www.tm.org) sponsored by the Transcendental Meditation movement argue that a group of meditators meditating in a specific area can influence peace, violence as well as the stock market in a nearby area—the field effect. While they use the language of science to justify this transfer (wave theory and the new physics), structurally it remains karmic theory. "Good" actions lead to "good" results. However, the definition of this goodness, for example, in the case that increased meditation in a specific area raises the price of the stock market, remains unproblematic to the Transcendental Meditation movement. Stock prices and human welfare are not necessarily synonymous except within a capitalist framework.

Karmic theory either is thrown out altogether as an impediment to development or is embraced entirely as ancient wisdom. The many uses of karmic theory, the meanings embedded in it and the politicizations of these meanings (who gets what and how do we know good and bad) remains undone. Interpretations of karma remain authoritative. Sarkar's effort has been to remove the control of karma from the priest and to attack renderings of it that blame the victim. He has chosen to redefine it.

But the larger philosophical effort of ungrounding karma—seeing how it is put forth in discourse, by whom and for what use, as Foucault has done for Western sexuality—has not been Sarkar's project. Thus, those at the top layer of society can and do continue to use it to justify the status quo. Hierarchy then finds philosophical substantiation. Prosperity means one has good karma. There is little discussion as to why good is related to prosperity. Indian philosophy on its terms should be read as good karma meaning that which leads to *ananda*, not wealth or privilege. Thus, birth in a rich family does not necessarily mean good karma, for wealth—if it leads the individual to identification with the material plane—could be read as bad karma (unless one sickens and then renounces the gross world).

Necessary to make karma intelligible over time is the notion of rebirth. This is important in Sarkar's thinking. He even develops hypotheses as to why we do not remember our previous births: lack of intuitional development and as a coping device for the young to avoid multiple-life confusion. While again this is not the place to restate Indian philosophy, what is significant for our quest in understanding Sarkar and the Indian episteme is that Sarkar appears to follow the classic Indian model, although he adjusts it for his particular PROUT. Thus, he counsels against readings of karma that blame the victim, rather he locates the site of karma not in the nation, the community, or the clan, or caste, but rather in the individual, in desire and responsibility. Batra (1978), in contrast, argues for a collectivist karmic reading of history: empires rise and fall because of good and bad karma. Thus, in the rise exploitation occurs and once karma "kicks back" there is the decline. But for Sarkar, karma must be reinterpreted lest it fall into nihilism, given that the dominant model in Indian thinking argues that nothing indeed is real.

Karma for Sarkar is related to desire. Within this model what one desires must be fulfilled in some form. Thus one must return, forever attempting to fulfill various desires. Indeed, one's birth in the next life is entirely dependent on the desires that need to be realized. The problems associated with this type of thinking are obvious: the ability to rationalize, to blame, to ignore, to create new nuances of karmic transfers to the point where the spiritual model is totally subverted by the supply/demand and costs/gains of the self-interest economic model. The result of this worldview is clearly not the invention of new models of greed (economic growth), nor new realms to conquer (expansion), nor equitable models of distributive justice (solidarity). Rather, what results, as one might expect in an idealistic worldview (as Sorokin uses the term), new and newer theories, of speculations upon speculations, fantasy upon fantasy, all tied together by a thin thread of logic, of reason.

A natural implication is the centrality of the free will versus determinism question, whether humans simply play out their role in the cosmic drama or whether they can improvise and prevail upon the scriptwriter to make alterations, or whether they can somehow break out and move outside of the script. In either case, within the Indian

context, there remains a very real and a surprisingly thick philosophical nexus that must be negotiated. Even if Sarkar simply calls
these theoretical extravagances, he too is forced to develop his own
theory based on the historical arrangements of knowledge given to
him by the various schools of thought. Even Jiddhu Krishnamurti
(1966) who rejects all metaphysics, asserting that self must simply
gaze at the self, ultimately developed an anti-theory along with various organizations that promote the Krishnamurti school of thought.
Samuel Beckett, not speaking to the Indian episteme, is useful here.
"What can you expect, they don't know who they are either, nor
where they are, nor what they're doing, nor why everything is going
badly, so abominably badly, that must be it. So they build up hypotheses that collapse on top of one another, it's human, a lobster couldn't
do it" (McCarthy, 1973, front page).

But for the Indian, there remains karma to explain why things
are going so badly. There is also life beyond karma, either through
individual enlightenment or through the redeemer, who will once
again bring dharma back.

Synthetic and Spiritual

In addition to (1) truth as bliss, (2) philosophy as ultimately therapy,
(3) the self as a goal directed social construction with karma as the
glue that links the self from life to life, there are other salient features of Indian thinking.

Indian thinking is synthetic in that the positions of various schools
are argued back and forth but they are not outright rejected. This
is true as well for the recent liberal/democratic and state socialist
ideologies. Sarkar, too, while he differentiates himself from various
schools, still can conveniently quote from seemingly opposed positions when they can inspire individuals to act, and think in accordance with the deeper goals of the Indian tradition: *bhakti*. And even
while he makes a strong distinction between the Tantric and Vedic
perspectives, largely arguing that Tantra is more individualist, struggle orientated, dynamic and pre-Aryan while the Vedic is more
group, prayer-oriented and Brahmanical, he can easily in the next
discourse quote extensively from the *Upanishads*. Similarly, he can
critique Buddhist philosophy for being weak on socio-economic theory and then use the Buddha's dialogs as assets for his own project.

Underlying this is the belief that nothing is totally good or bad in the relative universe and that nothing is totally outside of the Indian project. Of course, he quotes in a way to reinforce his activist and rational position on the good life.

Along with the synthetic approach is the privileging of the spiritual perspective. Only Carvaka and recent Marxist variants argue for an alternative perspective. While Orientalist critic Ronald Inden (1986) argues that generalizing Indian thought as spiritual or synthetic only reinscribes the notion that India is either backward, mysterious and irrational or mystical, exotic and erotic, nonetheless, as a starting point we do assert that Indian thought can but be described as ideational or idealistic). With respect to Western thinking it falls closer to Platonic and Kantian thinking than the Cartesian perspective. The central questions in Indian thought relate to the nature of the self, not is it materialist or spiritual, but how is it spiritual? The question is not: is there a consciousness beyond the material, but what is its nature and how does it relate to the creative force of *Prakrti* or the energy/actional component of the universe? Its orientation is fundamentally metaphysical. This is not to say there are no implications for the structure of power—polity, economy, and culture—that derive from this, but simply that the project is primarily one that has at its center the search for the Other. This Other is believed to be outside of space, time and the individual, which exists independently of our knowing efforts, but when known, through prayer, meditation, chanting, provides *the* solution to the problem of meaning. And, this Other at the same time is the self, the subjective, the internal. The Other then is both external and internal. What is, then, is more than what the senses perceive and, what is, then, is more than what reason can conceive. Moreover, once that which is beyond senses and reason is perceived then it can be transmitted. The perception of this self, however, is a project of many lives. Once realized, it accords one with the ultimate status, that of *guru*. The guru then can teach others how to realize the self and because of the difficulties of self-realization and because of the guru's prior experience, his or her status in Indian thinking, whether materialistic or spiritual, becomes central. Teacher as guru is also compatible with the Indian notion that reality is naturally multi-leveled and hierarchical. Each human can be placed on this hierarchy depending on his or her spiritual realization. We should then not be surprised at the centrality of Sarkar's leadership model and that Sarkar's model of leadership is not one that privileges philosopher-kings (the wise intellectual) but rather the spiritual-intellectual (the one who has all types and levels of knowledge and all types of social existence).

The critique of the Orientalist discourse (the Orient as either spiritual or erotic as an opposite of the rational economic model of the West) has merit in that the politics of Indian thought are often left examined such that, for example, caste is seen as an independent condition of Indian thinking instead of a category of inclusion/exclusion that developed with Kingship or from Aryan subjugation of the conquered Dravidians—the necessity to include them in the natural order, but obviously at a lower level. However, while a critique of Orientalism is useful in that it politicizes natural categories, we, however, take the position that the Indian project or mission is significantly different than the Western position, notwithstanding that most understandings of the Indian position have been packaged by European and American Orientalists, specifically, Western Indologists.

Knowledge or Philosophy

Also useful in understanding the Indian project is that there is no word for philosophy in Sanskrit. Philosophy, in the Indian perspective, is only one part of the overall dynamic—it is *vijnana*, knowledge derived from reason. The word used to describe the overall project is *darshana*, or to see, to a particular type of view. Thus, it is perspective. It is only with the political hegemony of the Brahmin class that philosophy becomes the highest branch of knowledge. Karma and *bhakti* then became located underneath *vijnana*. Implicit in the notion to see is that there are many ways to see and that there are many seers. It becomes an additive form of knowing, not an exclusive, first originator, the prophet model variety. Thus, it is quite understandable that there is no one book as with Western religions, rather there are a range of texts that have more than ordinary authority. This is similar with Sarkar's work in that there is no particular text that stands above other texts, rather his work exists in a textual unity. However, this is not to say that the texts are not authoritative, it is just that authority is not based on historical origination, rather, the texts are eternal, outside of time, indeed mythic, for the Indian, truth has always existed.

The Author

This is one reason why—as opposed to the Western project that finds its unity of discourse, the unity of the historical text, in the author, in the writer himself—in the Indian context, the author is removed from center stage in a move congruous with the death of the postmodern author. Instead of the author, there arise different views of the world. Specifically, the six orthodox schools and the three heterodox schools, with Indianized Marxism and liberal democratic capitalism as the latest entries to this project.

Authors are quoted only at points when authority is needed. While the author is important it is not the individual author that gives credence to a perspective but the perspective itself. But ultimately it is the reader who must give meaning to the text by reinterpreting his/herself, for the text finds its durability in its ability to change the self of the interpreter, not the reification of a particular pre-held concrete self. Again, truth is transformation, the realization of *ananda*, not a particular philosophical assertion. The location of meaning in the reader is similar to the postmodern project in which meaning is neither with the author nor the philosophy, but is moved to the point of contact, the point of thought, the point of significance—to the reader, the interpreter, the watcher.

But the Indian writer to be intelligible to history must speak to these different schools of thought, to the unbroken mass of tradition, of historical texts. To validate himself, Gandhi reinterpreted the *Upanishads*. He found the future of India in its past and made this past an alternative present (Nandy, 1983). Even Rajneesh who claims to be universal, speaks directly from the Tantric perspective, although his style has been the "left-handed" Tantra school which forces the liberation of the self through emersion into pleasure. Rajneesh's claim to universality is still bounded by his role as guru. He does not, cannot, stand outside the Indian context.

Likewise, Jiddhu Krishnamurti struggled to stand outside the Indian tradition. He was to be the avatar of the world, the point from which the knowledge of heavenly worlds was to pass through, but Krishnamurti rejected this purpose for him. What did he reject this power for? He did not turn to the *bhakti* schools nor did he turn to the karma schools, nor did he convert to one of the Occidental religions (Islam, Christianity, or Judaism), Marxism or Liberalism. Rather he argued that all systems of thought were creations of the mind, a mind that was essentially socially fabricated and thus ripe with deceit, anger, expectations. The way out was to simply watch one's desires, one's mind, and to even watch the desire to watch. Out of this, for Krishnamurti, comes the natural self that can truly love and truly experience the world as it is. But while this view rejects the orthodox grand system building schools, it falls very much in the Indian tradition. Krishnamurti's perspective is squarely within the tradition of natural versus artificial self and it can be seen as an interpretation of the Vedanta school or the negation of the self project of the Buddha.

For Vedanta the world is unreal, thus attachment to this world is a mistake. Electoral politics or creating a spiritual organization would be mistakes. Krishnamurti, like the yogis of the past, who had no attachments and thus could not be controlled, takes this perspective but critically applies it to the welfare state, to the Marxist project of reconstructing the political economy and the self. And while he attempts to go outside of the Hindu project, asserting that gurus create a dependence on the external, on form, his rugged spiritual individualism recapitulates back to the basic yogi myth. Finally to him, it is through understanding the self, that *all* is understood.

Sarkar is similar to Krishnamurti in that they both deny that their projects are hindu. Sarkar would assert that India has a spiritual tradition and that is why he takes his birth there. (Another feature of the Indian episteme, one is not born but takes birth, thus privileging individual action but the structure of karma too influences this choice). His movement begins in a particular soil but is universal. But both simply—albeit at a profound level—are engaged in massive reconstruction projects. Krishnamurti's is unorganized and only accessible to intellectuals and the upper-middle class as well as to foreigners (his homes were in Europe and the USA). While Sarkar opts for a major overhaul in the tradition at all levels—cultural, political, economic, philosophical—at the level of civilization. But as we continue to place Sarkar within this soup of Indian civilization, he is through and through Indian. As with Krishnamurti, attempts to move outside the Indian project eventually moves one back.

Returning to the problem of the unity of discourse, the privileging of schools of thought instead of a particular author is because the Indian discourse has no founder. While Sarkar argues that it was Shiva who systematized Indian thought and who led the matriarchal society from immorality to morality, others divide Indian thought differently. Central are discussions as to when the Vedas were written, what ideas were brought from where, but no starting point is given. While Buddhists date their mission from Siddhartha Guatama's enlightenment, "Hindus" see the Buddha as one among the many enlightened. In addition, Buddhism, it is believed, was vanquished by the monist arguments of Shankaracharya, possibly since Buddhism had been transformed to an ineffective, elitist nihilism. With the author pushed to the side, great figures in Indian thought soon become archetypes, they become gods. Their historical reality becomes less important. Even Mahatma Gandhi was perceived as capable of healing the sick and causing illness to those who took his name in vain, as Shahid Amin (1988) has argued. Gandhi too has become an archetype of the larger Indian mythic structure.

The Guru

The many gods of the Indian pantheon are also explained by the notion of multiple levels of reality of Indian thought. Center stage of this archetype is man or woman as god: the guru. This basic principle we see throughout Sarkar's writings and throughout Indian thinking. It is not the philosopher who can argue truth, or the businessman, or the political organizer, or the king who occupies the role of author, it is the enlightened one. Whether it is Sarkar's Shiva and Krsna, or whether it is the Buddha and the *bodhisattvas* that follow him, or whether it is Patanjali (the systemizer of Yoga), or the many gurus of this century, once the ultimate state is defined not necessarily by knowledge but by bliss, and once the transition to this bliss is located in a transmission from guru-disciple, then it is the guru that holds many of the keys to understanding Indian thinking.

While a sophisticated reading would argue that the guru functions as the Other in that the guru forces the individual out of the ego self into the transpersonal mystical self, the mythic reading is that the guru functions as the one who can personally liberate one from karma. He or she is the door between the expressed and the unexpressed worlds. Why the guru does not become author and thus become the anchor of discourse relates to the centrality of experience within the Indian discourse. The guru brings one to the mystical state. The guru guides and controls. His thoughts, words and actions must follow one another, ultimately, it is whether the guru can transform the *atman* of the individual to the supreme *atman* of Brahman that is the key.

In addition, the problematic nature of the self adds to the synthetic nature of Indian thought. With the self made concrete, there can be a founder. But with the self simply congealed desire, or a social construction, and the real self a universal self, then the writer cannot but be backstage. Writing indeed is not the individual writing, but the will or play of Shiva or Krsna at the populist level or by the Macrocosm as Sarkar would refer to it. The individual is but an instrument. Moreover, the self by following various disciplines ceases to be the self of time, place and person, of contemporary discourse, of the confines of the objective material world and its various descriptions, becomes a reflection of that which is true, of *ananda*. The true, however, is available to all and thus not assignable to specific individuals.

The discourse of guru is evident within the totality of Indian writing. Only recently has this been translated into what is called Leadership studies in the Occidental discourse. For Sarkar, there are different levels of spiritual leadership. First, there are the *taraka brahamas*, figures that restore the rightful balance in the universe. Second are the enlightened ones who bring people to the spiritual path. Third are the various scientists and inventors.

Sarkar's leadership model takes the enlightened one and makes him or her into an intellectual, then he takes the scientist or inventor and makes him or her into a sage. Finally he adds an activist dimension. This to him is the *sadvipra*, the spiritual intellectual. It is the *sadvipra* that can provide the leadership for transforming the world. That he would opt for a leadership solution to the human dilemma can be read many ways. Among them is that the leadership discourse comes out naturally from the Indian episteme. Only those in touch with the real, who understand struggle, are humble, follow basic moral principles can provide the extra-cyclical leadership to bring on the next revolution. These are Gramsci's organic intellectuals, but they now obtain a spiritual color. The problem of abuse of power by these leaders is handled by having group rule, the problem of the *sadvipras* simply becoming part a new super-class is not developed. The obvious analogy of the rule of the Imam becoming the rule of the ayatollahs is explained as exploitive vipra rule, but the failure of Iran as an event which can be read as an asset to the PROUT movement, as something that PROUT can learn from, is undeveloped.

The guru takes many forms in Indian thinking: as the *Taraka Brahma* in Tantric thinking; as the avatar in Vedic thinking; the *bodhisattva* in Buddhist thinking; the *satguru* (the pure, truthful guru, the one that is truly omniscient); and the plain guru who brings one along the path of spirituality. The categories of teachers in itself is fantastic. While some assert that the guru must be married and simple, others argue that the guru must be a monk and a renunciate. For Sarkar, the perfect guru must have the classic occult powers. These include: *anima*, the ability to become as small as possible; *mahima*, the ability to become as big as possible; *laghima*, the ability to maintain a composure of lightness even while carrying the responsibilities of the universe; *prapti*, ability to provide all with what they need; *iishitva*, omniscience; *vashitva*, the ability to be in control of one's mind; *prakamya*, the ability to translate every psychic wish into physical reality; and *antaryamitva*, the ability to enter the body/mind of anyone. What is significant for this discussion is not whether they are real or not but that they part of the legitimate criteria for a guru, that they are normal and rational. These attributes are not in the Christian sense seen as only the right of the Son of God, but rather they are seen as the potential attributes of every great guru. Of course those that claim they have these powers give reasons why they don't use them. The reason generally is that there are deeper karmic laws that cannot be violated. The manipulation of the physical world cannot be based on personal desire. The world is to be transformed through teaching others by example and action the true path, not simply changing all into ego conceptions of perfection.

However, and this is crucial to understanding Sarkar's pivotal role, Sarkar changes their meanings from their occult mystical definitions to social/other-oriented definitions. *Laghima* now becomes true understanding, for ". . . unless you understand how much pain and sorrow is accumulated in others' minds, how many tears well open their eyes, you cannot alleviate their sorrows and sufferings" (Sarkar, 1989, 6). *Antaryamitva* is retranslated as the ability to enter others' minds so as to know their desires and pains. Thus, the purpose becomes not the fantastic power insinuated, but the necessity to remove human suffering. However, Sarkar claims that these qualities are but natural characteristics of the Macrocosm in its bounded form, in *taraka brahamas* such as Shiva and Krishna. Alternatively, if one translated these to the claims made by the creators of the new information technologies (divine light as fiber optics, omniscience as the perfect information system, entering the body/mind as microscopic revolution) we would have a mirror of Western technology. Within the ideational worldview, it is then not surprising that one creates categories such as the above and assigns them potentially to the individual, conversely, within a sensate ideology, it is not surprising that they become assigned and embedded in various technologies. Alternatively, once the mind is seen as outside of the physical world, then the powers and abilities assigned to it can easily become unimaginable, only limited by our own episteme. In this sense Sarkar's and others' prediction of the good society that is possible once mental and spiritual potentials become tapped does not appear unreasonable, but a natural derivation from the Indian worldview.

Being, Structure and Agency

The question then becomes how to create a society where such possibilities can arise or in Hegelian terms, how to create a society where Being can realize itself? The situation of Being remains the primary differentiation of the various modes of thought: in matter, in spirit, outside both, in both and neither, in society, in the individual, in specific great individuals, in the state, in matter as technology, or in the movements of masses of people, that is, in mass populations. The Indian solution by and large has been in the individual self, not how can Being itself realize itself, but how can the many beings return to the original source, or how can they travel through *Brahmachakra*, the cycle of Brahma? The question of how Being acts in history and the problem of human suffering is ambiguous in Indian thinking. Sarkar, for example, in his theory of history avoids the intrusion of God in history, and yet in his more devotional tracts, it is very clear that Brahman in the form of the *Taraka Brahma* comes to the planet to correct evil. In his *Ananda Sutram*, however, he refers to this notion of divine intervention as not an empirical event, but as a concept that evokes *bhakti* among the mass.

The Redeemer may or may not ontologically exist, what is important is that the devotee believes that the beloved Other exists. Again, this type of thinking is indicative of the Indian episteme. Something does not have to be empirically (materially) real for it be of utility, as long as it has use value in terms of leading individuals to the right path through devotion, action or knowledge (*bhakti*, karma or *jinana*), it becomes rational and real. Truth, just as it becomes associated with bliss, becomes associated with education, history as *iti-hasa*, not history as *itikatha*, meaning to record, or history as the *puranas*, "mythological, not factual, but educative stories" (Sarkar, 1987a, 3: 26–27). Moreover, again truth in itself has numerous meanings, the earlier mentioned *rta* and *satya* distinction. This distinction is applied to history as well in the interpretation of events.

Simply said, the distinctions made in occidental thought of truth and falsehood, good and evil, free will and determination are not so clear. Sarkar (1981, 63–64) writes how after the *Mahabharata*, one of the mothers of the fallen *Kaoravas* asked Krishna, why this war had to happen if Krsna was omnipotent and omniscient. Why human suffering? Krishna's obvious reply—to teach all a lesson that virtue is victorious—was met by the intriguing, "well then why did my family have to die and yours live, why not the other way?" Krishna was silent. She then cursed Krishna, wishing his entire clan, his kin, would die in front of his eyes. Krishna responded by "so be it." Does this mean that Being is acts in history; does it indicate that an individual can change the course of the lives and deaths of many, or is it a reminder to the reader that there is a much larger drama at play and that it doesn't matter if one is victor or loser? It is this last interpretation that Ashis Nandy has favored. He begins his essay entitled "Towards a Third World Utopia" with the following quote: "Alas, having defeated the enemy, we have ourselves been defeated . . . The . . . defeated have become victorious . . . Misery appears like prosperity and prosperity looks like misery. Thus our victory is twined into defeat" (Nandy, 1987, 20). The story then can be read as a true story in the sense of aiding one in resolving the structure/agency question, or it could simply be read as a story to remind us that once the soul enters the body, it must live and die the death of the body. The tragedy of humanity exempts none.

In Search of Critical Thinking

But then within this all embracive worldview, what is the role of critique, of the intellectual discourse? When reality can be constructed in so many different ways what is the role of self-criticism? C. Kunhan Raja's classic *Some Fundamental Problems in Indian Philosophy* is instructive. His question, as the title might lead us to believe, does not attempt to deal with the problems of Indian philosophy from a critical perspective, that is, we are not told what is problematic. His questions are not what doesn't work, what is unreasonable, irrational, nonsensical (he does not develop a politics of order), but rather how Indian philosophy deals with problems. This lack of a critical commentary in Indian intellectual style is investigated by J.N. Mohanty in his "Indian Philosophy Between Tradition and Modernity" (1982).

He comments that Indian philosophy is not orthodox (which he defines as "the hypostatizing of the past into a lifeless, unchanging structure") (23) but rather that it is traditional. Traditional, for him, "is a living process of creation and preservations of significations" (23). Critique then should be done internally to the system. It should not question the grounds of the tradition itself. Furthermore, the " 'logical' itself is conceived as ancillary to . . . the scriptural, so that the tradition did not recognize the autonomy of the logical, be it in the sense of an autonomous, self-subsistence mode of being or in the sense of having an autonomous type of truth (i.e. formal validity, analyticity)" (240). Scripture, thus, cannot be contested, just lived.

Thus, we find Sarkar repeatedly returning to scriptural texts and indeed writing his *Ananda Sutram* as *sutras*, aphorisms that can be easily memorized and chanted. Naturally then India certainly has not created a Michel Foucault who questions the ground of all categories and thus denaturalizes the authoritative. We should not expect this. The questioning that has emerged relates to the location of identity: such identity is perceived as increasingly abstract, increasingly all pervasive, from personal ego, to family, to locality, to race, religion, ideology, to globalism, to universalism, and finally to that which cannot be symbolized by mind and thought. But how the notion of self and identity has been put forth and how it has been constructed and what are the implications of cosmology to "basic human needs and conditions"—the genealogical, the archeological, and structural—remain ignored problems.[3]

Moreover, recent critical efforts by modern writers to respond to this are likely to be doomed for the classical Indian will respond that the queries of critical theory simply privilege the intellect at the expense of other ways on knowing. For the Indian, there is sense-

---

[3] The work of Ashis Nandy and others of the Center for the Study of Developing Societies as well as the Subaltern Studies project are exceptions to this.

perception, reason, authority and intuition. And there is a fifth way of knowing that emerges and disappears in the collective and in the individual, it is *bhakti*, a way of knowing outside of criticism. Even intuition can be criticized as after the mystical experience there is translation into the language of the time, but with *bhakti* there is no translation, no criticism is possible. The devotional discourse remains pre- and post-discursive.

Thus, much of the critique of the Indian perspective has come from outside India. Primary is Orientalism, which have framed Indian philosophy as superstitious, irrational, and nonsensical. Also significant is the Islamic perspective that places Indian thought in the category of the primitive, since from the strict Islamic perspective there is only one God and Muhammed was the last prophet, thus eliminating the guru and Indian gods. The universal brotherhood of Islam is also fundamentally opposed to the caste hierarchy of the Indian structure. Still even with this ideological difference between Islam and Hindu perspectives, historically there have been numerous periods where muslims and hindus have lived in harmony, in a cultural ecology of intertwined beliefs and lives.

While at one level, colonialism has led to a fascination with the West: wealth, industrialism, sexuality and modernity, it appears not to have damaged India's philosophical spirit. Gandhi, Aurobindo, Tagore, Bose, and specifically Radhakrishna, among others, have kept this tradition going. This can partially be accounted for by the lack of division of science, philosophy and religion in the Indian episteme. It is holistic not atomistic. In contrast is the Western division where sense perception and inference are located in science, reason and authority located in philosophy, and authority and intuition located in religion. This division does not hold true in the Indian episteme, past or present. Rather the various ways of knowing the real do not contradict each other. Simply, science is seen as a particular *darshana*, a particular way of seeing the world. Thus, Sarkar can speak intelligibly about a science of intuition, a science of devotion, a science of yoga, a science of Brahman. To him, science simply means that there are causal reasons for various beliefs. They are not based on authority or tradition or intuition. They can be logically induced from the empirical world or deducted from his theory of consciousness. His work is scientific in that there is rational explanation.

However, he does make the implicit difference between the scientific and the irrational or primitive by asserting that his views are better then traditional Indian views because they are more scientific. But to Sarkar, this means that they are more systematic, and he provides a theoretical framework for the understanding of non-material entities, transmigration of the soul and so forth. But he does not make the next move and attempt to find proof within the empirical social sciences as the Transcendental Movement has tried to do. There are no mathematical methods or techniques that seek to prove that the mind has material, ego-rational, and transcendental capabilities. However, at the same time, the western notion of science: hypothesis testing, empirical verification, repeatability, objective disinterest from the results of the study or experiment, validity and reliability, and the vertical division of theory and data with values as outside of science is perceived as cultural not as universal. The Indian view of science is perceived as universal.

But Sarkar does to some extent move out of the Indian tradition. The role of authority is significantly diminished, especially in relation to various concepts he finds inappropriate—exploitive interpretations of the karma, and exploitive tendencies in monist schools of thought (as well as social systems that deny basic structural equity and material equally opportunity). In a remarkable statement—that can only be intelligible in the Indian context—he counsels his followers to reject the words of the mythical Brahma if he appeared in front of them if the words were irrational, yet to accept the wisdom of a child if sensible (Anandamurti, 1986, 79). Besides the implication that God can become human, it is an obvious theoretical move away from the authority of the *Vedas* and *Tantras*. Surprisingly and unfortunately, Sarkar does not historicize the rational and natural at this theoretical level. However he does develop a sociology of knowledge which argues that what is significant and real changes as society moves through its different eras, but the deeper tradition of the real within the Indian context remains steady.

Cycles of Creation

As mentioned earlier, this deeper tradition begins with the tradition of understanding the self and assertion that this understanding is objective. "In India, philosophers did not project their thoughts externally; the project of man's thoughts on the outside world had its counterpart in a similar project on the thoughts inward also . . . the result was that the understanding of the nature of the world became identical with the understanding of the inward nature of man himself" (Raja, 1974, 4). For Sarkar, this is evidenced in his theory of Consciousness or *Brahmachakra*. Creation is a cycle and has two aspects. Consciousness becomes increasingly dense until it becomes physical matter. The next phase is the development of "life" from matter and then through evolution the development of humans. Humans at this point can return to their animal heritage or move forward toward their divine destiny. The pull of evolution is the attraction to the eternal and the push is the dialectical physical struggle between humans and nature, and between the ideas of humans themselves. Thus, at this level of evolution, there appears choice: the binding force of *Prakrti*, the creative energy, can be resisted and transcended.

Of particular interest is that the human mind has the same structure as cosmic mind. Both have a witness function, both have an ego-integration function, both have a sense of doing and both have a mental plate in which all this occurs. In Indian philosophy, thinking must have a space to occur. This space is the mental plate or the *citta*. This would be a natural derivative of the classical episteme in which thoughts must relate to substances. In addition, once the mind is removed from the brain it must have a place wherein it can reflect, thus the invention of a plate.

Now for the Cosmic Mind, the mental plate is the universe itself. Cosmic Mind, as one might expect, is the category used after pure unbounded consciousness is bound by *Prakrti*, the creative force of desire and action. It is analogous in conventional Western thought to God, and in the Platonic thought to the Idea. But the Idea is not more real than its physical correspondence. Both are real at different levels, for at work is a cycle of creation. This binding function—Nature—is not the traditional Indian *maya* of illusion, rather it is an integral part of *Purusa* or consciousness. They are both real and inseparable. As Sarkar explains, they are "like two sides of a piece of paper" (Sarkar, 1967, 1). The why of creation is considered unanswerable since its understanding is beyond human mind—Mind cannot perceive itself—(yet the construction of cosmology, interestingly, is not). However, alternatively at the level of the devotional discourse, creation is explained by the loneliness of God. The universe was created so that God would have something to do—it was God's desire—the cosmic mysterious drama, ultimately unintelligible to the human mind.

As projected, the universe while in essence a thought of Consciousness is composed of basic fundamental factors: etherial, aerial, luminous, liquid, and solid. These are interrelated and can play different roles in the movement of space and substance. Sarkar, in addition, to this classical scheme, had added the theme of microvita—the minutest substance, thus making his thought holistic and atomistic at the same time.

Human Suffering

The question of human suffering is answered in varied ways as well. At the level of the individual, suffering stems from desire and attachment. Thus, choice. This, of course, leaves the structure of society (inequity, imperialism, and injustice) outside of the text. It is only the *avatar* who through his actions removes the wickedness in people. In this perspective, the moving force of history is external, for only the *avatar* can right the imbalance and bring on justice. The denial of this mythic structure—that of hope and faith in the external redeemer—is perhaps the real and awesome contribution of Marxian and neo-Marxist thinking, that is, the analysis of the structure of imperialism and injustice.

Sarkar includes the notion of the redeemer but steps outside the Indian tradition and borrows from critical Marxist thinking, most likely due to the influence of such thinkers such as M.N. Roy or Subash Chandra Bose. Nonetheless, this lack of structural analysis is the glaring weakness of Indian thinking. But then we should not be surprised at the particular social formation of the caste structure. How else could it have continued intellectually undisturbed. A structural discourse immediately exposes it. Thus, while Indian thinking has been strong at the personal, the moral and the abstract (ideational) levels of discourse, it remains weak at the structural level.

How is choice dealt with in the absolute discourse and in the moral discourse? At the outset, choice is negated insofar as one accepts that what-is is a creation and that humans are but actors in this larger drama. At this absolute level there is no choice. Thus, the inference that the guru (one whose mind is as the mind of the macrocosm) cannot make mistakes. Virtue is not a choice for him, his action inheres in virtue. Thus, animals do what is natural, humans fluctuate between the natural and the unnatural, but the God-man again resides in naturalness.

But there is a third level as well. This is the level of *Prakrti*; it is the level of creation or alternatively said, at the level of deep social forces. At this level there is choice and there is not choice. There is a war between virtue and vice, *dharma* and *adharma* which at any moment is unpredictable in its form and in its content. This situation is possible because at one level virtue represents the wish of God (of Krishna the godhead in Sarkar's earlier story) while at the same time represents the ultimate real, Brahman, who is beyond good and evil. It is beyond any notion of morality since morality is a human construction. Thus, the problem of evil and suffering is answered in a both/and perspective that is level or reality dependent. Agency and structure are not put in opposition to each other. Rather, they exist simultaneously as part of a larger issue, part of a larger coexistence that can be understood to some degree, but still remains ultimately beyond both agency and structure. Karma creates the conditions of what can be done, yet new karma is ever created and karma can also be broken by the grace of God. Perhaps this is unsatisfactory for the non-Indian mind, but it resides peacefully in the Indian.

The Layers of the Indian Mind

The model of the Indian mind too follows this both/and pattern. The classic psychological model sees the body, *Annamaya Kosa*, as the first layer of mind. This is the level of hormones, glands, blood and cells. Well-being is possible through the practice of the various *yogas*. The next layer is the *Kamamaya kosa*, the layer of physical desire, the instinctive level. It is controlled by breath. The *Manomaya kosa* is the rational/emotional level. It is concerned with four functions: memory, thinking, dreaming and the experience of pain/pleasure. It is controlled by concentration. The *Atimanasa kosa* is the transpersonal level of mind. It loosely corresponds with the Jungian collective unconscious. At this layer of mind, every individual is connected, thus allowing for various forms of group consciousness and collective change. *Vijinanamaya kosa* is the last level of individual mind. One's actions at this level correspond to those of cosmic mind. Thus, will and larger historical purpose are identical. The last level, *Hiranamaya kosa* is a "thin veil that separates one from pure consciousness" (Towsey, 1986, 103).

Table 2

Level of Mind	Corresponds to	Controlled by
Annamaya Kosa	Body	Yoga, Diet, Fasting
Kamamaya Kosa	Sensory and in-born knowledge	Yama and Niyama
Manomaya Kosa	Physical Desire/Instinctive	Breath-Pranayama
Atminasa Kosa	Memory/Thinking/ Dreaming	Concentration
Vijinanamaya Kosa	Capacity to discriminate reality	Wisdom through discrimination and non-attachment from other levels
Hiranyama Kosa	Transpersonal mind	Devotion-Meditation

Continuing in the perfect symmetrical model, Cosmic Mind (God) has similar levels of thought: the physical universe, the crude cosmic mind, the subtle, the supramental, the subliminal and the subjective cosmic mind. There exists then a perfect symmetry between the individual and the cosmic. But this mathematical perfection does not end there. Just as the mind is divided into layers, so too is the body. The five layers relate to five mental-glandular centers located in *and* out of the body. These control emotions and desires and are managed through spiritual practices. In addition, there exist layers of the cosmic mind, the *lokas*. Thus the body and mind of the individual and the body and mind of the universe (the layers of Cosmic Mind) exist in perfect ontological symmetry.

The why of this symmetry, however, is not explained since that would call into question the structure of the episteme. There have been many efforts (For example, Towsey, 1986; Wilber, 1995; Elgin, 1993) have been to apply this model to the western model of mind. Again, the above is a brief description of what are volumes of writings on the layers of the mind, each rich with philosophical commentaries and with populist versions assigning gods and demons to each layer. This model is then superimposed on various theoretical enterprises such that each theory is true at its level of existence—Freudian, Marxian, Jungian, but only the Eastern view which has ways to deal with all the layers is ultimately true.

Dharma, defined as "the way" emerges once one has merged with pure consciousness. Subsequently theorizing about the memory of this blissful merger begins. Theorizing after spiritual realization results in the authentically true. Given the unity of being that one experiences, theory then *prima facie* cannot be racist or limited, it must be outside of all boundaries. There are two contradictions not resolved though. The first deals with the historical realities of theorizing by enlightened ones as eventually resulting in various "isms." This is resolved, first, by the notion that once the truth is spoken it then enters the discourse of the world; second, by the assertion that there are different stages of enlightenment; and, third, by the assertion of the fall of man, from order to disorder, from golden eras to materialistic eras.

The contradiction not answered is that if the knowledge of past, present and future is known, then the universe is a closed system, yet consciousness is constantly being bound and souls are always remembering their true identity and merging in consciousness. How is this dynamic nature of the world resolved with the omniscient static nature of the world? Sarkar personally resolves it by not predicting the future and by asserting that all statements change given the relativity of time, place and person. Is then omniscience conditional? Sarkar philosophically resolves this question of the nature of the universe by asserting that mind cannot know pure Consciousness except through self-transcendence. In addition, using the metaphor of Shiva, the universe is considered in the constant process of creation and destruction—it is an open system! Yet a science of the currently known relative world is certainly possible.

Still, within conventional Indian philosophy, the problem of ethics and morality and the impersonal nature of consciousness, if only reconcilable at the level of individual choice, appears in contradiction with the model of the *avatar*, the savior, the *bodhisattva*. Leaving aside the arguments within this philosophical discourse, more significant are its implications. What results is a social formation that cannot but be vertical and frozen, ever so perfectly symmetrical, since karma privileges personal action and blame at the expense of structural analyses. Moving outside of karma comes not through utopia building, through revolution or governmental social welfare, but through faith in the soon to arrive redeemer.

The classic Indian response to the above critique has been multifold. The evocation of Maya, that social suffering is but an illusion, of the naturalness of *varna*, of the divine right of power, of the

king, or of the right of the Brahmin. It has been as one might expect
not a structural response nor a historical response, but a transcendental. It is a response that cannot be challenged within the framework of the space wherein it is uttered, thus allowing an escape only
to an alternative view, Buddhism or Islam, for example. Or more
recently Gandhism, which intends to make all shudras or liberal capitalism which intends to use in equality for the benefit of the majority, through trickle-down development economics.

Returning to the Indian episteme, central to its understanding are
the following seventeen points: *first*, history is cyclical but the cycle
has direction; *second*, there is a symmetry between the individual and
the cosmic, the body and the mind (as within as without: as above
as below); *third*, truth is defined as that which leads to physical, mental and spiritual growth, that is, philosophy as resolving suffering,
truth as therapy; *fourth*, there is a unity of discourse with the final
meaning resting in the interpreter; *fifth*, a both/and approach to contradictions; *sixth*, a view that there are multiple levels of reality; *seventh*, the privileging of the enlightened one; *eighth*, a strong vertical/
hierarchical dimension; *ninth*, the self is the center piece; *tenth*, karma
and dharma are the pillars that support the foundation; *eleventh*,
holism in that every aspect of creation is intrinsic to it with the
nucleus of the universe (since consciousness is everywhere and everything) simultaneously everywhere and in everything; *twelfth*, dialectical, in that there are forces in conflict and in tension with each
other (and out of these struggles qualitatively different levels of substances appear); *thirteenth*, consciousness leads to matter which then
dialectically evolves back to consciousness; *fourteenth*, there is a lack
of a critical spirit that attempts to question the episteme itself; *fifteenth*,
science is constructed as rational and causal and *sixteenth*, there are
five ways of knowing the real: sense perception, authority, reason,
intuition and devotion/love. And finally, *seventeenth*, the Indian episteme is additive. It has not radically changed through history, rather
new levels of reality are added to the episteme, thus transforming
the episteme and at the same time "Indianizing" the new discourse.

Episteme, Cosmology and Intellectual Styles of Knowing

To further understand the Indian episteme, we go outside of it and
compare Michel Foucault's analysis of the history of the European
episteme with the Indian. Foucault takes a marked historical view

of European cosmology and develops a history of epistemes. Of interest is that Foucault's description of the classical European episteme dominant in the 16th century shows a remarkable similarity to the ancient Indian episteme, which as just mentioned survives today, largely intact, notwithstanding the reformers, the liberals, the technologists, the Muslims and the British.

To Foucault, resemblance was the key that guided the dispersion of order and knowledge. ". . . resemblance organized the play of symbols, made possible knowledge of things visible and invisible, and controlled the art of representing them" (Foucault, 1973, 17). And in poetic language that in itself resembles the style of the Vedas.

> The universe was folded upon itself; the earth echoing the sky, faces seeing themselves reflected in the stars, and plants holding within their stems the secrets that were of use to man. Painting imitated space. And representation . . . was posited as a form of repetition: the theatre of life on the mirror of nature (17).

Of course, this view was to a large extent held by the Greeks as well, it was there that the macro/micro inter-relationship for the West began.

But the characteristics he uses to describe this resemblance, we do not see in Sarkar's prose and philosophy at all. Foucault's characteristics include *convenientia* or a kind of intermingling of nature, man, animal and plant. "We see plants in the antlers of stags, a sort of grass on the faces of men . . . The world is simply the universal convenience of things, there are the same number of fish in the water as there are animals, or objects produced by nature or man" (18). This is the ancient astrological worldview where everything is related and in mathematical perfection to everything itself. Just as nature has cycles, individuals have cycles, as do dynasties. Thus the social world follows the natural, individual and cosmic worlds.

The next aspect of this episteme, according to Foucault, is *aemulatio*, or emulation.

> There is something in emulation of the reflection and the mirror: it is the means whereby things scattered through the universe answer each other. The human face, from a far, emulates the sky, and just as man's intellect is an imperfect reflection of God's wisdom, so his two eyes, with their limited brightness, are a reflection of the vast illumination spread across the sky by sun and moon; the mouth is Venus, since it gives passage to kisses and words of love (19).

Space is abolished and the small becomes a miniature version of the large.

The other two characteristics are analogy and sympathy. The analogy model is similar to the model of the Indian body and the *chakra* system. The universe is held together in analogous relationships. "He [man] is the great fulcrum of proportions—the center upon which relations are concentrated and from which they are once again reflected" (23). Sympathy appears with antipathy and both are of a world in tension with each other, forces in harmony and disharmony.

In Indian thought it is the force of *vidya* and *avidya*—introversion and extroversion, in harmony and disharmony, expansion and contraction. It is also the three forces of *sattva* (pure), *raja* (active) and *tamas* (static) in equilibrium, until an equilateral triangle is created. From this shape, the seed of desire springs out and Creation begins. In classical Indian thought, the power of language was centered in the name: a name represented the ontology of a thing, a person. Thus the mantra. Mantras can kill. Mantras are secret. Mantras said correctly can give liberation. It is not a mere representation of the modern world, nor is a name a construction as in postmodernism and poststructuralism, rather the name links one to being itself: to ontological truth. Language in the classical episteme is real and it participates directly in the real: the relationship is ontological. Thus, the mind of the meditating person—while repeating the mantra—becomes that which is being said, since the underlying principle is: as you think you become. Exactitude in repeating the mantra is critical for the right saying evokes the internal Gods; the wrong saying the internal demons; alternatively, the right saying focuses the mind, the wrong saying distorts it.

In the modern world, however, language refers to the real: the real is objective and extra-linguistic. Language then has no intrinsic meaning or magical power in itself. Modern research on Indian meditation can then argue that it matters not what one says, it is the technical act of repetition, of slowing the breath that is critical. The ancient world is suddenly then appropriated by the modern: the enchantment of the word is lost for the objectivity of the world.

However, the poststructural perspective asserts that language participates in the construction of the real and in general takes a skeptical/agnostic position as to whether the real can be known in and of itself. Language then becomes not a vehicle to liberation, nor a

mere representation of liberation, but a tool which one can understand, toward which one can allocate resources, what might be called
God-talk, or liberation-talk. The mantra then becomes an asset for
the mind or in terms of social formation, for the priest.

Returning to Foucault's history of episteme, in the next era, the
modern era, these resemblances become notions of madness: magic
was hidden and a new form of rationality emerged that had different
characteristics. The word ceased to have ontological identity with its
referent object. The object stood alone independent of mind and
knower. Knowledge of it, however, remained possible with adequate
theory, reason and senses.

> Resemblances and signs have dissolved their former alliances: simili-
> tudes have become deceptive and verge upon the visionary or mad-
> ness; things still remain stubbornly within their ironic identity; they
> are no longer anything but what they are; words wander off on their
> own, without content, without resemblance to fill their emptiness, they
> are no longer the marks of things; they lie sleeping between the pages
> of books and covered with dust, Magic, which permitted the deci-
> pherment of the world by revealing the secret resemblances beneath
> its signs, is no longer of any use except as an explanation, in terms
> of madness, of why analogies are always proved false (48).

But while the West has generally moved out of the classical era and
entered the modern episteme of representation with language now
as symbolic of the real with good theory being fidelity of representation, in India the ancient/classical era continues alongside the
modern era.

In Indian thought, the modern episteme has not destroyed the
classical one. Social psychologists like Ashis Nandy and others use
the knowledge of this episteme as a foil against modernity, the
Transcendental Meditation movement hopes to legitimize the classical through the modern, but Sarkar, however, attempts to rationalize the classical, removing what he believes is magic and what is not
rational. For example, he does not locate witchcraft under women
wisdom (pre-modern) nor under superstition, rather his distribution
is knowledge used to attain the spiritual (*vidya*) and knowledge used
to obtain powers for ego-gratification. The ability to move objects,
cast spells, injure from a distance, spread social theories through
microvita, instruct meditators on the Himalayas to concentrate so
that a New Age can come into being is not contentious. Rather it

is utterly obvious. His project is to frame the classical in a new rationality, not of the modern, but of the planetary. Action at a distance is not seen from the view of analogy or sympathy, but rather the power one develops when the mind itself is focused and concentrated.

Again returning to Foucault, given these changes in epistemes and given that for Foucault man epistemologically appeared in the modern era and will soon disappear, our question becomes did "man" exist in ancient India? For Foucault, European man did not exist unto himself until the modern era, he was simply an image, a reflection of the real that was elsewhere, he did not exist in-himself. It is only in the modern era that man comes to be the measure of all things. In the classical episteme, there could be no *science* of man, no separate category of existence. However, man did exist in India in that man was an image, but that image of not above or near, or an analogy, or a sympathy, rather the body of man himself was the ground of experimentation. The practice of yoga, the search for the first desire, the division of man into sectors of control, wherein breath and mantras could manage the body, are indications that man did exist. He existed in India and not elsewhere because of the nature of the Indian episteme. The episteme was not antithetical to nature; everything had a soul; God had personal features and was impersonal; humans had a personal soul but were not really that soul; the goal was eternal life but not in a way that the self could enjoy it. It is a paradoxical worldview in that *moska* (the final liberation) can only be obtained when that which seeks to attain liberation disappears. The subject can be free only when it no longer is its own object, when it is no longer in the position of perceiver.

There are two dimensions to this. First, is the philosophical view of the mind realizing its limitations and transcending itself to become the Other. That is, liberation comes to be a state wherein there is no fear. The second is the classic worldview in which the actual stuff, the substance, of the mind is transformed. Mind is just not an idea, rather it has a presence that is real. Thus, in the Indian and in Sarkar's view, the mind is "alchemically" transformed into a new substance. The transformation of the mind thus is compatible to the classic symmetrical episteme, to the natural and the cosmological: seeds become trees, mind-stuff becomes god-stuff.

Structure and Cosmology

We now move from the theory of knowledge to the implications of knowledge. We will borrow mainly from the cosmological analysis of Johan Galtung. In his article "Religion as a Factor," Galtung (1983) compares and contrasts three main cosmologies (leaving aside African, Pacific Islander and others): Western, Oriental and what he calls Hindu, or Indian. He seeks to take religion from the transcendental and sort out its implications on four variables: direct violence; structural violence; distribution of wealth, force and meaning (remunerative, coercive, and normative types of power); and; economic growth.

We use his model to first locate Indian thought and then attempt to place Sarkar's thought in opposition to it and to ascertain whether the problems in Indian thought are resolved by Sarkar, and if so, within the Indian context, or outside of it.

Galtung's analysis is structural. He asks the question: "with which structures and processes in very concrete material and human reality would certain religious thought figures, idea structures be compatible" (Galtung, 1983, 1). Religion to him is a dimension of cosmology. This is the search for the deeper assumptions that underlie people's attitudes and behavior. For Galtung, a cosmology is a social grammar that defines how humans relate to each other as well as to nature, and these categories themselves (1981). It is embedded in individuals and can be seen as a social program. That which is isomorphic to the program is more easily accepted, understood, and followed, and that which is not, is rejected. These isomorphisms show up at the level of the individual view of mind, at the level of architecture (physical space) and naturally at the level of the view of space/time and the Other. Galtung's notion of cosmology is similar to Foucault's concept of and one can pose a chicken/egg question here: which is first, cosmology or episteme? There might be a dominant cosmology with different epistemes in it: antiquity, classical, modern and postmodern. At the same time, cosmological analysis in itself is a product of a particular view of ordering the world, of a particular episteme—precisely, the Western modern sociological one.

Cosmology for Galtung includes structure, culture and person. Certain types of actions, ways of seeing are compatible with certain cosmologies, thus restricting the likely possibility of action for individuals and other groupings. Finally, for Galtung, language is part of cosmology and predisposes various behaviors. It is similar to *Weltanschauung* (worldview) but broader and deeper and not assignable to a particular author, but provides the ground from which authors and others speak. Thus, cosmological analysis, like poststructural thought, does not take a stand on the materialism versus idealism dichotomy, rather, it is a search for deep structures and ideologies that become revealed once something is compared so that one can see how it differs from other cosmologies. In addition, cosmologies are discrete phenomena. Galtung's question is: Is it possible to be from a particular cosmology and create a new one? For Marx, the answer is that Marxism continues the basic Western formation but with new carriers of salvation (the party for the proletariat) with a new capital (Moscow at one time) and with similar perspectives on gender, nature, and time. With respect to Sarkar, answering this question is at the heart of this book.

Galtung begins his analysis by developing a religious map of the world. The first are the Occidental religions. The people of the book: Judaism, Christianity and Islam. They are understood by the following factors: personal god (describable by human features); singularist (only one god with "jealousy toward other gods"); universal (the religion is for all, the universe); personal soul (all human beings have a soul which is the link between the individual and God and can be developed further through right prayer and behavior); and the soul has an eternal life (either in heaven or hell, depending on the behavior). In terms of epistemology it is atomistic (searching to endlessly divide phenomena) and deductive.

Galtung argues that they have developed one after the other (Judaism, Christianity, Islam) and that the present form is secularism, or humanism in its various forms: liberalism, conservativism and Marxism. In humanism, there is no God, man is the measure of all things, but the prophets remain, whether Adam Smith or Karl Marx.

Furthermore, within the Western cosmological model one has to choose between one of these ideologies at the expense of others. No contradictions are permitted. Finally, the main project is that of sorting good from evil.

In contrast, and this brings us to the next portion of the map, Oriental thought is additive. Contradictions are allowed and are seen as a source of enrichment. Good and evil can coexist, indeed, dichotomies are dialectical inseparable. Nothing, then, is entirely good or bad in this world. Epistemologically, Oriental thinking is holistic and dialectic, searching for totalities and their essences. Things are explained not in terms of their logical interrelationships but in terms of inner forces and processes that in turn follow the whole and are discovered through empirical intuition (nature and spirit together). Sarkar's thought to a great degree follows this pattern, but he intends to be utterly rational as well, and thus, attempts to find a place in-between and beyond both these perspectives, a space which as we will discover Galtung argues is still fundamentally Hindu.

In Oriental thought, there is no soul, there is no god, other faiths are not excluded, and it is collectivist. What is critical is the mind working out its problems, its desires. It is thus godless but has many symbol systems of the gods exist within; it is pluralist (other gods are allowed to exist); particularist (dependent on the observer, space and time); soul-less; and the goal is the nirvana (a place where there is no desire). The key is the description of reality through metaphors rather than the creation of exact maps of reality, for as the Zen story goes, one should not confuse the finger pointing at the moon for the moon.

While the above map is highly useful, what needs to be added is that Islam too is also highly collectivist, high on the fraternity side and that Buddhism (and Hinduism) ultimately lead to a cosmic accounting scheme. Individual realization is lost at the expense of the search for merits to negate one's demerits so one can enjoy the next life. What starts out as a transcendental (yet derived from the empirical) investigation of the self, becomes epicurean in its practice. Instead of the transcendental what is left is prayer to the external Buddha (functioning as the Western God) to absolve one's karmas (or sins). However, this merit/demerit conversation is different than that of the Christian perspective in that there is less of a priesthood to extract the merits. Nonetheless the similarities in these two cosmologies possibly point to a deeper more universal human structure. This structure can be characterized by a desire for immediate sense-oriented rewards (and class or caste power that uses religious messages to extract meanings—obedience, respect, acceptance—labor, or wealth) and a real desire for some type of reality that is beyond the immediate, the temporal, and the sensate. This is the tension of sensation and the ideational so well developed by Pitirim Sorokin (1970). The similarity between these vastly different cosmologies also might point to the fall from heaven hypothesis, wherein each idea begins pure and then power, ego, fame finds a way of remaking that idea to fit the reality of the world.

Alternatively, in Confucianism, "there is no promise of heaven or threat of hell, only the hypothesis, verified in social reality according to the adherents that by following these rules a decent stable society will ensue. It is an ethical code that does not exclude religion" (Galtung, 1983, 11).

Shintoism is quite different from the above. "Here there is a clear doctrine of the Chosen People with the Sun Goddess finding her abode in the Japanese Emperor, setting the Japanese people apart from the rest of the world. It is particularist in that they (the Japanese are chosen) but not singularist (in that Japanese combine it with other religions relatively easily)" (11).

In this mapping Hinduism, however, has elements of Occidental and Oriental thought. Of [Hinduism] one may say everything: there is a personal god, even more if one wants to see it that way, and there is no god if one wants to conceive of them metaphorically. They may be said to exclude other faiths, but they are also rich and complex that they can easily be said to include others, through some little act of redefinition. They may be said to be for the Hindu space only, but on the other hand, because of that richness easily comprise the whole of the world, because any religion should be able to recognize its basic figures and thought structures somewhere in the tremendous variety of Hindu thought (13).

Now what of Indian social space? At the outset, for Galtung, it is cruel in the way power is distributed. This is the caste system. This structural violence led to the Buddha's and later on Gandhi's effort to reform it—to make all equal. Ashis Nandy (1987) here has argued that Gandhi's effort was to simply make all into shudras; Marx's was to put the shudras in power, while some like Ananda Coomaraswamy have tried to defend the caste system, arguing that it is less cruel than the Western class system—Coomaraswamy, however, forgets that India has both, a double cruelty one might say.

Sarkar: Indian, Occidental or Oriental?

What of Sarkar? Is he Indian, Occidental or Oriental. One gets a complex mix. First, he is universalistic—he has written a divine command that states that it is the duty of all followers "to bring all to the path of bliss," to the path that leads to *ananda*, to the good life, righteousness. Thus, it is not as particularistic as Indian and Oriental thought. Secondly, it is not simply singularistic since there is a

non-dualistic position, it is not there is God and separately there is
nature, rather God and nature exist together. It is non-dualistic.
However, god is not personal, except in the form of the *taraka brahma*,
who is not an ontological person, but functions as real qua *bhakti*.

At the same time, Consciousness qua God is indescribable: beyond
space, time and observer. When the infinite is discussed, the guru
becomes dumb and the disciple deaf, as the infinite cannot be
expressed. The soul has eternal life with the goal—not being the
cessation of desire, as in Buddhism—the transformation of multiple
desires into one desire, that of cosmic consciousness. Thus, here is
a critical difference between Buddhism and Sarkar" thought. The
goal is not to think of nothing (to not objectify the eternal subjectivity of the world, the I-Thou relationship), but to think of the
infinite, since first, the mind must always think of something by its
very a priori nature and, second, since what the mind thinks, it
becomes. Since the mind cannot by definition think of the infinite,
it ceases to (for the time being) exist as before, and goes into a state
of *samadhi*, and thus attain bliss. Thus, Sarkar's model is first and
foremost mystical. This is not to say there are not any concrete
visions of the material world. For the material is real, but it changes.
Thus, it is not absolute. With the world real, the goal then is to
reduce human suffering by finding ways in which individuals can
achieve their spiritual destiny. This is obviously compatible with
Indian cosmology: utopia is a place where the self can realize itself,
its true nature. Utopia, on the other hand, in the Western model,
is where all one's desires are met (alternatively, where one meets
one's ancestors, a basic desire). For Sarkar, it is the place where one
has no desires since there is self to desire them. The realization of
the natural self—*atman*—is irreversible for the particular individual—
it is the death of death.

In moving to the politics of utopian thinking, Galtung asks: *who*
will bring about the new world, *where* will this struggle take place,
and *how*. What are the specific messages that are embedded in cosmologies with respect to remunerative and coercive power? And,
where do they stand with respect to the problem of growth and distribution and the problem of structural and direct violence?

Galtung argues that Hinduism and Buddhism are weak at creating economic growth—Hinduism because of the notion of karma
and the structural rigidity of the caste system, and Buddhism because
of its focus on distribution. Islam is also weak at encouraging eco-

nomic growth largely because of its doctrine against interest. Christianity obviously is strong on the growth dimension.

Galtung next develops the distribution dimension. This is a concern with the allowable level of inequality. Buddhism by positing right livelihood and the middle way advocates a doctrine of floors and ceilings. Hinduism, however, has no clear-cut right livelihood, nor indications of floors and ceilings, rather because of karma, its economic principles are certainly ripe for exploitation. Although growth is possible in the short run, there is no comparable redistribution mechanism (demand function) in the long run. Here, of course, Sarkar differs from traditional Indian thinking in that his ideology, PROUT, is growth and distribution oriented (It has maxi-mini wage limits, limits to wealth accumulation, simplicity in living, but encouragement of incentives, and of accentuating the maximum use of physical, mental and spiritual resources).

With Occidental religions, there is a tension between salvation through deeds and salvation through faith. This deeper dilemma finds its expression in Indian thinking in the contradiction between one's own action leading to enlightenment and praying to the gods for assistance in resolving the problem of the material world.

For Sarkar, this tension is directly dealt with. Although liberation is an individual affair, one has a basic responsibility to the universe, one cannot rid the ego of ego unless one is involved in good efforts. However, gold chains or iron chains, those of good and bad karma, are still chains. Effort simply creates more chains. It is devotion that leads to the realization of the unity of self and the infinite. But, in Sarkar's thinking, there must be a balance between the individual and the collective. One does good to the individual to reduce the misery of the individual and to create a better world, where the collective mind can develop. Thus, Sarkar develops an alternative politics that brings the spiritual back to the earth and earth to heaven (Inayatullah and Fitzgerald, 1999: 19–23).

What of violence? Hinduism is low on direct violence with its emphasis on *ahimsa*, but high on structural violence because of the caste system and the dynamics of karma. Islam, with its call for fraternity is low on structural violence, but given its historical development—defending itself against other civilizations and modern de-colonization—is high on direct violence.

However, Galtung argues that both Christianity and Islam have deep codes in them toward the non-believer that can be used to justify both direct and structural violence. These attitudes are not found in Buddhism and Hinduism. Hinduism, however, has in its structure, patterns directed against those at the bottom are not found in Buddhism either. Sarkar again directly seeks to reform these patterns.

For Sarkar, revolutionary efforts should not be directed against capitalists, but against the system of capitalism. For in a system where the reincarnation of the soul is accepted, simply killing another (as in State execution) does not resolve the problem for the seeds of the problem remain in the individual mind and collective mind. The task must then be to correct the mind through spiritual practices or structural constraints and transform society. Indeed, at the mystical level, Earth itself is a schooling and testing ground. His comments on exploitation and on violence in general can be traced to Tantric doctrines of struggle. However his acceptance and condoning of Subhash Chandra Bose's program ("to free India") also presents a side to this thinking that is far from Gandhi's passive resistance. Sarkar's would engage in active resistance with violent struggle acceptable but as a final resort. However, even in violent resistance or struggle the goal would remain, *ahimsa*, that is, the *intent* not to harm others.

Finally, Sarkar distances himself from Jain and other totally non-violence perspectives by reminding us that the entire universe is violent, each particle/wave living and dying. Concretely, Sarkar accepts the warrior role of Krishna in the *Mahabharata* and Shiva as destroyer when evil grows on Earth.

But perhaps Sarkar's key contribution to traditional Indian thought is his redefinition of karma. While Sarkar has argued that karma should not be used as a justification for blaming the victim, it is his conceptual jump that is far more useful than his humanistic exhortation. This is partly as his redefinition of karma counters blame-the-victim politics but as well because exhortations simply in the long run reinscribe that which is being fought against whether by stating the issue in the same language or by concentrating on that which is wrong, instead of that which needs to be done. Sarkar adds the concept of imposed *sanskara*, karma or *A'ropita* (Anandamitra, 1967, 181), or to use sociological language, structural karma. Thus, one is in a particular socio-economic space because of past life *sanskaras* (desires and reactions that must be worked out) *and*, this is the key, because of the social structure around one, that is, the environment. Thus, the child born in Calcutta and made to beg is not blamed for having bad karma, but rather the structure of society has made it such that bad karma is imposed on the self of the boy. Thus, social environment (as well as physical surroundings) became central in his theory of action and reaction, of causality. This keeps the necessary structure of Indian thought (escaping the wheel of life) yet adds a structural dynamic to it. Because of this, changing the environment—social and political—becomes an appropriate strategy. For an appropriate social and physical environment can then lead to a quickening of one's *karmas* and a quickening of the process of enlightenment. Karma (how it is expressed and its severity) can be transformed through social service, helping others. This redefinition of karma becomes a potent weapon against *jhat*, caste.

Finally, Galtung includes the secular ideologies in his argument. Marxism is high on distribution, high on direct violence, but low on structural violence. Liberalism emphasizes economic growth. It is not concerned with the other variables and sees them as somewhat natural, part of the system, as laws of societies, the cost of having left the Garden of Eden.

In India, the most recent effort to reinterpret Hinduism has been Gandhism. Gandhi worked directly to reduce direct and structural violence so that human development and non-violence became inseparable. For Galtung, Gandhism is much closer to Buddhism than Hinduism, both come from the same soil, but both have been forced to leave it (should we predict the same with Sarkar?).

Finally, the modern ideology of social democracy accepts growth and expansion and the need to reduce both direct and structural violence, thus, making it an ideal system for Galtung. However, from Sarkar's perspective, social democracy experiment is non-transcendental and thus does not appropriately deal with the spirit, with meaning, and with the environmental world, the rights of animals and plants. Moreover, he would opt, especially in the third world, for a revolutionary agenda instead of the slow speed of democratic socialism.

Sarkar's goal, then, is to develop an alternative political-economy, theory of distributive justice, that draws its theoretical sustenance not from modern economic theory, but from his spiritual conception of the real. Sarkar's model is growth oriented in that its basic principles assert the need to expand wealth, to find new ways to increase material wealth, and it is essentially humanistic in that it asserts a need to continuously redistribute wealth to all members, human and non-human.

On a critical note, the question that must be asked is, does Sarkar have any hope of achieving his transformation of the Indian social formation given the resilience of this structure? How will Sarkar's law of the social cycle and the centrality of spiritual leadership escape the highly vertical structural tensions of Hinduism. Will Sarkar's spiritual leadership simply become yet another way of legitimizing *Brahmanism*; will the cycle be used not to challenge the present leadership and exploitation but further concretize the caste system? For while Sarkar intends to create a rupture with Indian cosmology, the deeper cosmological grammar of India may force it to become compatible with Hinduism in the long run (if indeed it has any success in transforming the Indian system). However, if PROUT is successful without transforming Hinduism, it could create a global Hinduism that is potentially as destructive as the last few hundred years of Western colonialism.

From Sarkar's perspective, however, his philosophy is quite different from Occidental, Oriental and Indian thinking altogether. It is Hindu in that it accepts karma and reincarnation but radically redefines it to include a structural component; accepts the unity of individual self and supreme consciousness; accepts that salvation from the world of suffering is possible; and accepts the multiple view of reality perspective. However, Sarkar's system rejects caste and indeed finds it as one of the strongest divisive aspects of life. He rejects the Vedic tradition of prayer to gods, idol worship, temple rituals, and pilgrimages. He rejects its non-growth orientation, indeed, Sarkar asserts that a society's level of productivity is a measure of its vitality and through the maxi/mini perspective and its assertion that nothing can be owned since everything is owned by the Macro entity, develops a distributive justice dimension. His rejection of the Indian model, however, is not merely a theoretical move—Sarkar argues that the movements he has started are structured precisely in ways to develop an alternative cosmology. For while other groups may speak against the caste system, Sarkar's PROUT has methods to avoid the re-inscription of caste, for example, intermarriage, forbidding members to attend a marriage where caste or dowry are considerations, and the abandoning of all caste identifications before joining any of his movements.

In terms of person-nature articulation, Sarkar argues that plants and animals have rights, that nature has mind in it (naturally since everything is essentially Brahman). In addition, he takes a humanistic stance on the person-person dimension arguing that most injustices in this world are a result of man's inhumanity toward man, which is especially tragic since humanity is fundamentally one. However, his hierarchy comes through in that he argues that since intellectual and spiritual potentials are rare, those with those attributes should be afforded more incentives to provide work, indeed, should be in positions of governance. But he intends to decrease the inequality of humans toward humans through economic means (PROUT), through cultural means (localism universalism, and cultural movements), and military means (overthrowing genocidal/corrupt governments, in this sense, he is more Western interventionist, than classical Indian) and through spiritual means (developing ways to transform inferiority/superiority, inclusion/exclusion models). He is thus Indian, but seeks to redefine Indian cosmology. Yet other efforts to transform Hinduism have failed. Because of its maturity, argues Galtung, Hinduism is resilient. Modernization efforts will most likely reproduce caste hierarchy (in this capitalism would work perfect there, a ready-made proletariat, but perhaps not as industrious as those of the Oriental cosmology, as well, high-tech capitalism will likely merely product techno-Brahmins instead of a more equitable society). Both Gandhi and the Buddha challenged the hierarchy of caste and both were marginalized. Will Sarkar find his work far more accepted outside India than within India?

In summary, Sarkar takes Indian cosmology but develops an economic dynamic with socialist and spiritual base wherein all property is owned by the supreme consciousness. He reduces structural violence through his structural changes, yet increases the potential for direct violence (calls for revolution). What emerges is a model that is less market driven, more equitable, but probably more interventionist.

Intellectual Styles

We gain further insight into the Indian episteme and Sarkar's location in it by examining intellectual styles of knowing. We borrow from the model developed by Galtung in his essay, "Structure, Culture and Intellectual Style" (1981). In this essay, Galtung examines four intellectual styles: the Saxonic, the Teutonic, the Gallic and the Nipponic. Summarizing, in the Saxonic (American) style the key question is how does one operationalize a hypothesis. It is data-run,

preferring quantitative studies and mid-level hypothesis. It is weak
at paradigmatic analysis, but the tradition encourages debate and
discourse. The Gallic (French) style is more concerned with the elegance of the theory not with the empirical level of analysis. Does
the theory follow a certain grammar: how does it sound in French?
What does its linguistic construction reveal? According to Galtung,
the Gallic style is strong on theory formation and paradigm analysis. Alternatively the Teutonic (Germanic) tradition accentuates the
theoretical with deductive reasoning and strong schools of philosophy as the center piece. The style is highly elitist with strong divisions among the various theories. It is very strong on theory formation
and strong on paradigm analysis, but it is weak on proposition production. The Nipponic style is more ambiguous, concerned with
social cohesion and compatible with the Hindu and Buddhist acceptance of contradictions and differences among theories. It is weak
on paradigm analysis and weak on theory building, but strong on
empirical quantitative work (especially mathematics) and very strong
on commentary about other intellectuals. Also central in this style is
the search to understand who is the Master of the particular intellectual—what is one's social-intellectual location?

Now let us briefly comment on Indian philosophical thought and
then Sarkar's thought. First Indian thinking, at least in the frame of
reference of the modern world, is comparatively less developed than
the Anglo-Saxon or Teutonic. This is largely because of modern
colonialism and subsequent transformation of intellectuals into feudal bureaucrats—a composition of the agricultural and the factory
model of knowledge—as well as other problems that correlate with
the underdevelopment of the academy. Intellectuals that do become
leaders leave the Indian soil and assimilate into alternative intellectual styles. Nonetheless, historically it is weak at the empirical proposition level, but very strong at the level of theory development, much
like the Teutonic style. Thus there are six orthodox and three heterodox schools (and the three alternative more recent schools, Islam,
Liberalism and Marxism). While in Teutonic thinking, there is only
inter-subjectivity within schools, in Indian thought, there is inter-
subjectivity between all the schools thus allowing for an agreement
on the overall project, individual enlightenment, *moksa*.

Finally, lineage is central. Who is one's guru? Whose guru was
he? While in Germany it is the Professor at the top, in India it is
the guru. Although the liberal social science model is changing this

to some extent, nonetheless the deeper hierarchical, if not feudal, structure continues with the listing of innumerable degrees after one's name commonplace. The attempt to gain legitimacy through "degree-dom" is an example of cultural inferiority. It is a fetish response to colonialism. The guru thus becomes the professor who then seeks to become the government minister.

There is also compatibility with the colonial British aristocratic style and the Brahmin intellectual style as both are hierarchical and conservative. Entrance into this world is limited by birth (Brahmin), the appropriate schooling (elite universities) and the appropriate fields (economics). Thinking outside the arena (myths, inter-disciplinarian work) is discouraged. It is above all a style of tradition and authority.

But in general, in the Indian context, while at one hand there is a perceived intellectual inferiority in terms of the modern world, at the same time, there is also a belief that only India has what is ultimately significant, the assertion, that it has all been already said (everything originated in India). The Vedas, it is commonly asserted, contain all knowledge for past time and future. A correct reading can indeed lead to understanding nuclear energy and man's landing on the Moon. There is thus a glorification of time past where all knowledge was available. This was *Satya Yuga*, the era of Truth, not the present *Kali Yuga*, the era of materialism and grossness. Concomitantly, there is a hope and a search for someone who can regain the Vedic glory and bring India back to center stage.

In the meantime, the Indian style constantly evokes past commentaries, past *sutras*, and one establishes one's own linkages, legitimacy and credibility by commenting on them. In this sense it remains static and can be described as underdeveloped, particularly social science knowledge, since that space is occupied by philosophy and religion. A science of society mirroring a science of the natural world has yet to develop. From the modern social science view, the regime of astrology and the world of endless cycles are propositions that lack evidence, yet endure because of tradition. The style of this old world comes through in the proposition par excellence in Indian thinking: it is the *sutra*. A short phrase in Sanskrit which states a basic truth. *Shiva Shaktya'tmakam Brahma*, or cosmic consciousness, is one but has two aspects: a cognitive and a creative dimension (Sarkar, 1967, 1). Following the sutra is the purport, a brief explanation of the sutra. The Indian intellectual, especially the wandering yogi, does not need to know complex theories or empirical data; rather he can memorize thousands of *sutras* and simply recite and interpret them at the appropriate speaking engagements. These *sutras* then form the data packages for the intellectual as well as the yogi.

Sarkar remains in this style as well. His book on cosmology, *Ananda Sutram*, is spoken in the *sutra* form (and then written down by his students). Moreover, it is just not the content of what is said that is important but the sounds of the words themselves for they are in the ancient Sanskrit. Reciting the *sutras* affects the basic *chakras* of the body and in itself leads the mind to the subtle. Remembering the *sutras* then places one in a spiritual and intellectual context: one remembers the truth, the body feels the sound of the truth, and one speaks the words of truth. Language then does not simply refer to the spiritual, rather it ontologically "vibrates" at the same level of the truth. The word then is truth, not a construction, nor a referent. It more than participates in the real, it *is* the real.

Commentary on past intellectuals is different from the Saxonic, Gallic, Teutonic and Nipponic style of intellectual interpretation (quoting sources, writing reviews of others), it is a commentary on intellectuals of the long past, not of the present. Finally real knowledge is either practical (that is industrial and leading to increased efficiency and wealth) or spiritual and thus available from the gurus and the other wise men. These wise men in turn are placed in various schools of thought which coexist and eventually the gurus are memorialized as enlightened souls—their words are remembered for what they have achieved as they have realized the soul. The truth packed in *sutras* can then be legitimately remembered and recited over and over, for that which is stated by someone who has left the lower levels of mind to the higher levels must be speaking the ancient truth, the primordial truth, the first truth.

Sarkar, too, speaks this style. He does not write, but rather speaks constantly with students who record his utterances. He quotes and speaks of times past. In addition, unlike the Teutonic or Gallic or Saxonic, he speaks counter to the intellectual tradition, speaking often more like Mao asserting that intellectuals are parasites. Especially in his analysis of the Vipran era, he argues that most theories of intellectuals should be judged on their impact on human welfare: did a certain theory lead to material prosperity *and* spiritual realization? If not, the theory is worthless. The jugglery of words—central to the Gallic style—is ridiculed by Sarkar as a game of the ego. A favorite story is that of intellectuals and devotees in front on a mango tree.

The intellectuals analyze the tree (counting, dividing, theorizing on the beginning, the middle and the end of the tree), while the devotees simply eat and enjoy the bliss of the mango fruit. Intellectuals then waste their lives in petty arguments at the expense of their larger duty. Ultimately for Sarkar, the style of the intellectual must be that of working for the masses, creating theories to aid in human development, and finding ways to transcend the intellect. For him, intellectuals who are not associated with social service work, with some effort outside of their mental activities, develop an enlarged sense of self-importance and arrogance, forgetting that it is the Cosmic Entity that is the ultimate knower, and that the minds of intellectuals are in comparison small. Their intellects are imprisoned in the wall of ego, in their own creations—unaware of the external material world or the internal spiritual world. Their intellects are in need of liberation. His counsel is to know oneself and thus know everything. One might conclude here that Sarkar's project is anti-intellectual, but perhaps like the Chinese he is reacting to Mandarin/Brahmin rule at the expense of the workers and others. However, Sarkar attempts to place the intellect in the larger spiritual model of knowledge and praxis. The intellect now becomes a tool for social transformation, not the study of knowledge for its own sake, or for personal aggrandizement. His book *Neo-Humanism: the Liberation of the Intellect* (a remarkable title in itself) develops this placement of the intellect.

What Foucault has done for the body—shown how it has become medicalized, bureaucratized, domesticated and made docile by power and professions in various forms, Sarkar does for the intellect. Sarkar shows how the intellect has become imprisoned by various monumental historical structures: namely, egoism at the center (the world as an extension of the self), the personal family, geo-sentiment (one's place of residence and one's nation, which leads to geo-politics, geo-strategy, geo-economics and so forth), socio-sentiment (associations in group, gender, ethnicity, ideology, or religion) and then humanism (humans as the measure of all things, the planet exists primarily for humans). Outside the bounds of concentric circles is neo-humanism, a spiritual humanism based on the principle of social equality, a respect and dignity for all forms of life, humans, plants and animals. The greater the liberation of one's intellect, the greater the empathy one has with all life, the increased desire for social welfare and increased levels of un-differentiation as well as a re-identification of the self. At present, however, the intellect remains

in an ego-politics with the goal of maximizing self-interest instead of
collective welfare. When the intellect is totally liberated then it can
reflect pure consciousness perfectly without any other intervening
sentiments and identifications. The intellect then is free, no longer
in ego-politics, not in the center of all these circular prisons, but
outside of itself.

Sarkar's texts are certainly strong on theory and paradigm analysis and weak on empirical indicators as one might expect in the
Indian style. The style is macro with a great deal of commentary
on other Indian traditions. Finally, its structure remains hierarchical
with intuition and service above with intellect below. Even though
he speaks of the need to develop the intuitional intellect that can
benefit humanity, he discourages the creation of philosophical schoolism,
rather, as per the Indian episteme, the goal is the realization of the
self. Sarkar simply adds a social service and a revolution dynamic
and thus makes the intellect goal-driven and the intellectual style a
mixture of praxis, acceptance of spiritual authority and intuition.

Yet this preference for action at the expense of analysis, since
Sarkar has already provided the theory, has obvious dangers. We
are then not surprised that his most prolific student, Batra, has written numerous books on Sarkar with not one comment that is critical, that is doubting, that is testing. He seeks not to look for that
which is not explained, for a politics of exclusion, but rather he seeks
to convincingly prove the all embracive nature of Sarkarian thought.
He seeks not to critique the text but to uphold it. For example, in
Batra's writings on Sarkar's social cycle, we find perfect symmetry
between history and Sarkar's theories. There are no anomalies, exceptions, or personal interpretations; rather there is a perfect matching
between the world of theory (totally expressed since Sarkar speaks
from the intuition of macro-consciousness) and the world of sense
perceptions, time and place. India and other civilizations—all civilizations!—miraculously every other civilization, culture, society, or
nation state have followed this pattern perfectly, even while an alternative reading of Sarkar's thought suggests that Sarkar's argues that
the universe is open and that space, time and observer damage our
ability to see things as they are in themselves, not to mention Sarkar's
willingness to speak of exceptions to every rule. But for Batra, what
is remembered is not social theory, not the context of discourse, nor
the construction of discourse, but the search for data that proves
once and for all that the truth has arrived, and India has regained

Vedic glory (notwithstanding, Sarkar's privileging of the Tantric, practical tradition). Weaknesses in the theory—the role of artists, periods in history where a trading community has dominated, or moves in power that appear out of order—are reordered.

While it can be argued that there are various strains of anti-intellectualism in PROUT culture (students primarily writing to uphold the texts of Sarkar), the goal is not against the intellectual discourse per se, but against the vertical spatiality of where the intellectual places him or herself. The intellectual discourse has its secret codes, claims of universality, often implicit authoritarian structures, and in general, in the present age exists to serve the vaeshyans. Moreover, the nature of the intellect itself leads itself to cynicism and nihilism, to philosophies that are intelligible in the rarefied atmosphere of theory, but—to continue this spatial metaphor—do not touch the earth of hunger and the hunger of earth. Just as capitalists make properties their own, intellectuals make knowledge their own. They hoard it, misuse it and then place themselves in inclusive categories forgetting that the intellect is a gift to be used for the people and that moreover, one day this gift will disappear in the personal oblivion that is death. Thus, Sarkar's effort is to liberate the intellect.

This vertical intellectual structure is countered by Sarkar with a horizontal approach wherein the only qualifications needed for the obtaining real knowledge, the realization of the self/Brahman, is a human body. A developed intellect, various degrees, professional positions are not required for eligibility. The solution is a benevolent intellect guided by spiritual principles. Indeed, it was this benevolent intellect that, for Sarkar, led to the invention of spirituality. It is this benevolent intellect that Sarkar places as one of the most important categories in his theory of leadership. The *Sadvipra* has a pure intellect, guided not by sense perceptions, not by authority, but by intuition—an intuition unlike the theoretical of the *Vedas*, but a practical, historically developed intuition of the *Tantras*.

Finally, the narrative of Sarkar remains within the intellectual style but speaks not from the position of the Brahmin, but the guru. It is commentary-oriented, strong on paradigms, and weak on empirical theory, but strong on empirical action. The intellect is placed then in the context of the body and spirit, in the context of Sarkar's model: knowledge and purpose. The intellect thus functions to help the self gain self-realization and help create a society where the spiritual can be optimized.

We conclude this chapter by comparing Sarkar directly to Indian schools of thought. Our guiding question is: Is Sarkar part of the Indian tradition, and if so, is he orthodox or heterodox? If heterodox, will he become yet another guru, important for a brief period, and then forgotten shortly thereafter?

Locating Sarkar in Indian Schools of Thought

Western thought in general does not divide itself into heterodox and orthodox schools. Rather Western philosophical history is the victory of one paradigm over another: for example, the Church over Science, idealisms over materialism, the rationality of the enlightenment over the dogma of the Christian, and Marx's historical materialism over German idealism. The division of heterodox and orthodox is useful within fields in terms of the phases of which ideas have currency, but not within the entire history of Western thought itself. Rather Western thought begins with the Greeks, and then is traced sequentially forward until the current economism/developmentalism and their models of progress. In general, it has been atomistic-deductive, progressively linear and obvious as to who is included in the faith and who is excluded. Heterodoxy is not stated as such, rather it is placed in the category of the primitive and the irrational, often the Asiatic. The Orientalism of the past two centuries has in fact created a mirror opposite in Islamic and Indian thinking. That which was normal in the West could not to be found in the East since the East was the site of the abnormal (Said, 1979). The East could not be included in the authoritarian but inclusionary model of Western science since the East was thrown out of the bounds of the real, rational and normal, except as a time past when men and women were ruled by nature and mistakenly took the powers of nature as the powers of gods. The history of the West from the West's own perspective can be read as history of the ego. The super-ego was then the Christian church and the East, the Id.

The history of India, however, cannot be framed in this model. Rather, it is the history of the Fall of Man, from the Age of Gold, to Silver, to Copper and now to Iron. It is the transcendence of the spirit into the body and the final imprisonment of the soul in the body. The promise of the future lies in knowing that what-is, is from the very beginning to the very end, a cycle and that what lies ahead is a golden age. The initiator of the Golden Age remains in doubt. But this doubt is not the doubt of the empirical question: will it be a planned economy or a market economy? Rather it is the doubt of patience, of waiting for redemption, of waiting for the fruition of untold penances and sufferings, of wondering whether it will be Indian nationalism, American liberalism, Soviet Marxism, Gandhism, the Brahmo Samaj, a returned Krsna, or an avatar yet to be named that will usher in the future.

This history, however, is met with an alternative history and future. The new faiths of natural science, liberal capitalism, social science and Marxism promise an end to the cycle and a beginning of upward economic and political progress—a possibility of creating a world without karma, where all flourish through following their *dharma*. While it might not be the *moksa* of the masses—the grand enlightenment of the millions falling backwards into hitherto unimagined *samadhis*—it still promises an era where corruption is gone, wealth is here, and the vested interests (a classic Indianism) are forever vanquished and the equality originally promised by *varna*, from each according to his duty, to each according to their need (not to each according to their karma) is available.

The history of the Indian episteme, as we have developed it, is inclusionary philosophically, but exclusionary at the level of power, caste and class. Thus, Islam, which attacked power, caste, and class, did not dent Tantric and Vedic philosophy, although it could be argued that the emphasis on equality and fraternity found in Sarkar, and others, is picked up from the Islamic influence. Indian thought has been philosophically inclusionary as the larger project has been the same. All the schools have been either Ideational (the real is the idea or the Diety or a totality embracing concept of Being) or Idealistic (inclusionary of both ideational and sensate perspectives). Only Carvaka has been through and through materialistic, and that school is often dismissed with quickly. Marxism, however, has been more difficult to dismiss. PROUT cadres, among others, argue that only a socialism that is spiritual and thus part of India's history, whether popularly constructed or scholarly/elite constructed, can solve India's moral, economic and political problems.

In Sarkar's numerous articles but especially in *Namami Krsna Sundaram* (1981) and in his "Views of Other Faiths," (Sarkar, 1987b: 3) he locates the various schools and places himself within these. The faiths he chooses are the six orthodox and three heterodox, as well as

Marxism. His location of Marxism in "Faith" is that he argues it is
an ideology, albeit an incomplete one, in that spiritual practices are
not an integral part of its text and actions. Moreover, it privileges
one class at the expense of others, it is not a true revolution for all
the classes.

The primary question of the Indian schools is the nature of Being.
Is it singular or dual? And, if so, is there one mind or many minds?
Is the energy that creates the universe more important or less important than consciousness? Does mind emerge from basic fundamental factors or is a reflection of cosmic mind? Is the self concrete, an
expression of various forces, or an illusionary reflection of the real?

Sarkar's approach is two-fold. The first is to argue with the Indian
schools by searching for various contradictions or conditions that
expose a fundamental flaw. The second is to expose the implications
of these philosophies on the economic and spiritual well being of
the masses. He is especially critical of what has become the dominant school, Shankaracharya's Vedanta. Specifically, its assertion that
only Brahman is real and the world is illusion, with *maya* as the
force that creates this illusion, in itself also unreal. First, is the problem of understanding *maya*: if it were creating an illusion, how could
it be real itself; if it was real itself, then Vedantic monism becomes
dualism. Second, is the problem of the cruel world of escapism; a
philosophy which denies the material world creates. Sarkar quotes
a story about a loyal *mayavadin* (one who supports the view that the
world is unreal) who is in Kashi (Varnasi), a place famous for bulls.

> The *mayavadin* began to flee at the sight of the approaching bull. A
> logician happened to be standing nearby. He addressed . . . [him] say-
> ing [Well sir, if you say that this world is unreal, then the bull is also
> unreal. Then why do you run in fear? The [*mayavadin*] would not
> accept his defeat in logic. He replied, "My running away is also unreal!"
> (Sarkar, 1981, 80).

In terms of the structural implications, those who are beyond *maya*
become then the holders of special truth and privilege that others
steeped in *maya* do not. Moreover, all economic gains, all gains to
the body and to the mind find themselves not situated on a plane
of significance, but as fundamentally false and thus not important.
The costs to society of a totally ideational society wherein only the
Absolute idea is real and all else is a mirage can be cruel, to say
the least, from Sarkar's view. In addition, Sarkar points out other
weaknesses in the Vedanta cosmology such as the inability to explain

the evolutionary development of unit minds. In contrast, he asserts that his position is that the world is a changing phenomena not a mirage or a false phenomena. Sarkar also says: "Simply by playing on words and thereby confusing the people, a section of so-called learned people may derive intellectual pleasure, their intellectual thirst may be quenched, but the human heart remains unsatisfied" (Sarkar, 1981, 92). And:

> One cannot escape these realities by resorting to philosophical rigma-role. It would be a great blunder if the great potentials of the *jivas* [individual souls] is underestimated. It is incorrect to say that all these *jivas* have come out of nothing. As I have already said, something cannot come out of nothing, and nothing cannot come out of something. Something which exists will continue to exist through undergoing metamorphosis. Similarly nothing that does not really exist can never have an expression. All of you feel that you are carrying some warmth of life, some life-force in you. You feel that you have a mind, that you have so many feelings and sentiments, hopes and aspirations, pains and pleasure—so many susceptibilities and sensibilities... These are not burdens, but the bliss of joyful living. The value of humanity goes unrecognized in this [Vedanta] philosophy (168).

Thus for Sarkar, Vedanta (and other related perspectives) negates the sufferings and the joys of humanness. His project, however, is a spiritual humanism that embraces not rejects suffering and joy. For him, there is no *maya* except that of change, there are simply forces that lead within and forces that lead without.

Sarkar also places various Buddhist schools with Vedanta for they too deny the existence of the self and the existence of Absolute Being. Within Sarkar's devotional discourses, he refers to life of the Buddha and the spiritual lessons one can gain from Buddhism positively; but at the intellectual level, he questions the belief in the transmigration of the soul asking what indeed is migrating if there is no self. Buddha's silence as to the existence of God is explained by arguing that Buddha was asserting that God is beyond the mind, or supramental.

Also, Sarkar differs from the Buddha in the centrality of *dhukha*, sorrow. Sorrow is a relative truth for Sarkar as it is the mind that experiences it. Sarkar divides and analyses the numerous schools of thought within Buddhism, attempting to explain how the self is articulated, the self appearing to be concrete because there is a continuous flow of waves in a "quick succession of ... creation and destruction" (Sarkar, 1987b, 3: 67). He is especially critical of the Shunyavada (Nothingness school of Buddhism) as it leads to a type of cynicism wherein the end all of life is a state of nothingness, utter and total nihilism. In contrast is Sarkar's view wherein the soul completes its journey through the realization that the individual self is indeed the cosmic self. Thus, Sarkar is neither atheistic, nor uncertain about God, rather Being is central to Sarkar's ideology. Indeed, it is the rational. The rational is Consciousness but Consciousness is inexplicable.

But, at least, Buddhism is practical—among the reasons why the Buddha was successful is that he spoke to the common man, used common language, and provided a concrete way out of suffering. In contrast, Vedanta is utterly theoretical, although all its proofs of God are metaphorically based on the material world, the so-called world of illusion. Sarkar's counters this theoretical orientation with his own Tantric perspective. Tantra is based on observations of the material from which theories of existence are derived. They are not based on "intellectual extravaganza" (Sarkar, 1987a, 6: 18). Indeed, this is Sarkar's criterion for a good theory and thus a good science—practice prior to generalization. For him, Indian thinking suffers from this overly theoretical approach. It remains imbalanced.

> So many theories have been expounded through out the history of India. . . . Many soar[ed] high without having any concern for the practical plane. . . . In medieval India, many scholars of Nyaya [of Gautama not Kanada] uselessly researched year after year the question whether the oil is in the pot or the pot is in the oil. This has nothing to do with the real world. Some people may wonder why there was not more development in Pathan India, in spite of a high population of scholars. The reason is that Nyaya philosophy, the philosophy divorced from [the practical world], had too great an influence on life (Sarkar, 1987b, 6: 18).

In Sarkar's model, most theories are incomplete in that they do not speak to physical, mental and spiritual planes. A good theory must deal with all these levels of reality. In fact, it is this epistemic principle that Sarkar later uses to develop his social cycle. What is true at the level of the natural world and the individual world is also true at the level of the social. There is a congruity between the observable laws of the individual (breathing, cycles of rest and movement, ups and downs, life stages) and in the natural world (seasons, cycles of pause and speed) and the social world as well (rise and fall of nations, periods of growth and then contraction). It is only at the level of the spiritual where the cycle completes itself and the self finds eternal rest in pure consciousness.

This emphasis on observation is characteristic of all the Indian schools except Mimamsa and Vedanta. Yet according to Indian historian Romila Thapar, it was the Vedanta that came to be dominant in the Indian discourse, internally and through Orientalist scholarship (Thapar, 1966, 162). We then should not be surprised that Sarkar spends extensive textual space attacking the notion that only Brahma is real and the world is illusion and associated arguments that indeed the Real is pure nothingness.

But he also rejects Carvaka as Carvaka rejects the transcendental dimension, the soul, supreme consciousness, karma and indeed, the entire Vedas. For Carvaka, mind arises from the material factors: water, air, fire and earth. In addition, only perception is accepted as a form of knowledge. Sarkar summarizes the Carvaka view like this:

> As long as you live, you should live in joy and happiness for we do not know what happens after death. As long as one lives in the world, one should live in comfort and happiness. One should even eat *ghee* by incurring debts, for there is neither heaven nor the reactions to actions, nor *atman* or soul, nor the world beyond death. After the body is cremated, how can it be born again (Sarkar, 1987a, 6: 65).

The Mimamsa School is also rejected by Sarkar since it developed as a reaction to the fear that the Vedas were being rejected. Mimamsa focuses on rituals, believes that heaven and hell are not metaphors but real empirical places. Inasmuch as the after-world is real, Mimamsa posits that sacrifices will lead humans there. Finally, the *Vedas* are considered outside of history; they are eternal. This then is the classical Brahmin viewpoint. For Sarkar, rituals are thrown out for meditation; heaven and hell become states of mind; the *Vedas* are used for their educational value, but they are rejected as the supreme authority. Indeed, Sarkar's entire approach is an afront to the classic Brahmin priests, from Sarkar's acceptance of the material world, his attack on caste, his criticism of vipran Indian rule, and his attempt to build a non-theocratic but spiritual society. As contentious from the Brahmin viewpoint is Sarkar's refusal to accept the nation-state as a foundational entity/community, and thus his refusal to enter the "India will arise and lead the world" discourse.

Sarkar also rejects the Nyaya formulation as it is ultimately dualistic, individual being and the supreme being will always remain separate, their unification is impossible. Thus, Nyaya is dualistic theism. In addition, while it takes a common sense approach to language, with language simply describing reality, Sarkar takes a symbolic approach to language with language attempting to express the ultimate Idea, but failing. Language participates in the real in that it is a reflection, albeit incomplete reflection of the real. Sarkar does not go as far as the Buddhist position, where language constructs the real.

The Vaisheskika School, often paired with Nyaya, also is dualistic and theistic in principle. Both schools are atomistic in their orientation, rejecting forces, and positing that atoms combine to create air, earth, and the other elements.

For Sarkar, the building blocks of life are microvita, but these are not concrete atoms, rather they have a degree of consciousness and can be manipulated by higher levels of consciousness as well. In addition, the basic structure of life is ultimately pure consciousness itself. Microvita are its emanations.

Sarkar comments as well extensively on Sankhya and Yoga. Sankhya is essentially atheistic (although a God as controller was later added on to gain adherents and solve various contradictions). According to Kapil, its founder, the world is made up of twenty-four basic elements. There is a basic dualism between body and mind with consciousness only being imminent in individual souls, not independent or outside of unit minds. God is the catalyst agent which sets creation into place. For Sarkar, Sankhya is defective because there is no cosmic consciousness, only individual consciousness and thus no place for *bhakti*. Moreover, consciousness remains only a witness with no attributable and personalizable properties.

Sarkar's critique of Yoga is similar. A major difference between Sarkar's Tantra and Yoga is that in Yoga the desires of mind are suspended, that is, the self is in a state of hibernation, thus allowing a state of perception of bliss. For Sarkar if there is total suspension, who is there to perceive? In Sarkar's Tantra, the self (a flow of knowledge, or a flow of existence, or desire) is not suspended but channeled towards Being. Witness-ship then moves to the next level of existence until ultimate witness-ship is unification with pure consciousness. In Sankhya and Yoga, enlightenment is only available to those who can perform penances, while for Sarkar through *bhakti* the mind becomes fixated on its goal and thus realization is possible.

As to Jainism, the other heterodox school, Sarkar sees it is impractical, especially its view of non-violence. Sarkar's approach is vegetarian, but it accepts that all life is struggle and argues that Jain attempts to monitor one's breathing to avoid the killing of microbes is nonsensical. In addition, Sarkar is more "rational" and claims to be scientific. While the Jain approach is far more probabilistic. There are, for example, seven truth possibilities for every statement: (1) Maybe x is; (2) Maybe x is not; (3) Maybe x is and is not; (4) Maybe x is inexpressible, (5) Maybe x is and it is inexpressible; (6) Maybe x is not and it is inexpressible; and (7) Maybe x is and it is not and it is inexpressible. The richness of the above thinking has led Pratima Bowes (1982), among others, to argue that this view, the quality of may-be-it-is is central to the entire Indian construction of reality. Reality is then multifarious and its nature expressed in many ways. Reality then can only be partially known. Sorokin (1970) has taken this view and used it to argue that all social systems have seeks in them of their own transformation since they only express a portion of reality (its ideational, idealistic, or sensate attributes). While Sarkar does not comment on this aspect of Jainism, he would criticize it for its atheism and fear that the multiple reality view could degenerate into unnecessary intellectual-talk instead of necessary spiritual-talk. The main problem for Sarkar with respect to Jainism is its ethics of non-violence, again for Sarkar, an ethics which is ultimately impractical.

Sarkar In and Out of the Indian Episteme

The texts that Sarkar uses to differentiate himself are Indian texts and while he criticizes them, he remains within the Indian episteme. He speaks to the Indian tradition, but through his alternative model and his social movements intends to radically revolutionize it. Sarkar keeps the goal of *moksa*; of truth as bliss; of karma; of cycles; *varna* (historically as ideal type or color of mind); of the guru; of the redeemer; of philosophy as human therapy; of the symmetrical relationship between the natural, social, individual and cosmic worlds (as above as below; as within, as without); of the relationship between individual self and cosmic self; the three approaches of devotion, action, and knowledge as well as the epistemological avenues of sense-perception, authority, reason and intuition. But Sarkar rejects absolute monism; rejects the dualism of Sankhya and Nyaya; rejects the materialism of Carvaka; rejects *jhat* (or caste); rejects the various atheistic approaches; rejects Yoga and other approaches that exclude *bhakti* or that re-categorize the spiritual to the technical or sacrificial; rejects the privileging of sorrow; and rejects the schools of nothingness.

Finally, Sarkar reinterprets karma; reinterprets *varna*; develops a balance between the individual and the collective; articulates a dynamic balance between the physical, mental and spiritual (*prama*); reinterprets violence; develops a structural approach to poverty and inequity; reinterprets the cycle of creation; and develops new theoretical constructs such as microvita and neo-humanism.

Sarkar clearly places himself in the Indian project we have outlined. In many ways he is square within it, in other ways he is radically outside. And although presently he is not a son of India (seen as controversial and primarily as a guru not as a philosopher), if we learn anything from Indian history, it is the ability of the Indian view to take the revolutionary and radical and make it part of its doxa, as heterodox or as orthodox. This is especially so after the guru has passed away. It is thus not surprising that since Sarkar has passed away, his life works are increasingly heralded by the Indian aesthetic and scholarly community.

Notwithstanding his neo-humanism or his spiritual socialism (his influence from Marx) or his view of progress (liberal influence) or his view of equality (Islamic), Sarkar, by speaking to the Indian tradition and privileging the views of Shiva and Krsna, at once attempts to recover the truth of the self, the truth of tradition, and at the same time is attempts to transform Indian thought to make it spiritual, rational, scientific and ready for the future. Foucault described Marxism as a fish in water in the 19th century, Sarkar can be described as the same for the late 20th century, but given the history of the Indian project, to place a temporality on his boundaries would be a mistake.

The above has been a positive reading of Sarkar's thought, we have left silenced some of the most obvious problems. It is noteworthy that Sarkar describes his project as scientific, rational, while others are irrational and dogmatic. His philosophy is comprehensive and practical, while others are limited and overly theoretical. His path includes devotion, action and knowledge, while others only include one of the above, or are overly sentimental, escapist and dogmatic. Silenced also is the problem of having the centerpiece an ideology of the transcendental and thus putting it outside of history and thereby outside of debate and dialog. Is this not bringing back vipran—Brahmin—rule, theocracy, or Sorokin's Ideational system? Finally, Sarkar rejects authority, yet his whole approach places himself as an authority. And while Shiva and Krishna are perceived as great originators and bringers of *dharma*, the analogy to himself creating a new cosmology are obvious. Moreover, although he is critical of the *avatar* theory, his own theory of *taraka brahma*—albeit meant as a devotional concept—restates the *avatar* theory itself. And although he attempts to take the Indian tradition outside of itself by using *varna* as central to his theory of social change, he allows for the possibility of the re-inscription of caste, even though he utters and practices against it. By asserting theorems that can only be accepted on Sarkar's "divine" authority, he re-inscribes the belief in authority instead of the realization of the self. And by accepting the Indian concrete self, the *atman*, he regresses and reifies a self the Buddhists and poststructuralists have temporalized.

To our question is Sarkar Indian, we can but answer, he is, and of course, given his attempt to revolutionize the project, he is not. This "both" situation perhaps makes him ultimately utterly Indian. When we compare him to other civilizational projects, we will examine if he is more than Indian, or solely a product of Indian thought, practices, and discourses. Certainly his cosmology uses the language of Indian thinking, not the concepts of the Greeks, the Romans, the Renaissance, the Enlightenment and Modernity. He does not speak to the Western project, except to remind one that democratic theory, atomic theory, and other perspectives began in India. Nor does he speak to the Chinese, Japanese, Pacific Islander and Islamic, except to call for a spiritual universalism based on a progressive socialism grounded in planetary ecology and the meeting of human needs and rights. But, perhaps that is enough for one person.

CHAPTER THREE

SARKAR'S CONSTRUCTION OF HISTORY

While the previous chapter situated Sarkar in the Indian episteme, this chapter focuses on the Indian construction of history. This chapter specifically will overview a range of classical, idealistic, nationalistic, modern and critical theories of history as well as recent hybrid approaches such as those of Buddha Prakash, Sri Aurobindo an Romila Thapar. Through these approaches, we seek to understand the context of Sarkar's own theory of history.

The discursively dominant Indian model is the idealist, theistic model drawn from the *Gita*. This has served as the departure point for Indian theories of history. In addition to this model, the other dominant model has been Hegel's and Marx's developmental model. The rest have largely been commentaries on the traditional dynastic history style with various calls for more nationalistic history, or less nationalistic history, attempts to be less idealistic or more idealist.

Romila Thapar's *A History of India* remains, however, the modern classic. Her work traces the social movements, the dynasties, and the philosophies and thus develops a balanced approach. What she primary privileges is the historical narrative, and so her history is a modern history, which while Indian and written sensitive to Indians, comes from the dominant linear, evolutionary, actor-oriented Occidental social science episteme. It thus leaves vague the question of structure or the problem of periodicity in history, explained only as a meaningless division of time, as inappropriate grand theory. The most recent critical approach is that of the Subaltern group which springs from the works of Gramsci and Foucault and writes a history of the dominated, the subaltern. The Subaltern writers consciously do not privilege a philosophy of history perspective, rather, they prefer to search for the ways in which power has suppressed, oppressed and hidden the narratives of peasants and workers. They seek to hear the voices of the poor; voices that have become silenced by accepted forms of historical evidence and by dominant notions of what is considered significant. Finally, they remain undecided toward the issue of structure vs. practice, that is, the grand scheme versus the micro occurrences, the teleological versus the day-to-day history. Using exemplary texts from the above narratives, we locate them in Sarkar's meta-structure of four types of history—intellectual history, economic history, workers' history and dynastic history.

The Yugas of History

To begin with, classical, or, perhaps better, traditional Indian thought follows a cosmological dimension to time.

> Hindu thinkers had evolved a cyclic theory of time. The cycle was called a *kalpa* and was equivalent to 4320 million earthly years. The *kalpa* is divided into 14 periods and at the end of each of these the universe is recreated and once again *Manu* (primeval man) gives birth to the human race. At the moment we are in the seventh of these 14 periods of the present *kalpa*. Each of these is divided in 4 *yugas* or periods of time. The *yugas* contain respectively 4800, 3600, 2400, and 1200 god-years (one god-year being 360 human years), and there is a progressive decline in the quality of civilization (Thapar, 1966, 161).

Besides the size of the numbers, cosmic time is distinct from historical time in that certain numbers have magical properties (in the classic episteme, numbers participate in the real, they are not mere representations) and there is no end to time. Thapar characterizes this total orderliness, however, as unreal, meaning absurd and unbelievable and not modern. From the classical world, time had to relate to the consciousness and the natural/social worlds since the entire universe was mathematically perfect. While there is no end to time, there is a regeneration of time, brought about by the redeemer. Vishnu, Krishna or some other god takes birth to terminate the inequities of *Kali Yuga*. While Thapar (1986) believes that this redeemer was not taken seriously as evidenced by the lack of millennial movements in Indian history as compared to the Judeo-Christian tradition, other Indian philosophers take the redeemer quite seriously. A redeemer comes, sets the world right, but then the natural process of decay and degeneration continues, until the redeemer returns. Sarkar's own order appears to be a 3500 year cycle: Shiva was alive 7000 years ago and Krishna 3500 years back. Is it time again, according to this pattern?

Mircea Eliade in his *The Myth of Eternal Return* takes a slightly alternative reading.

> What is important to note in this avalanche of figures, is the cyclical
> character of cosmic time. In fact, we are confronted with the infinite
> repetition of the same phenomenon (creation-destruction-new creation),
> adumbrated in each yuga (dawn and twilight) but completely realized
> by a *Mahayuga*. The life of Brahma thus comprises 2560000 of these
> Mahayuga, each repeating the same phases (*Kṛta, Treta, Dvapara, Kali*)
> and ending with a Pralaya, a Ragnarok ("final" destruction, in the
> sense of a retrogression of all forms to an amorphous mass, occurring
> at the end of each *kalpa* at the time of the *Mahapralaya*) (Eliade, 1971,
> 114–115).

This end is then a return to a beginning from which the cycle starts
again.

> In addition to the metaphysical depreciation of history—which, in pro-
> portion to and by the mere fact of its duration provokes an erosion
> of all forms by exhausting their ontologic substance—and in addition
> to the myth of the perfection of the beginnings . . . what deserves our
> attention in this orgy of figures is the eternal repetition of the funda-
> mental rhythm of the cosmos: its periodic destruction and re-creation
> (Eliade, 1971, 115).

What then is the way out? The first is to wait for the redeemer and
while waiting to increase one's life chances by following one's destiny and by doing good works: *dharma* and karma. The second is to
escape the whole cycle of cosmic time and move to a point outside
of time—*moksa* or liberation. This could be at the ontological level
of the self actually undergoing a sort of alchemical transformation
and becoming eternal *or* a type of perceptual change in which nothing is feared, all is embraced, and thus liberation is achieved.

Sarkar uses the cyclical notion of time in his social cycle, uses the
notion of the redeemer but appears to keep it at the perceptual level:
as a way of knowing, devotion, *bhakti*, but then he reifies it by pointing to an apparently real 3500 year cycle. Ravi Batra (1988), in his
interpretation of Sarkar's macrohistory, resorts to the perfection of
numbers in his various cycles—30 year cycles and seven year cycles.

Buddhist time, in general, follows the same pattern as well. However
there is a difference that is more similar to Sarkar then to the traditional Indian model. Buddhist time like Christian or Islamic time
has a beginning. It is the death, the *Mahaparinirvana*, of the Buddha.
"Because of the claim to the historicity of the Buddha there is a single, central point to which all events relate chronologically" (Thapar,

1986, 376). And here we see even more isomorphism with Sarkar's thought.

> Change within cosmological time is emphasized further by the cyclic movement of time taking the form of a spiral, in that the cycle never returns to the point of origin: and a spiral if fully stretched can become a wave. The rise and fall within the cycle purports constant change and even the fall carries within it the eventual upward swing of the cycle (Thapar, 1986, 376).

For Sarkar too there is a beginning to history. At the level of the theory of *Brahmachakra*—the cosmic cycle of creation—history is endless and indeed beginningless. But humans have an evolution, and there are times of degeneration where great personalities change the world, they begin new ideologies that cause new waves of ideas, which lead to new changes. At truly desperate times, historical redeemers are born. But it is just not one redeemer as with Buddhism or Christianity, or Islam, rather, there have been two already. At the root personal level, the model is cyclical, since only spiritual progress counts. Sarkar's preferred macrohistorical pattern, however, is a spiral, wherein the duration of the phases of exploitation are reduced. Or stated in traditional Indian terms, the *(Kali) yugas* decrease in time, while the other *Satya* or *Krta* (golden) *yugas* increase. This wave pattern remains one of Sarkar's favorites. In this sense he speaks ancient body-talk as his metaphors are all of the body, indeed, the notion of *yuga* in itself comes from the life cycle of the personal body.

While Sarkar takes a layered perspective, distinguishing what is cyclical and what is spiral, in the traditional Hindu perspective, the cycle can never become a spiral for time is beginningless, thought itself is beginningless. For Eliade, "The conception of the four *yugas* in fact contributes a new element: the explanation (and hence the justification) of historical catastrophes, of the progressive decadence of humanity, biologically, sociologically, ethically, and spiritually" (Eliade, 1971, 118). Eliade even sees the basic theory as "invigorating and consoling for man under the terror of history" (118). For now, man has information that he is to suffer in this epoch and thus must either resign himself or take the opportunity to enter the spiritual path and escape through *sadhana* (struggle to achieve liberation). The cycle thus becomes accessible, allowing for transcendence.

As with Sarkar's use of Indian philosophy, we see how he uses Indian history as a point of departure and then attaches a new range meanings to it—some additive and some organic. His social history

is cyclical as well. But the cycle must be approached from vantage
points. As mentioned earlier from the cosmic view of Creation, it is
endless. There are two parts to it. The first is the "downloading" of
consciousness and its binding into matter; the second is its unbind-
ing, the reawakening of consciousness (the phase which Western evo-
lutionist theorists spend a great deal of their textual space on). But
there is no natural or rational progress since with every technological change there are new social problems created. Every change is
a change in frequency that alternatively leads to a disturbance in
the field of waves. New technologies increase and reduce choices;
they expand and they limit; they solve old problems and create new
ones. Real change is change that leads to a re-identification of mind
in an alchemical transmutation of mind. For Sarkar, and the Indian
project as a whole, real change is that which ends the cycle, that
calms the final wave. Sarkar uses time in different ways. There is
the cosmic cycle at one level, the generation, degeneration and regeneration of time, at another level, there is the individual escape from
time and entrance into no time or infinite time. And there is the
social level wherein exploitation can be reduced through social transformation, thus allowing for individual escape from time.

In a short talk entitled, "In Kali Yuga, Strength Lies in An Organized
Body," (Anandamurti, 1987) Sarkar speaks to the classic division of
Indian time, that of the four *yugas: Krta, Treta, Dvapara*, and *Kali*. The
first era, *Krta* is redefined as *Satya Yuga*. In this golden age the attainment of the *atman* is the cherished goal. The following passage gives
us a sense as to what he sees as important distinctions.

> Regarding the right to do spiritual practices, they would not discrim-
> inate between anyone, not even between friend and foe. They toler-
> ated everyone. They would even give special opportunities to their
> sworn enemies to learn spiritual practices. In this regard, they never
> lost their collective spirit (Anandamurti, 1987, 7: 65).

This is, without a doubt, Sorokin's ideational era (elaborated in chapter five).

In the *Treta Yuga*, or the silver age, instead of the attainment of
the soul, the mind itself becomes more significant. For Sarkar, there
was some degeneration (from spirit to intellect), but in general the
larger collective harmony continued and in battles they "never harmed
great scholars or learned people in any way" (65). This would be
Sorokin's idealistic, dualistic age, where the real is described in a

both-and metaphysic, spiritual and material. Alternatively, using Indian eschatology—not Sarkar's—one might call this the age of the Brahmins.

However, because differing perspectives (in spirit there is unity, in intellect there is difference) the next era begins. Of importance again is the organic relationship between the eras: they emerge from each other. Naturally.

> Due to these differences, there was a further degeneration and human-ity entered the Dvapara Yuga, the so-called Copper Age. People became more body oriented. At the least provocation they would annihilate their enemies. It is evident that body-oriented creatures are more degen-erated than mind-oriented creatures (66).

This is the first phase of the sensate era in Sorokin's terms, or Sarkar's Ksattriyan era. Phase two is the dark age of destruction, *Kali Yuga*. The present age is *Kali Yuga*, the iron age, or Sarkar's *Shudra* era. "People of this age are food oriented and grossly mate-rialistic. Eating plays such an important part in their lives that, if there is a shortage of food, they think they will surely die" (66). This era is hightened by an individualism which runs counter the collec-tivism that is needed to solve the global problematique. "This requires a collective, organized effort following the spirit of 'in the olden days the gods used to share their food' " (67).

Instead of the four ages, one might use the three binding forces to develop a theory of history: *tamas* or static, *rajas* or active, *sattva* or pure. History starts out in *sattva*, then degenerates to *rajas* and finally lapses into *tamas*. It then begins again. This coincides with Sorokin's sensate (*tamas*), *rajas* (idealistic-dualistic) and *sattva* (ideational).

Sarkar, however, does not use these historical eras, or phases, to define a person's life, rather the static, active and pure forces are always acting on humans. Moreover, Sarkar asserts that he does not believe in the empirical division of time into *Krta, Treta, Dvapara*, and *Kali Yugas*, "although I do admit that there is some truth in the underlying spirit" (67). They are useful in judging what phase one's own life is in but not as predictions of the future. Thus their util-ity is not in as predictive theory, but as devotional-inspiration dis-course. For Sarkar, the key is to become individually enlightened and personally enter the golden era and secondly for the world to enter a new era.

Sarkar believes a new *Satya Yuga* is about to commence again, one in which people will once again be soul-orientated. Thus the cycle of history will be reasserted. However, instead of relying on an endogenous dialectic, a natural flow to the next era—as Indian thought tends to—Sarkar resorts to collective human agency. "Satya Yuga will start as soon as you implement the socio-economic ideology (PROUT). By your collective efforts let Satya Yuga be established on this dusty Earth as soon as possible" (68).

For Sarkar, the traditional view is significant largely as a tale that leads to individual and societal action—his is a radical reading of Indian thought. Thus it is useful in its description of the decline of spirit into mind and then into matter, collectivity to individuality, and justice into injustice. Far more important is the notion that after the dark age, there will be a return to the soul era. The cycle will continue.

Rethinking the Yugas

In his exemplary, "The Hindu Philosophy of Life," Buddha Prakash (1958) takes the classic Indian division of time and uses it not as a personal metaphor or a call to action, but applies it to history itself. The tale of the *yugas* for Prakash is an empirically accurate rendering of history that must be explicated.

For Prakash, history has two aspects: the first is "the ascertaining of facts on the basis of a critical and scientific investigation of the evidence left by the past," (Prakash, 1958, 494) and the second is the finding of correlation and interconnection among the facts thus established" (494). And thus while we wait for a history that is inductive in character, Prakash immediately makes a move to the philosophic. He reminds us that the Hindu view of history is process-oriented and organic (like a seed sprouting into a tree whose development is dependent on the environment and the potentiality of the seed). The Hindu view also places cosmic forces first, as in the *Gita* where "the role of the individual is only to act as a means to execute his will" (497). Thus,

> Hindu philosophy . . . is something that develops of itself in an autonomous manner transcending ad carrying in its sweep the individuals and participating in it. . . . historical evolution is a flow and convergence of impersonal or transpersonal forces, which are capable of being expressed in organic or biological images (497).

History is an interaction between the cosmic, the social and the environmental. But, echoing and perhaps influenced by Hegel, "this interdependent development of human spirituality and material development finds its expression in a series of individuals who chance to be at the points of vantage that qualify them for their respective roles" (497).

History then is impersonal and transpersonal, but it occurs through individuals and behind the backs of individuals. But, instead of Sarkar's *varna* derived social cycle, Prakash takes seriously the division of the real into *Krta, Treta, Dvapara,* and *Kali*. These eras are essentially interpretations of a divine moral order; a structure which decays over time. Prakash, however, does not fix mathematical immutability to it, rather the duration of the ages depend on the actions of human beings, thus structure and agency. Here, we have a noteworthy comparison to Sarkar, as he too, in his social cycle does not assign time spans to the particular eras, rather the duration of the cycle is agency affected.

Prakash further articulates the *Krta* to *Kali* cycle using Jain theory. In this, there are six periods: (1) the period of great happiness, (2) the period of happiness, (3) the period of happiness and sorrow, (4) the period of sorrow and happiness, (5) the period of sorrow, and (6) the period of great sorrow. On the cosmic level, this is the day and night of Brahman. Progress: Degeneration. Eternally.

As with other narratives of Indian philosophy, the texts are based on the metaphor of the body. Prakash quotes the *Aitareya-Brahmana*, a *Rigvedic* text, wherein Indra says:

> the fortune of a sitting man is static, of an idle man, it becomes still, of a sluggard, it sleeps and of a moving man, it moves forward. *Kali* is sleeping. *Dvapara* is shaking off (of the sleep), *Treta* is rising and *Krta* is moving. The moving man gets the honey and tastes the fruit of the *Ficus glomerata*. Look at the glory of the sun who never stops moving (499).

The biological model is associated with the psychological and then the social. It is also associated with the cosmic: Consciousness is first asleep, it awakens, and then actively creates the universe. This is an extension of the *sattva, rajas,* and *tamas* model, although Prakash uses the words of awakening, active and sleep, instead of pure, active and inert/static. For Prakash, "there is a unique harmony and symmetry between the tendency of an individual and that of a group of them" (500).

Prakash next develops the various ages: *Kali* becomes sleep, *Treta* and *Dvapara* become the age of awakening, and *Krta* becomes the age of activity. In the age of activity through the union of social contract individuals form a government. Moreover, this government is strong, popular and legitimate. Upward mobility is natural, institutions are open, allowing people to express their urges. In the age of activity, there are developments in science, philosophy, technology and art. And, of course, consistent with the spiritual nature of the Indian project, when the people as a whole are energetic, they are moved by a faith that leads them to creative activity. "When they cease to be active that faith dries up and gives place to escapism and apathetic indifference" (501).

From an age of activity, an age of sleep emerges. Government becomes dictatorial existing without active popular support, institutions are closed, the social horizon narrows, cultural expression is stunted and an atmosphere of imitation with respect to philosophy and technology develops.

> And when people struggle to be active, to assert themselves in political affairs, to make the social institutions mobile, to render the arts and humanities creative and to treat religion as conducive to social good, the 'age of sleep' passes into the 'age of awakening' (501).

The structure of change is cyclical, the process is organically dialectical and there exists a unity of discourse at individual, social and cosmic levels.

Prakash applies his theoretical scheme to the events and trends of Indian, Western and Islamic civilizations. We will simply summarize his main points of transition. Indian history can be seen as active prior to the seventh century. Its economy was expanding and its polity just. "When tyrants ascend the throne, they are disposed, when royal dynasties detract from the norm of conduct, they are overthrown" (502). However by 647 A.D. with the death of Harsa, religious intolerance and tyranny increase, arts and philosophy lose their innovativeness, "castes grow tight, contact with the outside world is shunned, religions preach escapism and a sense of weariness broods over the people" (502). Islam establishes its hegemony in 1198 and even though there were spurts of awakening, India for Prakash remains asleep and dominated. The awakening begins with the suppression of the 1857 "mutiny" against the British. The awakening is concluded in 1947 with independence. "A glance at modern independent Indian reveals the jazz and buzz of a new age of activity that is attaining its full momentum" (503).

While Prakash operates from the biological/spiritual metaphor of sleep-awakening-activity, it is the political discourse that is central for Prakash. He appropriates the traditional spirit-mind-matter decline and rearticulates in the language of modernity. Prakash attempts to fuse the traditional territorial state-centered model of history with the idealistic model of history. Unfortunately, there is no attempt to explain economic exploitation, poverty, and hopelessness in India today. Awakening is simply nationalism; activity becomes industrialism. This runs counter to Sarkar's view in which India is currently in *Kali Yuga*: the dark age of materialism.

Prakash's history of Europe begins with the age of activity as reflected in the ancient Greeks and their contributions to science, art and philosophy. By the beginning of the Roman empire, the age of sleep sets in. The common man is exploited, and "Caesars appear as gods incarnate and compel the people to worship them as such" (503). Christianity does not change any of this as tyranny remains. The age of awakening begins when Islamic thinkers bring Greek thought to Europe and revitalize the Western project. "As a result, there was the Renaissance, the Reformation, the progress of science, the great conquests of the ocean and the discovery of new lands" (503). The age of activity begins again with the French revolution and continues today.

In China, the age of awakening dawned in 1911 with Sun Yat Sen, in Islam with the Westernization of the Middle East through leaders such as Mustafa Kemal Ataturk. Again the age of activity is represented by the rise of nationalism, industrialism and the scientific revolution. Every country and culture follows this pattern. While it appears that Prakash argues that history perfectly represents these stages, in his conclusion he moves a step back. He asserts that these stages are not empirical laws, rather, his aim is to show that a moral dimension must be given to the natural process of history. To Buddha Prakash, the Hindu philosophy of history stresses

> the moral aspect of the historical periods besides their chronological conception . . . the way in which this view was possible was the belief in the rise and fall of virtue (dharma) as the basis of the succession of ages. When virtue (dharma) was once accepted as the basis of the periodic arrangement of history, the freedom of human will and effort followed as a corollary (505).

What is important then is not the actual stages, but the synthesis of natural history and moral principles. Moreover, these moral principles are not divine, that is, outside of human creation, but rather they inhere in human actions. But the divine, as we have developed in the previous chapter, can be located within *and* without human consciousness, thus, there is a moral structure to the universe and humans create and interact with it.

In general, Prakash takes the classical model of Indian history from the *Gita* and applies it to world history. But unlike Sri Aurobindo who presses the role of God and the *avatar* in history, Prakash remains focused on periodicity in history. Sarkar, also, uses the *Gita* metaphor (that of the *avatar*) but situates it in the devotional discourse, not the empirical one. Moreover, Sarkar follows the classic *Gita* division of the four *varnas*, but makes them central to his theory, not peripheral introductions. However, both function as naturals. In the *Gita*, Krishna evokes *varna* to remind the reader that there is natural in history, that man has a duty. Sarkar uses this concept philosophically to remind one that although there is individual will, there remains a deep structure.

Like Prakash, Sarkar, too, represents historical narratives as primarily educational, as a way of illustrating deep moral dilemmas and principles. However, Sarkar adds a dimension of the vision of the future (**PROUT**) and while he uses the biological discourse to explain his theory—the breath, the life cycle, hills, waves, and the body— he takes this discourse not as metaphor but as the real. His stages become in some fashion, laws. But laws in the Indian episteme are perceived differently than the laws of the western social sciences for truth and knowing are constituted differently. Like Sarkar, Prakash does not bother to focus on the historical narrative, the data seems almost incidental. The categories of description are far more important. Indeed as empirical events they are highly contentious from a variety of viewpoints. What is central is how one age follows the next and that progress is cyclical.

For Sarkar, more important than the narrative of events or the problem of the periodicity of cycles is the silencing of the stories of suffering. Sarkar's history is a tale of the inhumanity of humans, of their attack on each other, of their ability to punish and mutilate the weaker among them, of their creation of theories and economies to nourish a few while justifying the silent destruction of the tongues of the majority. His story is one of the betrayal of ideals by each subsequent type of leadership. Each leadership type comes to power, promises much, achieves little, and then uses military, cultural or economic power to stand above others. Yet, leadership always fears that those who have supplied strength, legitimacy and labor will suddenly and certainly tear the wealth from their bodies and palaces.

For Sarkar, every age has periods of activity, sleep, and awakening. But these categories are not eras in themselves. In addition, activity need not always be good, for example, imperialism and other "isms" come about through great concerted activities.

Both, however, emerge from metaphors of the body, of what is immediately seen. Compare this with the approach of the modern, Occidental Sorokin who develops his system not from the body, but from rational thought. His first question is: What is the real? The answering of the question forms his divisions of history, perception and self.

Cosmic History

But Prakash's is not the only interpretation of Indian history, there are other significant versions as well. Staying within the traditional, body-spirit view, contemporary Indian philosophers Sarvepalli Radhakrishnan and K. Satchidananda Murti offer useful idealistic/theistic descriptions. For Radhakrishnan, history is a meaningful process.

> Those who look at it from the outside are carried away by the wars and battles, the economic disorders and the political upheavals, but below in the depths is to be found the truly majestic drama, the tension between the limited effort of man and the sovereign purpose of the universe (Radhakrishnan, 1967, 40–41).

History is teleological. It is abstract. Existence affords man the possibility to continue the awakening process and differentiate the eternal from the temporal. "The soul has risen from the sleep of matter, through plan and animal life, to the human level, and is battling with ignorance and imperfection to take possession of its infinite kingdom" (Radhakrishnan, 1967, 41). The purpose of history then is to recover truths and discard falsehoods, what is, exists, so that humans can "attain mastery over it and reveal the higher world operating in it. The world is not therefore an empty dream or an eternal delirium" (41). For Radhakrishnan, suffering finds meaning in the subjectivity of the individual and his or her attempt to give an idealistic, spiritual meaning to it, or more correctly, to find the meaning sequestered in suffering.

K. Satchidananda Murti articulates why history must be cosmic. With a cosmic-centric view, "We are freed from humanism, localism and parochialism" (Murti, 1967, 44). The sovereignty of the subjectivity of man is thrown out, the locale of history shifts from cultural, national and civilizational history to world-as-history. For Murti, history is the expression of the divine in space-time. The individual observer is removed. This truth is the message of every religion, Occidental, Oriental or Indian. When pressed as to the finality of this process, Murti stays his ground and responds that this is an anthropomorphic question. "God has nothing to realize. . . . For Him, no aim, no purpose" (44–45). To explain the why of creation, again the *Gita* is resorted to. We are told that it is the play and sport of God—*Lila*—meaning that it is a dance that humans cannot understand, for ultimately as long as we remain humans we cannot know. Only by becoming Being, the Real, can we know. Once there, however, we cannot communicate in a language that is intelligible to others, since the "language" of Being is not human based.

Thus no progress for humanity as a whole is possible. But unlike other Indian writers, Murti does not look backward to a previous historical golden age. Unlike Sarkar, he does not posit a future golden age. Rather the lesson of history is to turn inwards.

Radhakrishnan's and Murti's macro perspective removes humans from agency, except insofar as they re-identify with the soul. Two of the implications of this view are obvious: (1) a Vedantic-type lack of concern with the material world and (2) a rejection or unconcern for technology since it has not increased happiness or the moral nature of humans. While Sarkar begins with this view—that progress is essentially spiritual—he counters with a blueprint for an alternative material construction that makes the possibility of the realization of a good society more likely. More possible. In this sense Sarkar's history is closer to the Marxist and the Subaltern perspective. In these critical views, the goal of history is explicitly to change the present. It is not the rendering of myths, it is not the repetition of genealogies, it is not the noting of that which was recorded in texts that still exist, rather it is the uncovering of structures and practices that make possible an alternative tomorrow and, indeed, an alternative yesterday. Moreover, Sarkar takes a macro perspective that explicitly attempts to explain the movement of forces, ideas, and matter through time. It is not a mere categorization of stages. The stages relate to each other in more than a perchance spatiality.

Finally, Sarkar's model places all Indian constructions of history in their temporal positions, a placement we will investigate once we outline other interpretations of Indian history.

Aurobindo and God in History

Sri Aurobindo (1872–1950), influential philosopher, activist and exemplary for our own comparative purposes in understanding the Indian construction of history, takes the *Gita* model of history and melds it with the Hegelian and Nietzschian models, that is, the placing of God in history and the centrality of the superman. Aurobindo begins with the idealistic view but dislodges the *maya* of Vedanta thus allowing a role for humans and economic/social development in history. Yet it is the Cosmic that defines history.

> When we withdraw our gaze from its egoistic preoccupation with limited and fleeting interests and look upon the world with dispassionate and curious eyes that search only for the Truth, our first result is the perception of boundless energy of infinite existence, infinite movement, infinite activity pouring itself out in limitless Space, in eternal Time, an existence that surpasses infinitely our ego or any ego or any collectivity of egos, in whose balance the grandiose products of aeons are but the dust of a moment and in whose incalculable sum numberless myriads count only as a petty swarm. When we begin to see, we perceive that it exists for itself, not for use, has its own gigantic aims, its own complex and boundless idea, its own vast desire or delight that it seeks to fulfill, its own immense and formidable standards which look down as if with an indulgent and ironic smile at the pettiness or ours (Aurobindo, 1967, 361).

Thus, for Aurobindo, behind the "confused torrent of events and personalities or a kaleidoscope of changing institutions" (Varma, 1960, 33) lies the Supreme Being. Aurobindo asserts that "the history of the cycles of man is a progress towards the unveiling of the Godhead in the soul and life of humanity; each high events and stage of it is a divine manifestation" (Varma, 1960, 34). While this establishes a grand perspective, the question remains: what forms does Consciousness use to express Itself in the material world? In the *Gita*, the form is the individual, each person is but an instrument. Aurobindo, however, borrowing from Hegel, not only assigns instrumentality to historical individuals but also to groups, associations and collectivities. Nationalism—specifically Third world independence movements—

itself now becomes part of the divine drama. It becomes an extraordinary event that represents the will of Consciousness in creating
a better human condition. Thus God for Aurobindo not only works
through *avatars* such as Krishna but as well through nationalistic
movements and other associations as well.

But if all history is the expression of the Divine, then why are
some events, associations or structures privileged over others? Moreover,
if creation is but Divine expression, then how is human suffering
explained? This classic question has had numerous responses. The
Vedantist response is that suffering is an illusion, merely a matter
of perspective. Alternatively, the Occidental response has been the
location of the cause suffering in man, in choice. God then for both
the *Vedantist* and the Occidental does not cause suffering; *maya* is to
blame or the choices men and women make is to blame. Choice,
then, becomes karma in the Indian worldview. Suffering is caused
because of unknown actions by the self in this or in previous lives.

Aurobindo eventually recourses to a technical position with respect
to the problem of evil. The choices to him are twofold. First is the
devil, but as Thapar has brilliantly stated, "The fundamental sanity
of Indian civilization has been due to the absence of Satan" (Thapar,
1966, 15). The second is redefining *maya*, illusion, as ignorance. Writes
Aurobindo: "It is often God's will in us to take through the mind
the *bhoga* of ignorance, of dualities, of joy and grief, of pleasure and
pain, of virtue and sin, of enjoyment and renunciation" (Varma,
1960, 37). At the level of collective action, it is imbalance that leads
to evil, it is the ego that perhaps begins in God's light but then goes
too far. The ego becomes consumed by itself and not by any higher
purpose. But ignorance leads to possibilities to learn and thus perform penances and eventually good karma might result. In this way
Aurobindo redefines God's purpose as that of learning and teaching.

The classic Indian response from the *Gita* is similar. Humans are
only instruments. Morality is no longer a ground for action *and* the
yogi who has accepted the divine acts in the flow of the divine. The
individual will becomes merged with the Cosmic reflecting only that
which God deems is possible. In the cosmic march of history suffering
then is incidental. It is real, but cosmically useful in that suffering
leads people back to the truth. In either case, there is a larger purpose and pattern that should not be seen in human terms. Humans
exist to fulfill that purpose. But in this classic view, there is no men-

tion of associations or God working through collectivities. There is simply the rise and fall of dharma.

On this point Sarkar takes quite a different tack. Given that the real is perceived from different levels in various ways, problems arise when there is an attempt to ontologically engage in discourse-travel, understanding one level from the vantage view of another. While there is a larger purpose, ultimately it is unknowable. Yet at the same time, to see history totally from the perspective of the individual (God as within the inner self, the *atman—paramatman* symmetry) leaves out the larger cosmic drama, forgets the role of past lives in creating the present. The results is a perspective that forces one into locating purpose in family, group, community, race, nation, social group, or religion—all spaces that limit and bind the intellect. In this sense Aurobindo takes a risk that Gandhi, for example, was unwilling to take. Gandhi could afford to use the divine in politics at the level of metaphor and the level of strategy, but Aurobindo as a philosopher could not do the same. He had to work out the philosophical implications for such a view. He had to work them out given his view in the absolute, his view of the *Gita* and his associations with various movements. But this view of Spirit in associations could not be found in Indian texts, thus his recourse to Hegel.

Returning to Aurobindo's division of ignorance and knowledge, Sarkar takes a similar tactic, but defines it as *vidya* and *avidya*. Introversion and extroversion. Introversion leads to increased clarity, to compassionate action that emerges from the desire for social equality. Extroversion leads to sin or the misuse of spiritual, mental and physical resources. Introversion calms the perturbations of the mind, leading to right thought and action.

Suffering in this model becomes an asset as it makes a person stronger, developing inner strength. Gandhi uses this philosophical perspective to justify the least-violence movement. Evil now becomes located in self not in a concrete entity, thus allowing for what appears to be an utterly agency-less model to suddenly allow will. And yet, when convenient, Sarkar and Aurobindo (and Gandhi) can move to the layer of the absolute, wherein every action is purposeful. What that purpose is can be defined in different ways. The safest way to define it is that it is unknown, thus purpose cannot be appropriated, and reality made less authoritative and more negotiable. Sarkar alternatively uses the different ways of knowing to find purpose:

intuition, reason, sense-perception, authority and *bhakti*. Yet he is
also authoritative, at least metaphorically, for the *Taraka Brahma* has
perfect knowing of the real.

Aurobindo takes an alternative route, again borrowing from Hegel.
For Aurobindo, divine determinism implies the "Godsent leader"
(Varma, 1960, 41). "This is the greatness of the great man, not that
by their own strength they can determine great events but that
they are serviceable and specially forged instruments of the Power
which determines them" (42). The hero thus emerges in critical periods of history and brings on the next stage in human evolution. The
hero is the agent of the active part of Consciousness, *Prakrti* or *Kali*.
While for Hegel, the hero is unconscious, for Aurobindo he or she
is conscious.

For Sarkar, too, his *sadvipras*—intellectuals motivated for the greater
good and grounded in spiritual consciousness—are conscious of their
role and the drama unfolding around them. They are used by
Consciousness, but as consciousness is also inside them, their ego
can move forward with this Desire or back away from it. For
Aurobindo, however, at a certain state there is choicelessness. Krishna
gave Arjuna no choice: the cosmic drama demanded that he fulfill
his role and engage himself in battle at *Kuruksetra*. Understanding the
political dangers of a cosmic amoral view applied to the world, Sarkar
attempts to balance the Cosmic view with an appeal to rationality—
humans must follow reason. Reason, however, is defined as that which
leads to self-expansion, not merely the logical or non-emotive.

By attempting to frame the divine in history, Aurobindo can then
easily justify the French revolution as an act of God with Mirabeau,
Danton, Robespierre and Napoleon serving their respective parts.
Napoleon is finally destroyed by *Kali* for putting his ego first and
forgetting the greater historical cause of nationalism. For Sarkar this
would be an irrational reading. Only that which is outside of boundaries—which transcends family, society, nation, race, species—can
be ultimately rational. The nation-state as an organizing entity is not
a necessary part of human evolution. God does not prefer any particular political structure over another. But for Aurobindo, Napoleon
did serve God.

Thus Aurobindo takes the model of the *Gita*—specifically, Krishna's
conversation with Arjuna—and uses it to justify the battles of other
cultures and other world-historical figures. Again, Sarkar differs. His
history does not privilege world-historical figures, only Shiva and

Krishna are given special status and then only for the specific period of time they lived and ultimately only from the view of the devotional discourse. Sarkar moves in and out of different discursive spaces. These spaces, levels, include: (1) the rise and fall of *Dharma*; (2) the level of structure; (3) the fall and rise of particular classes; (4) and the individual level at the struggle of the self to realize itself and to serve humanity. In contrast, Aurobindo privileges the nation-state by asserting that Indian nationalism cannot die for it is a creation of the divine will. What follows from this perspective is an India constructed as the chosen people. Indians had suffered and now were casting off their yoke ready to fulfill their destiny of bringing spiritual light to the world. Sarkar again avoids the location of a destiny in a specific people, no particular group will bring about a renaissance. Revolutionary activity—spiritual and political—abides in those who are willing to suffer and challenge the present irrespective of various sentiments such as nation and religion. Aurobindo believes India will lead the world in the future because of her spiritual legacy. The rise and fall of nations in the long run can be traced to their spiritual state. Its recent problems are because India has not been following her spirit adequately. From this association of the spiritual and national destiny, Aurobindo develops a theory of the rise and decline of all nations.

Aurobindo uses this perspective to develop a general theory of the rise and fall of cultures. For him all cultures traverse three periods. The first is the period of *formation* where the fundamental practices emerge. In the second phase, the *structure* develops. In the third phase, there is *decay and disintegration*. At this point, there are two possibilities: a renaissance or a slow decline. In India, the formative period was the Vedic period; the development phase was the Epic period; and now, India is in decline awaiting a renaissance. In this theory, Aurobindo does not directly follow the classic end of *Kali* and return to *Kṛta*. Rather, culture can fall into disintegration and collapse. The highest possible integration is where the nation follows the Spirit. But there need not be only one divine nation per epoch as with Hegel. There is no such hierarchy with Aurobindo.

Sarkar does not locate the progressive and the good in the nation. Writing at a time when the nation-state is already established (if not declining) and indeed oppressive of minorities and individuals, Sarkar finds the good in revolutionary cultural, linguistic, local economic movements *and* in a spiritual globalism (in fact, in spiritual universalism).

Aurobindo writing at a time when the Indian nation needed to be theoretically buttressed resorts to the Gita and Hegel for help. To a certain degree, then, their differences can then be explained by the events of the time.

The last aspect of Aurobindo's philosophy of history that is useful in our comparison to Sarkar is the notion of the superman. Vishwanath Varma in *The Political Philosophy of Sri Aurobindo* (1960) juxtaposes East and West titling one essay "The Superman, the Vibhuti, the Avatara, and the Philosopher King." Varma argues that Aurobindo takes Western concepts of leadership and brings Yogic interpretation to them. For Aurobindo, the Superman is one captured by divinity, not solely rationality. He is not power, but divine, following the natural flow of cosmic mind. He is not the great military leader, but the man who is forced to transform because of his meeting with the inexpressible. This definition of leadership is similar to Sarkar's in that these leaders are not incarnations of the divine, but resultant of concrete historical conditions. Yet they are part of the unfolding of the human evolutionary drama, the next stage for humanity. Aurobindo wrote, "Either man must fulfill himself by satisfying the divine within him or he must produce out of himself a new and greater being who will be more capable of satisfying it. He must either himself become a divine humanity or give place to Supermen" (Varma, 1960, 417–418). But while Sarkar looks toward a society where exploitation is replaced by the just *sadvipra* administration of government, Aurobindo calls for nothing less than a Yogocracy. In this interpretation, Aurobindo downplays the power of Hegel's historical figures since ego is paramount in them, Nietzsche's transcendence of man is accepted but this transcendence is divine, not of the individual ego.

Generally, Aurobindo begins with an absolutist spiritual view of history, places God in history, explains suffering by inner ignorance at the level of the human and individual learning about God. From the level of the absolute, Aurobindo sees divinity acting through associations such as the nation-state and finally through a spiritual community of supermen, through whom the cosmic mind can act.

Certainly Aurobindo's system is massive and synthetic, but he is exceptionally weak at structure, remaining at the idealistic level. His theory as little explanatory value (in terms of explaining the causes behind the events and trends of history), but nonetheless is useful in understanding the type of thinking that emerges from pressing and extrapolating the Vedic model. Sarkar, too, attempts a synthesis and also is equally influenced by the Indian classics. However, instead of Hegel and Nietzsche, Sarkar looks to different Europeans, namely, Marx and the Marxist notion of structure, class and exploitation. But like Aurobindo, by resorting to a *sadvipra* or a superman, Sarkar falls out of the liberal camp of democratic politics, a liberal politics that has attempted to move God outside of history and move science and technology inside history with balance coming from the opposition of many interests (pluralism and interest group theory). But this balance is rejected by Sarkar as yet another attempt by the capitalist class to keep the exploiting *varna* dominant long after it has served its usefulness.

But especially hazardous from Sarkar's view is the writing of history with a concrete God, a God that is not a metaphorical, but represented as real, a God that is not a functional theoretical tool, but rather an actor with omnipotent agency in history. The hazard is that this God can easily become appropriated for once God is introduced there must be a vehicle for his/her talk and actions. Whether it is the prophet, the nation or other associational forms, as long as it moves away from God solely as presence or inspiration then the danger of interpretation, of power, of conquering, of defining and extracting becomes increasingly and ominously everpresent. God in History cannot help but become ideological. Is the alternative then to leave God outside of history or present but only at the level of emotion, of poetry, of conscious metaphor, that is, in poststructural language, at the level of God-talk—concrete at the cosmic but internally subjective at the individual level?

However from a broader poststructural view, one need not be worried only about God, for all "history" is interpretation. God in history is simply one authoritative definition. Conversely one might impose an order of science and rationality, or of a self-interest market model. There must be some order to history to make our world intelligible. This ordering cannot help but be, once available, appropriated. Who will appropriate it and how then becomes the far more crucial question. This is Foucault's question. Aurobindo, however, is not interested in this question. Sarkar is. His history is an answer to the question of how the real is interpreted and appropriated at the expense of other interpretations and interpreters. Like Foucault

his question becomes not so much of developing a scheme of God
in history, but more of the price of history. Not solely content with
analysis, Sarkar develops a way of economizing the price, of reducing the price of history. But in the process, one can critically ask
does Sarkar not raise the cost of history again by imposing yet
another transcendental model that can be appropriated by other than
the harbingers of good-will?

Interpreting Indian History

Can Sarkar's social cycle be applied to Indian history? Sarkar, unlike
Prakash and Aurobindo, does not attempt this, but Batra does. Batra
does not care for questions of epistemological price. His effort is to
fit Sarkar's theory to Indian history. He applies Sarkar's theory to
the Aryan civilization leaving aside the older Indus valley civilization given lack of evidence for that culture. The Aryan Vedic period,
beginning around 1500 B.C. when they invaded the Indus valley
inhabitants (the Dasas), is for Batra the first *Ksattriyan* Era. This was
a society of clans each organized around a warlike male or group
of males. Initially caste was more a general category, based on "like
father, like son" instead of a means of political and economic inclu-
sion/exclusion. Females in this society still retained a level of rights,
possibly as there were still vestiges of matriarchy. As the Aryans
expanded and established an empire, the superstructure became composed of warriors and eventually priests. By the end of the *Brahmanas*,
Batra believes that the cycle had shifted and India was now in *Vipran*
era. True power was ideational and in the hands of the priests. It
was then that the caste system developed, although the *ksattriya*
remained as top. Peasants now had to support priests and aristocrats. However, at the same time there was a philosophical explo-
sion of new ideas, largely the perennial philosophy of the *Upanishads*.
With the invention of money there was increased trade. Eventually
merchants gained in power and became the most respected class.
This was the Buddhist era, from 700–400 B.C. This era also saw the
development of the *Sangha*. Central in its expansion was the pur-
chase of land and construction of temples. To Batra, there was little intervention from the State and a sort of free market prevailed.
The authority of the Brahmins decreased, and that of wealthy merchants increased. Wealth became concentrated with the Nanda dynasty

who were particularly oppressive. As we might predict with Sarkar's cycle, next is the worker's evolution or revolution leading to a new centralized state. Batra's interpretation of Indian history naturally follows Sarkar's model. Thus Chandragupta Maurya lead a workers' revolution in 324 B.C.

This then starts the next warrior era. It begins to decline with Asoka's death in 232 B.C. With the power of the kings after Asoka in decline, the Brahmin's power increased. This was also the time of the writing of the *Manu-Smriti* which celebrates the power of intellectuals. By the third century B.C., Batra describes a new capitalist era that lasts until Samudra Gupta. The decentralization of the polity that occurs in capitalist eras ends and the polity becomes centralized. Power is centralized but rights increased.

The Gupta period is seen as a golden age for Indian, a spiral continuation of the structure of the Mauryan times. With the death of Harsha in 7th century there is a decline of the *Ksattriyan* era. For Batra, the 9th through the 10th century is the onset of another *Vipran* era, largely because of the writings of Shankaracharya. The next period sees a rise in the power of landlords, not traders or merchants, and thus a rise in Feudalism that Batra takes to be the *Vaeshyan* era again. The weakness in the polity makes it easy for the Muslim invaders to colonize India. What follows is an evolution into an anarchic *Shudra* era. Finally, with Alauddin Khilgi, the *Ksattriyan* era begins again. Power is centralized in kingship and the era of the warriors continues until Akbar—the spiritual synthesizer—begins a new *Vipran* era. Power passes to *vipran* ministers and kingship declines. The British period marks the next capitalist era, which, notwithstanding Independence and India's socialist efforts, continues today. This in the near future is to be followed by a new centralized polity, but with the intervention of Sarkar's ideology one which will regain the economic and human rights of the exploited as well as increase the spiritual, intellectual and material wealth of the nation. Thus, for Batra, India is in the final stage of the third cycle.

There are certainly numerous problems with Batra's interpretation. Huge spans of history are covered in one era with minor to deal with problems in interpretation either at the level of epistemology or at the level of conventional readings of Indian history. Batra is especially weak on the role of the *shudras* in history and on their efforts to create the next era. The new king to be, whether Chandragupta Maurya or Sumudra Gupta, is privileged.

Nonetheless, Batra provides an alternative reading to the cycles of Indian history. Now, for example, one can trace the classic battle between brahmin and king and include the merchant as well.

Ancient, Medieval and Modern

In contrast to Batra's macro approach, most Indian historiography has not been concerned with the history of epistemes, or paradigms, nor with the theory building enterprise itself. Indian historiography has largely been concerned with middle range and micro theory. It has been a project of various empirical and classification approaches, rather than of deep structures or patterns. But nonetheless an implicit structure has emerged. While the traditional idealistic or spiritual view is that of the life cycle of the soul and body, the usual or dominant historiography has been a classification of history into three periods. These are ancient, medieval, and modern. Ancient is seen as Hindu, medieval as Muslim, and modern as British. These categories are natural derivatives from the dynastic interpretation of Indian history, largely as a result of the discovery of India by British and European scholars. According to Thapar,

> Those who were most directly concerned with India in the nineteenth century were the British administrators, and the early non-Indian historians of India came largely from this group. Consequently, the early histories were 'administrator histories', concerned mainly with the rise and fall of dynasties and empires. The protagonists of Indian history were the kings and the narration of events revolved around them. The autocratic king, oppressive and unconcerned with the welfare of his subjects, was the standard image of the Indian ruler . . . As for actual governing, the underlying assumption was that British administration was in fact superior to any known to the history of the subcontinent (Thapar, 1966, 17).

Therefore, instead of the cosmic cycle of Krishna, of the *Gita*, the linear evolution model of industrialism was adopted. Indian history was placed in a development scheme with England ahead and India behind. This history was not one of epics, nor of the philosophical schools, but of constructions of those rulers who managed to domesticate time and worker and thus somehow were isomorphic to the British perspective. The Indian could not have his own theory of history, since there was a larger theory of social evolution in which all Indian theories would find their place. Alternatively, Orientalism attempted to glorify the mystical, the romantic, the erotic and exotic in Indian practices and thought. India was now pre-history and Europe became history. Even Marx did not escape this or more aptly especially Marx did not escape this. India was the child with Britain the adult. In Marx's theory of progress, "Childhood innocence serv[ed] as the prototype of primitive communism" (Nandy, 1983, 12).

> India to him always remained a country of 'small semi-barbarian, semi-civilized communities' which 'restricted the human mind within the smallest possible compass, making it the unresisting tool of superstition' and where the peasants lived their 'undignified, stagnant and vegetative life.' 'These little communities ... brought about a brutalising worship of nature exhibiting its degradation in the fact that man, the sovereign of nature, fell down on his knees in the adoration of Kanuman [sic], monkey, and Sabbala, the cow' (Nandy, 1983, 13).

Given this, it was possible for Marx to state that "whatever may have been the crime of England she was the unconscious tool of history" (13). In the scheme, the first stage in Indian history was a sort of primitive communism, then Asiatic Feudalism, then British rule. This rule was imperialistic, but necessary to set into motion capitalism. Once capitalism matured, India could then become socialist and then eventually join the communist community. Unfortunately, India, instead of becoming a mature capitalist society, became a peripheral society and a colony to the European core.

Nonetheless, the sequence is the same: ancient, medieval, and modern. Modern for Marx meant capitalism then socialism, for liberal writers it meant capitalism in various stages (pre-growth, take-off, growth) or agriculturalism to industrialism. Prakash too follows this line of reasoning, as he assigns the present as a golden age of activity, instead of the traditional view of the present as Kali. However, he gives a more sympathetic reading by calling the Indian mutiny of 1857 an awakening.

Looking at the same division but from the viewpoint of the history of philosophy, that is a view that is primarily based on the Indian episteme but overlaid with an Occidental historical, linear narrative, we can divide Indian history from a slightly different angle. The ancient system can be divided into four stages. The first is the *Vedic* (6000 to 2500 B.C.) where Indian thought moves from polytheism to monotheism and then to philosophical absolute monotheism. The second phase can be seen as the *Epic* period (600 B.C. to

200 A.D.). This is the era of the *Mahabharata*, the *Dharmashastras*, the *Ramayana* and the beginning of Buddhism and Jainism. The next era is the *Sutra* (100 B.C. to 600 A.D.) where the six schools of philosophy are developed. The final era, which continues today, is the *Scholastic* where the role of philosophy is to comment on the original systems. It is only a few rare individuals who have attempted to start their own systems, Aurobindo, for example, from the spiritual perspective and M.N. Roy from the Marxist perspective.

Alternatively, David Kinsley (1982) in his *Hinduism* calls the first phase the *Formative* period. This to him is the Vedic period (2500–800 B.C.) with the writing of the *Rigveda* dated at 1200 B.C.. In this period, priests play a strong role in defining norms and reality is represented through ritual and sacrifice. The next stage is the *Speculative* period from 800–400 B.C. This is the telling of the *Upanishads* wherein Indian thought becomes clearly associated with the desire for *moksa* and renunciation becomes a central theme in Indian culture. Following this from 400 B.C. to 600 A.D. is the *Epic/Classical* period when the *Mahabharata* and *Ramayana* were both written. The *Dharmashastras* as well are written at this time.

> It is in this literature [*Dharmashastras*] that the definition of the ideal society as *varna-ashrama-dharma*, the duty [dharma] of acting according to one's stage in life [student, householder, spiritual life and renunciate] (ashrama) and position in society (*varna*) is arrived at (Kinsley, 1982, 16).

His next era is the *Medieval* period (600–1800 A.D.) defined—not as the Islamic medieval as the Indian historian would write it—for the development of the six schools and the rise of Tantra. Sarkar, of course, would place Tantra 7500 years ago. He does not use the division of time based on the birth of Jesus Christ refusing to enter into that discursive space. However, he would agree with Kinsley's redefinition of Tantra. "The *Tantras* . . . often criticize established religious practices and the upholders of these practices, the Brahmins" (Kinsley, 1982, 19). The *Modern* period from 1800 to the present is characterized by the Hindu revival of the 19th century (Arya Samaj, Ramakrishna, Brahmo Samaj) and the Independence movements as well as the introduction of the Indian worldview to European and American society.

There is, however, no attempt to search for a deeper order to history. There is no teleology. Nor are there any ruptures in thought as Foucault might search for. Rather thought is seen as one continuous flow from ancient to present. Other than Sarkar, Prakash, and Indian Marxist interpretations and to some extent Aurobindo, there have been few attempts to place Indian history within an evolutionary, theoretical scheme, that is, a theory and philosophy of history—macro-history. Indian history either has been classified by philosophical eras or dynastic eras, for example, the Nanda, Mauryas, Guptas, Moguls, the British and the recent Nehru/Gandhi dynasty. There have been few attempts to search for the underlying causes of historical change—the key variable has remained the power of kings. Alternatively, it is argued that Indian history has no meaning or pattern, only its philosophical schools have meaning and that as an escape from history. In this regard Sarkar stands out as radical break, a rupture from past Indian thinking. He finds—imposes—a pattern, but not based on an import from Marx, but rather a local knowledge pattern, and one that is, as Indian thinking claims to be, universal.

But Sarkar is not the only one to critique Indian historiography. Among those, K.M. Panikkar writes:

> The study of local dynastic histories, without reference to the conditions of Indian as a whole has led us to the exaggeration of local patriotism which is one of the most dangerous tendencies today. . . . It is time we also discarded finally this attempt to build our history on monarchs and dynasties, and viewed it from the point of view of the evolution of the Indian people (Pannikkar, 1967, 35).

To him, the fascination with the Aryans has led to the Aryanization of the country and of history. What is needed instead is a history of India that looks at the social evolution of Indians.

This search for a pattern is further developed by D.D. Kosambit. To him Indians need to take seriously the charge that India has had some episodes but no history (Kosambit, 1967, 37). The way out is a study of the means and relations of production. But this need not be Marxist or European, especially with Marx's belief that India has no history, that it is not part of the progressive movement of power, technology, and structure. Indian history must concentrate on changes in technology and the resultant changes in power between classes.

> The more important question is not who was king, nor whether the given region had a king, but whether its people used a plough, light or heavy, at the time. The type of kingship, as a function of the property relations and surplus produced, depends upon the method of agriculture, not conversely (Kosambit, 1967, 40).

The philosophy of India, its classics, its culture cannot be divorced from the objective economic conditions. In a passionate quote, he reminds us that:

> The subtle mystic philosophies, tortuous religions, ornate literature, monuments teeming with intricate sculpture, and delicate music of India all derive from the same historical process that produced the famished apathy of the villager, senseless opportunism and termite greed of the 'cultured' strata, sullen uncoordinated discontent among the workers, the general demoralization, misery, squalor, and degrading superstition. The one is the result of the other, the one is the expression of the other. The most primitive implements produced a meager surplus that was expropriated by a correspondingly archaic social mechanism. This maintained a few in that cultured leisure which they took as a mark of their innate superiority to the vast majority living in degradation. It is necessary to grasp this in order to appreciate the fact that history is not a sequence of haphazard events but is made by human being in the satisfaction of their daily needs (40).

Jawaharlal Nehru in his *Glimpses of World History* develops this Marxist analysis as well. To him real history must be the history of progress; of how humans overcame challenges and struggled against the elements, just as today they must struggle against economic inequity. His project was to fuse the nationalist spirit with the international proletariat spirit within the context of an objective science of history, a science of life. But Nehru did not remain within the confines of Marxist thought. He was clearly additive in his thinking.

> Marx's general analysis of social development seems to have been remarkable correct, and yet many developments took place later which did not fit in with his outlook for the immediate future. So while I accepted the fundamentals of the socialist theory, I did not trouble myself about its numerous inner controversies. . . . Life is too complicated and, as far as we can understand it in our present state of knowledge, too illogical for it to be confined within the four corners of a fixed doctrine (Nehru, 1967, 48–49).

This statement typical of the Indian episteme, one that we would not expect a neo-liberal to state as his guiding philosophy. Assuming Sarkar's thought does become the model of Indian thought in the next century, we can but posit that this pattern will continue. The overall stages will be used. Predictions that are incorrect will not change faith or use of Sarkar's intuitional science or his theory of evolution. Just as we can see with Nehru, 19th century European thought had infiltrated the Indian episteme making words such as struggle, progress, and science current and valuable in discursive transactions, we can expect the same appropriation of Sarkar's cosmology, if it gains currency.

While Nehru uses Marx's language to speak to a history of India that is class based, K.M. Munshi attempts to develop a nationalist interpretation of Indian history. Indian history should be about how the Indian nation has been created. All forces, economic, cultural, geographic, political, philosophic, spiritual must lead toward the creation of a collective will. Indian history, for Munshi, has been the history of foreign invaders, of Alexander, of the Sultans of Delhi, of the British. The occupation of India is only matched by the occupation of Indian history. As a true nationalist, Indian history must not show how "she underwent foreign invasions, but how she resisted them and eventually triumphed over them" (Munshi, 1967, 34). Thus the unit of analysis now becomes the Indian people themselves, independence then becomes the fitting crown to Indian history. Agency moves to the collective, not to a particular *varna*, an episteme, class relations, technology, or the people. But his is not a mere rejection of foreign culture, but how Indians have absorbed the invaders and made their ideas their own while at the same time keeping their original authentic selves. This to him is Indian history.

Of course, Romila Thapar and others critical of Orientalism do not believe India has been that successful at all. India may have achieved nationhood but her history and her present is still perceived through the eyes of 19th European century writers. India, and her history, as created by the West, is one that is essentially centered on kingship and mysticism (as in superstition).

> In the imagination of Europe, India had always been the fabulous land of untold wealth and mystical happenings, with more than just a normal share of wise men. From the gold digging ants to the philosophers who lived naked in the forests, these were part of the picture which the ancient Greeks had of the Indians and these images persisted throughout many centuries (Thapar, 1986, 15).

But when Europe prospered taking its place as Core in the emerging world capitalist system and India concomitantly declined taking its place as periphery, India became less known for its gold and spices (they had been expropriated) and more for its poverty. And as Europe rejected the classical world and embraced the modern, it created its opposite in India and the Islamic world. Europe became rational and progressive: India mystical and regressive. The West had a balance between civil and political society, India, instead of institutions and government, had only the caste system (civil society) while China had only the state (and Islam perhaps neither state nor civil, but the worst of both, "oriental despotism" and a backward religion imagine Orientalists). While Edward Said (1979) has brilliantly developed this argument for the Islamic world, it is to Ronald Inden (1986) that we turn to for an understanding of the Orientalization of Indian history.

In Inden's article "Orientalist Constructions of India," he places much of the blame on Hegelian thought. It was Hegel who took the Vedantist interpretation of Indian philosophy and made it hegemonic. As with Marx, India for Hegel was prehistorical for "History is limited to that which is an essential epoch in the development of Spirit" (Inden, 1986, 425). Prehistorical people for their own good must enter history. According to Hegel, "the English, or rather the East India Company, are the lords of the land: for it is the necessary fate of Asiatic Empires to be subjected to Europeans" (426). But the paradox for the West has been why has India retained its own self while having been conquered? In Vishwanath Prasad Varma's brilliant *Studies in Hindu Political Thought and its Metaphysical Foundations*, he writes the following summary:

> In [Hegel's] dialectical scheme of historical evolution, while China represents understanding, India represents phantasy and sensibility. China, so to say, marks the beginning of oriental history. But the Chinese are in the condition of legal immaturity.... Contrasted to China, India represents the growth of idealistic philosophy. It has, certainly, a conception of spirit (*Geist*) but it did not develop into an idealism based on rational concepts. Its idealism is rooted only in imagination. China represents the spirit at the level of sleep. But although India typifies the awakening of the spirit, it is not the full rational awakening. Consequently, instead of deliberate efforts at the formation of distinct concepts, in Indian thought, one only finds profuse imagination, dreaming and fancy (Varma, 1974, 379).

Consciousness thus maintains itself in "pure abstract sameness," according to Hegel (379).

The real remains overly imaginative with no concrete manifestations in great historical figures nor in a developed polity-state. Of course, here Hegel was responding to the hegemonic position of Vedantic philosophy: the other Indian philosophical schools were far more empirical and practical in their orientation. In this reading, this lack of development of the rational State has led to the conquest of India, over and over again. For Europeans, this was to be India's destiny until it could finally be molded into German rationalism, or later into British empiricism.

In his *The Intimate Enemy*, Ashis Nandy asks why India has this central paradox, why she has been conquered yet managed to retain its ancient culture. For Nandy, while the Aztec priest would die and lose his culture, the Indian Brahmin would accept the foreign culture, yet transform it so in the long run, by defeat, he could be victorious. By compromising, by being weak and passive (in the minds of Orientalists) he arrested the psychological victory—the Indian did not become a heroic enemy that the West admired. He did not internalize the value of the victor. Rather he stayed outside of this discourse, "Better to be a comical dissenter than to be a powerful, serious but acceptable opponent" (Nandy, 1983, 111). There is no fear of loss of identity, for the self, as we have argued, is constructed differently. That which is eternally real can never be colonized. And in the long run, it is the cowardly Indian who, in his passive resilience, will be victorious. This, for Nandy, is paradigmatic of Indian behavior.

Like Foucault, Nandy's writings show that every interpretation has a cost, a price that must be paid. Victory has a price, as does victimhood. "Orientalism" ultimately then is a price that the West pays. Of course, India too pays the price in terms of what Sarkar calls psychic exploitation. Indians see themselves as a less real representation of history and the real, while the West sees itself as a more truthful representation of progress. The way out for Ronald Inden is for historical scholarship to place itself in the context of a multiple view of the true perspective, decidedly an Indian perspective. Among other goals, this is the purpose of this book. However, Inden would object to the casting of the Indian episteme in spiritual terms, or with what he would call, societalism, that is using *varna* as agency in history. This, to him, forgets that caste is a product of kingship, not something inherent in Indian thought. It is only Orientalist constructions that have placed caste and other abstractions prior to individualism. But here he misunderstands the Indian episteme, forgetting its unity of discourse. He criticizes Orientalism and its construction of Indian history, yet he does so from the epistemological viewpoint of modernity. Ultimately, the problems he raises for the Orientalist discourse are problems for the West, not for India. Although

deconstructing Orientalism is useful, far more important is to develop
alternative interpretations of Indian history and global history. As
important is to show how the West has been constructed in India:
as a land of gold, sex, and individuality, but with no culture, history and spirituality. People with money, but not quite refined yet.

Equally concerned with not being subjected by the history of the
dominator, of the discourse of domination, is the Subaltern project
(Guha, 1988). In this project, the purpose is not to create a new
structure, a new pattern of history; rather, its aim is to write Indian
history from the view of the dominated classes, not the elite or the
colonial. This is the history of the class that has had its perception
of itself penetrated by the interpretations of others, that has only
spoken through the recorded narratives of others. This is then not
a nationalist history against external forces for domination can occur
within nations or peoples as well. This is the history of workers and
peasants and how they have constructed the great movements, the
great changes of history. In the words of Ranajit Guha:

> [This is] no history of ideas, no calmly Olympian narrative of events,
> no disengaged objective recital of facts. It is rather sharply contestary,
> an attempt to wrest control of the Indian past from its scribes and
> curators in the present . . . And if there can be no actual taking of
> power in the writing of history, there can at least be a demystifying
> exposure of what material interests are at state, what ideology and
> method are employed, what parties advanced, which deferred, dis-
> placed and defeated (Guha, 1988, vii).

Influenced by poststructural thought, Subaltern studies intends to
supply the missing narrative of Indian history. It is not the official
story, but the development of a new story that intends to plainly
state the price of the dominant historical narrative of the nation, of
dynasties, of schools of thought, of philosophies. Thus, there is not
one India, but many Indias. Not one interpretation, but many interpretations. It is a change in the site of history, an attack on the evidence of history, an attempt to denaturalize Indian history. It is an
attempt to see the world from the view of the subaltern classes, to
ensure that their actions of courage, of defiance to a larger will are
not ascribed to an other agency. Historiography then becomes strategy, a way of taking back consciousness. But it is not simply an
attempt to relativize history, to move to a position of epistemological relativity, rather there is a clear will to politicize in Subaltern
writing. Subaltern studies is an effort to avoid a historical amnesia

toward those who have suffered in the production of dynastic or philosophical histories. Subaltern studies is not a move to a higher level of generalization but a remembering of memory.

Sarkar's Metahistory

Besides writing a template for an alternative history of India, Sarkar's theory of history can be used to contextualize the various interpretations of Indian history. Just as there are four types of mentalities, structures or types, we can construct four types of history. First, there is the *shudra* history, the project of the Subaltern group. It is done however not by the workers themselves but clearly by intellectuals. Second, there is *ksattriyan* history: the history of kings and empires, of nations and conquests, of politics and economics. This is the history of the State. This is history of great men and women. Third is *vipran* history. This is the philosophy of history. This is the development of typologies, of categories of thought, of the recital of genealogies, of the search for evidence, of the development of the field of history itself. This is the attempt to undo the intellectual constructions of others and create one's own, of deciding is their one construction or can there be many constructions. And fourth, there is *vaeshyan* history. This is the history of wealth, of economic cycles, of the development of the world capitalist system, of the rise of Europe and the fall of India.

Sarkar's own history attempts to write a history that includes all these types: peoples, military, intellectual and economic. Marxist history also is broad. While it is directly located in economic history, it is written for the *shudras*, and warriors bring about the Marxist State, and it is an intellectual who created the type of discourse.

These types of history are certainly interlinked, and of course, as history itself has been a discourse owned by intellectuals, history should be *vipran* heavy. Alternatively, one can use a model to talk about diachronic (through time) history using the dichotomies of individual/collective and intra/inter. Most Indian history has been intra/individual (biographies and genealogies) as well as inter/individuals (comparative elite history, a comparison between the various Moguls). There has been little emphasis on collective/intra (deep structures and processes) or inter/collective (macro-comparative history). While Sarkar develops deep structures, he is weak on comparative macro-history with little effort to trace the structure of the social cycle though various civilizations. Batra simply applies the cycle to each unit of analysis, but does not take the next step in comparing the development of the units to each other (in writing world macro-history). Sarkar's excellence is that he uses structure but not from an Orientalist view, it is a local knowledge perspective that moves to the universal. Moreover, it manages to provide a framework in which histories of each group are possible—of workers, kings, intellectuals, and of economic forces. And at the same time it provides a framework for a history of structure at a point in time, through time, within and across cultures as well.

Sarkar's Ideal Historiography

Before we develop Sarkar's history of history, we articulate his views on the ideal historiography. For Sarkar, past history has privileged kings and monarchs—the dynastic model. "If the chronicles of history merely describes who succeeded to the throne and when, who plundered the neighboring countries or kingdoms, and who became a minister, they will be of no important what so ever, nor, indeed, of any interest to the common masses" (Sarkar, 1987a, 4: 63). But history is not only *ksattriyan*. "Similarly, the history of the Vipra era is full of praises for the glorious deeds of the vipra leaders, and the history of the vaeshyas contains an abundance of stories about the wonders of the vaeshyas" (67). History thus is interpretative and purposely written to validate a particular mentality, a "particular vested interest" (67).

Sarkar believes history should be written about how humans solved challenges. How prosperity was gained. "History . . . should maintain special records of the trials and tribulations which confronted human beings, how those trials and tribulations were overcome, how human beings tackled the numerous obstacles to effect great social development" (64). History then needs to aid in mobilizing people, personally and collectively toward internal exploration and external transformation. Thus history should be a "resplendent reflection of collective life whose study will be of immense inspiration for future generations" (66). True history is about value.

> You should remember that in human society nobody is insignificant, nobody is negligible. Even the life of a 100 year old lady is valuable. In the universal society she is an important member—she is not to be

excluded. We may not be able to think that she is a burden to society, but this sort of defective thinking displays our ignorance (Sarkar, 1987a 7: 45).

Sarkar's own history is meant to show the challenges humans faced: the defeats and the victories. His history shows how humans were dominated by particular eras, how they struggled and developed new technologies, ideas, and how they realized the *atman*. It is an attempt to write a history that is true to the victims but does not oppress them again through avoiding providing a vision of the future. His history then is clearly ideological, but not in the sense of supporting a particular class, but rather a history that gives weight to all classes yet attempts to move them outside of class, outside of ego, and toward neo-humanism.

Sarkar's history then attempts a balance between spiritual idealism and social structure and develops a model to locate the various approaches to history.

Sarkar's Theory of History

We now summarize Sarkar's own theory of history. As argued earlier, it has different components: (1) the four varnas; (2) the dynamics of history; (3) leadership in creating an alternative future; (4) and the centrality of spirituality.

Sarkar's theory of history is that there are four types of people and four epochs in history. Each epoch exhibits a certain mentality, a *varna*. This *varna* is similar to the concept of episteme, to paradigm, to ideal type, to class, to stage, to era and a host of other words that have been used to describe stage theory. Sarkar alternatively uses *varna* and collective psychology to describe his basic concept. He writes, "Human history is made by the collective urge of collective psychology" (Sarkar, 1987a, 7: 44). This then is a reflection of desire, of the basic nature of mind. It is social desire. There are four basic desire systems. The four *varnas* are historically developed. First the *shudra*, then the *ksattriya*, then the *vipra*, then the *vaeshya*. The last era is followed generally by a revolution of the *shudras*. During the final phase of the *Vaeshyan* era, all the other *varnas* become *shudra* in terms of their economic standing. All are exploited mentally and economically by the capitalist class, even though their *varna*, the way they approach the world, remains either *shudra*, *vipra*, or *ksattriya.* While the order is cyclical, but there are reversals. There can be a counter-revolution in any era. From *vipran* to *ksattriyan* or a counter-evolution. Both are short lived in terms of the natural cycle since both move counter to the natural developmental flow. But in the long run, the order must be followed because it is naturally and historically derived.

History is but the natural flow of this cycle. By natural Sarkar means evolutionary. That is, at every point there is a range of choices, once made the choice becomes a habit, a structure of the collective or group mind. Each mentality with an associated leadership class comes into power, makes changes, and administers government but eventually pursues its own varna-class ends and exploits the other groups. This has continued throughout history. In *The Human Society*, Sarkar asserts that so far one cycle which has passed, but in other articles he implies that different nations have followed many cycles (Logan, 1988). His unit of analysis begins with all of humanity, it is a history of humanity, but he often refers to countries and nations. In contrast, Batra (1978), borrowing from Toynbee, refers to civilizations.

The relationship to the previous era is a dialectical one; an era emerges out of the old era, because of the old era. Thus history moves not because of external reasons, although the environment certainly is a factor, but because of internal organic reasons. Each era comes to its limit, becomes inauthentic—does not allow varna expression—and then the new group comes in, to use Sorokin's (1970) principle of limits. The metaphysic behind this movement is for Sarkar the wave motion. There is a rise and then a fall. In addition, this wave motion is pulsative; that is, the speed of change fluctuates over time. The driving force for this change is first the dialectical interaction with the environment, second the dialectical interaction in the mind and in ideologies, and then the dialectical interaction between both, ideas and the environment. But there is also another motivation: this is the attraction toward the Great—the individual attraction toward the supreme. This is the ultimate desire that frees humans of all desires.

Clash, conflict and cohesion with the environment lead to the *Shudra* era becoming the *Ksattriya*; and then clash, conflict and cohesion with ideas leading to the *Ksattriya* becoming the *Vipra*; and then the dialectical clash of environment and ideas leads to the *Vaeshyan* era. The attraction to the great is the solution or the answer to the problem of history. It results in progress. For Sarkar, the cycle must continue for it is a basic structure in the mind but exploitation is not necessary. Suffering can be reduced or ended by placing the *sad-vipra*, the intellectual who has qualities of all the *varnas* but works for the benefit of the whole, at the center of the cycle. Sarkar's metaphor are the life cycle of the body and nature *and* the ancient wheel, that is, technology. Thus, there is the natural and there is human intervention. There is a deep structure and there is choice. It is Sarkar's theory that provides this intervention. He legitimizes this theory partially by his neo-humanistic ideology and partially by appealing to the Indian belief in extraordinary leadership, in the knowing abilities of the guru. Sarkar's theory of *varna* is an empirical claim, a claim of reality correspondence (within the context of the Indian episteme as argued previously). The *sadvipra* acts from the center, attempting to create a permanent class revolution, not in the sense of Trotsky who meant that it could not just stop in one country, but in the sense that revolution must be forever, since humans are constituted by *vidya* and *avidya*, introversion and extroversion. Humans are in essence desire. There is a range of desires that presently constitute humanness—fifty at the present level of evolutionary development. Their expression can lead humans toward power, control and fear or toward justice, compassion and love. Without periodic and systematic revolutions, the new era promised by every group will swiftly turn into an old era of exploitation. For Sarkar, the four types are natural and thus must continue. But the apolitical administration of power must not become the abuse of power. Politics must continue but it must be a politics of negotiation and economic, cultural and human development, not one of extraction of wealth from the many to the few, not one that denies human's intellectual rights and spiritual potential. This is Sarkar's theory of PROUT wherein he develops a theory of ownership: everything is owned by consciousness, humans can only "rent" it.

In this preferred future vision, there must be basic guarantees of human rights and basic needs. These are to be increased through the economic dynamic that results from the increased use of physical, mental and spiritual resources. The use of these resources must be based on the desire for the collective good, not the good of any particular individual mind or particular environment. Finally, individual initiative must be rewarded preferably in the forms of advantages that can lead to increased public good. An increase in the wealth of those that are advantaged must correspond with an increase in the wealth of those who, although all there needs are met, are proportionally less well off. This system, however, can only occur, at present, through a *Shudra* revolution. PROUT then is the future for the world; a new alternative political economy. In addition, based on other trends such as internationalization and the globalization of problems, the appropriate governing body would be a world government but with strong regional linguistic, cultural, economic bodies and associations. Indeed, it is these local movements that are at the heart of Sarkar's movement to create a new society. From these movements and his various organizations, he intends to create leadership that has the characteristics of all the *varnas* and is benevolent. Again, the *shudras* are controlled by the environment. The *ksattriyas* control the environment. The intellectuals control the environment and the other two varnas through understanding, not power. They theorize and develop answers to questions of meaning and thus use these theories to increase life chances for themselves and their progeny. The last class—the *vaeshyans*—uses the environment, not conquers. It turns all the classes into resources for its project. The environment becomes not something that one is dominated by, not something one conquers, not something one theorizes about, but something one commodifies, uses to increase one's life choices, through accumulation and investments.

Sadvipras have all these qualities but again use them for the other. Sarkar does not investigate they the sadvipras might use their exceptional qualities for their own class interests, since they are outside of the cycle. They will not exploit or transform it into another Marxist *ksattriyan* rule, or a vipran rule of the Brahmins. Nor will they transform innovative entrepreneurial activity into predatory capitalism or make science and technology into yet another tool of class, or become experts beholden only to their own interests. Rather they will represent the interests of the whole. Or so hopes Sarkar.

He believes they will not exploit since to become a sadvipra they will have to undergo revolutionary training, spiritual training. And while Sarkar posits a structural theory of mentalities based on the interaction with the environment, he remains in the spiritual rise and fall of dharma model. Humanity has suffered enough and now it is time for the next era. This is the revolution that he is to bring about. This new era is not about the end of rational man (modern man) as Foucault and Nietzsche have written—Indian man was never modern man, rather it is about the continued evolution of humans toward Cosmic Consciousness. And it is not about a new "race" of supermen who transcend man himself, nor is it about Aurobindo's divine man, or Teilhard De Chardin's divine man; rather it is closer to Gramsci's organic intellectual: activist, self-reflective, and critical of class. Sarkar, however, adds a spiritual dimension in terms of the concrete practice of spiritual disciplines that empirically change the individual mind and lead to the resultant ethical changes—the *yamas* and *niyamas* of Yoga.

Sarkar believes his contribution is revolutionary in that it is outside of the cycle. His theory does not support any one class: the workers (communism), warriors (monarchy, force), intellectuals (liberalism and various utopias), or acquisitors (capitalism). It is an attempt to transform this classic structure and develop a classless society where unity is based on the spiritual ideal, the unity of humanity and nature. Thus Sarkar presents an alternative Indian construction of history which coherently uses the spiritual, the critical, the structural, and the historical facets of Indian historiography but envelops them to create a new theory.

Varna and Caste

In order to understand Sarkar's reconceptualization of *varna*, we need to deconstruct his use of *varna* and place it in the context of the various meanings of caste in Indian thought. Once this is done, once we are aware of Sarkar's construction, then we can examine his prose and his writing of history.

Caste, like death, is ubiquitous in the Indian context. One's practices cannot but be framed within the discourse of caste. Indeed the modern history of India as deconstructed by critics of Orientalism shows how caste has become the definition of Indian society. Caste is the agent of history, the agent of leadership and of economic decision-making. While rulers and philosophies may come and go and economies may rise and fall, caste remains. In *Capital*, Orientalist Marx writes:

> The simplicity of the organization for production in these self-sufficing communities that constantly reproduce themselves in the same form,

and when accidentally destroyed, spring up again on the spot and with the same name—this simplicity supplies the key to the secret of the unchangeableness of Asiatic societies, and unchangeableness in striking contrast with the constant change of dynasty (Varma, 1974, 44).

Instead of market and State, caste is eternal. Kingship and other Indian political institutions have been dismissed by the Orientalist. From the outside caste has been perceived as "both the cause and effect of India's low level of political and economic 'development'" (Inden, 1986, 403). As mentioned earlier, to Hegel this meant that India was *a*historical. It was a people, but had no State, thus no rationality nor any possibility for freedom.

The alternative Orientalist view has been what Inden calls the romantic India, not the irrational people outside history, but the spiritually evolved people whose entire culture is essentially idealistic. The romantics take the features that the rational-utilitarians find backward and praise them. The romantics search for a greater unity, a larger myth to explain caste. Joseph Campbell, for example, represents caste not in political and economic language but in spiritual mythic language.

> There is therefore in Hinduism an essential affirmation of the cosmic order as divine. And since society is conceived to be a part of the cosmic order, there is an affirmation, equally, of the orthodox Indian social order as divine. Furthermore, as the order of nature is eternal, so also is this true of orthodox society. There is no tolerance of human freedom or invention in the social field, for society is not conceived to be an order evolved by human beings subject to intelligence and change, as it was in advanced Greece and Rome and as it has in the modern West. Its laws are of nature, not to be voted on, improved upon, or devised. Precisely as the sun, moon, plants and animals follow laws inherent to their natures, so therefore must the individual [follow] the nature of his birth, whether Brahmin, Kshatriya, Vaishya, Shudra or Pariah. Each is conceived to be a species. And as a mouse cannot become a lion, or even desire to be a lion, no Shudra can be a Brahmin; and desiring to be one would be insane. Hence the Indian work 'virtue, duty, law,' *dharma*, has a deep, a very deep reach. 'Better one's duty ill performed,' we read, 'then that of another, to perfection.' The Greek or Renaissance idea of the great individual simply does not exist within the pale of the system. One is to be, rather, a *dividuum*, divided man, man who represents one limb or function of the great man (*purusas*) which is society itself (Inden, 1986, 434).

The metaphor of the body is the classic representation of caste. A late hymn of the *Rig-Veda* provides a mythical origin of the castes:

When the gods made a sacrifice with the Man as their victim.
When they divided the Man, into how many parts did they divide him?
What was his mouth, what were his arms, what were his thighs and his feet
*   called?*
The brahman was his mouth, of his arms were made the warrior.
His thighs became the vaishya, of his feet the shudra was born.
With Sacrifice the gods sacrificed to Sacrifice, these were the first of the sacred
*   laws.*
These mighty beings reached the sky, where are the eternal spirits, the gods
(Thapar, 1966, 39–40).

Caste is divine. Natural. The first law. Sarkar, as we might expect, has this to say about the *vipras* and their creation of caste.

> At other times they [Brahmin priests] resorted to blatant falsehood and said: "These are the commandments of God. Those who contradict these commandments will be damned to eternal hell-fire . . . Your eyes will develop cataracts and your throat will contract goitre if you don't read the scriptures and pray to God every day . . . If the offerings made to God touch your feet, or if you do not touch your forehead after handling consecrated food, you will develop leprosy . . . It is God who has made caste divisions.' (Sarkar, 1987a, 15: 16).

The alternative reading of caste is racial. But even within the racial discourse, there are many readings. Thapar writes that the Aryans were composed of the three classes, not castes: the warriors/aristocracy, the priests and the common people. Profession was not hereditary, there were no rules limiting intermarriage, and there were no taboos on social practices such as eating. It was thus an economic/social division of labor. Caste emerged with the interaction between Aryans and the local *Dasas*. The first caste distinction was thus between Aryan and *Dasa*, with the Aryans being the twice born class (birth and then caste status). The *Shudras* resulted from the Dasas and those of mixed Aryan-Dasa origin.

According to Thapar, at first the warriors/kings were on top (as Sarkar would argue) and later when the priests recognized the power assigned in caste, they put themselves on top. Thus, the above hymn and Sarkar's commentary. Thapar, thus, places caste in a historical significance narrative, thought to have developed first from class, then from race, and finally through class/caste power struggles. Eventually, the earlier divisions were secured through actual taboos and over time *varna* became of little significance, while *jhat*, sub caste became extraordinarily important in the day to day life of Indians. Vertical mobility became almost nonexistent and movement through

the hierarchy was only possible for the *jhat* as a whole, not for the
sole individual. In this sense both schools of Orientalism, the Europe
as superior and India as mythically spiritual, touch on real interpretations of the caste, but they do not historically trace it, and thus
do not notice the similarities of caste with class, that is, with the
division of labor, wealth and power. With structure.

Relevant to the question of caste is the "great conundrum of
Indian social thought: whether the Brahmin or king had precedence"
(Dirks, 1987, 10). To speak to this question, Thapar again takes a
decidedly historical view. For her, we must first examine when caste
or the political state was primary and then examine the respective
role of *varna*.

We can understand historical consciousness and the history of caste
by examining the various types of societies that existed in India. In
lineage societies where descent and birth was the main form of social
ordering, then one can argue that caste was primary. "The evolution of *varna* stratification is rooted in the lineage-based society of
Vedic times" (Thapar, 1986, 357). Therefore, one could argue that
in lineage societies caste or religion was primary as Louis Dumont
(1979) asserts. In State societies, kingship—or what is conventionally
seen as the political—is primary. In these State structures, the Brahmin
thus is not more powerful than the *Ksattriya*. But this political, historical interpretation of caste has received far less attention than the
religious by Orientalists and modern historians. Caste as class or as
deep structure or as understood from Galtung's cosmological analysis has little currency.

In lineage societies history is myth. It not only records but creates the totality of the past (Dirks, 1987, 58). In state societies, history is the story of dynasties. The king and conquest. In addition to
history as myth and history as the rise and fall of dynasties, Thapar
presents a third form of history. This is chronological history. She
dates this from Buddhist times when the *Sangha* developed. This is
the post-Gupta era where history did not simply narrate the lives of
the Buddha but also "described the building of monasteries, the
amassing of property, and the rights to controlling these" (Thapar,
1986, 374). This to her is externalized history. For Thapar the form
of historical consciousness changed significantly through time. Mythic
consciousness decreased in importance over time; kingship became
more important than questions of caste; and finally ownership increased
in importance.

Thapar thus moves toward Sarkar's understanding of caste, as forms of knowing the world. For Sarkar there are different epochs in Indian history and different stages. Caste comes about largely in what he calls the *Vipran* era. To stay in power, the Brahmins reified caste, alternatively putting themselves on top, and then the *Ksattriyans* on top when their own power base was threatened. That is, agreeing to movements in the structure, but keeping the structure that guaranteed them eternal economic advantages. Not just for themselves, but for their future generations.

> Here it should be remembered that the words shudra, vaeshya, ksattriya and vipra have no connection with the *Varn'n'shrama* oriented social order of the old Hindu society. Those who became vipras by virtue of their intellectual power in order to perpetuate their vested interests declared the vipras an hereditary caste. Out of a little compassion (actually, we should not call it compassion at all as their ulterior motive was to employ the ksattriyas to their own advantage), they gave the next highest status to those vanquished ksattriyas, who had sold themselves out and surrendered at their feet (Sarkar, 1987b, 5:22).

Thus for Sarkar caste was a creation of the Brahmins who then used myth and scripture to normalize their location in the social order. Those who see caste as the primary tool for understanding India forget that India has gone through various epochs with power located differently in each epoch.

Fundamental to Sarkar's project is his attempt to overthrow caste. But here he uses caste as *jhat*, the various rules of marriage, relationships or vertical practices that exist in India today.

Overthrowing caste is as essential as overthrowing communalism, nationalism and other boundary structures. Caste violates the essentials of a good society. It is unjustified economic privileging not based on any contribution to the social good.

For Sarkar a good society must have the following components: peace (through spiritual practices); unity (a common ideal, a casteless social structure, and no capital punishment); and, social security (no economic exploitation based on gender, race, and class, with wealth considered the property of the universe). The project then is not simply to transform a particular social formation called caste but to transform the privileging of various vertical structures. To him this is the oldest vice: dividing people up so as to gain benefits. His way out is the spiritual approach yet at the same time the basic functions embedded in caste are useful: that is to serve, to develop the mind, to confront adversity and to engage in economic activity. The goal then is to develop a society through structures and practices that are horizontal in nature. His aim is to transform caste and class relations into a new social formation, not one based on classifying humans according to their trade or their capacity.

The caste system as a power structure was an attempt by a particular *varna* to exploit other *varnas*. Sarkar specifically attempts to distinguish between his use of *varna* and the classic use of *varna*. Among other strategies, he changes the English spelling and instead of Brahmin he uses the word *vipra*. Unfortunately, *varna* meaning mental color in Sanskrit remains his description of his structure. However neither ideal type, episteme, paradigm, nor color appear to satisfactorily capture the essence of *varna*. Sarkar keeps the idea of *varna* but reinterprets it to mean collective psychology, or group mind, group desire. *Varna* now translates as fundamental group desire no longer as a social division of labor, or caste, or myth.

Cosmology, Caste and Politics

Galtung (1981c) has a different view of *varna*. He takes a civilizational perspective examining time, social space, and social relations. For him all civilizations have vertical relations in that there are steep differences in power and privilege. He explores how exploitation is carried out at levels of meaning (how the real is constructed), war (who must fight for the State), labor and wealth. He develops five classical caste systems. Feudal Europe with nobility (landowner and military) on top, clergy below, burghers (traders and merchants), peasants (workers) and a fifth bottom highly marginalized group of gypsies, Arabs, jews and women. The Feudal Chinese model has the *shih* (nobility and scholars) on top, the *nung* (farmers) a step below, then the *kung* (artisans), the *shang* (merchants) and finally the fifth group of nomads, barbarians and women. Japan's Tokugawa system had the *shi* (samurai, military, low nobility) on top, the *no* (farmers) a step below, the *ko* (artisans) lower, the *sho* (merchants) next and the *dowa-chiku*, the foreigners and women at the very bottom. All these are seen as castes since they follow rules such as endogamy, commensalism, and, "of course, like father, like son" (Galtung, 1986, 143).

Table 3: Five Classical Caste Systems—Johan Galtung (1986, 143)

Feudal Europe	Classical India	Feudal China	Tokugawa Japan
Nobility (landowners, military)	Brahmins (priests, religious teachers)	Shih (nobility, scholars)	Shi (samurai, military, low nobility)
Clergy	Ksattriyas (warriors, aristocracy)	Nung (farmers)	No (farmers)
Burghers (traders and merchants)	Vaeshyas (traders and merchants)	Kung (artisans)	Ko (artisans)
Peasants, workers	Shudras (farmers, workers)	Shang (merchants)	Sho (merchants)
Gypsies, Arabs, Jews, women	Pariahs, women	Nomads, barbarians, women	Dowa-chiku, gaijin, women

In addition, India's system was more explicit and because of the Aryan invasion developed the notion of pollution. The structure of verticality continues today with capitalists-bureaucrats and intelligentsia on top (Sarkar would agree whole-heartily for the end of the *Vaeshyan* eras finds intellectuals enthralled by the *Vaeshyan* mentality and thus fitting in their structure). For Galtung, the key is looking within cosmologies and searching for structure. Traditional merit was derived from birth, while the equation today is education. Each cosmology has vertical and horizontal relations, each orders the world differently, with various real human and social costs.

Rajni Kothari (1970) in his *Caste in Indian Politics* reminds us that caste is one among many ways of ordering the world, in engaging in politics. Politics is about the negotiation of power and meanings. While the modernizers want to rid India of caste, they forget its relationship to order. Indeed, they want to rid India of politics, and thus replace it, with an alleged value-free, non-privileging, economics. Here Kothari moves toward the poststructural view which defines politics not as the competition over resources, but of the ways in which the world is ordered, more precisely the ways in which order is ordered. In this way caste is neither seen as apolitical, outside politics, nor is it seen as reactionary in the sense of damaging class politics. Kothari also argues that *jhat*—the myriad associations, relationships, and lineages that are what is perceived as caste—is far more relevant today. The traditional category of *varna* rarely is intelligible. The question in India is what is your *jhat* not what is your *varna*.

Sarkar wants to replace caste and class with an alternative spiritual, socialist structure. His strategy for this is politics in the sense of creating an alternative discourse, perhaps even cosmology, and through his organizations creating a new society from concrete day-to-day living experiments in social reform. His history then can be seen as a way to delegitimize any particular power structure, to situate it in change, and thus damage its normalizing power. Thus, his various epochs. And thus, *varna* is *varna* and it is not *varna*.

Sarkar uses the various constructions of Indian history but attempts to develop a broader, more general overlay that consumes them. At the same time, he calls for a history that listens to the voices of the exploited and that tells the stories of the challenges humans faced. Finally, Sarkar reinterprets *varna* and uses it to develop a cyclical and linear theory of history. The prose of this theory constitutes the next chapter.

CHAPTER FOUR

SARKAR'S PROSE OF HISTORY

In this chapter, we review Sarkar's *The Human Society* wherein he articulates his four-stage theory of history. Our strategy will be to summarize his theory with a special eye to style: the language and the metaphors he uses. In this regard we will quote extensively, letting Sarkar speak for himself.

Movement or Stasis

As with the ancient Greeks, Sarkar begins with an analysis of motion asking what is fundamental, movement or stasis. He concludes that both are inextricably related to each other such that every entity (person or society or cosmos) goes through periods of motionless and then movement. True stability for the person is only possible once the roots of the mind (desire) have been extinguished. Within the world of relativity, however, every action is systaltic. Every movement has expansion and contraction phases; velocity and motionless. They are characteristics intrinsic to what-is. However, the relative world realizes itself not through achieving a state of total unity (pure consciousness) but through the relativity of movements. In this world of movement, true individuality is impossible given societal constraints. Paradoxically true individuality is only possible in the spiritual world where the self merges with cosmic consciousness. The motivation or desire appears to be the real units of agency. For example, "The vibrational fluctuations of the resultant motivity of the various motivities that can well be called the motivity of the social order are somewhat shorter than those of the unity. It is this shortness thereof that paves the way for evolution or revolution" (Sarkar, 1967, 6). Therefore, by increasing one's wave length of mind—identifying with that which is grander than oneself—social change is possible. One's identity changes. In addition, "When the waves of the unit mind lag behind those of the cosmic mind or move toward opposite directions, we call it the downfall of the unit. When they move at a par with the latter, we call it the natural movement of the unit-mind and when they travel faster than the latter, we call it advancement or progress" (Sarkar, 1967, 5).

For Sarkar, as we might expect given his location in the Indian episteme, the universe has a natural flow; an internal movement toward cosmic consciousness. *Vidya* increases one's flow and *avidya* leads one against this internal flow. Spiritual practices increase the natural speed, while engrossment in the material world reduce the natural speed.

Just as humans die when there is no new vital flow during the pause phase —"the length of the state of motionless is adjudged as death only when the old structure is unable to hold and appropriate the vital force of motionless" (7)—societies die when there is a loss of identity between phases. Hence, Egyptian civilization died because of the overwhelming strength and cohesiveness of the Islamic wave. And Islamic civilization expended its "energy" with the conquest of Egypt ("it had to ingest the thought waves of Egyptian culture") and thus could not conquer Europe. To maintain its own structure, it had to resolve the various cultural, political and economic conflicts that arose once it conquered Egyptian civilization. There was a period of pause that transformed the Islamic flow.

The metaphor Sarkar uses to describe this process is that of the breath or a series of rolling hills. Besides expansion and contraction, onward movement is based on pause. It is this rest that allows the next phase. There does not exist—except at the level of the infinite— any continuous uninterrupted linear straight line function. This is true for all levels of the real. For example, economic trends must follow a cyclical pattern in Sarkar's metaphysical scheme. But the peaks and valleys of the cycles can be managed, for example, with respect to economic cycles while there are periods of expansion and contraction, a depression is unnatural, symptomatic of a grave imbalance in the distribution of power and resources—knowledge, capital and labor.

The Shudra Era

From these metaphysical assumptions, Sarkar takes the next step and describes the origin of his first collective psychology, his first way of knowing and viewing the real. This was the shudra mind, which must be distinguished from the shudra class during the capitalist era when all the classes function economically as workers, although their mental posture might be different. In Sarkar's language, "When the waves of the unit mind try to maintain adjustment with the waves of crude matter without attempting to assimilate them, the unit mind gradually becomes crudified" (Sarkar, 1987b, 5: 1). The shudra mind is dominated by the material world and takes it to be the ultimate reality.

The Shudra society was a loose collection of individuals. "As conjugal relations were based on relationships of the enjoyer and the enjoyed, no sense of permanence or humanism was involved" (1). And:

> Shudras live for material enjoyment. To put it plainly, the life of a shudra is based essentially on gross materiality, preoccupied with sensual pleasures. Ideology and logic have little meaning for them. Of the three divisions of time—past, present, and future—only the present is important for them. They have neither the time nor the desire to think about the past or the future (2).

The main emotional characteristic is fear and the desire to gratify the sensual mind. Thus they follow animism and other forms or worship. "Like merciless nature, survival of the fittest is the main feature of the Shudra society, which recognizes no pit and compassion for the weak" (3).

This is a significantly different reading than those that argue that the past was a golden age of plentiful resources with little conflict, or a type of ancient pure communism. Rather, it is a world of individuals existing for themselves against the environment. Sarkar paints shudras as a non-creative class, best suited for mechanical laborious work. However, society was not brutal.

> Life was brute and non-intellectual. Nature was the direct abode and physical strength ruled the day. The strong enjoyed at the cost of the weak, who had to surrender before the voracity of the physical giants. However, the sense of acquisition had not developed in them and they worked manually and there was no intellectual exploitation in that age. Though life was brute, it was not brutal (Sarkar, 1978a, 80).

The Ksattriya Era

But the mind can also triumph over matter. "At the embryonic stage of the human race, when the sense of humanity arose out of animality, human beings . . . found only two paths open to them—the

path of inertness through constant obsession with thoughts of mate-
riality and the path of triumph of material[ity] and the path of
Ksattriyahood (Sarkar, 1987b, 5: 1).

Sarkar defines this mentality as one that conquers the environment. "Those even struggling individuals who have acquired the right
to direct matter at will are called ksattriyas" (4). While a shudra
stops in front of a mountain, a ksattriya will conquer it.

In contrast, a vipra will chart it, explore, attempt to understand
its relationship to rivers and built various theories of nature. A
vaeshyan will see a resource in front of him or her and find ways to
convert matter into more matter, to convert into resources that can
be used for the future and for other types of matter—luxury items,
for example. What is now commonly called economic development.

But the ksattriyan sees only matter in front of him or her. Sarkar
does not, as Western writers do, attempt to translate matter into its
other form—military technology, whether the ax, the spear, the sword,
the gun, the missile, or the nuclear warhead. Sarkar's history is not
a technology-led theory.

All is matter in different forms that the warrior uses to control
the world. While for ksattriyas conquest is primary, they did however begin the evolutionary development of humanity. But how did
the two classes relate to each other? "The greatness of the ksattriyas—their prowess and valor—struck the shudras with wonder.
The cowardly shudras of feeble intellect humbly submitted to the
bravery and spiritedness of the ksattriyas and accepted their superiority" (5). But when order is formed there is an exchange of rights
and duties, of hierarchy and solidarity. "The ksattriyas for their part
took over the responsibility of the safety and protection of the shudras by virtue of their valor and gained a lot of work from them"
(5) in return.

The strength of the ksattriyan leads to the exchange of work for
protection, for in this society protecting the distressed and dependent is of considerable honor. It gives value to the self and indeed
is part of the ksattriyan's self-image.

Protection for work was the basic social formation. At the top
were those who had physical and technological power, the ability to
make, in Sarkar's language, matter a slave of mind. In addition, this
ordering of labor and group mind can be seen as natural considering
the classic Indian episteme or the classic Western feudal arrangement.
Sarkar's prose is a matter-of-fact story, not an analysis or hypothesis-
building, but written more from the perspective of a television docu-

drama of human history, except that within the Indian episteme, it is Sarkar as guru who directly perceives this historical narrative.

This evolutionary step is what Sarkar calls socio-psychic mutation. As with other places in his text, what this means (either through definition, comparison, analogy) is not attempted. It appears to refer more to the idea that a new field of behavior was developed from the level of the social to the level of the psychic.

Sarkar's ksattriyan era was first matriarchal and then patriarchal. This partially resulted from the development of the family, the decreased role of females and their consequent dependence on the male. Much of the emphasis on marriage resulted from the male desire to perpetuate the legacy of heroism and wealth accrued by the ksattriyans to their children. Phallic worship is a representation of this desire for an increased population largely so as to increase the number of potential soldiers. In later times, as viprans are apt to do, this symbol of fertility was reinterpreted in religious language and made symbolic of *purusa* and *prakrti*, of *shiva* and *shakti*.

But while the greatest of the ksattriyas leaders are forever remembered (Alexander, Genghis Khan, Napoleon), shudras "come and go unnoticed and unsung, having little impact on life" (9). While Sarkar hopes that the historiography of the future will be written from the perspective of the common person, in this 1967 tract, he laments that "alive or dead they [shudras] mean nothing to collective humanity" (9). Most of them are engaged in pursuits that privilege only themselves, they "look upon everything as an object for their own gratification and run after one and all with greedy eyes" (9). They will not impact the world and deservedly so for they only work and run after matter, never conquering it, or understanding it, nor using it to create more matter, to construct value. Sarkar certainly does not glorify the worker. Ksattriyan society brought them protection and a social order that stopped the anarchy of war, and even though power was centralized, the quality of life, in many ways, improved. Indeed with every social order, Sarkar sees points of general good and areas of fantastic exploitation.

The development and numerical expansion of ksattriyas leads to the Ksattriyan era. This society is defined by its domination by those of Ksattriyan mind, Sarkar does not problematize the issue whether the society as a whole is different from all its members, whether it consists incrementally of its members, or a function of group mind. We must turn to Pitirim Sorokin and other much more rigorous sociologists for clarification, but in defense of Sarkar, he believes his role is to present the general theory and leave it to the intellectu-als—who delight in such tasks—to work out the analyses, the minor points. It is outside of the Indian construction that we must go to for a microscopic empirical analysis of macro-structures and func-tions. Even with the voluminous works of Shri Aurobindo, there is little detail, little application of the general theory to specific "empir-ical" (as defined by the dominant discursive formation) historical events, trends and process. Minor details in Indian thought are ignored for more important are the fine philosophical points. And where there is fine historical detail it is outside of any grand theory framework, merely acontextual description.

Sarkar's *varna* can also be differentiated by how time is perceived. Shudras live only in the present while ksattriyas live in the past and present. "Without bothering their heads about the future repercus-sions of their deeds, they jump right into the licking flames of a fire, leap from the lofty precipice of a mountain and run in pursuit of planets and their satellites with rockets" (10). The past serves as a feedback mechanism for future decisionmaking: it provides them with inspiration and a record against which they must seek revenge. Viprans exist in all three times, past, present and future. But the future time of the vipran is different from the future time of the vaeshyan. For the vipran the future is often transcendental: always ideological, related to the *Idea*. For the vaeshyan, the future is related to resources, to investments and to savings. In fact, it is the ability of the vaeshyan to *use* the future—to commodify it—that gives him or her superiority over the other types.

But returning to the Ksattriyan era, Sarkar argues that govern-ment administration grew from the clan Father to the king so as to avoid internecine battles. The final centralization of this development is what Toynbee has called the universal state: one ruler, highly dis-ciplined, with a strong emphasis on territorial expansion. Because the world is at the end of the Vaeshyan era, Sarkar can but pre-dict a new global superstate with expansion in two areas: outerspace and innerspace.

The dictatorships of present "communist" societies in this theory are seen as prototypes of the original clan Father and then later King structure. Whether the world government of the future will be of this type is unclear although Sarkar's preferred *sadvipra* society is closer to an oligarchy.

This ancient Ksattriyan society was significant for Sarkar in that it was the first unified social system with its own logic. And like other social systems the elite of the system continued to uphold and expand the system long after its evolutionary use.

> Through this system perhaps the chariot of rapacity may tread upon the weak with unabated speed, perhaps the hunger of millions of people may provide opportunities for one person to live in plenty and abundance, or perhaps instead of fraternal relations between human beings the relationship of rulers and ruled may be established, but nevertheless it is a system after all. Regardless of its merits and demerits, it is the characteristic of the ksattriyas to try and make it stand (15).

The Vipra Era

From the Ksattriyan era grew the Vipran era. "Ksattriyas want to rush forward with an all-conquering attitude. In ignorance they challenge their opponents to battle without ascertaining the strength of the adversaries, with the result they often have to leave the world prematurely, mauled and mangled. The history of the ksattriyas is one of blood not of the light of intelligence" (16). In that history there is valor, high spiritedness and gallantry, but not clarity of vision or wisdom—not the support of any subtle intellect. "That is way after the continuation of the Ksattriya age for some time, intellectuals began to control the ksattriyas by dint of their keen intellect. Persons of intellect told the ksattriyas to look where they had never turned their eyes before, and kept explaining to them what they had never understood" (16).

Eventually power passed on to the hands of the viprans from the ksattriyans. There was a change in *varna* and concomitantly in the elite. Through mythification—by creating truth claims in which Brahmins were to be worshipped—the vipras consolidated their power. According to Sarkar, even when monarchs ruled, most often it was the chief minister who held real power. The kings were mere puppets while normative and strategic power was in the hands of the intellectuals. For example in Indian history, Chandragupta was a puppet to his minister Canakya. The polity was divided into two: the religious order and monarchical structure. Power was transferred, although not so obviously, for much of the wealth remained with various kings. Kings that tried to exert their previous powers were removed by the vipras.

This transfer was as in all transfer of powers—in Sarkar's world-view—one where the previous *varna* had no idea of the horrors ahead.

> The most amusing part of [the Peripheric Evolution, the cycle] is that after the unprincipled Shudra age when the Ksattriya age came into being, the shudras took this as a great blessing. The brutal side of the ksattriyas or the image of their rapacious exploitation did not enter their vision. Similarly, when all the power of the ksattriyas was sold to the vipras, at the time the ksattriyas did not even realize that they were being sold . . . [into] slavery. And then again in a later period when the vipras sold themselves to the pelf of the vaeshyas—when Sarasvatii (the mythological goddess of learning) was made a slave of Lakshmii (the mythological goddess of wealth)—the vipras at first did not realize that their value was going to be measured in terms of money (17).

Each era this proceeds from the previous era since each varna is incomplete—what appears as weakness becomes strength in the subsequent.

> The power of speech and intelligence of the vipras are much subtler than the physical strength of the ksattriyas, and that is why the vipras do not find any difficulty in enslaving the ksattriyas brawn by circumstantial pressures. Those who establish themselves by a blatant display of power are sure to have vanity. This weakness of the ksattriyas derived form power was employed by the vipras to their advance through their intelligence (19).

This use of opposites is echoed in the *Mahabharata*. "Alas, having defeated the enemy, we have ourselves been defeated . . . The defeated have become victorious . . . Misery appears like prosperity, and prosperity looks like misery; Thus our victory is twined into defeat" (Nandy, 1987, 20). In this way, although Sarkar's history is at one level intended to be a true representation of the real, it is also a moral educational tract reminding those in and out of power that success is but the last rung on the ladder of failure (Batra, 1988). Power, in this classical view is short lived, for it is of this world, of the ego, of *avidya*. Ephemeral.

Thus the cyclical nature of Sarkar's social cycle. Each collective mind is dominant and a new way of knowing which as it evolves changes the various social, political, economic and power relations. As each varna solves a particular problem—the need for order, the need for victory, the need for understanding, and the need for wealth—it enslaves the previous class or classes. The need for justice then begins the cycle anew. As the cycle progresses, the next new Ksattriyan era maintains a similar social structure since the basic collective mental structure is the same—expansion oriented, disciplined, dualistic—but now that it is at the next level of the cycle, it keeps the learning of the previous phase with it. As an example, communist nations have a strong sense of the future, a carry over from the vipran and vaeshyan eras, as well as a result of the ideological impact of a vipran ideology. In this regard although some things change, the deeper structure remains the same.

Although Sarkar gives some indications how each era transforms into the next, his use of terms such as the ksattriyas or the vipras does not make necessary distinctions within the *varna* between the different types of vipras. Differences such as leaders versus followers, artists versus teachers, groups and individuals who have more than one mental wave are not crucial to him. More relevant to him is simply the distinction between *vidya* and *avidya* intellectuals. He favors the moral discourse and not the social science discourse. The distinctions he makes between a ksattriya and the ksattriyas or ksattriya leadership and finally the structure of ksattriyan society remain undeveloped. Another question unanswered is at what level do various individuals represent the true *varna*.

Sarkar's chapter on the Vipran era takes up most of the narrative of his *The Human Society*. Instead of physical struggle there is mental struggle. But society is not totally ideational in this world although the real would certainly be described in mystical, absolutist terms, to borrow from Sorokin. Rather, as with every other *varna*, there are numerous aspects to each class. Vipras want to enjoy the glory of victory as well, but they also find ways to place the ignominy of defeat on to others.

In addition, "the ego of vipras" (Sarkar, 1987b, 5: 20) leads it to sensuous enjoyment and the accrual of material wealth. However this is not the end all for them, they also wish to amass psychic resources. But while some vipras develop a pinnacled intellect, that is, one that touches the spiritual realm and is thus inventive and can be progressive, "most vipras are parasites, busily engaged in amassing objects of enjoyment with the help of others' crude strength" (21). The path of the intellectual is not direct as it is with the other previous *varnas*; rather it is crooked and hypocritical with very little honor. Indeed here Sarkar faithfully follows the classic *Gita* degeneration of morality theme. Dishonesty increases in every era until it reaches its apex in the Vaeshyan era. Following its advent in the

origination of the Ksattriyan era, there is a regressive decline of basic
goodness until a Shudra revolution reinstates honesty, thereby initiating the cycle again.

While the ksattriyas enter into an exchange relationship with the
workers, and enslave those whom they conquer, the vipras continue
their unbalanced—overly intellectual life—"by sucking the vital juice
of others like parasites" (23). Just as increased use of physical powers develops the body, increased use of mental power develops the
mind. However, in the case of vipras this only increases their parasitical tendencies. While in the beginning there is an openness to
ideas, by the end any broad mindedness is totally lost. The Ksattriyan
go from protectors to enslavers, the viprans from the pinnacled intellect (benevolent) to the parasitical intellect.

In between Sarkar's exegesis of the Vipran era, Sarkar develops
what might from an empirical perspective be considered possible
indicators. His thesis is that those who truly represent their *varna*,
who are authentically intellectuals and then there are the intellectuals who come to that position because of heredity. This is also true
for the other classes as well. Thus at the end of each era, there
develops an increased number of false ksattriyas, vipras and vaeshyas.
"The ksattriyas and vipras . . . realized that since nothing in the world
is unchangeable, their predominance will also come an end some
day due to their lack of capability" (24). That is why the classes
"give more importance to hereditary rights than personal merit and
individual capacity" (24). For Sarkar, kings desire their sons to keep
power, intellectuals want their descendants to command respect and
power, and corporate heads want their families to continue the tradition notwithstanding the personal merits of the individuals. Each,
of course, uses his class site to privilege offspring. But eventually the
true representation of *varna* declines. Ibn Khaldun—whom we will
feature in the following chapter—observed the same phenomena.
Speaking to what Sarkar would call the Ksattriyan era, he argued
that over four generations royal power weakens exceedingly. By the
fourth generation, the unity and solidarity derived from the struggle
with the harsh environment earlier had turned to laziness and expectation of power without the consequent training and correct mental
framework. At this point the dynasty is weakened from within or
taken over from outside. While Sarkar does not speak of decline
within ksattriyan or viprans cycles, clearly he is speaking to the same
phenomena—the decline of a particular power elite, ruling elite.

Once *varna* becomes caste, that is, reified, then the cycle must rotate for oppression peaks. Thus:

> It is impossible for these unworthy people to preserve their power. These were the opportune times when power passed from the ksattriyas to the vipras and later on, from the vipras to the vaeshyas. And when the predominance of the oppressive vaeshyas became intolerable in the society, the general mass opened up a new chapter of the social cycle through direct revolution (24).

Returning to possible indicators, Batra has argued that since the collapse of the US markets in 1929, the capitalist economy has been saved for its natural Shudra evolution or revolution by these false vaeshyans—intellectuals who use their theories to support an exploitive system. Through their policies (Keynesian economics, for example) they have simply prolonged the process by more than a half century. But as we learn from his *The Downfall of Capitalism and Communism*, this elongation of destiny is about to end with the next stage ready to erupt. One can look at history for indicators of a passing on of power from the founder, or as Ssu-Ma Ch'ien (Watson, 1958) has called the sage-king to the tyrant—or from the Buddha to the *Sangha* or the routinization of charisma to use Weberian language (Etzioni and Etzioni-Halevy, 1973). For Sarkar this degradation of power, this degeneration of natural *varna* to a false consciousness is inexorable and unstoppable. The role of *sadvipra* is to intervene at this time and revolutionize the cycle—creating a bifurcation—such that order, invention and wealth creation are maximized and enslavement, dogma, commodification minimized.

Fortunately, Sarkar does not oversimplify these already general classifications. Just because a particular locale is moving through the vipra era does not mean there is no territorial expansion. Rather:

> the vipras, being fully aware of their physical and mental weaknesses, allure then with food and money, or with slogans of hollow idealism, and force them into a war of immense destruction. Thus, in the Vipra-predominant age, the ksattriyas meet a tragic death while the diplomatic Vipra ministers get triumphant ovations (Sarkar, 1987b, 5: 25).

To Sarkar "history is not concerned with how many soldiers died in the battle field or how many people, while facing the cannons, saw their golden dreams fade into darkness" (25). But when the political leader dies, "flags are flown at half mast, and marble statues are erected at important points in public parks" (25).

Sarkar's language for these types of intellectuals is direct and from the moral discourse. "All the great war-mongers, the pompous politicians of the world belong to this satanic brood of Vipras" (25). This is especially true today in the Vaeshyan era.

> These wicked vipras, these agents sheltering under the capitalist vaeshyas, have led and are leading millions of people along the path of death and destruction. These fiendish vipras continue to offer oblations into the fire pit of the vaeshyas' demonic lust. Neither the shudra mass nor the warring ksattriyas are responsible for the plight of millions of homeless refugees around the world, or the piercing cries of the mothers, wives and children of the soldiers killed in battle, or the licking flames of communal and racial riots, or the sectarianism, provincialism, nationalism and casteism prevalent today (25).

He continues: "The responsibility lies with the vipran diplomats who, out of petty selfishness, have instigated such monstrous brutalities. This meanness, this fiendishness of theirs, makes a mockery of their intellect as it stages the devil's dance in the graveyard" (26). Sarkar's site of discourse again is clear.

Surprising then that Buddha Prakash can speak about this age not as the age of Kali but that of progressive activity. And it is not so surprising that Sarkar can conclude that humans have failed at building a decent society in the past few thousands years, that real progress is only possible in the spiritual realm given the human tendency to violate others.

Viprans then come in various guises: many as priests, some as philosophers, some as diplomats, and currently many as technocrats. Particularly in India, Sarkar asserts that appropriating the world after death, they increased their income in the material world. It was this that Marx objected to, religion used to sedate the masses. The creation of mantras, gods and demons all served to empower the vipras. However, at the same time the belief that "service to the vipras was the stepping stone to the attainment of celestial bliss" (31) was "instrumental in the stability and building of a society" (31).

The creation of order and unity are central to Sarkar's notion of the good, although they must be contextualized by neo-humanism. Yet order through history creates during the Vipran era the possibility for spiritual development and internal inspiration.

> Those shudras, ksattriyas or vaeshyas [and vipras] who trod the subtler path gave spiritual inspiration to the human race and molded spiritual philosophy. From this group genuine sadvipras had emerged in the past, emerge in the present and will continue to emerge in the

future. While criticizing the vipras we must not forget that the pin-
nacle of mental development, human fraternity, universal outlook and
material development [among the ingredients of a complete ideology]
were the outcome of the Vipra era (32).

However, notwithstanding some bright moments, most philosophical
treatises were mere justifications for privilege. Humanism did not
increase, and most importantly the position of females declined dramatically. While in the Ksattriyan era, especially the first part of it,
women were equal to men, by the Vipran era they become but servants, mere objects of male enjoyment. They lose their spiritual privileges, their role as clan mothers and their role as intellectuals.
According to Sarkar, this was the beginning of prostitution. "Few
keep count of the millions of women who wept and sobbed themselves to death in the darkness of many a sleepless night. They were
leveled flat like the soft earth under the administrative steamroller
of the vipras" (37). While a few females managed to regain some
rights, most were stripped of their dignity. Elsewhere, Sarkar has
argued that females themselves gave certain privileges and rights to
men in a sacred bond of trust that was immediately violated. To
regain them, force is necessary for "nobody gives anybody rights on
a platter. One has to establish one's rights by dint of one's own
force and power" (35).

In Sarkar's entire historical scheme each *varna* creates a new order
and then spends its energy maintaining that structure. "Whomever
wanted to make large or small changes in the social structure [female
or male] in the interests of the people, only broke their heads against
the hard rocks of the social edifice or had to hammer its strong walls
with their clenched fists" (37). While the oppressed greeted these
reformers, the ruling elite was less amenable. Among those who
attempted to recreate this order, Sarkar mentions Krishna, Buddha,
Mahaviira, Muhammed, Mahaprabhu Caetanya, Rammohan Roy
and Ishvarchandra Vidyasagar. All these leaders attempted to overthrow the vipran order, they all attempted to increase the rights of
minorities, females, the elderly; and each tried to develop not the
principle of egoism but that of social equality. The result was that
each was brutally attacked. "Even personalities like Lenin, Bernard
Shaw, M.N. Roy and others, who have been regarded as modern
moral leaders were subjected to severe criticism and false propa-
ganda for their revolt against prevalent dogmas and superstitions"
(39). At these times, when a new ideology emerges, the usual lack
of unity among vipras transforms to a unity against the new ideology.

They support social change unless their own class is threatened, then they attack mercilessly. Each new vipran group oppresses the new. For example:

> In the Medieval Age fanatic Catholics uses to burn non-Catholics or infidels alive. Many an obstinately orthodox Mullah decreed that killing a Kafir or infidel was not a sin. The orthodox Sanatanists, a section of Hindus, tried to murder Lord Buddha. During the reign of Bimbisar, power Buddhist monks used to oppress the Hindus. Both the Hindu Brahmins and the Muslim Mullahs were equally spiteful of Mahatma Kavir (61).

But Sarkar is not disheartened by this, rather he resorts to karma and the moral discourse in giving relief from his history of the betrayal of human dreams. When Sarkar was in jail he wrote this 1977 New Year's Day message: "The struggle between the good and evil forces terminate in the latter's rout. This you have seen, are seeing, and will see as well" (Anandamurti, 1982, 43). And:

> The humans of today are possessed of spirited intellect and accomplished wisdom. They are keen to advance with rapid steps shattering the shackles of dogmas. They will no longer be entrapped by an illusion of opportunism. The rays of a crimson dawn of a new humanity on the eastern horizon have started weaving textures of colors on their eyelids and in the finer cores of their minds. For those who have been dreaming so far to keep humankind imprisoned by dogmas, their days are numbered, their blissful dreams are being shattered to pieces (Anandamurti, 1982, 48).

For Sarkar there are real principles in history, among them is the hypothesis that every new ideology is tested and if it survives this challenge, it flourishes. At the same time the lesson from the history of vipras is clear as well. Each new vipran ideology destroys the old order and then often creates a new one that degenerates until a new order is created. It is the rise and fall of truth. Sorokin (1970) would say it differently. Each truth is only a part of the real. Over time it exaggerates and that which is denied then affirms itself. Thus society becomes overly ideational, next after becoming dualistic, it exaggerates, becomes materialistic and returns to ideational.

The control of truth is how vipras privilege themselves and their world. "Where intellectual and technical literature failed to convince the general people of the greatness of the vipras, they produced a countless number of awe-inspiring, colorful legends . . . warning the people at the same time that non-observance or questioning their truth would inevitably land them in a frightful inferno" (Sarkar, 1987b, 5: 41).

The real was represented not at the level of physical, but as an expression of the world of Idea. Food, instead of providing basic needs or strength, became an offering for the Gods. And of course "a sizable part of the offering destined for the sacrificial fire found their way into the coffers of the vipras" (42). This is what Sarkar in his later writings would call psycho-exploitation. Psycho-exploitation leads to the construction of a self that perceives its self as inferior to the superior self of the dominator. This to him is far more deadly than the classic economic exploitation, for it is psychic-exploitation that keeps the other classes from rising and overthrowing the ruling class. This psychological exploitation is essentially cultural exploitation. As Sarkar has written in his *The Liberation of Intellect: Neo Humanism*: "It is proper for human beings to struggle for political freedom, for social emancipation; but if their cultural backbone is broken, then all their cultural struggles will end in nothing" (Sarkar, 1983, 55). God was put forth in discourse as a way to accumulate cultural and ideological power, the interpreter of this sign becoming then the authoritative sign, from which only he could grant limitless "celestial bliss . . . or the horror of endless perdition in hell" (Sarkar, 1987b, 5: 43).

However, in the previous Ksattriyan era God was constructed differently. For the

> ksattriyans . . . religiosity was the result of their infatuation for greater and great acquisition and expansion. In other words, they thought that by having faith in God they would receive a lot of the world's wealth for their gratification. . . . The vipras . . . thought spirituality would give them such uncommon powers that they would be able to grant boons to the people and do good to those who would give them a fat share of their wealth. The vipras thought spirituality would earn them the power of cursing and harming people and that people would offer baskets brimming with commodities at their feet for their enjoyment out of fear and devotion (58).

In Sarkar's reading, "God bore the footmarks of the vipras on His chest" (59).

Each class tries to build memorials to itself in the hope of stepping outside of time, space and person/observer. However, for vipras, they are often unrecognized in their particular era. Sarkar explains this by asserting that "attraction towards the old is inherent in human beings, so whenever any new thing is presented or introduced by any vipra genius, the rest of humanity . . . cannot take it with equanimity. They cannot adjust with such a new rhythm of movement. In fact, they stick to their old strain" (46). Thus the attacks on new intellectual ideals.

Intellectuals exist in different spheres of time. Past, present, future and transcendental time. Most, however, exist in the past and in the transcendental future. In addition, they excel at creating philosophies that privilege the mind. But again there are moments of genius. For Sarkar, these moments include government by the constitution and creation of societal discipline based on universal concepts of morality. Efforts to move rule back to the ksattriyan kings were, as we might expect from Sarkar's grand theory, counter evolutionary or counter revolutionary. The era of centralized government cannot come again until after the shudra revolution or evolution (albeit at a global level).

The Vipran era is less unified and less disciplined than the social formation of the Ksattriyan era. However, vipran society has greater social ideals (though not followed) and greater individualism. But there are more wars in the Vipran era! "The great wars and bloodshed that took place in the world as the result of the Ksattriyan lust for domination waft into insignificance before those that took place in the Medieval Age at the direct or indirect incitement and instigation of the vipras, the standard bearers of faiths and religions" (54). And:

> For these wars are fought without the traditional Ksattriyan rules and conventions. A veritable stream of blood flows in the world, but not even a scratch bruises the body of the vipra . . . vipran history is one of ingenious treachery. In that history there is intensity of intelligence but not nobility. Their . . . cowardice and ingratitude—and also cleverness—are fouled with the stench of selfishness (63).

The Vaeshya Era

But this cowardice and more importantly, this desire for subsistence without labor "eventually turned them into parasites of the vaeshyas" (59). Accompanying this desire for wealth without labor was overconfidence.

> Overconfident of their own presence of mind, the vipras do not take the future into account, and so there is hardly any effort on their part for accumulation. They think that conditions will continue according

to tradition. But this overconfidence becomes the cause of their own ruin. When real danger comes, their presence of mind fails to cope with it and they have to sell themselves to anyone having any kind of means and resources. With the capital of their wealth, the vaeshyas of lesser intelligence start bossing the vipras (64).

But there is another reason as well for the development of the next era, Sarkar's version of social evolution. "During the Vipra-predominant era those who used to lose in the battle of wits, valor and physical abilities, tried to find some other way for their self-preservation and the establishment of their prestige in the society" (81). That is, they constructed a self that would still meet basic needs of recognition. "The special kind of emotional clash which these efforts awakened in their minds was responsible for the development of their money-making intellect" (81). Thus, with the other avenues of success closed, various individuals opted for money making and then in times of crises, the very intellectuals who had humiliated them, had to go to them for loans and jobs.

The final reason for the development of the next era is again intrinsic to the vipran mind. Intellectual development and discourse can hardly foot the bill in the world of reality. The vaeshyan Finance Minister solves this problem and the vipras get an opportunity to go about their vocations with a light heart. But vaeshyas never invest without self-interest. Their ulterior motive is to establish themselves over society, and this brings about the end of the Vipran era (66).

Significantly, Sarkar does not resort to external variables to explain the transition into the next era. It is not new technologies that create a new wealthy elite that can control the vipras, rather it is a fault within the viprans themselves. Moreover, it is not that they did not meet a new challenge, they did not as Toynbee would write, respond appropriately. Rather, Sarkar's reasoning is closer to Khaldun and other classical philosophers. They create a theoretical world, use it to take care of their needs, but when changes come, they are not prepared for they themselves have degenerated. These changes might be the technological (new inventions, discoveries of resources, lands and labor) but they are not the significant variables, rather it is the mindset of the vipran him or herself that leads to his or her downfall. Indeed Sarkar places the discoveries that one might normally associate with the Vipran era in the Vaeshyan era, for the intellectuals who create these new wonders are but workers for the accumulators of capital. "They are mostly dependent on the pittance of the vaeshyas for food and clothing" (66). Or as Marx and Engels would say it, "The Bourgeoisie has stripped of its halo every occupation hitherto honored and looked up to with reverent awe. It has converted the physician, the lawyer, the priest, the poet, the man of science, into its paid wage-laborers" (Marx and Engels, 1975, 36). Indeed, much of the section about the Vaeshyan era is reminiscent of *The Communist Manifesto*. The style and the content of the prose are remarkably alike.

The vaeshyans keep their power through the very forces of the previous eras. In Sarkar's words, "The funny part of it is that the vaeshyas, buying the vital force of the ksattriyas and the intellectual force of the vipras on the strength of their money, establish themselves with the help of these very forces and thus keep the ksattriyas and vipras enslaved for a long time" (Sarkar, 1987, 5: 71).

With capital, the vaeshyans dominate the viprans, and the viprans use their efforts to aid the vaeshyans in amassing wealth. The intellect and methods for "the evasion of taxes, black-marketing, smuggling, adulteration of food and medicine or inflating figures of profit by bribes" (64) are provided by the intellectuals. "In the vaeshya predominant society such vipras, like the shudras and the ksattriyas are nothing but sequacious hacks and drudges" (64).

In the new era the intellect of the vipra remains active, but not for its own class, but for the creation and development of theories that aid the capitalist class. "So the very day when the vipras submit to the vaeshyas, the Vipra age dies, though not the vipras themselves. The blood-sucking vaeshyas get volumes of philosophical books written and truth tactfully and artfully perverted and distorted with the help of the paid vipras" (65). The main role of the intellectual then becomes system justification. "Attempts are made to portray those who oppose the vaeshyas for their self-preservation as base and vile wretches" (65).

Thus the cycle continues: exploiter becomes exploited. But with the advent of the vaeshyan there are now three classes to use against each other, to extract different types of labor.

How does Sarkar define the vaeshyan? While the other classes desire to enjoy matter, the vaeshyan insists on accumulation. They desire to possess matter. But not just matter, they want to possess the other classes and individuals, not just as tools for production, but as objects for their own pleasures. However, the vaeshyan does not use theoretical schemes in his or her appropriation of matter, unlike the vipra who must first theoretically justify. The intellect of the vaeshya sees the world through the eyes of avarice and greed.

"They even look at the mental and spiritual world through the eyes of the trader" (75). There is little desire to develop the pinnacled intellect, rather at best their religiosity is derived from a fear of God, a carry over from the previous era.

Sarkar places this description in the language of Indian meta-physics. The vaeshyan are *rajasik* and *tamasik*; meaning they are active and inert. They are defined as active because of their efforts and inert because of their focus on matter, the environment. But the location of agency is not the individual but the mind which is imma-nent in self and environment, in the social ecology. For Sarkar, as with Spengler, once the money-making intellect is developed, it has its own logic.

> For money they can sacrifice all scruples about vice and virtue, right and wrong in a moment. Thus in order to save [the other classes] their money, the only prop of their influence and authority, must be snatched away from them. It would, however, be wrong to suppose that by dispossessing the vaeshyas of all their money, the problems will be solved. Inspite of their being divested of all their money, their money-making intellect will still remain (77).

Thus, the alternative for Sarkar is to create a social structure in which their intellect can be channeled and not used to exploit the other groups in society.

The exploitation that began thousands of years ago continues even more forcefully in the Vaeshyan era: honesty and other values defined by the ancients continue to degenerate, unity continues to decrease, excessive wealth leads to "debauchery on one hand" (79) and "poverty forces women" to prostitution on the other (80). The level of exploita-tion takes an astronomical jump in the Vaeshyan era. "Social human-ism gradually fades from their minds as they turn into bloodsucking leeches" (81). And: "In the history of struggle, if the role of the vipras is one of parasitic dependence on others . . . the vaeshyas are murderous parasites of the social who want to kill the main tree by sucking out all its sap" (78). They are thus in contradiction with their own goals, to prosper they must exploit, but eventually they destroy the entire system, thus making exploitation impossible. But like the intellectuals, the capitalists know that they are parasites. As the Vaeshyan era continues, "they grow desperate under the intox-icating spell of accumulation" (81). They "bloat their stomachs with the vital juices of others . . . forming a vicious circle of their own" (79). What can one expect but "a horrid picture of hell" (79). Or, elsewhere, as Marx has written, "veiled by religious and political illusions, [the bourgeoisie] has substituted naked, shameless, direct, brutal exploitation" (Marx and Engels, 1975, 36).

For the vaeshyas the preferred governmental system is democracy. Under a democracy, the economy is easier to control as are the other classes. In a democracy the vaeshyans use the viprans to get themselves elected. Under a dictatorship or an imperialistic administration, the populace will support the leader as long as "they do not do anything serious against the public interest" (Sarkar, 1987b, 5: 64). Thus, for Sarkar no political system in intrinsically better than any other one. Primary is *varna*, the dominant discourse, the way of dealing with the world. It is during the Vaeshyan era nationalism emerges. This is not the centralized monarchy of the ksattriyan era, nor the vipran ideology of the nation-state, but rather global economic imperialism, which Wallerstein (1983) and others have called the world capitalist system; one world economy with many nation-states, with capitalists using the nation-state for advancing their own accumulation projects or denying access to other capitalists. In this system, "the boot-licking vipras wield sufficient authority," (67) but for Sarkar the finance minister is always a true vaeshyan. The intellectuals remain as planners and as civil servants, but the accumulation and accounting of wealth goes to one who is first of all an accumulator of wealth, not ideas.

And when intellectuals organize to change the system through the use of the divide and rule strategy, they are kept in their place. The rebel intellectuals are defeated by the intellectuals who work for the capitalists and by the military and police force of the capitalist state.

Significantly Sarkar departs from the classic Hindu image of the vipra as the head, the shudras as the feet and the ksattriya as the arms, by placing the vaeshya not as the thighs but as outside the person or machine. They provide the machine with energy and then extract labor from it. It exists to perform labor and can be thrown away once the capitalist is tired of it.

Just as power is controlled by the elite of the particular *varna*, the responsibilities are also theirs.

> Whatever ills are perpetrated in society are in a great measure created by the vaeshyas themselves. To fatten their bank balances, the vaeshyas create an artificial scarcity of consumer goods such as food, clothes, etc. and make huge profits in the black market. Those who cannot afford to buy high priced food and clothes are forced to steal and commit armed robbery and through other shady ways to meet their basic requirements (79).

Again, this passage is Marxian. "In these crises there breaks out an epidemic that, in all earlier epochs, would have seemed an absurdity—the epidemic of over-production. Society suddenly finds itself put back into a state of momentary barbarism" (Marx and Engels, 1975, 40). But it is not the capitalists who are apprehended for any illegalities. "The rich vaeshyans slip though the trap on the strength of their wealth" (Sarkar, 1987b, 5: 7).

Things to the vaeshyan have no—what Sarkar calls—practical value. They have accumulation or hoarding value. The practical value of things decreases as the Vaeshyan era continues: money loses its mobility and the disparity of wealth continues to increase. "The vaeshyans are always in a minority because worldly wealth is accumulated by the few at the cost of the many" (76). Eventually, of course, "when these bands of slaves [the other *varnas*] [are] unable to tolerate the exploitation any more, [they] desperately leap into a revolt," (76). The Vaeshyan era ends. "It takes a long time for the downtrodden mass to realize that the vaeshyans are the parasites of society, and that is why a tremendous effort is needed to sound the death bell of the Vaeshyan era" (76).

It takes a long time because of several reasons. First, real wealth is created by the capitalists. "Whenever efforts are made to raise the living standard in national, economic and social life, capital becomes a necessity whether it comes from within the country or from outside" (83). Wealth must have a controller. This is the vaeshya. If it is used appropriately, it can increase the standard of living for everyone, if it is dominated by the state or the individual or the corporation, then only a few will gain.

In addition to the economic advance of the developed countries, second, the system is difficult to dismantle because it has taken the vaeshyas a long time to build it. Thus, "under such circumstances, to expect that they can be moved by entreaties and supplications or that they will suddenly take the path of the renunciate wearing nothing but a loin cloth is utter lunacy" (87). Thus, for instance, for Sarkar, the absurdity of the Indian Bhudan movement.

Third is the strategy of capitalists to give funds to charities and other associations so as to satisfy various interest groups. Fourth is the development of the false vaeshyas. These are intellectuals who are influenced by the capitalists and work to keep the capitalist system going.

> They drag out the vaeshya legacy to the last days of vaeshya dominance, [but] they end in utter ignominy and humiliation. In order to

carry on with their rapacity unchecked and uncurbed, they also try to employ all other intellectual endowments, apart from their economic intellect, for economic exploitation, and finally even seize the power of the state by whatever means necessary. . . . The entire society gets pulverized under that cruel grinding machines (82).

To save money for their descendants, they not only continue to exploit the entire society, "but also hoard large amounts of unutilized capital" (82). Finally, it is arduous to succeed in this revolution as one must defeat the vaeshyans and their various followers in the other classes. "Those who want to strike a blow at the vaeshyan framework have to confront all three vaeshyan slaves, the vipras, the ksattriyas and shudras" (88). For example, the vipras now exploit others for themselves and for the vaeshyans as well. Thus, the ideology of fatalism, and thus the context of comments (according to Sarkar) by Marx against religion, for he understood that it had made them "impotent and dispirited by instigating them to submit to a vicious circle" (89).

But while the opposition is stronger, so is the suppression. It is stronger because it takes more effort to maintain the structure. To maintain the ancient ksattriyan social formation all that was needed was superior physical strength and then allegiance from other warriors. Now in subsequent Ksattriyan eras instead of simply physical strength other factors come into play: numerical strength and the use of military/police are more significant and eventually technological strength in terms of offensive and defensive weapons are critical. The move from the ancient Ksattriya era to the Vipra era was natural in that they, the ksattriyas, to continue the structure of dominance had to learn new skills. The Hero had to go to the sage and later the strategist. "Subsequently, this learning was not confined to use of arms only and extended to other spheres, such as battle craft, medicine and forms of organization and administration, so essential for ruling any society" (Sarkar, 1978b, 2: 136). The dependence on intellectual strength led to real power passing on to a new class that eventually becomes aware that it is a class, albeit it fights among itself in the arenas of religion, philosophy or ideology. But intellectual exploitation is more difficult to maintain as the intellect can easily develop through equal access to knowledge centers. Thus, the development of caste systems, feudal systems, and other "false consciousness" schemata to maintain power.

For Sarkar, this continued extraction of wealth and self resulted in the development of communities which dealt only in goods. Eventually producers and traders became the ruling elite. This abstraction is even easier to learn and thus requires greater effort to maintain its structure. Indeed, ideology and military are necessary to maintain the economic structure for without it, labor would work for itself not for capital. In each case the ruling elite becomes smaller and smaller with the worker base of capitalism being the largest and the monied top the smallest. At this phase all become shudras in terms of economic class, even if in terms of mental wave they are distinct. Again as Marx would say, "Our epoch, the epoch of the bourgeoisie, possesses, however, this distinctive feature: it has simplified class antagonisms. Society as a whole is more and more splitting up into two great hostile camps, into two great classes directly facing each other: Bourgeoisie and Proletariat" (Marx and Engels, 1975, 33).

But this vaeshyan exploitation finally ends. "The oppressed and tortured people who are reluctant to succumb to such a ignominious death rise in revolt. The shudra revolution [thus] takes place during the period dominated by the dishonest vaeshyas" (Sarkar, 1987b, 5: 82). Possibly because of the concentration of wealth even the capitalists have a difficult time earning money. Thus, "the vitality of the Ksattriyan era surrenders to the intellectuality of the Vipran era, and the intellectuality of the Vipran era gets lost in the monetary figures of the Vaeshya era," (83) which gets overthrown once all the other classes have become shudras by economic class. While the evolutionary model is by definition more gradual, the shudra revolution is violent and disjunctive.

> They become desperate and one day they, the blind, conscience-shorn, mind-bereft public pitilessly break the Vaeshyan edifice to pieces. They do not contemplate the whys and hows of their act, nor how the society will be reconstructed after the destructive uprising. They leap into struggle merely for self-existence. They think that since they cannot live at all, let the end of life come nearer. During this reckless revolution the mental state of the vipras, vaeshyas and ksattriyas remains the same. It is then useless to expect any humanism from them (85).

Or again in the words of Marx: "They direct their attacks . . . against the instruments of production themselves; they destroy imported wares that compete with their labor, they smash to pieces machinery, they set factories ablaze . . ." (Marx and Engels, 1975, 43).

This then is the shudra revolution where the cycle, the wheel, rotates forward once again, and so returns to the Shudra era. At this point among the objections, the obvious one is that revolutions do not always occur when is exploitation its at its peak. There are other variables, for example, revolutions occur when there are collective unmet expectations, a change in needs, frustrated expectations. Galtung, among others, argues that "revolutions are structurally conditioned but not predetermined," (Galtung, 1978c, 3: 313). For him,

> The idea is that true revolutions are directed against vertical interaction and feudal interaction structures, that they have their origin among the groups that are most highly frustrated by these structures [workers, peasants, females, barbarians, outcasts], the rank dis-equilibrated groups and certain segments of underdog groups, the organization of either and of the contact between them is indispensable, and once these conditions are present then non-structural factors such as ideology, charismatic leader, frustrated expectations, precipitating incidents and new cooperation patterns, will be among the final ingredients sparking off the revolution (313).

While this is not the place to develop his thesis, the main point is that Sarkar's theory initially appears to be overly general. While one might defend it by arguing that Sarkar is speaking from far above, sighting the large waves, the vast movements of ideas and structures and epistemes, nonetheless, severe exploitation, so far, is not a useful predictor of revolution.[1]

But Sarkar is sensitive to such criticisms. For Sarkar, oppression, as defined by poverty, inferiority complexes, and the inability to realize the true self, are necessary factors, but not sufficient factors. In his words, "it would be futile to expect the revolution just because it was the ripe time. Conditions relating to place and person are also important factors" (Sarkar, 1987b, 6: 1). These conditions are the various variables that Marx and other sociologists have attempted to describe. In the last chapter of his *Human Society*, Sarkar does give us two social indicators. These are the *viksubdha shudra*, or the discontented workers. These are the labor leaders, the intellectuals who are struggle to dismantle the system, Gramsci's organic intellectuals, or the value-oriented intellectuals. They are the vipras and ksattriyas who have been forced into a laborer existence and are self-conscious of their class.

> . . . revolution will be brought about by vipra-minded and ksattriya-minded shudras, and for this a lot of effort and preparation will

---

[1] "So far" is the key here. While there have been movements in the cycle in various collectivities, in Russia, for example, from capitalist to worker revolution to warrior, the entire world economy has not yet experienced a world shudra revolution. However, the anti-globalization movement contesting that, for example, a handful of people—250—own has much wealth as 40% of the world's population, may yet create the conditions for the transformation of the world vaeshyan system.

have to be made by them, they will have to suffer a lot, sacrifice a lot and fight against the opposing groups and doctrines.... The vanguard of revolution, the ksattriya-minded or vipra-minded shudras will have to learn discipline, take proper training for the revolution, build their character, and become moralists (Sarkar, 1987b, 6: 2–3).

The other indicator Sarkar gives us refers to violence. For him bloodshed is not inevitable. "If the majority of the discontented shudras are ksattriya-minded or if their martial influence is dominant, revolution does occur through sanguinary clashes... Bloodless revolution can only occur if the number and influence of the Vipra-minded among the discontented is very great" (5). Unfortunately, "popular emancipation is blood soaked" (5).

Sarkar's Spiritual Leadership

Sarkar's effort is to transform these disgruntled individuals into a new type of leadership, the *sadvipra*, one which will continue the revolution permanently across borders and space. While to explain this concept he does not use any developments in leadership theory he does develop an impressive list of qualities of the ideal leader.[2] The sadvipra is a bodhisattva of sorts, willing to construct a self that has all four classes—servant, protective, intellectual and innovative—and highly evolved spiritually, but outside of the fame, power, lust and wealth matrix. While he speaks for a non-violent revolution, a revolution even if it is violent is more preferable than a slow evolutionary process into a society where capitalists have their power reduced.

---

[2] Sarkar presents the following as some necessary qualities of the spiritual revolutionary. They are translated from Bengali. In English the text comes out in the male gender; for "he" include "she" as well. We quote at length:

(1) He should always think in terms of Ideology and collective interest and never in personal terms. Generally a stroke of difficulty, a blow to personal prestige or position diverts one's attention towards oneself, thus forgetting the great ideology. This feeling may be either positive or negative but it preoccupies a large portion of man's mind and thereby creates too much self-consciousness which makes a man lazy and vocal. He chats about himself, his difficulties and his relations with the persons surrounding him and incidents. He loses balance of mind. In short, he thinks all the time about himself, forgetting his Ideology and task.

(2) He should never criticize anybody. The tendency for criticism comes only due to lack of ability and patience to withstand difficulties. It is sometimes only due to false personal vanity or sense of prestige wounded by someone that one criticizes others. If you point out some mistakes of a pseudo-scholar, for instance, he loses his balance and becomes angry.

(3) He should always try to please his co-workers through his actions and behavior. Words cannot convince them. People can only be convinced by actions.

The qualities of Sarkar's desired leadership are primarily moral, although the ability to labor, fight, calculate and account are crucial as well. The qualities he takes directly from classic Indian texts, the *yamas* and *niyamas*. They include: not causing suffering through thought, word or actions; actions and words with the aim of helping others; nonstealing; simplicity and only acquiring those things that are required for basic needs; commitment to the unity of consciousness; inner contentment; purity of thought and body; willing-

---

(4) A dull brain cannot be a revolutionary. He should be put in the most adverse and difficult circumstances and should be left alone to come out of them by his own efforts.

(5) If any point of differences arises, it should be solved tactfully and with cooperative zeal. No use of grumbling over it. It will just worsen the matter.

(6) There should not be any attachment with any individual. He should love all but should never have unnecessary sympathy for anybody in particular. Some persons try to create tender feelings in the heart with ulterior motives. A revolutionary has to be aware of them.

(7) He should be guided by his own conscience and should never yield to others' opinions. He should hear all but follow what his own conscience says. The leadership of a great organization is constituted by only one person. There may be ranks inbetween. A revolutionary has to obey his immediate superior, yet for details and for checking the morality of his superior, he should never lose faith in his conscience.

(8) He should never think about his power or position. But he should be aware of the importance of his fate and the method of the best utilization of his power, position and faculties.

(9) His mind should be cool and calm every moment. He should never react to any stimulus immediately, though he should keep proper knowledge of his environment. To have a cool and calm mind, one needs spiritual practices. Without the strength of mind achieved through spiritual struggle, nothing can be done.

(10) Never lament any loss. Try and make up the loss suffered with double strength. Be optimistic even in the most adverse circumstances.

(11) Before starting any scuffle or fight, assess your strength. But if calamity comes, don't worry. Face it with patience.

(12) Don't be moved by others opinions. Try to judge them on an objective basis. Don't be disturbed by what others are saying or thinking about you. Opinions are something outward. Be brave, make yourself strong, disciplined and fearless.

(13) If there are any anomalies, don't criticize. But try to remove it by proper action immediately.

(14) Live by principle (*yama* and *niyama*). One who deviates cannot succeed despite his best efforts. Stick to your decisions but be careful while taking a decision.

(15) A revolutionary should always think about Ideology. Not a single moment should be wasted in: (a) useless thinking, (b) useless gossip, (c) meaningless action.

(16) No one wants to tolerate the hegemony of others. Let no one get the impression that you want to keep one under your leadership. He should accept your leadership due to love and dedication.

These were made available to me through a personal letter from Acharya Maheshvarananda Avadhuta, January 12, 1990, upon reading an earlier draft of this chapter.

ness to struggle to achieve the goal; and understanding the essence of spiritual texts. Sarkar's sadvipra must moreover be versatile.

> The sadvipra is not an inactive witness. He is an active participant to see that no person or class exploits the reset. For this, he may have to resort even to physical violence because the sadvipra will have to strike at the source of the power which is tending to become the exploiter. In case the ksattriya class is becoming exploitive, the sadvipra may have to resort to physical force and in an age where the intellectual or vipra class is dominating, he will have to bring a revolution in the intellectual field. In case the vaeshyas are dominating, the sadvipra may have to contest and win elections because the vaeshyas class rule by democracy and the democratic set-up enables them to accumulate undue gains (Sarkar, 1978b, 2: 141).

While the *sadvipra* concept is a natural outgrowth from the Indian episteme and the Indian construction of history, and from Sarkar's theory itself, Sarkar does not entertain the notion of the *sadvipras* becoming a class in themselves, or given his reading of history as incredibly oppressive and unjust, of tyranny and tradition, on becoming the new oppressor but at a level previously unimaginable since they contain the abilities of all classes. Super-leadership can lead to super exploitation.

While one knows that he speaks from the spiritual perspective as does Aurobindo or Teilhard De Chardin and thus sees this in the context of a new society, nonetheless given his believe that the cycle/spiral shall continue endlessly, why not the sadvipras becoming part of the class they are trying to overthrow? For Sarkar, they will not become a class, rather the sadvipras will become the ksattriyans after the shudra revolution and then disappear to reappear when the ksattriyans become exploitive. But where will they disappear to? This, of course, is another way of stating the classic question of who will guard the guardians? While the democratic method attempts to find a way to pit the classes constantly (checks and balances) against each other, Sarkar believes the capitalists simply use it for the economic expansion. In the ideal world Sarkar believes "if the Sadvipras alone had the right to vote, there would be no difference between the real world and the heaven of imagination" (Sarkar, 1987b, 6: 5). Again this is not Plato philosopher kings, or Nietzsche's superman, they are *sadvipras* primarily because of their willingness to struggle and suffer. It is the Hero institutionalized within grand theory.

But Sarkar does not enter a critical discourse with respect to the sadvipra, except that he argues for a group of sadvipras sharing power, not a one sadvipra rule. Moreover, this is not a theocracy to him, since morality cannot be legislated; rather the polity can become theocratic in a particular age, especially the Vipran era.

Sarkar, thus is not giving us a rigorous social science theory; rather, he speaks from a mountain, yet from the view of the oppressed, but not any particular class, he surveys history, storytelling, using history to present his preferred world. But he is not only storytelling, these are laws that he describes, laws that when deconstructed are compatible with the Indian episteme, from his theory of consciousness. Just as consciousness follows a cycle, becomes bounded then re-emerges from matter, becomes human and then finally becomes unbounded and realizes its authentic but unalterable self, the social cycle too follows a clear cycle. Attempts to move it backward through counter-revolution or evolution (from vaeshyan to vipran, Iran, for example) go against the natural and thus are short lived. And:

> The world is a transitory phase or changing phenomena with the scope of Cosmic Mind. It is going in eternal motion and such a motion is the law and nature and law of life. . . . Hence no power can check the social cycle of evolution. Any force external or internal can only retard or accelerate the speed of transition but cannot prevent it from moving (Sarkar, 1978b, 2: 139).

Again, the social, biological, individual and spiritual all exist in a unity of discourse that cannot be broken. But given that the real ultimately is beyond good and bad and that humans desire a world without exploitation—oppression is historical but unnatural—it is possible to manipulate the structure such that rulers administrate, not extract.

But the ages themselves will continue. The thesis of the Ksattriya age will be countered by a sadvipra antithesis leading to a post-revolution vipra synthesis. Forever.

Concluding his classic *The Human Society* in poetic form, he writes: "The downtrodden humanity of this disgraced world is looking to the eastern horizon, eagerly awaiting their [the sadvipras] advent with earnest zeal. Let the cimmerian darkness of the interlunar night disappear from their faces. Let human beings of the new dawn wake up on a new world" (Sarkar, 1987b, 6: 8).

CHAPTER FIVE

COMPARING SARKAR: THE VIEW FROM ALL AROUND

Introduction

The task of this chapter is to take the essence, the central themes of Sarkar's thinking and place it in the context of other grand thinkers. We intend to move out from the Indian episteme and enter other epistemes, other methods of constructing past, present and future. Our methodology is simple. We search for similarities, for differences. Are Sarkar's contributions unique and unprecedented or have others entered similar domains and found like or different conclusions? Can understanding these thinkers aid in understanding Sarkar's theory, the purpose of this effort? Can they aid in understanding what Sarkar's theory is missing; what is needed; what is weak or not clear?

Central to this task is answering the question, why compare? We compare—through history, across episteme and cosmology and from writer to writer—so as to distance. To take a step forward or back-ward in space and time so as to better understand the object of understanding. In this distancing, we can find similarities and differ-ences. We understand something not only in its own terms, but in an alternative context. We see not only what it is, but more impor-tantly what it is not. How it is defined and how it not defined. Through comparison we also engage in an empathetic understanding: we move closer and search for similar efforts, for universalities in thinking and for peculiarities. We thus distance and gain proximity.

Who to Stand With?

The thinkers to whom Sarkar can be compared with while vast are certainly limited. Our effort has been to choose those from other civilizations that generally have a clear theory of history at the macro level, a macrohistory. Secondly, we include thinkers who can aid us in understanding his theory of leadership and elite rule. Some of these thinkers are invited for dinner in that they specifically relate to Sarkar and many will be invited for tea but not for dinner in that they show up to contribute a sentence or two, a thought or two, and then disappear via the back door. With the dinner guests we will be more exhaustive in our comparisons, with the tea guests we will be briefer.

While ideally the style of this chapter should be an inter-civiliza-tional and inter-epochal conversation between authors, we will remain within the third person narrative, using the language of social sci-ence commentary.

First we will set the stage or the dinner table to push this metaphor. We will use concepts in the social change discourse borrowing largely from Johan Galtung (the macrohistorical approach), Irwin Lazslo (basic concepts), and Eric Voegelin (the types of truth and the imma-nentization of the spiritual in history). Eric Voegelin is especially use-ful as he, like Sarkar, is concerned with all of the history of humanity and the nature of the self. His insights augment Sarkar's. We also reintroduce Foucault, who will be our ahistorical gate crasher—as he is prone to do—arguing for an alternative politics of history that searches not for transcendental continuities but for temporal dis-junctions. We also examine his history of epistemes and make pre-liminary comparisons with Sarkar especially as it relates to Foucault's notion of the changing nature of the rational and of punishment for those who move outside this nature. Fred Polak's monumental research on the image of future (optimistic and pessimistic images) and the ways that humans have historically dealt with the real will be our final arrangement. This will set the stage for the first guests.

From Chinese historiography we invite Ssu-Ma Ch'ien and Chang Hsueh-Cheng. Ssu-Ma Ch'ien's historical approach is dynastic, thus at one level dissimilar to Sarkar, but like Sarkar he is concerned with the rise and fall of virtue. Moral discourse is an integral aspect of historical discourse: it cannot be and should not be separated. Among others, Chang Hsueh-Cheng's contribution to Chinese thought is the question of how does the tao function in history? Also cen-tral to Chinese thought is the notion of the natural and of balance. There is a harmonious way of the world. For Sarkar too. Moving from Chinese historiography, we will examine Ibn Khaldun's thought, especially his foundational *Muqaddimah*. Khaldun, perhaps the founder of modern sociology, sees history as the rise and fall of *asabiya* or unity. His is a general theory of the rise and fall of civilizations. We give Khaldun more textual space, a dinner guest who will stay the entire evening, as his work still remains the prototype for other cycli-

cal theorists (wherein the rise or expansion in itself causes the fall
or contraction), especially the numerous European thinkers who come
after him. Like Sarkar his theory is cyclical, like Sarkar his own life
was tumultuous politically, and like Sarkar he speaks from a spiritual
perspective—Khaldun from Islam and Sarkar from Tantra. Moving
from North Africa across the Mediterranean we will compare the
stages of Vico with those of Sarkar. Both have four stages: for Vico
the ages of Gods, Heros, Men and Barbarians; for Sarkar the social
cycle. Both exist in a social science that is outside the present positivistic tradition. Vico historically so, Sarkar consciously so.

After the humanistic science of Vico, we examine the positivist
science of Comte. It is Comte who ends the cycle and articulates a
finality in history. Hegel follows neither as a dinner or a tea guest,
but as a guest who saw history too seriously, who was invited out
of politeness, but took the invitation seriously and stayed for the
entire meal. From Hegel, we attempt to understand the problems
encountered when the absolute is taken concretely. Sarkar moves in
this direction with his theory of *Taraka Brahma*, but appears to stop
short of disaster but smack into a messianic political activism, useful for mobilizing the masses and myth creation/generation, but
potentially disastrous for a self-critical utopian theory. From Hegel
we then move directly to Marx.

It is Marx who should with Sarkar cut the main dish and both
present a theory of history with, we believe, the expressed intention
to change the future. Both present grand systems, Sarkar is more
comprehensive, but Marx is far more detailed and scholarly. As this
event has been constructed by other writings on PROUT we will
summarize, not gorge. But we will use his forerunners, Gramsci for
understanding of the organic intellectual and Wallerstein for his analysis of the future of the world system, albeit as with Braudel merely
in passing, more like chutney then dinner or tea. After Marx and
his development of elite theory, we will continue this analysis with
Pareto and Mosca. Both Pareto and Mosca provide a more rigorous treatment of elite theory than Sarkar cares to give us. Sarkar's
work improves with their language, specifically, the notion of the circulation of the elite. After our elite theorists comes Spengler, who
like Sarkar, forecasts the end of the modern world. In addition,
Sarkar and Spengler have other similarities such as the role of money-
spirit and the different classes.

We conclude with Toynbee and Sorokin. Both Toynbee and
Sorokin are used throughout this text. Coming in on dinner con-
versations, commenting during tea, and in general attempting to
translate the world into their language. But while Foucault might
impertinently spill tea on our Indian carpet thus making problematic the ground of our thought, Toynbee and Sorokin wish to be
heard and to add their worldviews to our own. Toynbee is significant
to us because of the similarities of his universal state and universal
church with the Ksattriyan and Vipran eras, and Sorokin for his
vast cultural rhythms and for his analysis of limits. Sorokin in many
ways comes closest to Sarkar and is someone who Sarkar can learn
from in that Sorokin's adds to the richness of Sarkar's theory. Both
augment Sarkar's work. Indeed there is enough here for a general
theory of macrohistory. At the end of the chapter, we point to
future discussions with respect to leadership theory with which Sarkar
could gain from in presenting his theory of the *sadvipra*. There is no
dessert.

Tools

All meals have utensils, we are not without them as well. Galtung
(1990), among others, uses the following as points of departure in
interpreting theories of change. He focuses on historical processes
and on causes and mechanisms. In terms of historical processes are
they linear, meaning that the critical changes are irreversible and
that evolution is progressive? Or are they cyclical, meaning that the
history has a rise and fall or expansion and contraction pattern in
that the more things change, the more they stay the same? Or are
they spiral, meaning that the shape of history folds back on itself in
that there is progress in some areas and cycles in other areas or
meaning that the cycle of history can be intervened, socially adjusted.
Thus, it is both linear and cyclical. Or is history transformational,
meaning primarily with respect to the future that what will be will
be *a*historical such that it cannot be understood with respect to the
present, that is, it is neither linear nor cyclical.

In addition to the shape of history, it is important to ask are the
variables that move or pull history exogenous (outside) or endogenous (inside) the model, or some version of both/and or neither.
That is, how do the causes and mechanisms of history operate?
Finally, is one's theoretical articulation ideographic (a unique case,

one unit of analysis with many explaining variables) or nomethetic (repeated cases, many units of analysis with one variable)? Also useful is the study at one point in time or through time, synchronic or diachronic. For our purposes, macrohistory is through time with often one or two essential variables usually attempting to explain one unit of analysis. Some attempt to follow the unit, a civilization, for example, and compare it to another across time, but that is rare. Sarkar does not attempt this. Batra attempts to apply Sarkar's theory to various civilizations, but does not entertain a cross space/time comparison. Macro-thinking is nomethetic and diachronic. It is the search for patterns through time and space. As with Sarkar, most of the macro-thinkers we are concerned with believe they are writing a science of the past, present and future, a science that functions irrespective of observer. It is not a humble enterprise analyzing, for example, the history of a particular village, or even one nation, rather it is an analysis of totalities, of an all-encompassing theory.

Critics such as Karl Popper (1957) point that out that such an effort misses too many significant details, removes choice and contingency and privileges structure over human agency. But for the macrohistorian, individuals are important but they exist in larger fields: epistemological, ontological, economic, cultural, which condition their choices. One might speak about preferred futures as modern futurists attempt to, but these preferences exists within certain structures: biological (of the brain), epistemological (the historical possibilities of what is thinkable), social (one's own culture and its history), technological (the material and social ways that one might express thoughts), economic (the ability to express them, that is, having an identity and personal wealth so as to choose and not be a victim of structure). The macro view is also concerned about systems as a whole. Sorokin develops a typology of these systems: (1) unrelated, (2) related because of spatiality, (3) and related because they have an axial principle. It is the system related by an axial principle that is of interest to him, here the parts of the system related logically to the whole and there is a deep isomorphism between the individual, the collective, the physical and mental. The meaning structures are apparent once the system—the cosmology or episteme—is understood as a whole. In the macro view then, size, structure (vertical, horizontal, or what now are seen as feudal or bureaucratic arrangements), relations (person to person; person to nature; person to society) are significant.

Macro-thinkers are rarely useful to the present as they represent change. Cyclical theories in particular are seen as pessimistic from the elite and the core nation and core civilization. Insofar as individuals choose based on much larger forces they can be seen as pessimistic from the view of agency.

Staying within the linear/cyclical, endogenous/exogenous model, Galtung (1997) identifies Weber, Spencer, Comte, Durkeim, Parsons as endogenous and linear. Khaldun, Vico, Pareto, Sorokin, Spengler, are endogenous and cyclical. Hegel is linear and exogenous (the spirit as an outside force impacting history). Cyclical and exogenous is rare occurrence although Marx when he speak of pre-historical societies speaks from that view. Toynbee is cyclical and has endogenous and exogenous aspects. Braudel as well as Wallerstein have linear/cyclical and endogenous/exogenous elements. Marx has linear/cyclical (spiral) dimensions when he speaks about the society to be. Ssu-Ma Ch'ien is clearly cyclical and endogenous as is Cheng and other Chinese thinkers, for the tao works in history not as an outside factor. Sarkar speaks from the spiral perspective. History is cyclical but through his preferred future *sadvipra* society, it will become a spiral reaching higher heights of the satisfaction of essential desires. At the same time, Sarkar's theory is mostly endogenous (the new phase comes on because of the previous phase) yet at the same time the role of the spiritual is at times an exogenous factor (the *taraka brahma* and the spiritual emanations of microvita) and geography plays a role. Events such as his predicted polar shift will lead to a spiritual society as these will impact the electromagnetic fields of the world (Sarkar, 1987a, 7:53). Given the Sarkarian episteme, a shift in the poles would impact the solar system, the earth, the planet's ecology and thus ultimately the thought waves of humans. This changing event will aid humans in becoming more meditative. It could also lead to an ice age in the long run. In preparation, Sarkar's advice is to move to other planets. A rare but cyclical geographical event such as the polar shift could thus fundamentally transform society. Thus for Sarkar geography, Braudel's (1972) *longue durée* (the long time), plays a role in history and the future. From the spiritual view, geography is stable but as it is ultimately but a reflection of consciousness, its stability is dependent on other factors.

Returning to our discussion on macro-thinking and thinkers before we begin the various comparisons, before the dinner begins, let us wander among other ways to structure macro-thinking.

Irwin Laszlo in an article entitled "Footnotes to a History of the Future" (1982), identifies some of the key patterns. To him there is (1) circular movement, (2) circular movement that rises or descends, that is, toward utopia or dystopia (the cycle with direction), (3) linear movement either negative or positive, and (4) jagged movement with stops and starts, forward leaps and fallbacks.

The circular pattern is exhibited in Ssu-Ma Ch'ien theory of the rise and fall of virtue, Khaldun's rise and fall of *asabiya* (unity, solidarity), Sorokin Ideational, Idealistic, Sensate super rhythm, Sarkar's social cycle, Vico's cycle, Spengler's culture/civilization cycle, and Marx's historical societies. The Helix or Coil (cycle with direction) is the classic fall of man view (from the golden age degenerating to the age of materialism and then returning to the golden age with this pattern perpetually repeating itself). Associated with this pattern in the Indian context is the influence of the God-man at the end of degeneration. Thus there is structure, but also agency, albeit a super-agency. Laszlo places Hegel as well in this Helix structure, but the present instead of the site of degeneration is the site of high point of civilization, the Germanic state. The linear model is the classic western model of increased rationality, economic progress, urbanization, secularization, national integration and modernization. Spencer, Durkeim and Weber have been the classic proponents of this historical march. But there are also spiritual linear perspectives as well. The fall of man from Heaven to Earth without redemption is one example. But history can be constructed with the ascension of man. For example, Teillard de Chardin saw history as a movement toward God. God pulled all toward Him. The technological changes of modernity for de Chardin were leading toward a compression of information, a noosphere, a place of shared spiritual information and insight. Sarkar too when speaking of the spiritual uses the linear metaphor. For him the cycle exists at physical and mental levels, but as the spiritual level can assimilate these other levels (that is the curvature of reality can be transformed into the unity of the Spirit) there exists higher and higher levels of progress.

Laszlo's ideal pattern is the systems science perspective. In this is a cycle and linear direction as well with the accent on progress. The long-term trend is toward complexity, differentiation, increased size, improved use of energies and the ability to store and access various energies.

This has been the pattern from the stone ages to the modern

period with only the Middle Ages as a reversal in the long-term
trend. The trend is thus directional but there are periods of stasis
and periods of movements. These long periods however are increasingly punctuated by frequent periods of revolutionary transformation. These trends become disrupted by chaos. It is not a mere cycle
or mere Helix, rather there are disjunctions.

   These periods of change, of chaos, however, do not lead to the
reoccurrence of the past as with cyclical theories. Rather a new order
comes in, and what results are new levels of complex structured systems, greater in size and with an improved capacity to access, store
and utilize energies and maintain themselves. The cyclical part of
Laszlo's pattern is unclear, but for cyclical theorists these chaotic
periods bring on the cycle again, albeit at a new dialectical level
(for Sarkar and Marx, but not for Khaldun and Ssu-Ma Ch'ien).
For Galtung, what is missing in the systems view is the expansion/
contraction dynamic. The Middle Ages were not a reversal but an
integral dimension of Occidental cosmology—the West in its contraction mode.

   With the above gloss of macro-thinking prior to proceeding on to
the actual comparisons, some assumptions should be explicitly stated.
To begin with, where a thinker stands to a great degree conditions
what he or she sees and stands for. For example, Ibn Khaldun's life
is similar to his historiography: both follow a rise and fall pattern.
Khaldun wrote in the final stages of the decline of Islamic empire
and thus developed a sophisticated theory of disintegration. Hegel
writing at the zenith of Prussian State developed an alternative perspective, outside of the decline discourse. Sarkar, writing from the
horror that is Calcutta, develops a cyclical theory with an exit based
on Indian spirituality.

   Implicit in the relationship between the author and the text he
creates is that all history is interpretative. Moreover it is often elitist and certainly male. The voices heard are those that have been
written (historical evidence), little of it is oral. The macro perspective then is not less objective than the traditional historical view, of
say the Vienna Circle, which argues that history is merely one event
after another. The meaning of history is but an imposition. Indeed,
the communication and the intelligibility of existence is but interpretation. In this, the macro view aids in making sense of the apparently fragmented and unified (again, showing our bias for order in
history) events, images and trends.

Next each historical thinker must make some metaphysical choices. In their language these are not choices but truths, Sarkar is certainly not immune from this. Useful are the choices that Eric Voegelin gives us (1987). History is *cosmological*, that is, it reflects the harmony of the deeper order that pervades throughout the universe. This, of course, is the view of the classic European episteme, Vico's Age of God, and the Indian episteme. Next is the *anthropological/philosophical* discourse with history primarily understood from the psyche, from the intellect; the perfection of the heavens is not a necessary condition. Last is the *soteriological*; this is history from the viewpoint of the Godhead, the divine. Here history is created by the transcendent through his grace, through his relationship with the finite.

From the view of most macrohistorians, once there is a pattern, then there are laws. These can be based on a cosmic order, or based on a theory of order that there is a natural waiting to be discovered or based on a revelation by a transcendent. Thus, *once a transcendent is created in history, it must have a way to speak.* Hegel spoke through the great leader and the perfect state (or in Sarkar's language: the vipra desiring the discipline of a ksattriyan society); Ssu-Ma Ch'ien spoke through the sage-king, while Khaldun manages to keep the transcendent more as a sign of textual respect. Allah gives his blessing to successful projects, but only after the fact. In the Vedas, history is evolutionary and speaks not just through one figure but through the many who are enlightened. These many are then placed in a system of hierarchy from the avatar to the guru. Significantly, the prophet is not the sole source of prophecy. For Sarkar, history is spoken through the collective mind of the particular group and history is harmonized through the great spiritual leader.

The metaphysical choices are then the following:

(1) All historical actions are a result of a transcendental will (this is the idealistic position);
(2) Only those actions at points of civilizational crises are transcendental actions (fall of virtue, dharma, righteousness). This is the view that God begins history, then disappears, but reappears in a variety of forms when things get worse. God reappears because of His omniscient knowledge or because of the call of the masses, their heightened suffering;

(3) Real history occurs despite one's own apparent free will. There is a deeper agency happening behind one's back, or in other words, all actions appear to be done by humans, but God uses humans to bring about the larger will of God (Hegel);

(4) History occurs through the individual leader or through the family of leadership (Khaldun and Ssu-Ma Ch'ien). For a variety of reasons, the leader or group of leaders (family, dynasty) is more creative or conscious of the transcendental (Toynbee's creative minority). The leader is thus somehow more in touch, harmonious, or reflective of the real than others;

(5) History acts not through a religious transcendent nor through royalty, but through the magic of the marketplace, through the natural and rational meeting of the needs of various individuals (Smith);

(6) History acts through the most developed State or the most developed empire (Hegel or Marx) or through the contending/rising States (the post-colonial Third World for Shri Aurobindo);

(7) History acts through world figures (Hegel), the Great woman or man (either as sages, kings, capitalists, warriors, or other configurations);

(8) Historical acts can be understood through natural physical and social laws. These laws can be eternal, epoch contingent, or derivative from previous laws: linear, dialectical, idealistic, materialistic or dualistic. The transcendent can be understood through patterns, its material traces, and what is empirically intelligible. A corollary of this view is that history, or the future, can be understood specifically through intellectuals;

(9) History moves through the image of the future, the ideal state that draws and attracts people to act (Polak);

(10) History occurs through the call of the divine or the attraction of the Great (as with Teilhard de Chardin and Sarkar); and,

(11) History begins because of the Prime Mover. But the Prime Mover is a mystery even though it provides a teleological purpose to evolution moving man to perfection (Spencer).

Foucault and the Real

Prior to deciding how the real speaks, one must decide what the real in fact is. Is the real "physical" or "spiritual, or is it both. In his *The Order of Things* and *Archeology of Knowledge*, Foucault gives us not the traditional continuities of grand theory, rather he moves outside of this frame and gives us ruptures, breaks in history, in which the very way in which things are known changes. Thus, history is not problematically placed within a politics of the natural and the real wherein epistemological possibilities and the problem of intelligibility take precedence. Thomas Kuhn writing from an apolitical history of science perspective develops the same notion but believes that the transitions from one historical era to the other occur rationally through varied community of intellectuals (Shapiro, 1981). That is science and history are contextual, but the changing context is still rationally derivative. Apolitical. For Foucault this transition in the constitution of knowledge is political in the sense that the naming of something as truth is a political utterance. His history then becomes a history of ways of knowing, epistemes. Speaking of traditional macrohistory, Foucault writes:

> For many years now historians have preferred to turn their attention to long periods, as if, beneath the shifts and changes of political events, they were trying to reveal the stable, almost indestructible system of checks and balances, the irreversible processes, the constant readjustments, the underlying forces that gather force, and are then suddenly reversed after centuries of continuity. (Foucault, 1972, 3)

But this history of continuity has been replaced by epistemological acts and thresholds. Here the notion of order, of "man," of the "natural" undergo fundamental changes. These epistemological thresholds:

> suspend the continuous accumulation of knowledge, interrupt its slow development, and force it to enter a new time, cut it off from its empirical origin and its original motivations, cleanse it of its imaginary complicities; they direct historical analysis away from the search for silent beginnings, and the never-ending tracing-back to the original precursors . . . (Foucault, 1972, 4).

Once history ceases to be a continuous flow of knowledge, where the present is ordered differently from the past in that knowledge of the past often merely gives us a shadow of the present, historiography is made irrevocably contentious. Interpretive. Thus, all that is left is to examine the cost of various interpretations and as well to demarcate, when possible, the ordering of order. Thus:

> the great problem presented . . . is not how continuities are established [the linking of dynasties, the analysis of the variables that lead from

one era to the next] how a single pattern is formed and preserved
[Sorokin's super rhythm, for example] . . . the problem is no longer of
tradition, of tracing a line, but one of division, of limits; it is no longer
one of lasting foundations [virtue as for Chinese historiography, for
example, again] but one of transformations that serve as new foundations, the rebuilding of foundations (5)

This is then the search not for a new grand theory based on a concrete eternal, but a theory that contests the ground of knowledge
itself. Thus Foucault, unlike Sarkar, is not seeking to discern the
true. Rather,

> . . . it is a discourse about discourses, but it is not trying to find in
> them a hidden law, a concealed origin, that it only demands to free;
> not is it trying to establish by itself, taking itself as a starting point,
> the general theory of which they would be the concrete models. It is
> trying to deploy dispersion that can never be reduced to a single sys-
> tem of differences, a scattering that is not related to a single system
> of differences, a scattering that is not related to the absolute axes of
> reference; it is trying to operate a decentering that leaves no privilege
> to any center (205).

Of course, as Foucault decenters, he creates an intellectual discourse.
This is the type of decentering one would expect at the end of a
Vaeshyan era, one that would not survive the disciplined and ordered
Ksattriyan era to be, in Sarkar's terms. But Foucault's intellectual
discourse is not traditional since he takes reason and turns it back
on itself—he limits reason making it one way of knowing among
many. In this way, Foucault is similar to the Indian. The yogi does
this as well. The mind is watched and that which is watching is
watched as well until there is a breakthrough into an alternative discourse, into an alternative way of knowing. Reason and the real
become suspended only to return when the experience must be made
intelligible to the "self" (or at least the reasoning self) and to the
other. But here the yogi, Sarkar and others, and Foucault part company. For Foucault:

> the role of such a discourse is not to dissipate oblivion, to rediscover,
> in the depths of things said, at the very place in which they are silent,
> the moment of their birth (whether this is seen as their empirical cre-
> ation, or the transcendental act which gives them origin) it does not
> set out to be a recollection of the original or a memory of the truth.
> On the contrary, its task is to make differences: to constitute them as
> objects, to analyze them, and to define their concept (205).

Thus we can see how although Sarkar and Foucault are comparable in their search for alternative ways of knowing, of their understanding of discourse, given Foucault's distance from the transcendental, we might expect their social theories to be radically different. For Foucault does not intend to create a new history or theory of history, rather

> ...the essential was to free the history of thought from its subjection to transcendence. For me, the problem was certainly not how to structuralize it, by applying to the development of knowledge or the genesis of the sciences categories that proved themselves in the domain of language (langue). My aim was to analyze this history, in the discontinuity that no teleology would reduce in advance; to map it in a dispersion that no pre-established horizon would embrace; to allow it to be deployed in an anonymity on which no transcendental constitution would impose the form of the subject; to open it up to a temporality that would not promise the return of any dawn. My aim was to cleanse it of all transcendental narcissism, it had to be freed from the circle of the lost origin and rediscovered where it was imprisoned; it had to be shown that the history of thought could not have this role of revealing the transcendental moment that rational mechanics has not possessed since Kant [in the Occidental perspective, that is] (203).

Thus Foucault's project, unlike the macro-thinkers we will preview, is *not* to take cultural totalities and impose them on history—"whether worldview, ideal types or the particular spirit of the age" (15). Rather he seeks to take a total history such as Marx's or Sarkar's or Sorokin's that seek to write on the face of history—the stages, the ideas logically related to a single axis (spirit, technology, dialectic)—and transform them into a series of dispersions. Said differently, Foucault's aim is to search for the spatial points of power that lie hidden in the larger grand theoretical project.

Paradoxically Foucault's epistemes can be seen as a grand theory, albeit one where the causal connections are purposefully not made so as to keep the theory disjunctive. Also paradoxically Foucault's epistemes resemble Sarkar's *varna*, although they use them in different ways and they arrive at them in different ways. This is most obvious in Foucault's *Discipline and Punish* and *The Birth of a Prison*. In these we see the ways in which humans have imprisoned change through history. Foucault traces the way that the rational has been defined as well as the types of punishment inflicted on those outside the rational have changed.

The control of the rational and control of punishment for Foucault is a demonstration of power. In Sarkar's Shudra era, there is no authoritative definition of power. There is no authoritative discourse save the biological, survival. Discourses to construct the real are forming. Eventually, the dominant discourse becomes that of the warrior. In the warrior era, the key was the Prince. The power of the King was inscribed on the body of victims. Given the biological discourse, it was the body that was central, not the mind or spirit. Through the might of the body, power was shown. By punishing the body, the King showed his power and thus order was kept. This is Sarkar's Ksattriyan era. Those that were considered insane, however were exiled for they had no obedience for the King, thus the exiled ship of fools. Rationality thus was defined as the willingness to obey. Once this was transgressed, humans were relegated outside of the newly formed civilization, they were thrown outside of the known discourse.

But in the Vipran era rationality and punishment underwent tremendous changes. In the Vipran era, the key sign was the priest, not the king or prince. Here punishment was limited to the confession. The transgressor had to admit to the truth. Thus the body was punished and tortured so that the soul could be saved. Thus the notion of the burning of the witch. There had to be a cleansing so that truth could persevere. There could be no exile since God's eyes were everywhere. Leaving the discourse as with the ship of fools would not solve the problem, there would be no confessional. God had been offended, the individual must repent. Truth was thus defined in terms of fidelity to God, in terms of good and bad. It is the moral discourse that characterizes the Vipran era.

In the Vaeshyan era, rationality is defined by work. Idleness is madness and to be controlled and modified. Prison was there to shape men into laborers. "As it was initially conceived, penal labor was an apprenticeship not so much in this or that trade as in the virtues of labor itself. [It was] pointless work, work for work's sake, was intended to shape individuals into the image of the ideal laborer" (Foucault, 1980a, 42). As one might expect, the prison was constructed in the image of the dominant understanding, it was to make man into a machine, to place him directly in the means of production.

Table 4: Foucault and Sarkar's Social Stages

	Rationality	Punishment
Shudra Era	No authoritative discourse	
Ksattriyan Era	Obedience	Body
Vipran Era	Moral discourse	Confessional
Vaeshyan Era	Idleness is madness	Work

While the above is a mere gloss, it does show some important similarities in the content of their thinking and adds a new dimension of research for Sarkar's students. The table asks questions as to how rationality is defined in each era and how those that step outside the bounds of the rational are punished. As Foucault has shown, rationality and the punishment that ensues changes dramatically from era to era.

Thus for Foucault the critical question is how is the real real, not why is the real real, and therefore what is the cost for the particular interpretation, constitution of the real. This in one sense continues the Marxian effort of asking how the real is used to dominate and control, but while Marx would uphold the material basis of society, Foucault would, if he is true to himself, not be willing to place the material above the spiritual, ontologically, that is. Khaldun's question then posed in this language would be how is the real used by dynasty to gain power and rise. His answer is that of *asabiya*. Sarkar, here more like Marx than Sorokin, begins not with the intellectual question of what is real, but rather with the question of the gaze. What is that which is immediately seen, the environment and how does one negotiate this reality: by being conquered by it; by conquering it; by understanding it; theorizing it and in many cases making it ultimately real or unreal; by using and investing it; and in the ideal *sadvipra* situation by using it in its proper balance. Now for Sarkar there is an underlying unity in these various ways of knowing, for Foucault, there is none, except insofar as they are different epistemes.

Foucault then adds a significantly tool for our analysis of macrohistory. This is the problem of the unit of analysis. For him the central unit is not the civilization, the culture, Being itself, a dynasty, a people, race, a world economy, a cultural ecology, a global ecology, the spirit, the individual, *but* the way that subjectivity, or knowing itself is constructed. For Toynbee, this was not problematic, the clear unit was the civilization; aborted and successful civilizations. The comparison between success and failure of a civilization led him to his theory. For Sorokin, the problem was finding a logical coherent unit, his was the supersystem with the logical unity of meaning, behavior and materials. Sorokin's question is how is the question of the real related to societies; it is a structural question, not problematized as to the role of author, text and interpreter, as Foucault would do. For Sarkar, it is the group mind and consciousness. For Voegelin the unit of history is Being and its self-interpretation. For Hegel, Being interpreting itself through the state and great figures. For Aurobindo, it is Being through the rising nation-states and the various enlightened ones. For many recent feminist thinkers, it is gender that is the key unit. Again the question of the unit of analysis is an effort to find the way in which history speaks to us is constructed. For Foucault, all the above are constructions that stabilize the self and do not contest the way in which the self itself is created by practices and discourse. Discourse not only limits the possibilities of the objective, but also creates the subject as well. Again, Sarkar's response to this entire Foucauldian exercise would be that Foucault is a predictable product of the end of the capitalist era: intellectual chaos. His thinking, however, is necessary for the reconstruction to come in the Ksattriyan era, in which the vaeshyan structure destroyed by the other classes is rebuilt.

Polak and Voegelin

Alternatively, Fred Polak, less focused on spilling tea and more on the elegance of the room, privileges the image of the future. To him, this is the key variable in social theory. What is the civilizational image of the future? Like Sorokin's construction, this serves to integrate society; it is the core. For Polak, there are a range of possible constructions. His ideal type has two elements—the eschatological and the utopian. According to his main interpreter and student, Elise Boulding, "The eschatological, or transcendent, is the element which enables the visionary to breach the bonds of the cultural present and mentally encompass the possibility of a totally other type of society, not dependent on what human beings are capable of realizing" (Boulding, 1971, 30). And, "the second element in the ideal type image of the future is humanistic utopian, or immanent element which designates men as co-partners with nature (or God) in the shaping of The Other in the Here-And-Now" (30). The ideal for Polak is the balance between the transcendental and the immanent, what Sorokin calls the idealistic, mixed type of society. For Sarkar this would the balance between materialism—capitalism and communism where only matter is real and brahmanism where only God is real). Both distort the real. Either God has been primary or man has been primary. To understand the tension between the spiritual and its presence in world history, Eric Voegelin is instructive. According to Voegelin, this has been the crisis of the West in the past few centuries, the misrepresentation of the eschaton of Christianity by Gnostics and the creation of a historical immanence that has lead to the positivistic movement (Comte), the communist (Marx and Lenin) and national socialist (Hitler) and the liberal (Smith and others). It was the reinterpretation of the trinity, Father, Son and Holy Spirit into ancient medieval and modern that is "led" to similar trine constructions as Comte, Marx, and Hitler. Western civilization has accentuated the material, immanent factor too far and has such been in the paradox of rising (technology and better material conditions) and falling (wars, colonialism, imperialism, moral decay) at the same time. The victory of immanence has been the death of the spirit (Voegelin, 1987, 131). For Voegelin this is what macrohistory is about. "Voegelin wants to understand history as men themselves participant in history have understood it" (McNight, 1978, 103). This is the interpretive perspective outlined by Vico, not the positivistic view desired by Comte.

> [Voegelin] is interested in the consciousness of particular men grappling with the problems of existence and with symbols they use to express their understanding of what it means to be human. The drama of humanity . . . consists in man's quest for the truth of order, a truth that has to be gained and regained in the perpetual struggle against the fall from it (McKnight, 1978, 103).

This theme we see in Sarkar, Ssu-Ma Ch'ien and other ancients as well as that of Sorokin. There is a rise and fall of truth or the fluctuation of systems of truth. For Voegelin the immanentization of history is cause of the decline of Western civilization. Immanentization leads to a position where history has a final epoch and where truth is certain. This is the view of positivists, Marxists, Nazis and liberals and is in opposition to the classic view of the uncertainty of the truth

of the world. History for Voegelin then is a spiritual decline. From
spiritual faith to enlightenment to humanism to secularism has been
the pattern of decline. The modern period can thus be characterized
as a belief in the end of the cycle, in the irreversibility of the path
of linear history and progress. From the spiritual view, the cycle ends
outside of history, in the transcendent. But with the immanentization of history, history now has a worldly end—liberal the end of
ideology, the communist state, the thousand year Reich. For Voegelin,

> The death of the spirit is the price of progress. Nietzsche revealed this
> mystery of the Western apocalypse when he announced that God was
> dead and that He had been murdered. The Gnostic murder is con-
> stantly committed by the men who sacrifice God to civilization. The
> more fervently all human energies are thrown into the great enterprise
> of salvation through world-immanent action, the farther the human
> beings who engage in this enterprise move away from the life of the
> spirit. And since the life of the spirit is the source of order in man
> and society, the very success of a Gnostic civilization is the cause of
> its decline (Voegelin, 1987, 131).

This to Sarkar is the cycle, the ancient principle that success in the
world leads to failure. Real progress is only possible at the level of
the spiritual, Sarkar's task is merely to make the spiritual view more
available to humanity by constructing structures wherein the needs
of the world: food and identity, can be met.

Galtung, however, with his emphasis on cosmology would assert
that Voegelin understand part of the macro picture, but is missing
a critical ingredient. It is not the bastardization of Christianity, but
the playing out of the Judaic-Christian cosmology that is the problem. It is a natural process. Part of the expansion and contraction
of the West. The expansion phase uses the Christian eschaton as it
structure: the workers of the world become the chosen few, Marx,
Lenin and (fill in your own) become the Father, Son and Holy Ghost.
All are inimical to nature, to females, and to the colonies. Voegelin's
contribution is showing the descent of the spirit into history and
matter from 12th century Joachim of Flora to Comte, to Hegel, to
Marx, and Hitler. It was Joachim who made the third stage, that
of the Holy Spirit, the final third realm. But while Joachim of Flora
saw this as a spiritual stage, eventually it entered the world. Suddenly
history had a finality, and thus humans could be sacrificed for this
finality.

Clearly, the balance Polak calls for between eschatology and immanence has, if achieved, been ultimately disastrous, for in the search for the final perfection of humans, the cycle of nature, and the very cycle of humanity itself has been forgotten. "Specifically, the Gnostic fallacy destroys the oldest wisdom of [hu]mankind concerning the rhythm of growth and decay which is the fate of all things under the sun . . . To every thing there is a season, And a time to every purpose under heaven: A time to be born and a time to die" (Voegelin, 1987, 166).

But for Polak, Voegelin's view is only one view. There are others that have been historically used. He distills five major orientations towards the Other.

(1) Life cannot be purely transitory: there must be something more enduring. Man hopes for future grace.
(2) Life cannot simply end in imperfection. There must be an Other realm which man can enter.
(3) Life should not be transitory and imperfect. Man rebels out of despair, but without hope.
(4) Life is not as it appears to be. This world is an illusion and the essential reality is veiled from man
(5) Life does not have to be the way it is. Man can reform and recreate the world after any image he chooses (Polak, 1973, 2).

This as we will see is a less elegant model of Sorokin's ideational, idealistic, sensate (and types of skepticism which cannot serve to integrate society). But Sarkar is not captured by Polak's five orientations and Boulding's four imaging patterns. The world is perfect *and* it must be reformed by man *and* it is transitory and there is future grace or transcendence. While the Indian episteme might favor one of these orientations, Vedanta, in particular opts for the fourth. Moreover, Sarkar moves from Polak's first image to the fifth, mixing the transcendental and human agency and provides a metaphysic (as with Chardin) wherein humans become co-creators with the force of Life. Also difficult to classify is the perspective Chang Hsueh-Cheng and Ssu-Ma Ch'ien arguing from the Chinese perspective show that the sage can do what is natural, what is balanced and allow the tao to work with and through him. Nonetheless it is a useful typology, albeit phrased in Western language, to keep in mind as we review the different macro-thinkers.

From this typology, Boulding develops four historical imaging patterns.

(1) Essence optimism combined with influence optimism. The world is good and man can make it better.
(2) Essence optimism combined with influence pessimism. The world is good but it goes of itself and man cannot alter the course of events.
(3) Essence pessimism combined with influence optimism. The world is bad but man can make it better.
(4) Essence pessimism combined with influence pessimism. The world is bad and there isn't a damn thing man can do about it (Boulding, 1971, 31).

While useful this does not completely capture the perspective of Sarkar and indeed other macro-thinkers. The world can be neither good nor bad and there can be divinity and choice, and there are different levels in which one can speak to this. The Indian episteme, especially the richness of Jain epistemology, allows various both/and choices at the individual level, and as Sorokin would advice, there are stages of history where there are mixed societies in which the real is seen as both material/spiritual; fixed and changeable; wherein optimism and pessimism can both exist. Nonetheless, Polak and Boulding provide us with analytic tools for a better understanding Sarkar. What Polak does add of great significance is the notion of the image of the future to the perspective of macrohistory. The society with a rich image of the future rises, without a vision of the future then the civilization declines, argues Polak.

Cognizant of the image of the future, the pattern becomes then not only an effort in which one can then predict tomorrow but create as well the possible society or the possible person, or find a way in which the individual and/or collective can harmoniously move with the discovered pattern. For the modern systems approach Lazslo prefers, once the pattern is found, the very act of discovery allows for agency, and a change in the pattern. Enhanced information changes the balance of the choice/structure equation. *For cyclical theorists, the only advantage information can give is humility in the face of the cycle of dynasty, ecology, virtue, dharma, asabiya or spirit.* Sarkar, however, makes the division within his cycle of innovation and exploitation. With ideal leadership the cycle can be maneuvered but as it is fixed (either as a law, or as Sheldrake would argue a morphogenetic field) it can not be changed.

The above has been an introduction to macrohistory and macro-thinking with glosses of various macrohistorians and their thinking, especially recent thinkers such as Foucault, Voegelin and Polak. Now that we have opened with the present we will return to the past.

We will now as promised earlier begin the dinner tea party. The first course will be a meeting of the thinking of Sarkar and two exemplary examples of Chinese thinking chosen for their cyclical theory and their reading of the spiritual.

Ssu-Ma Ch'ien and Chang Hsueh-Cheng: Virtue and the Tao

Ssu-Ma Ch'ien (145–90? B.C.) is considered the grand historian of China. His still classic work, the *Shih chi* or *Records of the Historian* is an attempt to place history in a philosophical narrative consistent with Chinese way of knowing. As with Sarkar, Khaldun and other macro-thinkers, Ssu-Ma Ch'ien aimed to "examine the deeds and events of the past and investigate the principles behind their successes and failures, their rise and decay" (Watson, 1958, viii).

In this section we summarize his thinking, bringing other Chinese philosophers, particularly Chang Hsueh-Cheng and then compare and contrast the Chinese macrohistorical perspective with Sarkar's.

As with Indian macrohistory where the past be exorcised, the Chinese historian must deal with problem of historical order in China's long past. Every writer must place himself next to Confucius, he must take or reject (or a mixture of both) the Confucian worldview. Every Chinese philosopher must deal with the basic data of Chinese history and thought: the dynasties, the great men, and the tao.

Ssu-Ma Ch'ien takes the Confucian ethic of virtue, morality, respect for family and authority and uses it as a guiding principle for his historiography. But while he adopts the above principles, he leaves Confucius' linear evolutionary theoretical structure. For Confucius, the first stage was *Disorderly*: "with its anarchy, continuous warfare, primitive conditions, lack of efficient social control" (Sorokin, 1970, 375). The next stage was of *Small Tranquility*, characterized by the institutions of family private property, egotism, social instability (375). The third stage was that of *Great Similarity* "marked by social order, almost common property, mutual benevolence, and reverence" (375).

However, while he disagreed with the Confucius' general theory, keeping in the Confucian spirit, he believed that history was not simply to record, but to teach the sovereign, to raise the level of morality of the people. As Burton Watson writes of Chinese historiography generally and the *Shi Chi* in particular: "History is a mirror of mankind in which the reader may look at the men of the past and observe their fortunes and misfortunes, and from this observation come to understand the fortunes of his own age" (Watson, 1958, 137).

As with other classical writers, the Chinese historian did not attempt to write an objective science of history nor was this considered possible. The author's personality was part of the historical effort, even if laws were found, there was no attempt at disinterest, rather history was through and through involved and thus normative. Sarkar, writing from the Indian episteme, continues this process. He too writes his history based on what has gone before. Both must speak to past schools of Chinese and Indian thought respectively. The ancients must be honored and spoken to and from.

Ssu-Ma Ch'ien particular saw himself in a lineage of historical writers. The writer properly instructed could recreate the world. Ssu-ma Tan, Ssu-Ma Ch'ien's father, for example believed—changing Mencius theory that every five hundred years a true sovereign would arise—that a new writer could arise as well to change Chinese history. First was Confucius, then the Duke of Chou, and now five hundred years after, perhaps it would be Ssu-Ma Ch'ien, hoped the father. The Indian awaits for the *avatar*, the bodhisattva or Sarkar's *sadvipras*, but the Chinese awaits either for the just monarch or the learned scholar to bring virtue and tao back to society. Clearly this is an alternative model of the cycle of the universe, of leadership and of balance, with greatly different political implications than those of the West, there either one waits for Jesus or for Godot.

Ssu-Ma Ch'ien like Confucius and other Chinese philosophers operates from the cosmological episteme (Voegelin language) or the classic Indian episteme. As above, as below. There is a unity of discourse wherein what happens in the cosmos, occurs in the natural physical world, and develops in society as well. Within and without. The sage can discern these fundamental patterns thus allowing humans to live in harmony with the natural. But the natural in this view is not always in balance, there is a disharmony as well, which must constantly be righted. This is the Chinese Yin and Yang or Sarkar's *vidya* and *avidya*. This is the principle of dialectics wherein there is a unity of opposites. Central to the classical view is the notion of the transformation of quantity to quality. Once there is order then a new relationship can emerge in society. With order (people thinking together, children and females knowing their place, and subjects and rulers following theirs') a new level of existence is possible. This principle is also applicable to the mind. Once the mind's thoughts are ordered, a new self can emerge. With concentration, personal transformation is possible. Without this ordering, one remains at a primitive level of mind. Or in Taoist thought with ordering, a non-self can emerge and by doing nothing (in terms of the reference of the old self in which there is strife and disorder), everything can be done.

This classical worldview has become current through present interpretations such as Fritjof Capra's *The Turning Point* use this principle to explicate the coming global transformation from *yang* values (expansion, sensate, male, industrial) to *yin* values (cooperative, spiritual, female, and post-industrial). For our purposes, the key comparative link is with vidya/avidya and yin/yang; both operate from similar spiritual ways of knowing. For Sorokin, as we develop further, this is the cycle of Ideational and Sensate and for Galtung, expansion and contraction.

Theory of History

The context then for Ssu-Ma Ch'ien's theory is the Confucian focus on virtue, the classic cosmological episteme, and the dynasty as the holder of virtue. For Ssu-Ma Ch'ien, as well, it is the function of the historian to prolong goodness by preserving its record, for good endures and evil destroys the doer.

Moreover, unlike Western thought, ancient Chinese thought did not recognize a datable beginning to human history. Their conception of time [like Indian time] is astronomical; time is a series of cycles based upon the movements of the planets and stars, the heavenly governors as the Chinese call them, and such cycles may presumably be conceived as extending indefinitely into the past or the future. The dates, then, of human history are recorded in terms of the years of rulers, who are the mortal counterparts of the Heavenly Governors (Watson, 1958, 4–5).

In the Indian condition, the dates are assigned by the Vedas. In Islamic history by the Hegira; in Christian history by the birth of Christ. Western history is dramatic, there is a particular event from which time begins or that the new world begins. History that is based on the stars can never have any real beginning or end, for the stars continue moving, forward and backward. But Indian history has both timelessness and time, there is the time of the cosmos and the time began by a dramatic event, the birth of the transcendental in the plane of the world. For Sarkar's students, this is, for example, the beginning of Ananda Yuga, the era of bliss.

What is the pattern of history for Ssu-Ma Ch'ien? While Khaldun looks to the strength of the Bedouins as the beginning to new dynasties and Sarkar looks for a unifying or negative distancing sentiment (the image of the enemy outside) in the context of the Ksattriyan era, central to Ssu-Ma Ch'ien is the belief that each dynasty begins with a sage king of superlative wisdom and virtue (Yu of the Hsia and Ch'eng T'ang of the Yin) and each dynasty closes with an unspeakable evil and degenerate monarch (Chieh of the Hsia and Chou of the Yin). *Between the good and evil are just a list of names of rulers* (5). The unit of history is thus morality, the universe has a moral structure that ultimately prevails.

This cycle then begins again when a new sage overthrows the tyrant and a new house is set up. But the pattern is not always so simple. According to Watson, it is "varied in the middle, as in the case of the Yin dynasty, by the appearance of worthy rulers who restore for a time the original virtue of the dynasty in an act called revival or restoration" (6).

This pattern as with other classical writers is no more than the reflection of basic and most fundamental observation of life—that things come into being, then grow, reach a peak, and then they in various formulas decline, until they die. All heaven and earth are characterized by this waxing and waning.

Ssu-Ma Ch'ien's task as he saw it was simply to arrange the accounts of the early dynasties and feudal states in such a way that this pattern of growth and decay could be most readily perceived. He reinterpreted history so as to make it easier to follow virtue. Thus the natural was ordered, good history made this order more intelligible.

While Khaldun uses unity/solidarity (the dynasty that stays united and does not indulge in luxury but remembers its nomadic existence stays in power), Ssu-Ma Ch'ien uses the concept of merit. As Burton writes:

An integral part of his accepted pattern of the virtuous founder and the evil terminator of a ruling family is the very old concept of *te* or merit. *Te* in this case has more than its later meaning of virtue, imply rather a kind of mystical store of power set up by the sage ancestor of the family. This power, or achievement, *kung*, or blessing, *tse*, flows from the ancestor down through his heirs, bestowing up upon them in turn power and good fortune in their rule. But like all others things of creation, this ancient deposit of merit is subject to the law of decay. As the years pass, the power wears thin and the succeeding rulers sink lower and lower into evil and incompetence. As the Chinese historian describes it, the power or the "way" (the Tao) of the ruling family declines. At this point it is still possible for a ruler, by applying himself to the practice of wise and virtuous government, to restore the waning power of the family. But if no ruler appears who will undertake thus to replenish the original store of power and merit, the reservoir will eventually run dry and the family will be destroyed by other families who are ascending in the cycle of power (7).

There are thus two central aspects to his theory. The first is the pattern of rise and fall, growth and decay, waxing and waning. This is imposed on the moral order and thus there is the pattern of the rise and fall of virtue. For Sorokin interpreting Chinese macro-thinking, this is "parallel with this cycle of a dynasty, [is that] the people are virtuous and happy when the dynasty is rising and attaining its zenith; and they become violent and degenerated when it declines. And so does the whole cultural . . . life" (Sorokin, 1970, 375). Instead of yin and yang, Ssu-Ma Ch'ien remembering Confucius, uses *chih* and *wen* or solid qualities and refinements.

Next each dynasty can be understood by its moral characteristic. Good faith for the Hsia, piety for the Shang and refinement for Chou. As each dynasty declined its virtue transformed into a fault. Good faith became rusticity. Piety becomes its opposite of superstition. And refinement turns into hollow show. The natural becomes unnatural, and the harmonious becomes out of balance. But why does it decline? And why does it rise up again? This is intrinsic to the model: it declines and rises because that is the nature of men, of nature, and of the cosmos itself. The learned sage has discovered this nature by watching the self, men and women, and the natural world.

As for Sarkar, transformation is possible. Ssu-Ma Ch'ien articulates four ways to restore virtue when it is in decline. But Ssu-Ma Ch'ien does not believe in a return to an ancient golden past. This

school of Chinese thought he rejected. The role of the scholar was
to advise the government (as Ssu-Ma Ch'ien did, he was a secretary
of the emperor).

> History to him was a constant process of growth and it was impossi-
> ble to think of returning to some static golden age of the past. What
> was possible, however, was the creation of a new golden age in the
> present by a wise application of the moral values appropriate to the
> times. (Watson, 1958, 143)

Indeed, Ssu-Ma Ch'ien believed that the future could best be created
by learning from dynasties that were troubled not by the golden ages
of the past. It is in disharmony that learning comes about. For Sarkar
this is rephrased as struggle leads to individual and societal growth.

Now as we can see there are some fundamental similarities between Sarkar and Ssu-Ma Ch'ien. Both use the cycle, the notion of
virtue, speak from the classic episteme (although Sarkar writing in
this century has access to various historical epistemes). Sarkar and
Ssu-Ma Ch'ien are also similar in the emphasis on the sage-king in
starting dynasties. For Sarkar this is the perceptor needed to start a
new ideology.

But the differences are enormous as well. Sarkar's history is not
solely dynastic. To him there is a dynastic period and there are intellectual periods. In the Chinese Vipran era real power was in the
hands of the Confucianists (and others) who emphasized merit and
scholarship not might and the divine mandate of heaven.

Rethinking Chinese History

How might Chinese history look when it is reinterpreted from Sarkar's
view? Using Batra's approach one could reorganize Chinese history
with many cycles. The fall of the Chin and the rise of the Han (who
were of a lowly class, shudras) would be a ksattriyan revolution. This
is followed by the establishment of Confucianism (the Vipran era),
and then the consequent rise of the merchant class, which the vipran
Confucianists thought little of. An example, illustrative of this division between intellectuals and merchants:

> In the later Han most of the official posts were filled by men who
> had secured their jobs on the basis of scholastic achievement. The pur-
> suit of learning, particularly Confucian learning, became the concern
> of all members of the upper class; even emperors and empresses were

students of the Classics. The merchant class, that had begun to be powerful an important in the early Han, was degraded to the position almost of social pariahs and the ... literati class became the unchallenged leaders of society (Watson, 1958, 37).

Continuing our gloss of Chinese history, the merchant era is followed by the Mongols who create another ksattriyan era. Eventually the British would come in bringing on a Vipran and then a capitalist era. Maoism is then another ksattriyan era. The stage is set for a new Vipran era with a strong democratic/spiritual/intellectual oriented one. Sarkar, of course, would see one long cycle with Buddhism and Confucian influences representing vipra eras. Batra would see many cycles with the expansion/political centralization being peak Ksattriyan eras. In this model, the rise of the merchant class or the external economic imperialists, as with the British, represent vaeshyan eras. Sarkar's four class division provides a highly useful tool in understanding past and present of China; among other things the distaste of the ksattriyan communists of the intellectuals can be seen in a proper historical perspective. Communism from Sarkar's position then becomes part of the social cycle; a natural part of China's history, not an extra-historical event, although its ideological strength in terms of Sarkar's factors in his theory of civilizations needed for a healthy civilization is great. Communism, for example, has a leader, text, socio-economic theory, and to some degree a social outlook (although this is not universal enough), but it is missing spiritual practices and spiritual ideology. Thus it will over emphasize the material world and eventually decline.

Alternatively, Mark Elvin (1973) argues that China's past is divided into three phases: early empire, middle empire and later empire. Appropriately his beginning chapter title captures the thesis of his work: "The Formation of the World's Largest Enduring State." In Sarkar's language, ksattriyan from the beginning to end. Finally, Chang Xie (Galtung and Inayatullah, 1997) uses Ssu-Ma Ch'ien's cycle of good faith-piety-refinement to argue that the next stage in China's future will be one of refinement. Using Ssu-Ma Ch'ien's basic model, we could also argue that the Maoist dynasty has now become its opposite. Its piety (the meeting of basic needs, cultural pride and unity) has now transformed into evil and thus the dynasty will end or a new sage ruler will lead it to its next era. Sarkar would assert that the next revolution will be lead by a sage/intellectual of sorts. The Ksattriyan era is in its final days.

Unlike Sarkar, Ssu-Ma Ch'ien does not resort to Gods (Shiva or
Krishna) or the spiritual in his theory of history. There is no transcendence. This is not a theory of the tao in history. Humans create history: man is the proper study of history, not the spirit. The
sage does not play a direct role of an epoch as with Sarkar, although
Sarkar uses the sage-king notion to develop his concept of the sadvipra, but Ssu-Ma Ch'ien's sage-king is closer to Plato's philosopher-
king than Sarkar's spiritually transformed revolutionary.

The Role of the Tao

In contrast is the historiography of Chang Hsueh-Cheng who adds
a spiritual dimension to Chinese history. Specifically he asks the question as to the role of the tao in Chinese history.

Chang Hsueh-cheng (1738–1801) wrote during the second half of
the eighteenth century during the Manchu dynasty. From Sarkar's
view, the Manchu dynasty can be seen as a ksattriyan attempt at
unification after the factional strife of the peasant rebellions of the
Ming era. Alternatively, for Toynbee, the Manchu dynasty can be
seen as the universal state that emerged once Chinese civilization
underwent various crises.

The influence of the Manchu era led Chang to hold the ideal of
the powerful state in high regard. Much of his reading of the tao
in history is its relationship to the state. The crux of Chang's theory is that when government is separated from learning than the tao
disintegrates. As Li Kuang-Ti (1642–1718) had argued, "the tao and
government had been united in the persons of sage-rulers; later, with
Confucius and Chu Hsi, Heaven entrusted the tao to sages outside
the state" (Nivison, 1966, 18). And in reference to the Manchu government, "the government and tao [are] again [to] be united, for
now knowledge and action, government and learning, were again
one" (18). There is thus a unified order, without factionalism, in
which the tao is whole again.

This search for a strong state and the tao's location in it can be
seen as the classic Confucian utopian vision.

> This utopian vision saw human society as the perfect family, where
> each member would play his part without enticement and pressures
> to advancement, where 'men's minds would be composed' in their
> quest for virtue, where there would be 'no corruption of empty works,'
> where none would be subject to extravagance of speech and compo-

sition, and none would 'strive for honor and advantage.' This ideal envisioned society as a harmonious organic unity (67).

From the liberal Western view, this is implicitly authoritarian for truth comes through competing interest, not the through the wisdom of hierarchy, respect and order.

We find this notion of society as a family in Sarkar's thinking as well, although he uses the concept for a theory of distributive justice, nonetheless the similarity is significant.

> Society is like a company of pedestrians going on a pilgrimage. Suppose one among them is attacked by cholera, do the rest go on their way, leaving him behind? No, they cannot. Rather, they break their journey at the place for a day or two, relieve him from the disease and help him to acquire strength in his legs. Or, the start out anew, carrying him on their shoulders. If anyone runs short of his subsistence, others give him their own. Together, they share everything with all. Together, they stream ahead, singing their leading chorus. In their eagerness to go ahead with others, they forget their trifling differences which in their families might have led to negative exchanges and court cases, even down to three generations . . . society is like . . . a batch of pilgrims gathering a strange power of mind in traveling together and with its help, solving all the problems of their individual and social life (Sarkar, 1978b, 2:114).

The essence of Chang's work is his writing on the tao: its rise, integration and disintegration. Like most historiography, Chang looks for that which is eternal in human history. For him, it is the *tao*. When man came into being, the tao existed in man himself, but he was unaware of it. "The tao began 'taking form' in human history with the first human family and continued as population increased and human society became more and more complex" (Nivison, 1966, 140). For Chang, according to Nivison, "the tao is therefore the basic potential in human nature for living an ordered, civilized life, a potential that gradually writes its self out in history and actualized itself in what man must come to regard as right and true. That tao is thus seen in human moral order" (141).

The tao lies embedded in and behind the historical process. It is the why behind events and processes. But Chang is practical. The tao is not the possibilities of what could be. It is not an *ought* condition. The tao is understood in its evolutionary process. The tao is distinct from matter and they are inseparable. This is similar to Sarkar's concept of Consciousness and energy, distinct but inseparable. However for the Indian Sarkar, consciousness can be known

by the god-man, by the enlightened one, while for Chang there is
no such being, rather the tao is seen from the natural unconscious
actions of ordinary persons. *Thus, the sage knows the tao, not because of
devotion, but because he watches the ordinary people.*

This tao becomes expressed through the meeting of historical needs.
As needs arise, they are met. But common people meet these needs
blindly. They do not know what they are doing. The sage, however,
by watching the yin and yang, the ebb and flow, of every day life
can see the workings of the tao, and thus can respond and create
appropriate institutions and laws. Thus, there is choice but there is
also structure. The actions of the sage are modified by the particular historical conditions. The evolving problem of man's life and the
accumulation of solutions from sage to sage is the tao taking form.
Is this Toynbee's evolutionary principle of challenge-response? Or is
it similar to Sarkar's physical and mental clash?

But the tao and the sage are not the same. Again, according to
Nivison's interpretation of Chang:

> The tao is so of itself, and the sage must do as he does. Are these
> things the same? They are not. The tao does nothing and is so of
> itself. The sage see what he sees and must do as he does. One may,
> therefore, say that the sage takes the part of the tao; but one may not
> say that the sage and the tao are substantially the same (145).

Thus, while in the Indian episteme, there is a unity of consciousness between individual and collective souls such that a person can
become the ideal, in Chinese and Chang's thought that distinction
cannot be broached.

The tao also does not function in an Hegelian sense either. There
is no historical cunning that uses great men to advance the cause
of history. For Chang, the sage takes the part of the tao, but they
are its free agents, not its unwitting pawns.

Unlike the Hindu context in which Brahman descends on humans,
"the tao does not incarnate in a sage" (145). The sage's actions are
limited by the historical conditions. The sage's creations are not eternally valid, nor are his utterances the tao itself. Again this differs
from Indian philosophical thought, in which the words of the guru
are the words of Brahma himself. But while history can be understood from the meeting of needs, needs quickly become desires. This
for Chang and others is when the tao is lost, as the critical distinction is between the natural and desirous. In the natural, the tao
thrives, government is good, and people are virtuous. In the desirous,

the tao disintegrates, government factionalizes, and people do not follow the classics. There is disharmony.

Confucius transmitted the tao by keeping alive the wisdom of the ancient kings. In doing so he

> simply considered that the tao of the ancient sages and kings cannot be seen and the Classics are just the material embodiment of this tao which can be seen. The classics then are not books that expound the tao but the matter (chi) that exhibits it, for the tao can no more be abstracted from the material world than a shadow can be separated from the shape that casts it (151).

Thus, while consciousness for Sarkar exists independent of matter, except in the absolute sense in which consciousness is but an aspect of matter, for the Chinese it is through matter that the tao can be understood. The unity of discourse is not found in the unity of the atman-brahman relationship but in the relationship of the tao to the material world. The tao is seen in rivers and mountains, not in the complex psychological states of Tantra and Buddhism.

Contrast this to the Western notion of the Divine which exists outside of time, space and individual. Chang's tao is Sarkar's Saguna Brahma (God in the world); however, at the same time Sarkar has a Nirguna Brahma (God outside the world, the formlessness from which form emerges). Chang by placing the tao in the world (as an evolutionary principle of sorts) misses this dimension. But this is not endemic of Taoism for the tao that can be spoken is not the real tao, that is, the real tao exists outside of discourse, outside of the world. Chang, however, does not use this prediscursive tao.

The Tao thus acts in history. It acts through the sage. The climax of this tao in history was the Chou state (1122 B.C.). The Duke of Chou was the last sage ruler, or in Sarkarian language, it was rule of the spiritual led viprans. Later, the tao disintegrated as philosophical states factionalized and each sought to hegemonize ideas. Each attempted to appropriate the Tao. With the intellectualization of the tao the unity of heaven, state, family is broken. "As different paths of thought more and more divide, the tao is more and more lost sight of" (152). For Sarkar, this is the beginning of dogma, wherein spirituality is appropriated at the loss of the personal experience of consciousness or in Maoist terms where what remains is the chatter of intellectuals, the valueless passing of gas.

The difference between Chang and, for example, Hegel (who too uses God in history) is that Chang's tao does nothing, needs nothing, in no sense uses humankind to realize itself (292). In this way, the tao is transcendental but evolutionary. It serves as an evolutionary principle, but also a guiding ethical principle, similar to Sarkar's *prakrti* or the active doing dimension of consciousness. Chang's contribution is the articulation of a guiding principle that does not slip into an appropriation of power.

Now Chang too has a cyclical dimension to this theory, and insofar as he is dominated by the vipran worldview, this cycle has three phases: philology, literary art and philosophical speculation. The pattern of learning, artistic talent and understanding continue endlessly through history with the breakdown of philosophical speculation then leads to philology again. Different humans become attracted to different types of works. At the collective level, each dynasty expresses each type of learning.

Chang's tao begins unified and then as the state (governance) and learning are separated, that is, as the role of the sage diminishes, the tao disintegrates. But unlike the Indian stage of the degeneration of Brahman, from satya to kali, from gold to iron, for Chang, this is a degeneration of unity and virtue. The role of the intellectual is to restore this balance for through the sage the tao can take form. The writer must not allow any tendency to become imbalanced (the Chinese ancient version of the modern checks and balances system of governance). Like Sarkar, and unlike Hegel, and unlike linear, evolutionary theorists, the "present" then is not the ideal state, but a state of imbalance that must be restored. For Chang this is through the understanding of the tao (by the sage); for Sarkar, this is through spiritual realization and selfless service to humanity. Both Chang and Sarkar, however, conclude, distancing themselves from Western democrats, that the unified state is ideal, for a centralized polity in touch with dharma or virtue can best keep the various fashions or tendencies (of intellectuals, merchants, warriors, barbarians, and others) from creating havoc.

Chang's effort then is to take ideational Taoism and place it in a sensate context, and thus develop a mixed system. By placing the tao within time and within specific dramatic events—the Chou dynasty, for example, he breaks from most Chinese thinking in which time is timeless. Like Sarkar, however, he finds historical events in which dharma or virtue reigns. Yet at the same time, both attempt to keep reality discursive, Chang reminding us that the tao cannot be spoken and Sarkar reminding us that consciousness cannot be expressed.

Both take a both and view of structure/agency; history and God. Both take a cyclical view of history, and both present the possibility for a new future, although this is more comprehensively developed in Sarkar.

Ssu-Ma Ch'ien and Chang Hsueh-Cheng are fundamentally similar to Sarkar in that they present cyclical theories. Ssu-Ma Ch'ien focuses on virtue, while Chang on the role of the tao in history. Sarkar argues that the ideal system is a centralized polity based on spiritual leadership. Ssu-Ma Ch'ien and Chang imagine an ideal polity is one where government and learning is unified and where the sage learns from the people. In Sarkar's language, they accentuate the vipran tendencies in society, but those of the exploiting vipras not the service oriented vipras. Indeed, Chinese history can be seen as alternating power between the warrior and intellectual classes. At present the struggle continues with China on the verge of the next phase of the social cycle; a phase which for Ssu-Ma Ch'ien and Chang is another one in the long cycle of history, hopefully one where virtue rises and the tao is unified in history.

How might Ssu-Ma Ch'ien and Chang respond to the grand cosmology of Sarkar? Our sense is that they would see his effort as continuing their project of understanding the reasons behind history so that virtue and goodness can rise and evil can be censured. They would be delighted by his use of the sage as a future model of leadership. Chang would stress that while the people look to the sage for advice, the sage finds the tao in the unconscious actions of the people. Likewise, they would find agreement in Sarkar's notion that the human adventure is ultimately about governing evolution, increasingly taking the functions of prakrti into the minds of humans. They would also, we believe, not object to Sarkar's division of humans into different classes, although they might be tempted to include the category of foreigner or people outside the varna. But given that these thinkers all emanate from the cosmological unified discourse, we should not be surprised at the similarity in thinking. All three has as their main project the return of harmony and balance to a world that has privileged expansionist materialism at the expense of natural mind and divine life or the life of the tao.

This next section will continue the comparison process but move from Chinese historiography to the thinker that exemplifies Islamic philosophical thinking. This is the work and life of Ibn Khaldun, who like Sarkar, is a cyclical theorist, spiritually inclined and who too wrote at the end of a major era. What follows then is an exegesis of Khaldun's theory of history and a comparison of Sarkar with it. Specifically we focus on Khaldun's concept of asabiya, the jewel of his thought. We will be more exhaustive with Khaldun than with other thinkers in that his model remains current (although it has now unconsciously translated in the language of the positive sciences).

Ibn Khaldun and Sarkar: The Main Course

Writing at a time of the disunity and the decline of the Islamic empire, the horrors of the plague and the conquests of the Mongol Tamerlane, Ibn Khaldun (732–802 A.H. or 1332–1406 A.D.) sought to understand the rise and fall of civilizations. Like Sarkar, and unusually for his time, Khaldun's theory of history is not merely descriptive, genealogical, nor in defense of a particular civilization— it does not seek to glorify Islam—rather Khaldun searches for the causes behind historical actions and movement. His is an attempt at a science of history. Like Sarkar, Khaldun distances himself from contemporary and historical thinkers of the time by rejecting the theory that history is a degeneration from a previous era of perfection. Khaldun also rejects the cyclical regression view of the ancients in which prophecy leads to caliphate, then to unjust kingship, then finally a return to prophecy. Sarkar appears, at one level, to use this classic model in his rise and fall of dharma model. Mencius, Ssu-Ma Ch'ien and others, as we have seen, used this model, although they did not define the routinization of charisma as declining from caliphate to kingship. Indeed, Toynbee in his classic study writes that because of the instability of the kingdom (the inability of the creative minority to respond appropriately to external and internal challenges), the kingship state can lead to a higher stability than that of caliphate or empire, which then as it becomes oppressive leads to the forming of a new church potentially the new universal church. Thus the Toynbee equation becomes civilization growing from various challenges, then leading to a universal state, and finally a universal church emerging from within. Obviously, an equation similar to the Ksattriya-Vipra transition in Sarkar's theory.

Now while Sarkar laments at the inequitable distribution of power in history and the writing of history, Khaldun laments at the banality of most historiography. To him, most history is simply about how "people settled the earth until they heard the call and their time was up" (Khaldun, 1967, 5). Khaldun's aim is to discover "[t]he inner meaning of history, [which] involves speculation and an attempt to get at the truth" (5). Specifically, it involves the "subtle explanation of the causes and origins of existing things, and deep knowledge of the how and why of events" (5).

As with other macrohistorians, the pattern of Khaldun's own life is critical in understanding his theory of change and his predictions for the future. Indeed, his own life is isomorphic to his historiography. Khaldun moves from political escapades, intrigues and efforts to maximize power to his own person, to efforts to play the role of learned advisor to kings and potential princes, and then finally to a distanced academic wherein he is not concerned with personality, nor with particular tribes and religions, but rather with the consistent forms or variables that stand behind them. With structure. Sarkar, of course, is far more purposeful in his career, being a student, serving in the army, serving in the railways, beginning a mystical school, transforming it into a spiritual organization, developing a theory of history and a theory of distribution, and then forming an organization to fulfill his entire civilizational program.

Khaldun, however, unlike Sarkar, does not develop a history of Being thus distancing himself from the prevalent theological discourses of the time. There is no separation as with Sarkar of devotional-mythic writing and critical historicism writing. Khaldun's is not the project of finding how Allah influences the course of history. God to him is a figure that stands in the background, providing inspiration and individual purpose, used in his text most often to begin a passage—"May God take care of us and of you . . . in the same way He takes care of those whom, as He knows in His prescience, He will make happy and guide a right" (206)—or as an after the fact explanation. It was Allah's will. God remains in the absolute. For Khaldun what is significant about God is that through religion, the sign of God, human can increase their unity or *asabiya* and thus provide the basis for their rise in power.

Personal History: The Rise and Fall of Families

Ibn Khaldun was born in Tunis on May 27, 1332. His family history was that of scholars and statesmen. The Ibn Khaldun family played an important part in the civil wars in Seville in the 9th century and help high posts in the subsequent Umayyad, Almoravid, and Almohad dynasties. In 1248 just before the fall of Seville and Cordoba, they moved to the northern coast of Morocco. Ibn Khuldun's father was an administrator and soldier eventually devoted himself to theology, law and letters. In 1349 the Black Death struck Tunis and took away both his father and his mother. This event was not lost on Khaldun. Ibn Khaldun's personal life followed the pattern set by his family. Khaldun spent time in government but by 1357 the Sultan Abu Inan suspected his loyalties and threw him in prison. Once the Abu Inan died, the wazir Al-Hassan ibn Umar reinstated him.

"The next eight or nine years, which saw much strife between the Merini and Hasfid dynasties in North-West Africa, were the most precarious in Ibn Khaldun's restless career. On the fall of Abu Abdallah, Ibn Khaldun raised a large force among the desert Arabs and entered the service of the Sultan of Tlemcen. A few years later he was taken prisoner . . ." (viii). Khaldun next entered a monastic establishment where he wrote the *Muqaddimah* finishing in 1377. He moved to Egypt where he served as judge and applied the idea of *asabiya* to Egyptian history. But the ups and downs of life did not end for subsequently his family died in a shipwreck in 1384.

It is not surprising then that he chose to write about the rise and fall of dynasties, their actual causes, and concluding that history follows a cyclical pattern. Making this similar point, Mushsin Mahdi has concluded that "[t]he picture of the Islamic world during the fourteenth century as depicted by Ibn Khaldun, and for the most part substantiated by other sources, on one of general decline and disintegration . . . Western North Africa, where Ibn Khaldun grew up and spent fifty years of his life before going to Egypt, was the worst part of the Islamic world in this respect. It presented him with a spectacle of chaos and desolation" (Mahdi, 1957, 26).

Sarkar too writes in what he perceives as one of the most desolate times for humanity: economic poverty, intellectual extravagance, and spiritual cynicism; a world dominated by the twin demons of capitalism and communism on one side and religious dogmatism in the form of non-universalism on the other side. While it is not the end of the Islamic world, it is certainly the end of the Western world, if not the entire world of modernity as we have known it in the last few hundred years. Sarkar too while not engaged in the politics of dynasties is involved in the present day version: the politics of social movements and their attempts to transform the discourse of power, from state power to community, individual and spiritual power. His has been a struggle with the Indian government, spending time in prison and like Khaldun finding his loved one distanced and finding his organization destroyed and then finally rebuilding it. We should not be too surprised at the numerous similarities in thought then, albeit Sarkar writes with the intellectual history of the past few centuries, and substantially develops the Khaldunian approach.

The Primitive-Civilization-Primitive Cycle

Khaldun begins his historiography with the state of nature. He finds two types of culture: that of the primitive and that of the civilized—the rural and city. They are near opposites of each other, with bravery, morality, unity, strong kinship ties, respect for parental authority describing the rural and cowardice, fragmentation, economic and social ties, individuality describing the city. But they are not unrelated, groups start as nomads and as they rise in wealth they construct or conquer cities, but in cities with increased economic activity and size new relationships emerge. This leads to a concentration on leisure and sensual pleasure which then leads to the breakdown of the city. Thus nomads are not genetically more pious, rather it is culture that emerges in a given environment which create the context for the different meanings and behaviors of city and nomadic life.

Asabiya begins with the ideal person in nature, the Bedouin nomad. "Man seeks first the bare necessities. Only after he has obtained [them] does the get to comforts and luxuries. The toughness of nomadic life precedes the softness of sedentary life" (Khaldun, 1967, 12). The Bedouins or Sarkar's ksattriyans are more courageous because they have to be. Living in the desert requires such behavior, while those in city resort to governmental laws and regulations and thus destroy their "fortitude and power of resistance" (95). Through environmental adversities, desert people develop increased solidarity. With compassion and the desire to protect those of the family, group feelings—asabiya—continues to grow and consolidate. However, inter-tribe conflict leads to numerous wars and anarchy.

> Once a superior solidarity emerges within a group, it tends to subdue lesser solidarities and bring them under its control. The result is a greater solidarity that unites the conflicting factions and directs their

efforts to fight and subdue other groups. This process of expansion
and unification continues until a point is reached when the newly
formed solidarity is able to conquer the dominions of a civilized state
or to establish new and cities and the institutions characteristic of a
civilized culture (Mahdi, 1957, 199).

The group with the strongest unity rules other groups. From kinship, kingship emerges. Kingship leads to the desire for more power
and the tribe expands its population and size, accumulating power,
riches and leisure. Kingship or Royal authority is considered a necessity so as to avoid groups fighting, to give social cohesion. Thus,
kings provide a superordinate authority. According to Khaldun, "he
[the king] must dominate them and have power and authority over
them, so that none of them will be able to attack another. This is
the meaning of royal authority" (Khaldun, 1967, 47). Besides kinship, religion provides asabiya. It creates new loyalties and a new
solidarity. Indeed, religion mixed with blood loyalty in the context
of just royal authority creates a formidable unity of mind and purpose, the ideal civilization.

For Sarkar, Khaldun accurately describes the shudra to ksattriyan
transition phase in human history and the rise and fall of ksattriyan
power. Unity is essential, but it can be developed not only from the
desert, but from being outside of the center. It can be in the shaman
as well (Nandy, 1989). For Sarkar, this asabiya can be developed in
the various social and spiritual movements, for they although existing in the city do not exist in the city of materialism and capitalism. Sarkar then would take Khaldun's desert/city differentiation and
treat it metaphorically. Elsewhere, William Irwin Thompson has
developed this tension as the central rhythm in history.

> When one believes in an alternative vision of history . . . he is stepping
> outside the city to see a pastoral vision in which the office building
> and the universities do not obscure the archaic stars . . . Those left
> behind in the city define themselves as responsible and sane and see
> the wanderer as a madman. The wanderer defines himself as the only
> sane person in a city of the insane and walks out in search of other
> possibilities. All history seems to pulse in this rhythm of urban views
> and pastoral visions (Thompson, 1971, 214–15).

Sarkar does not go that the far, within Tantra the process of wandering occurs in the mind irrespective of the city/rural distinction,
although certainly tantric monks reside in graveyards and thus develop
a vision of the world that hangs precariously on the edge of sanity.

But Khaldun uses the desert model to develop a collective identity through which power is appropriated, spiritual identity is not problematic for him, it exists within and through Islam.

Unity of Discourse: The Finite and Infinite

Like Sarkar, the episteme that Khaldun thinks from has a unified discursive field, although Khaldun given his Islamic influence places man at the center with nature below and God above. But what happens to the individual, happens to the group, happens to a city, and happens to a civilization. Individuals follow a birth, rise, adulthood and decline cycle as do dynasties, cities and civilizations. Only God stands above, but although everything is per his will, he does not privilege one group over another. Rather those groups that stay courageous, whose followers give leaders legitimacy, and who construct themselves as one people, last over time. Others find their fortunes in decay. When fortunes decay, those who have strongest group feelings, the primitives come back into control and power, thus continuing the cycle. In addition, Khaldun separates God and the world. Although individuals can attain various levels of spirituality, it is the tension embedded in choice that gives rise of the various alternative futures, not the will of the spirit. Said poetically and philosophically by Lenn Goodman:

> What answer then has Ibn Khaldun to the problem of values and of God in history? . . . the laws of human and social nature (if not those of human existence) bring men into conflict, cause them to overstep. In the dialectic of history each man in his society pursues what may seem good (and partly be such) which lead both to virtue and to vice (in a partial sort of way) and bring in their train, or rather contain, their own retribution and their own reward. For societies, as for individuals, crime and punishment, virtue and reward are inextricable from one another. . . . every empire or horde [must] live the life which is in its nature and die the death which of its nature (Goodman, 1972, 269–270).

But this finiteness is unacceptable to man. Man seeks to expand through "group feelings," through identification, in family, clan, dynasty and empire. While this is similar to the classic search for the Infinite, it has a structural basis in Khaldun theory for it covers all relations, it bonds. For Khaldun,

> The true answer to the problem of evil (and of failure) in history was
> to be found in the tragic finitude of men and all that they create, a
> finitude at once noble and degrading, which God in His wisdom and
> grace bestowed upon men and nations, allowing them to live and caus-
> ing them to die through a nature of their own. In the end it is God
> that is eternal (Goodman, 1972, 270).

In Khaldun's words:

> He is all powerful and nothing in heaven or on earth is impossible for
> Him or escapes Him. He raised us up from the Earth and gave us
> breath, let us live on earth as nations and tribes, gave us our portion
> and sustenance from the earth. The wombs of our mothers and our
> houses were our shelters. Food keeps us alive. Time wears us out, and
> our fate, which us been fixed in the Book, comes. But He endures.
> He lives and does not die (270).

Thus as with Sarkar, humans are rational and have choice. True at
the level of the absolute, only He endures, but this absolute does
not infringe on the world for Khaldun, and for Sarkar it only infringes
when righteousness has degenerated to a point wherein nothing can
be done by humans themselves. But again as we have suggested
Sarkar moves back and forth—with little attempt to resolve his various theories of history—between the language of the philosopher
and the language of the guru. There are times when only realizing
the infinite matters, but by and large, the purpose of his theories is
to construct a world wherein the infinite is made more accessible.
Human suffering is a result of a

> defective social order . . . this state of affairs cannot be allowed to con-
> tinue. The structure of inequality and injustice must be destroyed and
> powdered down for the collective interest of the human beings. Then
> and then alone, humans may be able to lead the society on the path
> of virtue. Without that only a handful of persons can possible attain
> the Supreme Perfection, but it would be extremely difficult to lead the
> whole community with quick speed to the Supreme Being (Sarkar,
> 1978b, 2:17).

For Khaldun, this state is possible with the Bedouins, in civilization
the external force eventually takes over and the dynasty declines.

Again this is quite different than the choices, for example, Hegel
constructs, epochs later. For Hegel, "world history exhibits the development of the consciousness of freedom on the part of the spirit,
and of the consequent realization of that freedom" (Walsh, 1960,
143). History in Hegel's view works behind the back of individuals,

that is, there is Providence and reason to all events. History is the spirit expressing itself (Manicus, 1987, 86–96). Moreover, this spirit expresses itself in world history through states. Thus history has a notion of progress, but it is a particular notion, one nested in the State. And every nation has a peculiar contribution which it is destined, in its turn, to make to the process of world history. Furthermore, this progress is facilitated by great individuals, the Napoleons. They are the chosen instruments of destiny. For Hegel, his Prussian State then was the will of the spirit, the finest expression of freedom.

Khaldun did not privilege a group because they were at the zenith of their civilization as the group chosen by God, although certainly he was partial to the earlier Islamic caliphate. But Khaldun's questions are not moral ones, nor does he try to construct a vision of an ideal tomorrow. He is a diplomat historian. Closer perhaps to Chinese grand historian Ssu-Ma Ch'ien.

Rise and Fall: Unification and Fragmentation

Khaldun's focus are the fundamental laws of history. Again, the central concept is group feeling, unity. The word literally means the fiber or sinew by which a group is held together. It is that which binds people into effective groups. Once this concept is understood, then we can understand history for the laws of group identity are the laws of history.

From a contemporary perspective, Joseph Campbell has similarly written in his *The Masks of God*:

> The rise and fall of civilizations in the long, broad course of history can be seen to have been largely a function of the integrity and cogency of their supporting cannons of myth, for not authority but aspiration is the motivator, builder and transformer of civilization. A mythological canon is an organization of symbols, ineffable in import, by which the energies of aspiration are evoked and gathered toward a focus (Campbell, 1968, 4:5).

Instead of aspiration, the term is solidarity at the horizontal level, legitimacy as given by the people to the king, and protection and the meeting of basic needs as provided by the king/clan. When asabiya is strong, there is legitimacy, when it is weak, then dynasties fall, empires are conquered, and a new group with a stronger asabiya rises.

Dynasties tend to disintegrate through in-fighting. With fights in the inner group, the ruler eliminates and humiliates the contenders, legitimacy is destroyed and asabiya weakens. What results is a new but much weaker group feeling. This continues the further decline. Eventually, people who do not share in the group feeling of the elite take charge, but their commitment is not that strong and the dynasty is split and can be easily overthrown. In addition, with expansion more funds must be paid out to the masses and with luxury, group feeling decreases. Thus, to deal with crises, rulers pay out more money, which hastens the decline. This is in sharp contrast to the beginning of the dynasty, when it had a desert attitude—with no extravagant expenditures, a sense of royal authority and with regular fasting and other spiritual practices by the leaders.

But luxury is not always the downfall. Khaldun is far more sophisticated than that. For example, in the beginning of a dynasty, luxury actually leads to increased group feeling and royal authority as it brings on more children. The population of the leadership expands. It is only in subsequent generations that the non-productive elite become problematic and bring on their own decline. For Sarkar (as well as Mosca and Pareto whom we will come to) this is true for all elites: ksattriyans, vipras and vaeshyas.

Dynasties, cities and civilizations have clear stages. "Through the conditions that are peculiar to a particular state, the supporters of the dynasty acquire in that stage traits of character such as do not exist in any other stage. Traits of character are the natural result of the peculiar situations in which they are found" (Khaldun, 1967, 141).

"The first stage is that of success, the overthrow of all opposition, and the appropriation of royal authority from the preceding dynasty" (141). Thus the new group does not have to start all over, it has learned from the previous. In this stage, the ruler is benevolent and does not claim all authority for himself. In the second stage the ruler consolidates power and makes himself the sole executive, so as to exclude others from their various claims of royal authority. At this stage, according to Khaldun

> [there is] kindness to subjects, planned moderation in expenditure, and respect for other people's property. Nothing at this time calls for extravagant expenditures. Therefore the dynasty does need much money. Later comes domination and expansion (luxury) caus[ing] increased spending. It calls for the increases in soldiers' allowances and in the salaries of the people of the dynasty. Extravagant expenditures mount (Brown, 1871, 27).

But before the decline there is the third stage wherein, "the fruits of royal authority are enjoyed: the things that human nature desires such as acquisition of property, creation of lasting monuments, and fame" (Khaldun, 1967, 142). It is in this middle stage where the kingdom is prosperous, unity is high, expenditures medium, the army loyal and the ruler just. In the fourth stage, the ruler imitates the previous ruler and becomes conservative, not departing from tradition and thus making the mistakes of the previous cycle. Then, in the fifth and final stage, there is waste and squandering. He loses legitimacy. This is the stage of senility and the dynasty is destroyed. ". . . at the end of the dynasty . . . crippling taxes weigh heavily upon the people and crush their incentives . . . when they compare their costs of the production and the taxes they must pay with their income and see what little profit there is in trade and business they lose all hope" (Brown, 1971, 32). "A general apathy and hopelessness," argues Khaldun, "steals over people when they lose control of their own destinies and become dependent on others. Such a dependent people will be conquered by the first fighting tribe they encounter" (28). Also at this time the elites—government official and private individuals—leave the city with the wealth they have amassed.

Thus dynasties rise, consolidate power, expand, grow old, become senile and then die. This rise and fall is the rise and fall of *unity*, *identity* and *legitimacy*, or in one word—asabiya. New dynasties emerge at the periphery among provincial governors or among rebels with a stronger group feeling. However, the new dynasty comes to power not through sudden action, but through perseverance. Battle after battle, until eventually the senility not to mention the pestilence and famine of city centers bring it down. And of course, then, the new dynasty will take the cycle of the previous one: it will rise and fall.

But before the end, there is a rise again.

> Group feeling has often disappeared (when the dynasty has grown senile) and pomp has taken the place it occupied in the souls of men. Now, when in addition to the weakening of group feeling, pomp, too, is discontinued, the subjects grow audacious vis-à-vis the dynasty. At the end of a dynasty, there often also appears some (show of) power that gives the impression that the senility of the dynasty has been made to disappear. It lights up brilliantly just before it is extinguished, like a burning wick the flame of which leaps up brilliantly a moment before it goes out, giving the impression it is just starting to burn, when in fact it is going out (Khaldun, 1967, 246) (emphasis added).

While Sarkar's history is not nearly as in-depth in describing the rise and fall of dynasties, Spengler and Toynbee take Khaldun's ideas and refine them. In particular, the notion of the Indian summer is used to describe the false rise are central to them. In addition, Toynbee advances Khaldun's of the creative minority eventually becoming a dominant majority. Like Khaldun, it is leaders from the internal proletariat or the external proletariat that bring on the new leadership. But while Khaldun refers to religions as increasing the fiber of unity, for Toynbee, a universal religion is one of the bonds that the internal proletariat uses to construct the new civilization. Toynbee, in addition, adds the notion that in the integration phase, leadership successfully resolves the challenges posed, while in the disintegration phase a vicious cycle begins wherein failure leads to more failure.

The Time of Disintegration

Khaldun gives us indicators of this theory using generational time. Khaldun's hypothesis is that dynasties last four generations.

> It reaches its end in a single family within four successive generations . . . The builder of the family's glory knows what it costs him to do the work, and he keeps the qualities that created his glory and made it last. The son who comes after him had person contact with his father and thus learned those things from him. However, he is inferior to him in this respect, inasmuch as a person who learns things through study is inferior to a person who knows them from practical applications. The third generation must be content with imitation, and, in particular, reliance upon tradition. This member is inferior to him of the second generation, inasmuch as a person who relies up tradition is inferior to a person who exercises independent judgment. The fourth generation, then, is inferior to the preceding ones in every respect . . . He imagines that the edifice was not built through application and effort. He thinks that it as something due his people from the very beginning by virtue of the mere fact of their descent, and not something that resulted form group effort and individual qualities (105–106).

The family thus revolts and finds a new leader. The new leader then grows, while the man of the fourth generation continues to decline. Khaldun provides a remarkable example of this. The children of Israel were told by God to go forth and conquer. But they did not. Thus they wandered forty years until a generation had passed away, and a new one that had not witnessed the humiliation by Egypt could take over. Moreover, this new generation was strengthened by adverse desert conditions, developed asabiya and thus could accomplish the destined mission ahead.

Dynasties follow the same pattern lasting on the average three generations or 120 years (three times forty, the age of maturity). The first generation "retains the desert qualities, desert toughness and desert savagery" (137). They live on basic needs, their unity and their desire for more goods keep them active and vital.

> Under the influence of royal authority and a life of ease, the second generation changes form the desert attitude to sedentary culture, from privation to luxury and plenty, from a state in which everybody shared in the glory to one in which one man claims all the glory for himself while the others are too lazy to strive for glory . . . The third generation, then, has completely forgotten the period of desert life and toughness, as if it had never existed. They have lost the taste for the sweetness of fame and for group feelings, because they are dominated by force . . . They become dependent on the dynasty and are like . . . children who need to be defended (177).

But this last generation continues the show of courage by having contests and shows, but their courage, for the most part is gone. In the final generation, they are overcome by a group with more solidarity.

Among others, Tarde and Toynbee use the principle of imitation to write of the rise and decline of civilizations. For Sarkar, imitation occurs when a different varna adopts the color of the dominant varna. Thus, capitalism leads to economic growth, new products and a certain societal dynamism, however, overtime the greed associated with this economic systems becomes imitated by the other classes, who then unconcerned with the dynamism of the epoch are simply interested in the profits to be made. In addition, in the Vipran era, warriors become devious. Thus, imitation again leads to a general degeneration.

For both Khaldun and Sarkar, the causes of historical change are endogenous. What causes the rise, leads to the fall. External factors are important but not essential. The cycle remains: primitivism, civilization, kingship and absolute power, leisure and functional economic relations, disintegration, and primitivism again.

Toynbee—deeply influenced by Khaldun—takes an external approach to his history. At center stage is his theory of challenge and response. The civilization's creative minority often rises to meet the

challenge. Once the creative minority becomes exploitive it perishes
or is taken over. For Khaldun, the creative response is dependent
on the particular stage of the family, dynasty, city or civilization. If
it is in an earlier stage then it can be successful. In the later stages,
then there is too much luxury, warriors fight for salary, not out of
religion, thus the response would not matter. But the royal authority for Khaldun, eventually translates into the universal state of
Toynbee. This is unified centralized kingdom where discipline is high
and power is centralized.

Sarkar's approach is similar to Khaldun's. Khaldun begins with
the necessary physical and natural environment that gives rise to
civilization, and then moves to asabiya; Sarkar too begins with the
natural environment. This is developed in his discourse entitled, "The
Future of Civilization," in *The Supreme Expression* (1978b). For him,
both individual and society are dependent on three factors, existence,
development and Bliss (asti, bhati and ananda). Asti is material existence and its requirements (obviously, shelter, food, clothing, education, and medical facilities). According to Sarkar, for the development
of a group of people, the following factors are needed:

(1) *Spiritual ideology* – the philosophy of self and consciousness, a theory of meaning and its origin;
(2) *Spiritual practice* – a way to experience the ideology at the level
of the person, a process by which the ideology can be empirically realized;
(3) *Socio-economic theory* – a theory of the distribution and growth of
value, the allocation of values, goods and services and a theory
of what and how wealth is created;
(4) *Fraternal social outlook* – that all are existentially equal and that all
come from the same supreme spirit, basically some ethic of solidarity, the larger the outlook the greater the chance for civilizational growth;
(5) *Texts* – theories written from the point of view of authority so
as to serve as agreed upon points of reference, thus again providing meaning and inspiration; and, finally a
(6) *Perceptor* – here Sarkar means that each society for its development must have a founder, someone who can show the way.
Again a recognized founder from which texts, ideology, and practice find their unity.

All these spokes are necessary. For example, without spiritual practices the spiritual ideology would become colonized or controlled by

a dominant group. The practices keep the ideology person and other-centered. However, without a spiritual ideology, there would be no basis for understanding shared experiences. With social outlook, the problem of an internal or external proletariat is eliminated, at least conceptually, for all partake and participate in the universal project. This is the Islamic concept of fraternity, but not just in the Western sense of only humans, but the inclusion of animals, plants, and other types of entities. The six spokes as Sarkar refers to them are necessary for a successful civilization. When some of them are missing civilization degenerate. Sarkar uses his analysis not only for civilizations, but ideologies as well.

For true development all these factors must be there. A socio-economic theory without fraternity is no use as it would advantage some over others, spiritual ideology without sadhana would be no use, as the spiritual tradition would become autocratic and colonized by a particular priestly class; moreover, without the practice the personal realization of truth would remain missing. Why does he emphasize scripture and perceptor? Most likely these two provide continuity, they provide inspiration and give a society focus—they provide a coherent center.

Civilizations die because they are missing particular factors. Other civilizations colonize civilizations but in the process lose their own vibrancy—thus the Islamic wave became weakened after it had over-taken Egyptian civilization and thus was unable to overtake Europe. And Sarkar argues that Roman civilization was lacking in social outlook (slavery), lack of "proper socio-economic theory had generated a kind of a fascist mentality. Those rolling in luxury from free labor became indolent. Naturally, they were defeated by a stronger and more strenuous force" (Sarkar, 1978b, 2:99). This appears very similar to group feeling, especially when defined as unity, identity and legitimacy.

Those groups that have these factors will lead them to Ananda or Bliss, that is a society where individuals live in peace and justice, and where spiritual development is possible. He uses the term bliss to denote not only a bright future, but to denote the spiritual. "The real progress is only spiritual. In the spiritual field, due to the absence of reactive momenta (desires and past experiences which impact the mind) there is no clash, there is only forward movement, and this is the nature of true progress" (105).

Instead of dynasties, Sarkar provides an overall framework. But in the warrior era, unity (discipline, social order and hierarchy) is the key; it is an era of gallantry and heroism, of the protection of the weak and the poor, as well as the butchery of other nations and tribes. It is this era, that Khaldun, from Sarkar's perspective, wrote mostly about. Thus, his emphasis on group identification.

But Khaldun also points to the usurpation of power by intellectuals in the decline of dynasties:

> When royal authority is firmly established in on particular family and branch of the tribe supporting the dynasty, and when that family claims all royal authority for itself and keeps the rest of the tribe away from it, and when the children of (that family) succeed to the royal authority in turn, by appointment, then it often happens that their *wazirs* and entourage gain power over the throne. This occurs most often when a little child or a weak member of the family is appointed successor by his father or made ruler by his creatures and servants . . . Eventually, it becomes clear that he exercises the control, and he uses the fact as a tool to achieve royal authority . . . All actual executive power are believed (by the child ruler) to belong to the wazir. He defers to him all these things. Eventually the wazir definitely adopts the coloring of the leader, of the man in control . . . Once a dynasty has fallen into the hands of the wazirs and clients, it remains in that situation. Rarely is it able to escape from it, because (such control by others) is mostly the result of living in luxury and the fact that the royal princes have grown up immersed in prosperity. They have forgotten the ways of manliness [the desert ways] and have become accustomed to the character traits of wet nurses, and they have grown up that way. They do not desire leadership" (Batra, 1980, 114–115).

The wazir (intellectual) then "even though he exercises full control . . . he disguises his control under the form of a ruler's representative" (Batra, 1980, 116). Also from Sarkar's perspective, indicative of Khuldun's influence by the warrior era, is his understanding of royal authority. Royal authority is considered a necessity so as to avoid groups fighting, to give social cohesion. Thus, kings provide a superordinate authority. According to Khaldun, "he must dominate them and have power and authority over them, so that none of them will be able to attack another. This is the meaning of royal authority" (Khaldun, 1967, 47).

For Khaldun, Sarkar six spokes are simply the ingredients of asabiya. The dynasty that has all these points will last and rule long, for it will have religion and this is the factor coupled with Bedouin rugged strength and simple ways will lead to continued power. Again, for Sarkar instead of the simple ways of the Bedouin, he has the simple ways of the yogi (non-accumulation of material possessions, non-attachment to power and ways of the world). But Khaldun's brilliance is that he asserts that the process of power building in itself leads to a decline in asabiya, for over time initiative leads to imitation, hard work leads to laziness, military strength for sake of family leads to military strength for sake of money. Thus, as with Toynbee over time the structure in itself disintegrates. The process is endogenous and cyclical. Khaldun has two types of power royal authority and religious, but leaves out economic power as an independent variable, merely arguing that rulers should treat merchants well. Khaldun's main problem with Sarkar's thought is that Sarkar's unit of analysis remain vague (sometimes he speaks of civilizations, sometimes of ideologies, sometimes of countries, sometimes of collective/group mind) and he is weak at his understanding of royal authority, the end-all of all collective actions. In addition, for Khaldun there is no era of the wazirs, it marks simply a phase in the degeneration of royal authority of true leadership to a false leadership. While this is true for Sarkar as well (the true-false distinction), it also eventually leads to the usurpation of military power to normative/cultural power which can be evidenced by a loosening of the royal power to ministerial power, from one person rule to oligarchic rule.

In addition, for Sarkar the identifications that Khaldun uses for his theory, from family to clan to dynasty are relocated in an ethical theory. They are part of the problem. What is needed is a theory that is not grounded in geographical, social, religious, or ethnic identities, rather the self must be freed from all limited identities. These notions of unity enslave the intellect in the final analysis. Sarkar comments: "Due to the bondage of various types of exploitation and tyranny against the intellect in the physical sphere, the human spirit bursts out, writhing in suppressed agony" (Sarkar, 1983, 70). These are but the dogmas of the mind.

Nation and Identity

But then what is a political entity, what is a nation, what is royal authority? Here Sarkar uses Khaldun notions of asabiya and develops it along the lines Benedict Anderson (1983) has used for his explanation of the nation-state as essentially an imagined community. In his "To the Patriots", Sarkar develops his theory of asabiya. Immediately Sarkar dispels the classic interpretation of nation—"similar manners

and customs, similar model of living, similar traditions, racial similarity, religious similarity" (Sarkar, 1987b, 4:29). And: "linguistic similarity is not an essential factor in forming a nation either" (29).
While these play a vital role, they are in themselves insignificant. "It
is sentiment and nothing else that creates a nation" (31). Thus nationhood resides in emotional perception, in feelings. To argue his position, he develops an alternative history of India that follows a dialectical
rise and fall of sentiment approach similar to Khaldun asabiya. We
now summarize this history.

With the Aryan victory of India, India became two nations, one
Aryan the other non-Aryan, both with different ways of living and
both at odds with each other. But once the non-Aryans were located
within the caste structure, in effect, there was no unifying sentiment,
no image of an enemy and Indian became nationless. At this point
India could have been easily conquered by a foreign invasion. But
the new sentiment came internally through Buddhism. This "civilization" united a group of people under the Buddhist construction.
Once they began to abuse their power, an anti-Buddhist sentiment
grew and two nations were formed, one Buddhist, one anti-Buddhist.
This anti sentiment was based on the Brahman perspective as articulated by Shankaracarya.

With the end of both these sentiments, the muslims found it easy
to invade India, although their vital force had been weakened by
their earlier expansion, and India's own history allowed it to absorb
Islam. In any case, with oppression an anti-muslim sentiment developed making India into two nations again: muslim and anti-muslim.
Eventually as with the earlier cases, both groups merged to some
degree and the other as enemy disappeared. When unity or sentiment
fell again, the British invaded. But while the muslims and British
were both imperialists, the muslims came to settle not to extract
wealth. With British exploitation, two sentiments developed again; an
anti-British and a British. But because of the structure of the world
economy and the rise of nationalism as well as the fear of local leaders that the independence movement would become revolutionary,
instead of the needed economic independence, the anti-British sentiment was dominant. Moreover, the fear of a violent revolution led
to political independence instead of economic independence.

Based on different variables, nations form (Aryan, Buddhism,
Muslim, British) and when they exploit, an anti-movement starts.
This negation creates two or more nations, eventually there is absorp-

tion or one is victorious. Overtime unity again disappears. Thus each
nation goes through numerous episodes of unity and disunity. It is
unified when it has a sentiment.

For Sarkar, the sentiment needed today is an anti-economic exploitation sentiment, against the global capitalist system, in general. This
sentiment can be used to develop local, regional self-reliant unity
and thus develop solidarity. The USSR and China both successfully
used this strategy. However, even an anti-exploitation sentiment will
disappear once the cause of exploitation is resolved. Thus what is
the answer for human unity. As with Khaldun, Toynbee, Sorokin
and others, the answer is spiritual (unlike Marx who believed that
once labor was free, man would be free and the State would not
be needed): "Along with the theory of spiritual inheritance [prop-
erty owned by the cosmos], one Cosmic Ideology will have to be
adopted and that ideology is that one Supreme entity—the Cosmic
Entity—is the goal of all living beings. This spiritual sentiment will
keep human beings united for all time to come" (45). For Sarkar,
"no other theory can save the human race" (45).

Thus unity rises and falls. Eternal collective unity can be formed
only through a shared theory of the spirit and a shared theory of
property, that is, a theory that has all the spokes. For Sarkar, it is
this that will provide the best future to be. Sentiment, thus, in the
poststructural perspective becomes the critical resource. An anti-
exploitation sentiment is Sarkar's preferred with the universal spiritualism sentiment as the ideal unifying force.

Returning to Khaldun, we see that like his personal history of rise
and fall and rise, he presents us with a history of the rise and fall
of civilizations. History is cyclical, moved by endogenous forces. They
key to history is social unity and solidarity. It is this and the search
for basic needs that lead to royal authority and the development of
the state. State power is held as long the elite are innovative, fair
and unified. But with size and civilization, lethargy, cruelty, impi-
ety, sensuality develop. Instead of kinship, functional relationships
become paramount. Instead of unity, there is fragmentation. Eventually
the group feeling breaks apart and those with a stronger group feeling rise and take state power. They too then follow the same pattern. While God does not work in history, the notion of God provides
unity to the people who have faith. It is this faith that leads to
strength and victory.

Khaldun's works form the basis of much of present sociological thought. In addition to Sarkar, one can find Khaldun's thought in Comte (the creation of a science of society) in Weber (the routinization of charisma and the politics of bureaucracy), in Spengler (the biological life cycle applied to society), and to Marx (the town and country distinction), among many others, especially those who use a rise and fall of model of power.

As Khaldun developed a discourse but was forgotten, Sarkar too has developed a new ways of constructing the world such that his work will be used as an asset irrespective of the correctness of his various theories, they will be used to frame new questions. In summary, both their works have a great deal of similarities:

(1) Positive toward the future;
(2) Cyclical;
(3) Use endogenous variables to explain change, (although they include external variables such as climate, plagues and the such);
(4) Spiritual in approach, but not Hegelian in upholding the state;
(5) Stress on unity as or among the fundamental factors of change;
(6) Personal lives that were filled with success and tragedy;
(7) Wrote at the end of epochs;
(8) Saw in the decline phase of a civilization the rise of materialism, lethargy, luxury;
(9) Believe theirs is a universal history for all time and space;
(10) Critical of spiritual traditions around them (Khaldun at the soothsayers who try and comfort);
(11) Write a history through time; and finally,
(12) Stress religion or spiritual ideology as leading to great dynastic (civilizational) strength. In contrast, Sarkar, writes a history of mentalities, Khaldun of asabiya. They write in different eras and stress different aspects of history and political theory.

Islam and the Future

As we did earlier with Chinese civilization, we will offer some comments on how Sarkar and others might construct the future of the Islamic world. Batra (1980) has argued that Islam is moving into the Vaeshyan era and thus will be the center of democracy, decentralized government and entrepreneurism. Present Iran, then, is simply a counterrevolution against the capitalist developmentalism of the Shah. Conversely, one might assert that there was a true monarchy in Iran and now the vipran clergy has taken over. Khaldun is more instructive. For Khaldun, Iran can best be understood as a decline in asabiya. The rulership lost its mantle, not from heaven, but because of misuse of resources, because of luxury, and then someone, as Khaldun would predict, from the provinces (Khomeni) came in and took over the leadership. He started a new dynasty, which, if it was the 14th century, would take, most likely, a hundred years to dislodge. From Khaldun's perspective, the Saudi dynasty is past its prime, potentially ready for usurpers. On the other hand, Toynbee or Galtung with his expansion/contraction phases for cosmologies might argue that while Christianity is about to enter a contraction phase, Islam is beginning a long-term expansion phase. Politics in the Islamic world is simply the working out of who will lead this phase and what type of power it will be: normative-ideological, military, economic, or laborer/worker.

From Sarkar's view, first, the task is to determine which era it is in; second, and most important is to reconstruct Islam such that it is neo-humanistic in its orientation, that is, its unity is based a global anti-economic exploitation sentiment, and then a global spiritual sentiment. The struggle involved in doing this project will develop the asabiya needed to manage the planet for a long time to come.

Enter the West

We now move from a discussion of Khaldun and Islamic thought to one where pivotal Western macrohistorians are introduced. Some of these have already been presented and given the many choices before us, we will not examine them in the same depth as we did Khaldun. They are not the main entree. We begin with Vico, develop Comte and Hegel, then settle down with Marx and Gramsci. From there we examine the elite theories of Pareto and Mosca and then conclude with Spengler, Toynbee and Sorokin. We locate their key thoughts, again, with the view of understanding Sarkar better, putting forth his theory in the context of other thinkers.

Vico

Vico (1668–1744) can be seen as a turn that the social sciences did not make. His was an attempt to develop an alternative, a new science to the developing natural sciences. This social science must be different since it includes human and their self-interpretation of the

world. Thus, the methods of the natural sciences should not be used
for the social sciences. This was the view of the counter-enlightenment, that the meaning of a particular situation could be understood
through empathy, imagination, and intuition. In this view, the objectivity of the natural sciences was not an appropriate model to study
humans, since humans are reflective beings and thus not only discovered the world but in their discoveries constantly reinterpreted
the world. In the Indian context, there was no necessity of this
counter-enlightenment as there was no enlightenment of scientific
rationality. Rather the first enlightenment was that of the Vedas,
with then the counter-enlightenment of Buddhism. The issue was
not the nature of inquiry but the construction of the self and its
relationship to the cosmos. The radical division that the Europeans
underwent was a non-event in the Indian episteme, rather the Indian
episteme can be seen as the history of the construction and deconstruction of the self. There are times when it is material, times when
it only spiritual. Sarkar's reconstruction attempts to locate it in both
simultaneously arguing for a self that is eternal and finite. Commentary
in Indian thinking has always been an appropriate form of knowledge, intuition has never been banished except in Carvaka. Carvaka,
however, unlike the culture of Western cosmology, did not become
hegemonic.

For Vico, human sciences were superior to the natural sciences
since they were about and through men. Moreover, as Marx would
later assert in *Capital*: And would not such a history be easier to
compile since, as Vico says, "human history differs from natural history in this, that we have *made* the former and not the latter?" (Marx,
1952, 181). History then is the history of man's and woman's construction of their own character. History then as in the Indian case
is interpretive. But this does then not mean that history is without
patterns.

History shows us how we have formed ourselves. Precisely Sarkar's
observation. The fourfold division of power is not so because it came
from the mouth of Brahma (as in the mythological interpretation)
but rather because it developed historically through the interaction
of humans with the environment and with each other, and ultimately
with consciousness itself. According to Robert Brown in his *The Nature
of Social Laws*.

> Vico thinks of his new science as a detailed account of the necessary,
> that is law-governed, evolution of human history. Once we understand

the pattern into which providence works that history, we can deduce the presence in it of certain large-scale sequences, and the repetition of certain cultural stages (Brown, 1984, 161).

Thus, laws can be constructed without resort to a natural science construction of the objective. One can be credible and correct while not being part of the enlightenment science project. Marx saw this as well and created a materialistic science linking the objective with the interpretative and eventually with the utopian political (in terms of recreating the future) stance.

Vico attempts to find that which is common in all humans, irrespective of locality. To him these are various triplicates, no doubt patterned after the classical Christian division. These are "the ideas of numen (God, his providence, religious rites and institutions), the idea of the necessity to restrain passions (the institution of marriage), and the idea of the immortality of the soul (the institution of burial)" (Attila Faj, 1987, 25). These beliefs form civil society. They are necessary conditions without which organized societies could not be maintained. They developed to counter an early humankind that was ferocious, ambitious, and avaricious. Based on these commonalities, then various ages or stages are possible, alternatively the imaginative, the heroic and the reasonable, or the age of Gods, Heros and Men. "Every nation is subject to such a cycle from its rise to its fall and its rise once again. It is in the presence of this inevitable cycle which allows us to deduce the presence of the general features of each stage from the existence of the previous ones" (Brown, 1984, 165). Like Sarkar, who posits basic types of personality, characteristics of what it means to be human, once accepted, the rest of the theory follows naturally and logically. Again according to Brown, for Vico,

> the cycle is inevitable because the customs and institutions which human beings produce in order to meet their basic needs have predictable consequences, social and psychological. The reason why these consequences are predictable . . . is that certain features of human character have law-like connections with certain types of customs and institutions (165).

Vico's new science reveals these to us, just as Sarkar's new interpretation of history reveals the laws of the cycle, the law of the six spokes, among other universals.

The ages themselves can be seen in different ways. At one level, Vico simply takes the classic decline of humans from the spiritual

golden (Gods) to the silver (Hero) to the copper (Man), and then
the in-between iron age (Barbarism). The cycle then starts again
with the Age of Gods. From an epistemological view, in the Age of
Gods, only God is real; in the Age of Heros, the leader challenges
this construction and becomes the Great Father; in the Age of Man,
humans then construct the world self-consciously placing themselves
in the center; and, in the Age of Barbarism, reality itself becomes
deconstructed, until once again God becomes the really real. Alternatively using Sorokin one can see Vico's ages as the decline from
ideational to idealistic to sensate. There are some similarities to
Sarkar's social stages as well. The Shudra era is the age of Gods
wherein agency was God and humans followed the cosmic principles. The Ksattriyan era corresponds directly to the Age of Heros,
the Vipra with the Age of Men, and the Vaeshyan loosely with the
Age of Barbarism.

But more significant than the actual ages is his analogy for change.
It is not the body of man (the breath or the arms and legs) nor is
it the mountain nor the life cycle of nature, rather for Vico it is the
river. Movement. Each stage moves and circles the next. But his law
is soft. Attila Faj explains it.

> The 'softness' of the law means that the successive figures of this
> roundelay are not necessarily unavoidable and are not independent of
> any condition and circumstance. Each historical stage streams into the
> following one and gets mixed with it, so we cannot distinguish them
> sharply. For a long stretch, the stages and everything that belong to
> them are mingled like the sweet water of an estuary with the salt water
> of the sea (Faj, 1987, 22).

This soft-hard distinction appears a more fruitful way of understanding the various attempts to demarcate human history. While
the modern social scientist might call it sloppy or vague, it is at the
same time realistic in that it allows some freedom for history to
move. Indeed for Vico, a nation about to enter its new barbarism
can be saved by a virtuous monarch. There are escape routes in his
historicism. While the river analogy is useful, it differs from Sarkar
in that Sarkar has both: movement and pause, both dependent on
each other, both cosmological universals.

Vico conditioned (or liberated by his Christian upbringing) as with
other modern writers, leaves not only an escape route but a way of
transformation from the structure of history. Like Sarkar's spiritual

revolutionaries or Marx's proletariats, Vico has his true believers. Just as the ancient "chosen people" averted the decline history, "a similar phenomenon will occur in the future: the hopelessly and tragically recurrent *corsi* and *recorsi* will be stopped by Christ's true followers, who will never again let their community or state relapse into barbarism" (22). The cycle is eternal, discovered through intuition and interpretation, but the spiritual allows a way out. Thus, humans can transform themselves and the natural obstacles that the face. But not all humans! This is what the theorist then does, points to ways in which those ready for the task can change history, can transform the cycle. But this transformation is different from the project of the Gnostics that Voegelin warns us of. Vico keeps the cycle, allowing its transcendence though the spiritual, while the humanists, conservatives, liberals and socialists challenge the cycle within time, through and with the material world, and thereby create the sensate world. Sarkar's and Vico's similarities is in their method of finding basic human characteristics and then developing stages from them that are cyclical, but which allow exits and escape routes. Moreover, these laws although eternal are soft, in that there are alternatives routes in them. Vico of course stays with the nation, while Sarkar shifts identity. Sarkar could use Vico's river analogy to soften his notion of laws (a theoretical move that we believe is implicit in the Indian episteme). This would allow more space to move within his theory and use his theory as an asset to reveal the richness of the real, instead of being beholding to one definition of history. The river analogy allows one to speak of movement and stability, since the river is different yet the same at any given movement, an analogy particularly useful for cyclical theorists.

But they speak from different eras and epistemes. Vico responds to the end of the classical episteme and the newly emerging scientific one, while Sarkar need not do so. In fact, Sarkar takes the interpretative approach and consumes the physical and natural sciences with them. He goes so far to argue that laboratory results for investigations in his theory of microvita will be different depending on the spiritual level (their mental state, peaceful, balanced and open to the emanations of the supreme) of the scientist. The best science can then occur with spiritually evolved scientists then. Rules and regulations and public testing are important, but what one sees is dependent on where on locates one's self.

Comte and the End of the Cycle

Taking the opposite tack, the idea of inevitable progress were, among others, Henri Saint Simon, John Stuart Mill, Herbert Spencer, and the writer we focus on—Auguste Comte (1798–1857). Raised and inspired not by the spiritual world, but the sensate and the academic world, Comte saw the age of men/barbarism not as a degeneration of history, but as the culmination of progress. This is the victory of Cartesian rationality and the scientific worldview. Comte's intention was to create a science of society and man: sociology and the social sciences in general. In his words, "I understand by social physics the science which has for its subject the study of phenomena considered in the same spirit and astronomical, physical, chemical . . . that is subject to natural laws, the discovery of which is special object of investigation" (Timasheff, 1965, 18–19).

Comte believed that there are natural laws that are progressive and historically derived. "The experience of the past proves, in the most decisive manner, that the progressive march of civilization follows a natural and unavoidable course, which flows from the law of human organization and, in its turn becomes the supreme laws of all practical phenomena" (Etzioni, 1973, 14). To him, unlike Sarkar and others, history is uni-linear and progressive. It is this way because of the "instinctive tendency of the human race to perfect itself" (17). Or, as Herbert Spencer would articulate later:

> Progress . . . is not an accident, but a necessity. Instead of Civilization being artificial it is a part of nature; all of a piece with the development of an embryo or the unfolding of a flower. The modifications mankind have undergone, and are still undergoing, result from a law underlying the whole organic creation . . . As surely as the tree becomes bulky when it stands alone, and slender if one of a group . . . as surely as there is any meaning in such terms as habit, custom, practice; so surely must the human faculties be molded into complete fitness for a social state; so surely must evil and immortality disappear; *so surely man must become perfect* (Manicus, 1987, 32) (emphasis added).

Thus there is one process that is necessarily moving toward perfection. For Sarkar there is perfection but only at the level of the spiritual. At the physical and social there exist forces in tension with each other. There is good and bad, if there is perfection it is a Zen perfection, perfection as metaphor, perfection as an idea used to accept those things that cannot be transformed. But speaking from the periphery, speaking as an Indian from Calcutta, history has not, indeed cannot be progressive, for the central indicator is the reality of suffering, and that is cyclical, except when the spiritual is touched. Contrast this view with Foucault's, who would place perfection in a historical discourse. "Perfection" is a social construction that ultimately tells us about who we are and how we construct the real. For Foucault there is no site for perfection, transcendental or worldly.

But returning to Comte, he believed that perfection was possible, indeed the final stage of history was the positive stage—earlier stages were mere building blocks. For Comte, these clear stages are indisputable. They are natural laws valid irrespective of observer. They are objective. While Ssu-Ma Ch'ien accentuated virtue, Chang the tao, Khaldun the spirit of unity, Vico the mythic, Sarkar the spiritual and the group mind, and Marx the economic, and Comte, history as primarily intellectual development. The task becomes that of organizing knowledge. Indeed his mission was to build a social science that [would] satisfy the twofold intellectual need of modern societies for order and progress (Manicas 1987, 64).

This mission was built with the famous three laws, which, when compared with Sarkar give them an alternative reading not found in most analysis of Comte and others that followed the French Enlightenment.

> In order to understand the true value and character of the Positive Philosophy, we must take a brief general view of the progressive course of the human mind, regarded as a whole . . . The law is this: that each of our leading conceptions—each branch of our knowledge passes through three different theoretical conditions: the Theological or fictitious; the Metaphysical or abstract; and the Scientific, or Positive . . .

In the theological state, the human mind, seeking the essential nature of being, the first and final causes . . . of all effects—in short, Absolute knowledge, supposes all phenomena to be produced by the immediate action of supernatural being.

In the metaphysical state, which is only a modification of the first, the mind supposes, instead of supernatural beings, abstract forces . . . inherent in all things, and capable of producing all phenomena.

In the final, positive state, the mind has given over the vain search after Absolute notions, the origin and destination of the universe, and the causes of phenomena, and applies itself to the study of their laws—that is, the invariable relations of succession and resemblance (Comte, 1875, 1:2).

There are thus three stages with the final stage that of the scientific dominated by reason and empiricism. These stages are evolutionary and represent the development of the social mind and civilization itself. In this Comte can be seen as a sociological Kant for there are different forms of consciousness for every epoch, different forms of knowing. This idea is plainly there in Sarkar as well. Collective psychology or varna is first of all a social phenomena even if it inhabits a morphogenetic field—it represents a group consciousness.

There is further similarity with Sarkar in that the earlier stages of consciousness do not disappear, they remain. This is similar to Vico's river analogy or Foucault's epistemes. While there is an over-whelming worldview or way of knowing, past societies continue in the present.

The main different between Sarkar and Comte is the obvious one. The scientific state is the end-all of civilization, the third realm, the end of history. In this way, Comte continues the Gnostic project that Voegelin criticizes, the demarcation of history into ancient, medieval and modern. Max Weber, as well, continues with history becoming increasing positivistic and rational, with religion relegated to the irrational. Voegelin describes this as the replacement of the era of Christ with the era of Comte, the Gnostic re-representation of the transcendental with the immanence of scientism (Voegelin, 1987, 127).

From Sarkar's view, Comte simply addresses different stages in the Vipran cycle as well as presages the Vaeshyan era. Comte thus correctly perceives the degeneration of the Vipran era, however, his history ends too soon. He forgets that the scientific era of capital-ism too will have a phase of degeneration. And again while Comte is correct to stress intellectual ideas, he misses physical clash and the attraction of the Great, although from Comte's view his tendency toward perfection is precisely that desire, although Comte would not state it in Sarkar's language. Indeed Comte would assert that Sarkar's speaks from the theological/supernatural stage. From Sorokin's view, again, Comte is touching on something very real, but misinterpret-ing it. The theological is simply the ideational supersystem, while the metaphysical is the in between mixed idealistic, and the posi-tivist is the present sensate. The mistake Comte makes is to confuse the present as the end state, forgetting as Sorokin would remind us, that each system approximates the real, but in its exaggeration reaches the limit of falsity, and then the next system or some mixed version comes into play. This is not so for Comte. History moves in one direction. The final stage is that of positivism, modernity.

Is Comte's theory of history solely intellectual? No, there are other forces and attributes at work. The theological state is related to the military epoch while the positive is related to the industrial. The metaphysical is a mongrel intermediate stage where the old begins to die and the new is born.

For Comte in the Theological, "all the social relations . . . are avowedly and exclusively military. Society makes conquest its one permanent aim. Industrial pursuits are carried on only so far as is necessary for the support of the human race. Slavery, pure and simple, of the producers, is the principal institution" (Etzioni, 1973, 18). A near exact definition of Sarkar's Ksattriyan era. Sarkar, however, while acknowledging the spiritual pursuits of Ksattriyan era keeps the Ksattriyan and Vipran era separate. There is a real change in that the group mind changes. Comte, privileging the role of social mind and ideas, does not see or feel the need to separate the two.

As with Sarkar, the eras are related and proceed from each other. For example, in the later theological state, there was a notion of natural laws since there was the category of "miracle," meaning that which transgressed the natural laws. In the earlier state, there are no miracles since myth, magic and the physical coincide. It is word literally of gods and goddesses. Moreover, the speculative activities of the ancient state, create the possibility of a special class of individuals who could contemplate the meaning of the universe. This led to the development of an intellectual culture and further progress for humanity, although eventually they sank into mental lethargy. The vipras became parasitic exploiters. Control of the spiritual world was linked for Comte with control of the physical. "Such then was the moral operation of the theological philosophy—stimulating Man's active energy by the offer, in the midst of troubles of his infantine state of absolute empire over the external world, as the prize of his speculative effort" (Comte, 1875, 137).

For Comte, initially the theologically worldview brought progress, but eventually theology began to suppress the mind. "Instead of uniting men, which was its proper function at first, it now divides them, so that after having created speculative activity, it has ended with radically hindering it" (139). These words were echoed by Chang earlier. Where there is unity, the tao is present. When philosophers take the truth and divide it, factions develops and the tao disintegrates.

For Sarkar, too, the correct path is toward synthetic philosophy, not analytic, for the synthetic unites, while the analytic divides. The ultimate in synthetic is the spiritual. For Sarkar, after the positive and its numerous benefits, once it exploits, then there is a return to the theological-military—a spiritually inspired Ksattriyan society. But Comte does not conclude this. "The function of reuniting, as of stimulating and directing, belongs more and more, as religious belief declines to the conceptions of positive philosophy, which *alone* can establish the intellectual community all over the world on which the great future political organization is to be grounded" (139).

This third positive phase is not one of the military, but one of science and industrial activity. Reasoning and observation overthrow imagination. "All the special relations have gradually established themselves on industrial bases. Society, taken collectively, tends to organize itself in the same manner, by making production its only and constant aim" (Etzioni, 1973, 19).

Moreover, this trend of industrialism, science, individualism would continue well on into the future. Comte's various predictions have led futurist Burnham Beckwith (1982) to rank him as one of the original futurists, with his work as one of the original efforts to predict the future.

For Comte, knowledge can help men see the real, and thus control it as well. This was the final positive epoch where knowledge would continue to increase, a science of history and future would flourish, and the theological would lie moribund.

While in the theological, the priest controlled the transcendental future, in the positive modern, science would be able to foresee and modify the future. The will of the spiritual sovereign was now to be in the hands of the modern subject—Man. Indeed, man is created in the modern world as a true subject, before he existed alongside the cosmos and nature, but in the modern world, Man now stands apart, the subject and object of the world (Foucault, 1973).

Thus, with Comte we have a uni-linear trend (law) from theological to metaphysical to positive and at the same time from God to man and from military to industrial. These stages grow from one another and they are progressive. Within these stages, however, we have a rise and decline. Each brings on progressions (in relation to the end state) and then becomes dysfunctional wherein the next stage beings, leading finally to the positive stage. This positive stage, as with the theories of other linear macrohistorians, since it is the final stage, exists outside of history, although it emerges from history.

While the broad stage is linear, there are cycles within the progression. From Sarkar's view, Comte has much of it right. Correct is the natural and deterministic progression from military to industrial (Ksattriyan to Vaeshyan) and the rise and then decline of the vipran era and the emphasis on the social mind in history. In addition, he was correct in pointing to the development of dogma within the theological approach. But where Sarkar then makes the distinction between actual spiritual practices, Comte remained at the social level and thus denounced the entire religious approach. Sarkar, in contrast, keeps the spiritual and attacks the religious, placing himself in this universal spirituality and others within the religious sphere.

In addition, from Sarkar's view, Comte is incorrect in that he only sees one level of the real and in his assertion that the modern positive era is the final stage of progress. Among other problems, the implications of this view, as outlined by Voegelin, are disastrous. With the end of the cycle and the adoption of the linear evolutionary model, then racism is inevitable since now the categories of advanced and backward societies have an ideological backdrop. We should then not be surprised at the following comment from Comte. "We must study exclusively the development of the most advanced nations, not allowing our attention to be drawn off to other centers of any independent civilization which has, from any cause whatever, been arrested, and left in an imperfect state" (Comte, 1875, 151). Once perfection becomes a worldly criteria—placed in the material discourse—then social space can be divided into modern and primitive. The modern can then judge the undeveloped and as Nandy (1987) reminds us can claim not only to understand themselves better, but the primitive better as well. There is nothing to learn from the undeveloped. They exist to be transformed, altered and patterned after the perfected society. In this case, this perfect society is Comte's rising technological and capitalist West.

As Comte writes:

> It is this selected part, the vanguard of the human race that we have to study; the greater part of the white race, or the European nations—even restricting ourselves, at least in regard to modern times, to the nations of Western Europe. When we ascend into the remoter past, it will be in search of the political ancestors of these peoples, whatever their country may be (Comte, 1875, 151).

This mistake was made by other progressives, including Spencer, Marx and Hegel, but not by Spengler and Sorokin, later on. Marx, of course, by speaking for an oppressed class managed to remove himself from the racism of Comte. Hegel, by using the notion of progress and laws with the notion of the spirit, commits Comte's error as well. Sarkar skirts on the edge of this. By calling for a new class outside of class he creates for the possibility of a privileged class that can control the laws of nature, yet by maintaining the pattern of the cycle he avoids the extra-historical discourse. Indeed, it is these types of theories that have led Karl Popper (1957) to savagely attack the poverty of historicism, for it freezes the future in the past, privileges structure over agency, determinacy over indeterminacy, and in the final analysis leaves man alone in a universe of conflicting laws.

Finally, like other macrohistorians, Comte speaks with arrogance, a sense of finality. "Social science has with all its complexity passed through the theological state, and has almost everywhere fully attained the metaphysical; while it is nowhere yet risen to the positive, *except in this book*" (132).

For Comte the truth has been discovered, now science can continue to develop it. Sarkar, speaking from entirely different episteme, does not have a uni-linear progressive worldview to shape his. Sarkar's lives in different times: spiritual, seasonal, and quantitative. And unlike Aurobindo, who placed time in the nation-state, Sarkar does not place emanation in nation, rather he speaks for a global synthesis. Writing after the French revolution and the American revolution, but before the Soviet, Comte could speak of the new modern era. He could speak of progress. And yet while Comte argues against the Catholic (vestiges of the theological state), in fact, he comes out as conservative. St. Simon is the Father, while Comte is the Son, and Science is the Holy Ghost. The Europeans are the privileged people above and outside the intellectual and physical world of nature. The other continents are there for man to transform in the image of the trinity. God has stepped down, and through science, Man has risen.

Writing much later, Spengler, influenced not by the expansionist phase of western cosmology, but the contraction phase and by the horror of the positive state, would write not of the rise of the West but of the upcoming decline.

Hegel, History and the Spirit

With Hegel (1770–1831) the notion of progress continues, but progress is now not only reflected in the material world but also in the history of the spirit. For Voegelin this is the continuation of the immanentization of the Godhead in history. Although both believe in progress, Hegel stands in sharp contrast to Comte in the sense whereas Comte rejects the notion of the spirit in history, Hegel moves it to center stage. In Hegel's words, "If it be allowed that Providence manifests itself in [animals, plants and isolated occurrences—miracles] why not in Universal History?" (Manicas, 1987, 87).

History for Hegel is a drama on a large stage. He wants to explain history, "to depict the passions of mankind, the genius, the active powers, that play their part on the great stage" (87). Now for Sarkar, the mystic, he would not use the word passion except as an attribute to transcend. Rather, Sarkar's ideal history is one that shows how individuals have braved challenges, but these are not the challenges of wars, but how individuals have courageously faced material and spiritual poverty. From the outset their work is different.

In general, Hegel has three important ideas of use to us. According to political theorist Manicas, first is "the idea of Freedom as the *telos* of history" (96). Secondly, "Hegel's empirical concern is with the realm of thought, the ideas, beliefs, or more generally, the culture and the 'spirit' of a State. These are embodied in institutions, to be sure and thus we cannot overlook institutions. But we investigate them so as to discover the norms, values, goals and beliefs that people live by, to grasp what motivates them by virtue of their institutions and their role in them" (96). Third, is "the mechanism of historical process are to be found by philosophy—in the dialectic of the idea" (96).

For Sarkar, the telos is spiritual realization; movement toward consciousness. His empirical concern is with changing the material conditions of society so individuals can pursue the absolute representation of the real—pure consciousness. Finally, the mechanism of history is spiritual dialectics, his theory of collective psychology, the metaphorical rise and fall of dharma, and the rise and fall of the sentiment that creates the nation.

For Hegel and Sarkar it is not just the spirit that is active in history. Humans too make history. Individuals make history but not

the way they intend to, because of the cunning of reason. History
has its own purpose, individuals play out this purpose. According to
Manicas, first, "in their effort to 'develop themselves and their aims
in accordance with natural tendencies, human beings build up the
edifice of a human society; thus fortifying a position of Right and
Order against themselves'. Here, Hegel stands smack between Rousseau
and Marx. For Rousseau, human are born free but everywhere live
in chains, for Marx, human history begins at just the point where
individuals collectively control the conditions of their lives" (87–88).

For Sarkar, humans are not born free—their historical desires—
instincts are with them, as are their samskaras, desires from previous lives. Moreover they are born into a particular structure which
frames the possibilities of what they can do or not do. For Sarkar
history begins not with humans, but with the imbalance of the cosmic cognitive principle and the appearance of the first desire that
began the universe. But this is at the cosmic level. At the historical
level, there are the social forces that condition and create the various selves, specifically the ideas of the various epochs. But there is
also the individual level of choice in that every human can decide
to move toward the spirit or away. Sarkar begs the question or the
conflict between choice and structure by opting for a both/and strategy. The question in itself can be answered in different ways depending on the level of reality in which one is asking and answering.
From the view of pure consciousness, there is no choice for there
is no individual mind, nor space and time. At the individual level,
there is choice although it is constricted by structure and history. At
the level of the social, there are clear historical laws that societies
move through, although even here there are alternatives. These
laws operate in nature and once begun then cannot be changed or
transformed by Consciousness. Karma and other laws of nature are
inescapable. Sarkar does not need an historical cunning, there is only
historical ignorance.

For Hegel, Providence works by means of the unintended consequences of our acts. Historical changes goes on according to Hegel
"behind the backs of persons" (87).

But most significantly is the location of history. For while individuals provide the 'energy' for historical process (88), according to
Hegel it is "in the history of the world, the individuals we have to
do with are Peoples; totalities that are States" (88).

Thus history takes place in between states. According to Manicas,
"pre-state people are only on the margin of world history, ultimately

subject to the acts of those entities which, by virtue of their size and organization, are capable of affecting the processes of world history" (92).

For Sarkar, world history is the history of the collective mind as it is expressed in the material world by individuals, that is, in their efforts to use mind to conquer, understand, and economize the material world. The state is not a force of agency, rather it is the battleground of the various classes and the various types of power: economic, ideological and military. The nation for Sarkar is a type of sentiment that comes into being through the unity gained either from ideology or a mutual enemy. Thus, Sarkar's history of the nation is a history of the collective mind, of the group sentiment. It is the sense of oppression or injustice that unites and creates a people. In this sense a history of the state, as Hegel would have, would be a useless history for Sarkar, for the state is not a concrete association, it is ever changing. The fundamental unity of Indian thought is consciousness as embodied in the individual and as reflected in various groups. The state is simply one association among other historical associations. Hegel's privileging of the state is simply a ksattriyan history. This ksattriyan emphasis becomes clearer in his upholding of world historical conquerors.

According to Manicas, a further implication of Hegel's view is that only individuals who are leaders of states are capable of influencing history (93). The national security state is the consequence. Hegel saw the state as an integrated system of institution rather than an aggregation or aggregation of individuals acting in consort to satisfy individual interests as Hobbes does or as Sarkar might.

Indeed by placing Prussia as the ideal state and then placing other historical states as either outside history or as phases leading up to history, Hegel commits the same developmentalism as Comte does. But while Comte locates finality in positivism, Hegel locates it in the modern German state. Suddenly the Germanic state becomes the guiding image for other states, and as in the Christian code, it becomes the chosen state, with the message of the spirit of modernity now to be passed onward to other less modern, less imbued by the spirit states. Aurobindo, as mentioned earlier, takes this idea but subverts it, finding the spirit conscious in the nationalistic movements against the old European states.

For Manicas, Hegel's philosophy is a realism in the sense that the empirical, the phenomenal, is concrete and is the manifestation of the Idea, the abstract, which is nonetheless real. As Charles Taylor says, "Hegel's idealism, far from being a denial of external material reality, is the strongest affirmation of it, it not only exists but *necessarily* exists" (96). There is, for Hegel, a reality which transcends appearance, and of which appearance is a manifestation. But this reality is Idea. Writes Taylor: "Absolute idealism means that nothing exists which is not a manifestation of the Idea, that is, of rational necessity" (96). For Sarkar, the rational is real. But Consciousness, when humans attempt to locate it in a particular human construction, becomes illusive and mysterious, indeed mystical, outside of the understanding of sense perception. Consciousness is not functional nor instrumental. The yogi cannot use it for ego or nation building, and if he does, there will certainly be a fall after the rise.

While for Hegel, the fundamental purpose of philosophy is the overcoming of opposites. Division and opposition present themselves to the mind in different forms, in different cultural epochs. Between soul and body, subject and object, intelligence and Nature. The fundamental interest of reason is the same, namely to attain a unified synthesis. For Sarkar, these opposites will exit forever. They are part of the very nature of existence.

Their philosophical differences are more apparent in how both Sarkar and Hegel perceive the Absolute. Writes Frederick Copleston in his *A History of Philosophy*, for Hegel, "the absolute is the totality, reality as a whole, the universe. Philosophy is concerned with the true and the true is the whole" (Copleston, 1963, 170). The absolute is subject, what is its object. Itself. Thought which thinks itself, self-thinking thought. Copleston remarks,

> in saying that the Absolute is self-thinking Thought Hegel is obviously repeating Aristotle's definition of God. But Hegel is not thinking of a transcendental deity. The absolute is the Totality, and the Absolute is a process, the Absolute is a process of self-reflection. Reality comes to know itself, it does so in the human spirit (171).

This is similar to Sarkar's philosophical thought, although for Sarkar prior to the absolute as thought is the absolute as pure awareness. From pure awareness the absolute crudifies into the next level of reality, Cosmic Mind. Cosmic mind then crudifies into nature. Cosmic mind is similar to Hegel's notion of the absolute. That their positions are different can be expected. For a philosopher like Hegel it would be expected that the absolute would be reason, while for a mystic like Sarkar, the absolute cannot be mere reason, rather it would have to be indescribable, only locatable through bliss. To know consciousness, one must transcend the faculty that seeks to know.

W. Walsh in *The Philosophy of History* writes that for Hegel, "Idea is part of a super-triad, of which Nature forms the antithesis and Spirit (mental life) the synthesis. The Idea, to be fully itself, demands concrete embodiment, which it finds by 'externalizing' itself as Nature and 'returning to' itself as Concrete Spirit" (Walsh, 1960, 141). Thus the spirit does not descend into matter as in traditional mythology, rather spirit-matter are part of a dialectical relationship.

Stages of History

This dialectical relationship is also in evidence in Hegel's theory of history. It is here that we find a more interesting contrast with Sarkar. Philosophy of history, for Hegel, is part of the philosophy of Spirit and the problem that confronts its exponent is that of tracing the working of reason in a particular empirical sphere.

While Sarkar argues that most history is ideological history, written to aggrandize a particular class, be it kings and warriors, capitalists and corporations, priests and ministers, he prescribes that history should be about how it resolved momentous challenges. History should about how structures have created human suffering, and how humans have fought back. History should be a people's history. For Hegel, ordinary historians confine themselves for the most part to the narrative of contemporary events, a few paint history on a broader canvas, but all in all they simply try and write the facts. For Hegel, according to Walsh, the historian must, "illuminate history by bringing his knowledge of the Idea, the formal articulation of reason to bear upon it, striving, in a phrase Hegel uses elsewhere, to elevate empirical contents to the rank of necessary truth" (143).

According to Hegel in his *Lectures on the Philosophy of History*, "World History exhibits the development of the consciousness of freedom on the part of Spirit, and of the consequent realization of that freedom" (Walsh, 1960, 143).

In the Oriental world, despotism and slavery were the rule; freedom was confined to a single man, the monarch. From Sarkar's view Hegel is simply reading a particular stage of Oriental history, the Ksattriyan era. In the next stage of civilization, despotism becomes impure. Power becomes shared by monarchs and priests, exactly as Sarkar would write it. According to Brian Shetler:

> India takes the despotic rule that succeeded in China and built a vast religious superstructure on it that at once preserves it and transcends it . . . Indian religion is an attempt to overcome the insecurity, suffering and bondage of despotic rule . . . Thus, the despot is not a single person but all of nature, under which a political ruler must also labor. The Brahmanic priests and later the Buddhists priests enjoy higher standing that the political rulers as authorities on what are the duties of the political ruler (Shetler, 1990, 10).

But these two civilizations exist still in prehistory. It is only in the Middle-East with Zoroasterianism and then in Judaism that history begins. History begins there as Freedom extends from the despot or the priests to supernatural laws. Again for Shetler, "the despot can be deposed of by anyone following the commands of this supernatural order" (10).

History continues in the Greco-Roman world with freedom claimed as a right of citizens, but not all individuals, that is, slaves. Writes Walsh,

> This process has been completed by the Germanic nations of modern Europe, who have accepted the Christian principle of the infinite worth of individual men as such, and so have explicitly adopted the idea of liberty, although as Hegel notes, this does not mean they have carried it to full effect in their institutions (Walsh, 1960, 144).

Thus it is in the Christian West that history finds its negation of negation, its synthesis. While the French state stopped before it could complete Hegel's dialectic (the synthesis of the rational, the ethical and the spiritual) it is in the Prussian state that all can be achieved. The Spirit can find its true home.

Thus history has a notion of progress, but it is a particular notion, nested in the State. And every nation has a peculiar contribution to which it is destined, it its turn, to make to the process of world history.

This progress is further facilitated by great individuals. Certain men, like Caesar, Alexander or Napoleon are the chosen instruments of Destiny. For Hegel, then the Prussian state is the manifestation of the will of the Spirit. But why should the plot end there? Walsh argues that it does not, he quotes Hegel as having said "America is the land of the future, where, in the ages that lie before us, the burden of world's history will reveal itself" (152).

For Hegel then, the state is the culmination of history. There is a clear progression from the family, to civil society and then the state. The family is prior to society, the members of the family are united by the bond of feeling, love. But the family has its own seeds of destruction, for children pass out of it and become individuals. Then civil society with its institutions emerges wherein as opposed to the undifferentiated unity of the family, civil society allows for particularity. It is in the state, however, that we find differentiated universality, that is, unity in difference.

The state for Hegel is divine, it is "this actual God" (Copleston, 1963, 213). Sarkar, of course, does not see the state or any political formation as idea or a particular expression of divinity except insofar as everything that is, is an expression of divinity. Moreover, the mistake that Hegel makes is to believe that there is a hierarchy of states and that states follow a cyclical pattern. Thus, even in Hegel's own terms one can articulate a theory of history where the idea of freedom moves through a dialectic, but one does not need a spirit which moves from empire to empire to nation. Nor does one need a history that privileges the Christian West.

But in Hegel's view, it is Sarkar's notion of consciousness that is mistaken, but understandably so given the primitive Indian episteme. However, Hegel would agree that Sarkar's notion of the coming global world state, for Freedom then could find its finest expression—there would be unity and difference.

Hegel privileges the state for specific reasons. For Hegel, the well-developed state preserves the principle of private liberty. The will of the state must persevere over the will of the individual, and inasmuch as the will of the state, the universal or general will, is for him in some sense the real will of the individual. It follows then that the individual's identification of his interests with those of the state is the actualization of freedom.

But the movement to a global state for Hegel would most likely include conquest and war. Here Hegel and Sarkar differ, for Hegel rejects Kant's notion of perpetual peace, and argues that war is a necessary rational phenomenon. According to Copleston, "It is in fact for him the means by which the dialectic of history gets, so to speak, a move on. It prevents stagnation and preserves, as he puts it, the ethical health in nations. It is the chief means by which a people's spirit acquires renewed vigor or a decayed political organism is swept aside and gives place to a more vigorous manifestation of the Spirit" (Copleston, 1963, 218).

For Sarkar, war is the darkest blot on humanity's history. War is fought by workers and warriors for the sake of the theories of intellectuals and the expansionism of capitalists. However, for Sarkar what is necessary, is struggle. But this struggle need not be against other states, for Sarkar the state is not the end of all existence; one can struggle mentally, or struggle to create new goods that can benefit the people. Without struggle there is death. For Sarkar, life is struggle. It is only in the cosmic state of enlightenment where there is no struggle, when the mind has found its existential death in Pure Consciousness, but it is not a sorrowful death, it is the death of all deaths, and the final realization of the soul, of its true nature.

Among Other Problems

The problems with Hegel's work are numerous. Copleston develops some of these problems. Among them are if any nation rises to the top, then all that occurs is justified by the very fact that it occurs; thus imperialism is easily justified after the fact. The spirit has moved a country to do so. Thus, if one nation succeeds in conquering another, it follows that its action is justified by its success.

Thus, while an individual leader who conquers others may cause suffering to man, however, from a historical viewpoint his deeds are justified for he accomplishes what the universal spirit requires. Thus the spirit of world history is that which judges all events. Hegel would remark, according to Copleston (224), that he is simply taking seriously the notion of Providence—that God operates through history. This is similar to the notion of karma. What happens was meant to happen, and thus all actions can be justified. But Copleston argues that what is missing is morality.

> Once the transcendent God has been transformed into the Hegelian Absolute and judgment has been made purely immanent in history itself, no escape is left from the conclusion that from the world-historical point of view all the events and actions which form movements in the self-manifestation of the Absolute are justified. Moral questions are then irrelevant (224).

Voegelin, to be sure, would echo this perspective. Hegel falls into the Gnostic trap of misreading the Christian eschaton and placing the spirit concretely in history. In addition, Copleston asks: Why should not the goal of spirit be a universal world state or world society where personal freedom would be perfectly realized within an all-embracing unity? "Even if Hegel wishes to insist that the universal is manifested in its particulars and that the particulars in question are national spirits, it would seem that the ideal end of the whole movement should be a world federation, representing the concrete universal" (225).

Obviously Sarkar does not approach it this way. He does not insist on showing the role of Providence in history, this is not the problem from the Indian view or Sarkar reconstruction of Indian thought. For Sarkar, the problem is that of developing a good society, where power does not lead to exploitation, where humanity can finally take a bit of fresh air, away from the sleepless nights of fear and hunger.

However viewing the above criticisms from a sympathetic Hegelian perspective, Phil Carspecken argues that the type of critique we have used for Hegel is misleading in that Hegel was speaking metaphorically. The divisions Hegel makes are philosophical not historical. Hegel's mistake was to objectify this metaphor instead of keeping it in movement, unfixed. Hegel's mistake was to write his metaphor of the Absolute out. But Sarkar's mistake is far more serious.

> Sarkar's metaphors . . . seem to both claim to represent truth (rather than lead the thinker into an experience of truth) and to guide action so that one can become truth. As representation we have all the claims about microvita, [layers of the mind], luminous bodies, varnas and so on which are certainly claimed to be really true—objective and external to unit beings. Sarkar's own epistemology is a representational, sense-based one. He claims that ideology, as opposed to idea, is fallible necessarily but he does not integrate this useful idea with the rest of his philosophy, much of which is image drawing and action-prescribing. The rest claims to be 'true' representations of the world (Carspecken, personal communications, 1989).

From this view, given that Sarkar has initiated movements and associations to construct this new world of his, his theory is far more dangerous and disturbing than Hegel's for Hegel's influence remained theoretical, while Sarkar, like Marx's, intends to change our material, intellectual and spiritual conditions.

Moreover Sarkar too speaks of God in history, although from an Indian episteme this is not a judgmental god favoring a particular group of people, nonetheless, the absolute has entered and for the enlightened person, like Krishna, morality does not exist, for in his person, all discourses find their unity. Sarkar's response would be one that points to the reality of present suffering and the inability of various ideologies to speak to them in a way that fulfills the human spirit and the human stomach. Thus it would be based on the real conditions of the present: physical, mental and spiritual.

There is one final important relationship between Hegel and Sarkar previously touched upon that we now develop. This is the dialectical relationship of spirit and matter. For Hegel, the negation is solved with the spirit in the Prussian state. First for Sarkar everything is consciousness and all living entities are reflections of the consciousness (even inanimate rocks but to a lesser degree). Spiritual consciousness cannot enter the nation, as it is but a human sentiment, a construct. While then it is possible to develop a hierarchy of spiritual individuals, thus again allowing Hegel's world historical figures, for Sarkar these are spiritual figures, who find lasting "fame" through leadership as servitude. The nation simply is another sentiment that prevents humans from seeing their essential unity in consciousness. In this way, all human associations are fundamentally instrumentalist.

The question for Sarkar becomes which ones can aid in the process of realizing spiritual purposes. Only the family ranks high here since it provides stability and protection. All other unions except those such as the Sangha are constructed as dogmas (although spiritual communities too fall into power). For Sarkar, first there is unity, then there is a separation between consciousness and nature. The separation is exacerbated in humans who have the choice of following the natural or recreating the natural. Most animals and plants do not have that choice as the follow their instincts, the natural. However, this unity is regained periodically with individuals and then potentially in the coming spiritual new era. According to Sarkar, as human beings evolve, they move from individual, to mental, to spiritual levels. As Acarya Ratnesh argues in his *Microvita: The Cosmic Seeds of Life*:

> Finally they realize that the responsibility for the care and unfolding of the potentialities of the whole universe is their joint responsibility with the Supreme Creator or Cosmic Consciousness . . . Individually, human beings should make efforts to merge their minds into the mind of the Supreme Creator, while collectively they should work for the development and utilization of all of the hidden potentialities of the universe (Ratnesh, 1989, 150).

Walter Truett Anderson in his *To Govern Evolution* presents a similar argument that humans now must consciously govern planetary evolution if they are to survive. Genetics and other technologies thought of as unnatural are suddenly part of the natural evolution of the species. Sarkar, however, instead of humans becoming managers, would privilege a spiritual discourse wherein humans are co-creators with *Prakrti* in human evolution. His notion of the social cycle as alterable falls in this line of argument. The natural has been understood and naturally humans can move and evolve with the cycle of creation, co-creating and constructing it for the future within the bounds of the structure of the universe.

Summarizing this section on Hegel and Sarkar, both these thinkers, while perhaps spiritually in proximity, in fact, stand far apart. They differ in the their definition of the spirit, of the state, of war, of world historical individuals and in terms of approach. For Hegel the spirit is the idea, for Sarkar it is multi-leveled but ultimately inexpressible. For Hegel the state is finest expression of freedom that resolves the contradictions of family and institutions. For Sarkar the state is another dogma, however, a world government is needed to balance nationalism. For Hegel, war leads to greater human expression, for Sarkar it is the darkest blot in humanity's history, although struggle is the most important characteristic in individual and collective development. For Hegel world historical figures are great leaders, for Sarkar Hegel's figures are but ksattriyans. For Sarkar the key historical figures are the spiritually enlightened ones, those who bring dharma and devotion to the world. Finally for Sarkar, Hegel is too idealistic, unconcerned of the material world, while for Hegel, Sarkar is too mystical and contradictory, for even as Sarkar criticizes Hegel, he uses Hegelian dialectics and calls for a world state. For Hegel, Sarkar is more Hegelian than Sarkar would ever admit.

Marx

Sarkar is also more Marxist than Sarkar would admit. Like Sarkar, Marx attempted to develop a theory to consciously evolve society into progressively fairer material conditions. Begun by Marx (1818–1883) and continued by Engels, Lenin, and Gramsci, this vision attempted to move away from the idealism of Hegel and construct a dialectical and historical materialism that had a vision of the future. Our focus here will not be an in-depth comparison as this has already been extensively covered in the PROUT literature.

Indeed, every PROUT publication tends to include a section so much so that it has become obligatory to compare Sarkar and Marx. The debt to Marx is thus huge. This book in itself has had Marx as a shadow throughout. Sarkar's section on the Vaeshyan era closely follows Marx's theory. Moreover, by calling his alternative theory Progressive Spiritual Socialism (PROUT), Sarkar places himself within Marxist critical thinking and places himself outside of it. Sarkar's work is progressive because history can be changed, because the future is bright. Sarkar's work is spiritual because the end all of reality is the spiritual, it is the measure of all things. Sarkar is socialist because he focuses on the marginalized, on collective self-reliance, limits to the ownership of wealth, and because his ideal society is cooperative in its orientation.

Sarkar himself speaks rarely of Marx. In his lecture on the views of other faiths, he simply asserts that Marxism is mistaken in that it removes the essential differences between people in its quest for equality; it can only thrive in poverty and exploited areas. Marxism has little tolerance for other philosophical points of view, and for that it is essentially violent. What is important here is that he includes his comments in his section on the view of other faiths or ideologies, that is, the location of Marxism as a real competitor with Sarkar's own cosmology. Noteworthy is that his students spent entire sections asserting the differences and superiority of PROUT. This emphasizes the debt owed and the attempt to distance PROUT from Marxism.

In another place, Sarkar asserts the following with respect to Marx.

> Centering round a remark about religion by the great Karl Marx, a class of exploiters goes hysteric and raises quite a storm. It should be borne in mind that Karl Marx was never antagonistic to spirituality, moralism and good conduct. Whatever he said was against the then religion, for he had visualized, understood and felt that the then religion had paralyzed man mentally, made him impotent and dispirited by instigating him to submit to the vicious circle (Sarkar, 1987b, 5: 89)

Sarkar's message is similar. Religions with their emphasis on fate and karma force individuals into social impotency. "Those who try to break the vaeshyan structure and show tortured humanity the path of salvation should advise them to avoid the narcotic influence of religion" (89). In this sense, both Marx and Sarkar take off from Comte in their critique of the theological stage of humanity.

We do not summarize Marx and Marxism as this has been accomplished in innumerable books. We simply point out some similarities and differences and then concentrate on two concepts that clarify Sarkar's thought, namely, Gramsci's concept of hegemony and the organic intellectual.

In his comparison of Sarkar and Marx, Batra points out the following which essentially captures the Sarkarian critique.

> Both Marx and Sarkar use a historical method of analysis, both believe in the inevitability of historical patterns of societal evolution, though not in the repetition of events themselves, and both agree that capitalism will be brought to an end by some sort of revolution, although to Sarkar this revolution may be bloody or peaceful, whereas to Marx it will be bloody and violent. Marx calls for the revolution of the proletariat, whereas to Sarkar it is the social revolution [or evolution] of the Shudras (Batra, 1978, 36).

In addition, both speak for the workers and peasants, asserts Batra. Other salient similarities include both believe oppression and injustice *can* be ended; both argue that it *will* be ended through struggle. For Sarkar this struggle is spiritual as well as physical, intellectual, and economic; for Marx, the spiritual would be critically down played or recast in the mold of humanism, given his critique of the clergy. Both accept violence as legitimate ways of ending oppression, both accept non-democratic means of governance. Marxists calls democracy bourgeois dictatorship, while Sarkar, although considering democracy the lesser evils of current political systems, still considers it (when it is devoid of a moral and educational basis, and controlled by clever politicians) "foolocracy," that is, "government of the fools, by the fools and for the fools" (Sarkar, 1987a, 2:12). In this sense both accept elite rule as beneficial for only it can control the power tactics of capitalists, aristocrats and others. In Sarkar's words, "when progressive socialism is established within the framework of democracy, then democracy will be successful" (12). Both accept that real change must be global, not isolated in any single nation, to a minor extent the Trotsky formula of permanent revolution. Sarkar is sympathetic to Wallerstein's (1984) assertion that the capturing of state power by socialist movements has only in the long run strengthened the world system as a whole. Thus to counter the statist nature of politics he has developed revolutionary strategies outside of state politics, including self-reliance movements, ecological movements, spiritual movements, womanist movements and other transnational as well trans-statist approaches to changing the cultural frames of meaning which exhibit the world to us. Revolution for Sarkar is about the rotation of the social cycle and the collective psychology, but it is also fundamentally internal. It is fundamentally cosmological.

Both Sarkar and Marx have significant differences in their philosophical thought. Sarkar comes from a theory of history and from philosophical schools that are Indian and thus ideational. At the same time, he writes not from Europe but from the periphery of Calcutta. Marx, conversely, wrote a century earlier, responding to the notion of social progress, the laws of evolution, as well as to Hegel. While Marx may have stood Hegel on his head, Sarkar makes them both sit down in meditation and then into social action (And no dinner either but strict yogic fasting).

The differences are obvious and many, we will simply gloss a few. Marx's theory is ultimately uni-linear with the ideal future state a higher order of an ancient state when there was no private property and thus no alienation and division of labor. History is dialectical and here Sarkar is in total debt to Hegel and Marx, although Sarkar does come to it through Tantra. For Marx, history is certainly not cyclical, and if spiral, then it is a spiral that abruptly ends once property is collectivized and labor recovered. The purpose of the State ends once this alienation ends. Man is himself again. For Sarkar, history is cyclical and the State will forever be needed. The dialectical conflict between

> vidya and avidya will continue forever. So the necessity of having police or military force in greater or lesser degree will be eternally felt. Of course with the establishment of a world Government, its necessity will decrease. With the perpetual fight between vidya and avidya, the class rivalry is bound to persist, more or less. Hence, those who fly on the wings of imagination for sitting idle and living a life in repose on the establishment of a classless society will have to become disappointed (Sarkar, 1978b, 2:87).

There is no finally synthesis—the battle between basic forces in the universe is endless. This is again the fundamental realization of the ancients. It is the fundamental lesson of all mythology: good and evil exist within. This is what leads Ssu-Ma Ch'ien, Khaldun, Voegelin to remain committed to the cycle. It is only in the European Gnostic division of time that evil suddenly ends and a synthesis is achieved, whether through Marxism or liberalism or a futuristic post-industrial version of post-scarcity robotism wherein all humans can finally achieve a leisurely life. For the ancients, the problem of the paradoxical nature of the universe could not be resolved at the collective level. No utopia was possible. However, individuals could leave society and find their enlightenment. Later with the concept of the bodhisattva, compassion for others forces the enlightened one to work in the world until the last blade of grass realized enlightenment. But for Sarkar, a collective and individual future better than today, is possible. In Sarkar words: "In the state of a perfectly harmonious social order, none shall run like a cur, run after name and fortune. The environment of the external world will help the attainment of harmony of the mind and the wants shall gradually be on the decrease" (Sarkar, 1978b, 2). Unlike Marx, for Sarkar the ultimate problem is not private property. While all property from Sarkar's view is nested in Cosmic Consciousness, humans can and should use it for the benefit of all. Tadbhavananda Avadhuta and Jayanta Kumar argue in their *The New Wave*:

> From a psychological viewpoint, private property is the natural expression of the instinctive tendency to satisfy selfish desires with no consideration for the needs of others. While the collectivization of private property can eliminate overt exploitation, it can never challenge the selfish, greedy tendencies in the human mind (Tadbhavananda Avadhuta and Jayanta Kumar, 1985, 70).

For Sarkar as exploitation is psychological, these selfish tendencies must find gateways into higher values, otherwise the same forms will find more destructive forms—surveillance, apathy, anomie, among other problems.

Furthering these critical comments on Marxism, or actually "vulgar Marxism", the Marxist notion of class misses the notion of collective psychology or group mind. Other sentiments such as religion, the idea, are neglected. In Marx's reconciliation of materialism and idealism, he over emphasizes the material, thus placing Marxism in a paradoxical situation wherein it cannot explain its own origination since it is an idea that has changed the social relations, not a new technology or force of production. For Sarkar, this is natural for ideologies change the way the world is constructed. Their forms are determined by the particular varna of the era. Thus Islam had to be more ksattriyan to succeed. Using Sarkar's six spokes of civilization argument, Marxism has a preceptor; Marx has texts, the Communist Manifesto and subsequent authoritative texts, Mao's red book; and has a socio-economic theory, which is, in fact, its strength. However, in terms of social outlook, it is humanist but does not express the needed concerns of plants and animals. It is not universal. Moreover it privileges one class over others, the worker class.

While rightfully so, for Sarkar, the liberation of all is the task. Thus the capitalist by oppressing the worker suppresses his or her own spiritual tendencies and thereby becomes in the long run a victim as well. The task is to liberate the capitalist as well. This task is essentially spiritual. It is finding ways to allow the capitalist to enter the deeper levels of mind. But if this impossible, then for Sarkar, force can be used. In this sense Sarkar comes out not as process or means-oriented as the Buddhist or Gandhian approach. Finally, Marxism is pathetically weak at spiritual practices and spiritual ideology.

Other significant differences are metaphysical. For example, for Marx the universe is a constant flux, for Sarkar it is in rest and motion with each association (self, society, civilization) finding inspiration or death at the point of rest. Also, Sarkar in terms of his ideal society would simply limit physical wealth and find ways to maximize the use and distribution of intellectual and spiritual wealth.

Notwithstanding these differences, the prose of Sarkar often is Marxian prose. For example, let us take the fundamental proposition of Marxism from the Communist Manifesto.

> That in every historical epoch, the prevailing mode of economic production and exchange, and the social organization necessarily following from it, form the basis upon which is built up, and from which alone can be explained, the political and intellectual history of that epoch; that consequently the whole history of mankind (since the dissolution of primitive tribal society, holding land in common ownership) has been a history of class struggles forms a series of evolutions in which, nowadays, a stage has been reached where the exploited and oppressed class—the proletariat—cannot attain its emancipation from the sway of the exploiting and ruling class—the bourgeoisie—without, at the same time, and once and for all, emancipating society at large from all exploitation, oppression, class distinctions and class struggles (Marx and Engels, 1975, 13).

This can be easily translated into Sarkar's lanaguage (our words below):

> In every historical epoch, the collective psychology of the era, and the socio-psychic organizations necessarily following from it, form the basis upon which is built up, and from which alone can be explained, the physical and material history of that epoch and consequently the whole history of humankind (since the awakening of social responsibility and warrior mentality) has been a history of class struggle—contests between humans and nature, between humans and humans, between humans and ideas, and between humans and nature, humans ideas and resources—contests between exploiting and exploited, ruling and

oppressed classes; that the history of these class struggles forms a series of evolutions and revolutions in which each class as taken power and then lost power. The history of humanity has been a history of suffering. No class can attain its emancipation—neither shudra, ksattriya, vipra, vaeshya—without, at the same time, and once and for all, emancipating society at large from all exploitation, oppression, class distinctions and class struggles. This is only possible through the sadvipras, the spiritual intellectuals, guided by the Attraction to the Great as they work from the hub of the cycle, allowing each class to progressively administer the whole, but never allowing any class to exploit the whole.

The ease of translation tells us a great deal. Moreover, Sarkar has no problem with Marxian comments such as "The philosophers have only interpreted the world, in various ways, the points is to change it" (Bender, 1972, 155). At the same time, Sarkar would comment that Marx is partially correct when he asserts that "In direct contrast to German philosophy which descends from heaven to earth, here we ascend from earth to heaven [and] Life is not determined by consciousness, but consciousness by life" (171). From Sarkar's view Marx is speaking of the second half of the cycle of creation, *Brahmachakra*. But Marx misses the first half when Consciousness crudifies into the Idea (Cosmic Mind) and then into Nature. Thus, Marx is simply incomplete, however this is critical as it neglects the higher layers of awareness and consciousness.

Moving to political philosophy how do these two thinkers speak the relationship of power and society? Again we find fundamental agreement when Marx asserts that the ideas of the epoch are those of the ruling class.

> The ideas of the ruling class are in every epoch the ruling ideas, i.e. the class which is the ruling material force of society is at the same time its ruling intellectual force. The class which has the means of the material production at its disposal, has control at the same over the means of mental production, so that thereby, generally speaking, the ideas of those who lack the means of mental production are subject to it . . . Insofar, therefore, as they rule as a class and determine the extent and compass of an epoch. For instance, in an age and in a country where royal power, aristocracy and bourgeoisie are contending for mastery and where, therefore, mastery is shared, the doctrine of the separation of powers proves to be the dominant idea and is expressed as an 'eternal law' (183).

For Sarkar, while it is true that ideas of the ruling class are the ideas of the epoch, this is not necessarily so because the ruling class controls the material forces, equally important is normative power. For example, during the Vipran era, the clergy control the relevant ideas (the shape the construction of the real); they may or may not have direct state power and direct economic power. However, there is an iso-morphism between the ideas of the age, the ideas of the ruling class, and the general group worldview. There is an interaction between the ideas of the epoch and the ideas of the elite, both create each other. This interaction is clear to Marx as well. The bourgeois "com-pels all nations, on pain of extinction, to adopt the bourgeois mode of production; it compels them to introduce what it calls civilization into their midst, i.e. to become bourgeois themselves. In one word, it creates a world after its own image" (245). Indeed, for Sarkar, each varna does this in turn. Each creates the world in its own image and then because of its own contradictions, a new way of see-ing the world comes into dominance with an accompanying elite, which again reconstructs the real in that image and then makes it natural. For Gramsci, this was hegemony, a cultural force which imposes dominance. Central to hegemony is the consent of major groups in the ideological control of one class over others. While Sarkar hints at this term, it would be useful to further develop hege-mony as a way to explain how the different classes are consumed by the dominant class, how their dominance comes to be seen as natural. Marsha Hansen explains hegemony as such.

> Hegemony is important to Gramsci in analyzing historical develop-ment. Rather than conclude that fundamental historical crises are directly causes by economic crises Gramsci offers that economic crises 'can only create a more favorable ground for the propagation of cer-tain ways of thinking, of posing and solving questions which involve the whole future development of State life' (Galtung and Inayatullah, 1997, 131).

In this way, the economic moves off center stage allowing cultural-ideological vectors to play an increased role.

But for Marx Sarkar makes the mistake of detaching the "ideas of the ruling class from the ruling class itself and attribut[ing] to them an independent existence" (Bender, 1972, 184). Sarkar's mis-take is that he does not emphasize the material conditions of pro-duction, the typical mistake of the idealist or the intellectual. They are removed from the real.

> [By] ignor[ing] the individuals and world conditions which are the source of the ideas, we can say, for instance, that during the time that

the aristocracy was dominant, the concepts honor, loyalty etc . . . were dominant [as Sarkar does], during the dominance of the bourgeoisie the concepts freedom, equality, etc. [were dominant] (184).

Marx's lasting contribution is his linking the actual forces of production and the power relations in society. This dialectic and his escape from it is his genius.

Both Marx and Sarkar are similar in their escape clauses from history. Both create theories with adherents committed to bringing about their particular vision. While these theories make for interesting social science research, they also raise numerous questions, while this is not the place to elaborate these, the problem of the Gulag is worth elaborating. Michel Foucault (1980a) has brilliantly made this point. His question is: What in various texts of Marx and Lenin made the Gulag possible? This question should not posed in that an error was made, but rather what within the discourse made the Gulag all but natural. Moreover, to state the question as everyone as their own Gulag does injustice to the reality of those that suffer. Ashis Nandy (1987), as earlier pointed out, raises the same issue of caste. One can see the violence of caste as an error in India or as a natural derivation from Hindu cosmology. How one chooses to see it is ultimately political. In this way, Sarkar and PROUT can learn from Marxists texts and actions. The obvious location of the "Gulag" is in Sarkar's theory of leadership, which although spiritual—the leader as simple, as servant, as having endured suffering—is at the same time technocratic. It places the burden of monitoring, forecasting, planning and engineering the entire social cycle, of the entire future of humanity, on the leadership. While Sarkar places responsibility not in any particular sadvipra but on the board of sadvipras, an oligarchy of leaders (dictatorship at times, democratic at other times, depending on the particular epoch), the potential violence (textual and possibly physical) required to move the cycle is tremendous. The cycle must be interpreted and interpreted authoritatively for its engineering to be possible. It must be interpreted based on various texts of Sarkar, and while Sarkar's texts are rich enough to allude would be totalitarian leaders, they are broad enough to allow a range of interpretations, among them to justify population control of the mentally ill, for example (Sarkar, 1987b, 13:44–48). The question of definition, Sarkar leaves vague. What horrors will be committed by these sadvipras against the other classes is not difficult to predict. The problem of determining who is the sadvipra, the progressive class, and who is the reactionary class, as Marxists have had to endure, is equally problematic. But remembering Foucault and Nandy, the question should not be left to for a Stalin to interpret, but rather from the outset should be confronted. As Nandy reminds us, utopian constructions must have escape ways built in them, such that their definition of the future does not force the closure of an entire generation. Does Sarkar's theory have these?

If our comparison with the above writers has merit, it does have a few escape paths: the notion of the cyclical change in power; personal non-violence; tolerance toward philosophical diversity; the different layers of consciousness; and, the soft laws of the Indian episteme. Yet at the same time, in its lack of clarity between metaphor and true representations of the real, as argued by Carspecken, these openings are few, the closures are many. While the cycle provides an escape route, at the same time, it provides the closure, for Sarkar places the sadvipra in the hub of the cycle, as the controllers. Once the metaphor is used that way, than those with complete mind can but be at the center.

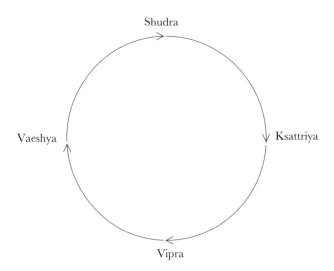

Historical Social Cycle

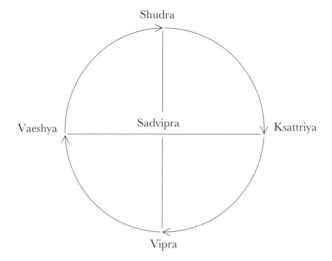

Ideal-Future Social Cycle

Also flowing naturally from the Indian episteme is the notion that leadership must be spiritual in terms of actual behaviors and it must reflect the cosmic. That is, this leadership must be have access to the divine either as enlightened ones, as bodhisattvas, as avatars, or to move to the western concept as Nietzsche's superman or Hegel's world historical figures, or Lenin's vanguard of the revolution (which Sarkar reinterprets as his *viksubdha shudras*), or indeed the more spiritual ideational interpretation of Teilhard De Chardin.

Alternatively and far less ambitious is another useful concept by Gramsci. This is his organic intellectuals. Gramsci holds that all individuals engage in intellectual activity, yet various intellectuals play a distinct political role. According to Carl Boggs in his *The Two Revolutions: Antonio Gramsci and the Dilemmas of Western Marxism*, for Gramsci,

> the more 'advanced intellectuals' would presumably take on a large number of indispensable ideological-cultural projects: subverting the illusions of conventional ideologies, introducing and disseminating critical views of social reality, presenting an alternative vision of the future (Boggs, 1984, 222–223).

This is different from the bourgeois definition of intellectuals as technical experts or learned men of culture. At the same time, for Sarkar, these intellectuals must be willing to work and live with the masses at their material conditions if they want to play a revolutionary role. But the key role of the spiritual intellectual is to aid in liberating the intellects of other intellectuals allowing them to move past nationalism and other conventional "isms" and toward spiritual universalism. Thus, Sarkar and Gramsci's intellectuals must declass themselves and not choose the elitist positions available to them.

In this way, these intellectuals would develop theory from action. "Only through the mediation of such organic intellectuals could an authentic revolutionary subjectivity be realized; they would provide the dynamic connecting link between theory and practice, the intellectual and the spontaneous, the political and social" (223). The problem for Sarkar, however, is that intellectuals see themselves as a special class and suffer from the psychology of superiority. They forget that the intellect is but a tool of the larger mind. The intelligentsia, moreover, remain aloof from the practical world, and for example, the understandings of workers and farmers. At the same time, while he is utterly critical for intellectuals who remain outside of the spiritual realm, and those who use the power of knowledge for their own class interests, he does see the role of intellectuals as increasing social economic wealth. For Sarkar, intellectuals who add value to services that increase the collective good should be rewarded. However, the writer, for example, must be ready to

> fight against the oppositions of thousands of superstitions and man's petty selfishness, his pen may break into pieces, his brush may be compelled to draw only lines of water on the canvas, his theatrical stances may perhaps end in mute gestures, yet his efforts shall not cease. [The writer] has to face humiliation and abuse every moment. But one who is afraid of such things cannot give anything to humanity. One who has no moral courage and no solid ground under his feet cannot provide a soothing shelter of bliss to others (Sarkar, 1973, 114).

The responsibility for Sarkar's spiritual intellectuals is high. "The true writer is not only a creator but a sage as well. As the representative of millions and as the architect of society, he cannot forget even for a moment the highest sanctity of his avocation. He is the messenger of the mute masses, the guardian of the society" (116).

Like Sarkar, who asserts that out of these intellectuals, a few sadvipras might emerge, not from the heavens but from the struggle ahead, for Gramsci, too, while he "conceded that intellectual defectors from the bourgeois would play a key role in the early stages of the revolutionary change, insisted that the crucial force over the long run would have to a 'new type of intellectual' generated through class struggle itself" (Boggs, 1984, 224). Both Sarkar and Marx declass intellectuals or reclass them, not as exploiters but as those who can play a historical role in promoting a new society. This is different from the role of intellectual as great philosopher or solely as critic, rather, the intellectual becomes part of the mass and works for the mass. For Sarkar, they must organize and mobilize so as to expose the hypocrisy of politicians, capitalists, and clergy in whatever epoch. At the same time, organizations devoted to the interests of academics and students need to be established which protect the rights of intellectuals and students from the State and Market.

For Sarkar, the source of revolutionary intellectuals is obvious. They are those who cannot pursue their intellectual abilities because of the capitalist system and those who have had their spiritual and social consciousness awakened. He warns intellectuals:

> It is far too easy to talk bit about revolution. . . . such tall talks may easily strike the listeners with wonder and may also draw applause from them, but to bring about a real revolution is not at all easy. The pioneers of revolution will have to learn discipline, take proper training for the revolution, build their character, be moralists—in a word, they will have to be what I call the sadvipras (Sarkar, 1973, 161).

And at the same time, Sarkar limits the role of the intellect of the intellectual, placing it as one step on the path of truth, one way of knowing, a necessary tool.

Elite Theory

The difficulty of transforming intellectuals though is obvious. Thornstein Veblen's *The Theory of the Leisure Class* articulates some of these. In his theory, he argues that in all societies there exists a leisure class that thrives by plundering the wealth of the other classes. Instead of pride in work, which was the natural state, the class became predatory. "Their work was predatory; they seized their riches by force or cunning and took no part in the actual production of wealthy by sweat or skill . . . far from being rewarded as wasters or spoilers . . . they did so with the full approval of the community . . . they were looked upon as strong and able" (Heilbroner, 1969, 209). Indeed, overtime, the leisure class gained respect.

Through history, there has always been a leisure class, with different methods but the same goal. For Khaldun this was a natural degeneration in leadership. For Sarkar as well. Leadership first desires to be progressive (meeting social goals), then over time it degenerates becoming solely concerned with its own goals. Each class displays its monuments: the warriors display their conquests (land and slaves), the intellectuals their theories and geo-political victories, and the vaeshyas their obscene wealth. Each group seeks to remain the leisure class. Instead of working for the mass, intellectuals and other groups find themselves working to increase their wealth and their leisure time, at the expense of the other classes. This is the same for the laborer class, who instead of revolution, seek to gain in material force and join the elites (most recently through the illusion of the national lottery system). Yet for Sarkar in the long run, this is impossible, and eventually, conditions create revolution or evolution. But the desire for leisure, wealth, a life of fame, remains part of the natural desires of humans. In the capitalist age, this mental malady becomes particularly brutal. For Toynbee and Galtung, the leisure class is the superstructure that eventually causes the downfall of the civilization as it increasingly becomes rigid and unable to deal with internal and external proletariat. This inability to negotiate terms with the other classes is structural, for production and ecological constraints can only support a certain group at such a high degree of consumption and wealth.

In addition to Veblen, who clearly augments Sarkar (and should be explicitly brought in to Sarkar theory) the two obvious two writers to compare Sarkar with and who add considerably to Sarkar's project are Pareto and Mosca. When Sarkar states that the Shudra era is to be followed by the Ksattriyan era, the Ksattriyan era by the Vipran era, and the Vipran era by the Vaeshyan era, culminating in a social evolution [or revolution] and "In the flow of the social cycle, a class is always dominant" (Sarkar, 1982, 166) the obvious comparisons are with Vilfredo Pareto and his theory of the circulation of elites as well as Gaetano Mosca's theory that in each and every group or association or structure, there is always a ruling elite.

For sure Sarkar speaks of two different things here: the social and psychological characteristics of the era and the characteristics of the class that is dominant in that era. His history is written largely as a history of the movement between eras—at the level of varna or structure. He is less concerned with the movement of leadership within a particular varna. At the same time there is a correspondence between the era and its leadership type. Leadership circulates with varna. Batra in his interpretation of Sarkar tends of focus less on the larger grand model—the supersystem—and more on the rise and fall of elites.

To further this comparison and to find ways to further develop Sarkar's theory, we closely examine, first, Pareto and then Mosca. Both writers were Italian, Pareto (1848–1923) lived to see the rise of Fascism and Gaetano Mosca (1858–1941) almost lived to see its end. Politically, they wrote in opposition to bourgeois democracy and to socialism. Pareto grounded his work in economics believing that society is governed by laws that can be modeled by economic equations. On the other hand, Mosca was clearly interested in power and political science, attempting to move beyond the traditionally Aristotelian classification of governments. For Pareto, the key explanatory concept is the circulation of elites, while for Mosca it is the balance of social forces. Both concepts are isomorphic to Sarkar's perspective. However, there are vast differences, in specific, Sarkar's project is spiritual, ecologically humanistic and socialist while Pareto and Mosca write with, if not a contempt, a suspicion of the working classes. While Sarkar is highly doubtful of the leadership ability of the shudras', he balances this stance with a concern for the marginalized and an appreciation for individual wisdom, although collectively for Sarkar the politics of shudradom is but mobocracy. With Pareto and Mosca, especially the former, little balance is exhibited in terms of the rights and the empowerment of the marginalized.

Pareto and the Circulation of the Elites

For Pareto, hierarchy is natural. All societies have elites. Writes Pareto:

> Except during short intervals of time, people are always governed by an elite. I use the word elite . . . in its etymological sense, meaning the strongest, the most energetic, and most capable—for good as well as evil. However . . . elites do not last. *Hence—the history of man is the history of the continuous replacement of certain elites: as one ascends, another declines. Such is the real phenomenon, though to us it may often appear under another form* (Pareto, 1968, 36).

The word elite is used in two different ways. It is first used as a measure of excellence in a particular field—those scoring the highest marks in whatever possible test—and secondly used to denote the rise and fall of groupings of power in history. Thus, we do not have the rise and fall of virtue, of dharma, of the tao, of the spirit, of power, but a movement in and out of elites. While Pareto uses this term largely for the government and economy, these terms can be applied to science, religion, art as well as ethics, for example. Thus, there can be an aristocracy of saints or an aristocracy of brigands, an aristocracy of the learned, an aristocracy . . . of the learned, an aristocracy of the criminal and so on. The totality of qualities promoting the well-being and domination of a class in society constitutes something which we will call simply the elite (Pareto, 1966, 155). Equality then for Pareto is impossible, there is always a movement to excellence, to difference, and thus to elitism.

To develop his theory of elites, the key analytic tool Pareto uses are the residues or sentiments or subconscious feelings. For Sarkar, these are simply the various desires in the body, the *vrittis* that constitute the human glandular system and the various psychic centers. For Sarkar, these include fear, lust, the Attraction to the Great, passion, envy, doubt, and so forth—the humanistic discourse of the self. But Pareto uses these residues concretely in his theory. He breaks these residues into six classes with two of these classes essential for his theory of elites. The first is innovation and the second is consolidation. Immediately, we should be reminded of Khaldun's dynastic model. The dynasty begins with the innovator and then eventually moves to a consolidation phase where it imitates past behavior. Indeed, as mentioned earlier, most rise and fall theories follow Khaldun's. These residues form the elite, the rest are the mass. The political structure lasts longer if the elite are open to upward mobility of others who are high in elite capabilities (as measured by some excellence index), thus allowing a faster circulation of elites. The best societies are those in which the elite circulate the quickest.

> Society is harmed not only by the accumulation of inferior elements in upper strata but also by the accumulation in lower strata of superior elements which are prevented form rising. If at one and the same time the upper strata are filled with inferior elements and the lower strata with superior elements, the social equilibrium becomes highly unstable and a violent revolution is imminent (159).

Like other grand theorists, Pareto uses the body as metaphor to articulate his theory. "In a certain sense, the social body is comparable to the human body which perishes very quickly if it cannot eliminate toxic elements" (159). The ideal situation is when elites are in rapid circulation and if the residues of his various classes are balanced. However, this does not always happen. What results is classic Khaldun, "after victory, the elite becomes more rigid and more exclusive" (86). The children of the elite come into power without adequate talents and thus the elite becomes decadent as they are no longer composed of the most gifted individuals.

But unlike Sarkar who gives us different social types, Pareto does not. Rather he rests his theory on the classes of residues, specifically, the residues of innovation and consolidation. This division has some similarity to Sarkar's work. The new leadership and collective psychology comes in and is innovative; it solves some problem, meets some struggle or develops out of the previous class, but eventually the class attempts to consolidate power. Each elite distributes and accumulates different types of power, then. Indeed, that is one way to see Sarkar's different eras. The new varna comes in and redistributes power and then over time consolidates its power. Over time, it abuses this power and then the next varna comes in to redistribute power.

However, the pattern that Pareto sees is not the cycle, rather it is the pendulum, power oscillates, moving between one type of residue to another. Innovative residues lead to a new system, but this new elite does not have enough consolidators, that is, individuals willing to use force to maintain the system. The innovative elite thus becomes soft. It speaks rhetorically for humanitarianism, but, in fact, is brutal.

> When an elite declines, we can generally observe two signs which manifest themselves simultaneously: (1) the declining elite becomes softer, milder, more humane and less apt to defend its own power, and (2) on the other hand, it does not lose its rapacity and greed for the goods of others, but rather tends as much as possible to increase its unlawful appropriations and to indulge in major usurpations of the national money (Pareto, 1968, 59).

And, "when we speak of the diminishing strength of the dominant class, we by no means refer to a decrease in violence; it even occurs very frequently that the weak are precisely those who are also violent" (70).

For Pareto, elite rule wherein elites are rapidly circulating is the best governance. Pleas for humanitarian equality have no value, since they would never be enacted. In fact, these pleas only weaken the elite and its various defenses of rights. In the following passage, we see Pareto's interpretation of this.

> It should be noted that Buddhism, which proclaimed the equality of all men, has generated the theocracy of Tibet; and the religion of Christ, which seemed especially made for the poor and humble, has generated the Roman theocracy. This was in its turn challenged by a new elite at the time of the Reformation, but since it was not yet entirely decadent, it suffered only partial defeat. The decline of the old elite and its increasing arrogance at the time of the Reformation can be clearly seen in the emergence of the robber barons. *As usual, the new elite leaned on the poor and humble; as usual, these believed in the promises made to them; as usual they were deceived, and yoke weighed even heavier on their shoulders than before* (87).

Thus, elites rule for themselves, not for anyone else. As with the non-withering of the Marxist state, Pareto appears to have made a telling forecast.

For Pareto, a high degree of circulation promises more wealth, while stasis, for example, as in any caste system, does not allow the best to come forward and take their rightful place as leaders. But the new elite do not come into power representing themselves, rather they claim to represent the people, or other legitimate political expressions. Here Pareto is clearly critical of the socialist parties. Government then does not remain neutral, rather it aids one class over another.

The privileging of the elite has one implication, not a necessary one, but one that certainly is explicit in Pareto. In Pareto's words: "Those who demanded equality of citizens before the law certainly did not foresee the privileges which the masses now enjoy . . . Those who demanded equality of taxes to aid the poor did not imagine that there would be a progressive tax at the expense of the rich" (Manicas, 1987, 154).

And speaking about the ideal distribution of differences, "A consequence of the heterogeneity of society is that rules of conduct, beliefs, morals, should be, in part at least, different for the different parts of society in order to obtain maximum utility for the society" (154). For Pareto there is indeed no evidence that equality is advantageous. For Sarkar, following John Rawls, inequality is only useful if it leads to more equality. Thus, his ideal political economy has a clear (but dynamically changing) upper limit to wealth accumulation as well as a minimum floor. Rewarding excellence for Sarkar should lead to the social good. Yet at the same time Sarkar's describes shudras as lazy, and prone to their instinctual selves. Linking this to democracy, again, Sarkar attacks it as a system which local leaders and capitalists can use for their own gain. The essence of the argument is that votes can be bought, politicians use the democratic platform for factionalism, and in the long run the best interests of all the classes are not maintained.

However, he sees democracy in a historical positive light perceiving it as a progressive revolt against monarchy. In countries with high educational levels it is indeed the appropriate form of governance. And until there can be leadership from spiritual, enlightened leaders, "democracy is a preference to other systems" (Sarkar, 1978a, 2:16).

At the same time, Sarkar supports a democratic world government, with a neo-Magna Carta. This new constitutional framework (1) guarantees purchasing capacity for all (economic rights); (2) protection for plants and animals, (ecological rights); (3) the right to follow spiritual practices, cultural history, cultural education and indigenous linguistic expressions (spiritual, educational and cultural rights); and, (4) that basic human values take priority with respect to the above three, for example, the saving of life takes priority over a cultural value that favor the taking of animal life (meatism, for example). Thus, he privileges basic rights as a way to deal with the abuse of power instead of locating the solution at the other side of the equation, public representation. Sarkar begs the public representation argument by first arguing historically that no democracy has ever had true representation since classes are always are always excluded and that representatives actually hold true power (accountability is bought off through normative, remunerative or coercive power). While he favors economic democracy, politically, Sarkar moves toward governmental centralization.

Sarkar's elitism is one that attempts to balance the elites, a concept that Mosca first originated when he reinterpreted Montesquieu's checks and balances (executive, legislative and judicial) governmental design. Conversely, Pareto's elitism is the application of Darwin's survival of the fittest to leadership theory. In this, he differs from Khaldun by preferring a rapid circulation of the finest, while Khaldun would prefer a long lasting leadership, one that stays true to asabiya.

Influenced more by human suffering, Sarkar uses elite theory as a way to unmask theories and behaviors that claim to represent the poor when indeed they use the poor as their fodder. Sarkar's history is only elitist (in the critical use of the word) in that the spiritual world has a hierarchical dimension to it. There is excellence and levels of knowledge, but the veracity of these levels is service to the poorest! Instead of the struggle of the fittest, Sarkar uses the metaphor of society as family. The strength of the society comes from how it treats its weakest members. But Pareto should not be seen as favoring the aristocracy of a particular class, rather his attempt is to find a formula in which society can continue to be prosperous.

> Human societies cannot exist without a hierarchy, but it would be a grave mistake to conclude from this that their prosperity increases in proportion to the rigidity of the hierarchy. Equally, the changing of aristocracies is advantageous to society, yet we cannot discount the advantages also of a certain stability. Selection should operate within such limits as to ensure advantage to the species without excessive sufferings for individuals (Pareto, 1966, 160).

It is this articulation of the balance of social forces that Mosca adds to Pareto's argument. Mosca writing at the same time as Pareto developed a similar elite theory. As with Pareto, he asserts that every government claims to exercise rule from a theory of representation: ". . . we find that all authority is being exercised in the name of the entire people, or of an aristocracy, or of a single sovereign" (Meisel, 1965, 5). But behind this theory of representation, there are always two classes. In Mosca's words, "The ruling class or those who hold and exercise the public power [who] will be always a minority, and below them we find a numerous class of persons who never, in any real sense, participate in government, but merely submit to it: they may be called the ruled class" (5). This class not only controls coercive power but ideological power as well. It determines the cultural level of the people. However, according to James Meisel,

> The ruled mass remains the humus out of which grow leading groups; the ruling class must never be considered as an isolate. Its ideology remains, if not epi-phenomenal, an aspect of the total social process until, at some point of class differentiation, the myth of the ruling class obstructs the evolutionary flow and becomes a mere 'class ideology' (21).

When the elite degenerate then the ruling class joins Pareto's classic phrase, "the graveyard of aristocracies." But from the viewpoint of elite theory this is not tragic (or a cause for celebration) for there is always another aristocracy waiting to represent the people. For Pareto, given this false representation, the best or ideal system is when there is a high degree of elite circulation such that excellence can find ways to reach governing power so that benefits can accrue to all.

And in Mosca's words, "Political power always has been, and always will be, exercised by organized minorities, which have had, and will have, the means, varying as the times vary, to impose their supremacy on the multitudes" (136). At one level, Mosca's theory provides an asset to those outside of power by locating all power relationships as essentially those of the ruler and the ruled. He also simultaneously reduces the power of those marginalized by power, for now master—slave and town council—citizen are constructed as identical social formations. From the view of liberal pluralist theory, elite theory misses the dramatic difference between domination and governance.

Mosca and Pareto strike at the heart of the Gnostic project, both liberal and Marxist versions. If history is simply the rise and fall of oligarchies, of elite rule, then a liberal democracy or the withering away of the state are but impossibilities. The pattern of domination can but continue. With such a cyclical theory (without an exit, a spiral of sorts, or a notion of spiritual progress) then the revolutionary asset that the Enlightenment gave the workers and the bourgeois and the asset that Marx and Mao gave to workers and peasants is taken back by the aristocracy, for minority rule is the constant. If the minority will always rule then why not continue that structure until its deliverance to Pareto's graveyard of aristocracies. In this way, Pareto and Mosca become neo-conservatives, much as one might read Sarkar as a conservative moralist, yearning for the days when old wise men, when the elders, ruled their respective tribes. But for Mosca elite rule is not a characteristic of the good society for the class that is ruled provides the ruling class with its means of subsistence. There is no horizontal relationship that benefits all equally here. There is clear exploitation.

Mosca's unique and lasting contribution is his analysis of the varying structure of the ruling class; a contribution more useful for us than Pareto's innovators/consolidators (or later on, rentiers and speculators). It is in Mosca's contribution that we see further similarities with Sarkar. First, like Sarkar, he reminds us that the era or the class in power cannot be recognized solely by those who hold the supreme power established by the law. For Mosca, "At times, alongside of the hereditary king or emperor, there is a prime minister or a major-domo who wields an actual power that is greater than the sovereign's" (Etzioni, 1973, 210). For Sarkar this is most often true in the Vipran and Vaeshyan eras. In the Vipran, the ksattriyan king is on top, but the vipra holds power. In the Vaeshyan, the vipra is on top, but the vaeshyan holds power. And in the Shudra era, there is anarchy, with the warriors ready to consolidate. It is in the Ksattriya era that power is faithfully represented by the ruling class of the era, for Sarkar. Thus Sarkar's general typology: anarchy (shudra), monarchy (ksattriya), republic (vipra) and democracy (vaeshya).

Mosca's classification breaks with Aristotle's (monarchies, aristocracies, democracies), and Montesquieu's (absolutisms, limited monarchies, republics) as well as Spencer's (militant and industrial states). His is a classification of the different types of oligarchies. The first historical category or social forces that Mosca's develops parallels Sarkar's. In Mosca's view, societies are initially controlled by the warriors and eventually are controlled by the wealthy—Sarkar's in between vipra stage is not used. Besides his description of rule of the warriors, he develops an economic model so as to explain the feudal structure. "As class became habituated to the practice of plow and spade, the warriors became nobles and masters, and the peasants, once companions, and brothers, became villains and serfs" (212). Once the warriors gain exclusive ownership of the land—and given that land is the source of wealth—"eventually, if other circumstances permit, a very important social transformation occurs. Wealth rather than military valor comes to be the characteristic feature of the dominant class: the people who rule are the rich rather than the brave" (214). Along with this change is the transformation of the feudal state to the bureaucratic state wherein public authority is used to protect private interests. "Once this transformation has taken place, wealth produces political power, just as political power has been producing wealth . . . if the powerful are as a rule the rich, to be rich is to become powerful" (214).

Using Sarkar-like language, but predating Sarkar, Mosca can be credited with describing the shift from Ksattriyan era to the Vaeshyan era. For Sarkar, the bureaucratic state is a vipran construct even if used in the Vaeshyan era. Mosca speaks of the vipras, but not as bureaucrats. "In societies in which religious beliefs are strong and ministers of faith from a special class, a priestly aristocracy almost always rises and gains possession of a more or less important share of the wealth and the political power" (Mosca, 1939, 59). But while priests become a social force, they are not critical in Mosca's theory of history. Nor does Mosca represent the priest as isomorphic with the modern technocrat, as Galtung sensitizes us to. For Sarkar that there is no specific political qua government structure for the Vipra stage does not perturb him, it is neither empire nor is it nation-state, rather it a phase wherein power is held by religious authorities. Power comes from guru or pope, irrespective of the political structure. The group mind, the collective worldview, is the independent variable, not government. Government is a reflection of the mentality of the epoch. Power thus is located in collective psychology, in varna, not in a particular government structure.

In these stages, ruling classes rise and fall. The reasons for these again are isomorphic with Sarkar's worldview.

> If a new source of wealth develops in a society, if the practical importance of knowledge grows, if an old religion declines or a new one is born, if a new current of ideas spreads, then simultaneously, far-reaching dislocations occur in the ruling class. One might say, indeed, that the whole history of civilized mankind comes down to a conflict between the tendency of dominant elements to monopolize political power and transmit possession of it by inheritance, and the tendency toward a dislocation of old forces and an insurgence of new forces (215).

As with Marx, it is this conflict that produces history. However what separates Marx and Sarkar from this analysis is their image of the future and their use of political theory for strategic purposes. But Mosca does have an ideal, a preferred polity. Instead of accepting Montesquieu's theory of the best government as a balance of legislative, executive and judicial, Mosca asserts that the best government is a balance between the different social forces. This is similar to Sarkar, except Sarkar constructs his theory so that each class rules the other in succession. Now what are these social forces? Arthur Livingston, in his introduction to Mosca's *The Ruling Class*, writes that: "A social force is any human activity or prerequisite that has a social significance—money, land, military prowess, religion, education, manual labor, science—anything" (Mosca, 1939, xix). By anything we can assume that these forces change over time as the civilization varies. Ruling classes are different in regards to the number of forces they control. The stability of a regime is measured by how many of these forces it controls and how many it does not control. Again this is a useful concept for Sarkar. To predict (relocating Sarkar to the empirical discourse for the moment) the next era one would look for indicators that reflect the inability of one varna to control the other varnas, that is, a politics of varna as reflected in representative government. However, progress in itself creates new social forces. Or as Sarkar would say it, the new era dialectically emerges from the previous. Thus, instability is natural. "Struggle [then] is one of the continuous and never-failing aspects of human life. Social forces, therefore, regularly manifest themselves in aspirations to power" (xix). And then in classic Sarkar: "Soldiers want to rule, and they are a hard group to control since they hold the guns and know how best to use them" (xix). Indeed, Mosca's theory emerges from this initial question: Why is it that the warriors are not in control? Given their control of the means of destruction, the natural state would place them on top of the other forces. Continuing Livingston's interpretation:

> Money wants to rule and it is hard to control money because most people succumb to the glamour and influence of wealth. Priests want to rule, and they have the weight of ignorant masses and the majesty of the mysteries of life in their favor. Scientists want to rule, and . . . they have dreamed of dictators who will establish their technocracy and their 'rules of the best.' Labor wants to rule and would rule did it not always encounter the law of the ruling class and fall into the hands of its leaders (xix).

For Mosca, the ideal political system is one where these forces are balanced. If one social force is dominant, as in Sarkar's model, then tyranny results and progress ends, since social forces emerge from progress. Fortunately, there are often checks.

> [M]ilitary power is checked and balanced by money or religion; or money, perhaps, checked and balanced by taxation imposed by land; or an obstreperous religious hierarchy checked and balanced now by superstitious sects which group up within itself, now by coalitions of external forces of enlightenment (xx).

But there are moments when force is progressively balanced, where each person can develop his or her potential, where "the whole infinite potentialities of human nature burst into bloom," (xx) writes Livingston. This is most possible when power is balanced by "habit, custom, morals, institutions, and constitution" (xx) or juridical defense.

History can then be understood as the expansion or contraction of social forces. While for Sarkar, an ideology may not expand because one or many factors are missing (from the six spokes), for Khaldun it is because of unity, for others virtue or force, while for Mosca it is because the proper balance in not kept. Thus, Islam declines because the caliphs failed to resolve the problem of the standing army—generals became independent. But for Sarkar, Islam simply over-expanded. To have furthered its expansion, for Mosca, Islam would have had to balance at least three forces: religion, government by law, and army. But the Islamic polity did not manage this. Thus, for Mosca, the measure for a successful government then is the balance of social forces as understood by some level of consensus legal authority. Sarkar would agree calling for a global constitution, a neo-Magna Carta, that enforces ecological, labor and cultural rights, the three sufferers of modern capitalism.

In this way, Sarkar comes closer to the theories of these two Italians (associated with Fascist thinking) then with the democratic tradition of Montesquieu and others. For Sarkar, however, the democratic discourse is not incidental, indeed, he bases his model of world government on a checks and balances, lower and upper house division model. But varna is about an analysis that is much deeper than government and ruling classes, it is an entire world view, comparable to Sorokin's cultural super system, to a social ontology of the real. Different types of government (again as with Sorokin) are but secondary factors in the larger system. Nonetheless, the conservative charges made against Pareto and Mosca have been made against Sarkar in India, notwithstanding Sarkar's attempt to position himself differently, but should we expect differently, when Sarkar's ideal polity is often expressed as a dictatorship of the enlightened? Out of context or in context depending how or where one speaks of Sarkar, he falls far from the mainstream of democratic thinking. But for Sarkar, democratic socialism is far too slow, what are needed are efforts that quicken the pace of change, which allow elites to circulate and social forces to balance, to evoke Pareto and Mosca. Democracy is useful, but too often, endemically, the larger capitalist structure and local political leaders imbalance it at the expense of the suffering poor. Moreover, for Sarkar what is important is responsiveness to human needs and the accountability of power, that is, a model of needs representation not representation by ballot. For the liberal, however, it is the ballot that eventually leads to the

representation of needs. Pareto and Mosca then offer useful insights
for Sarkar, but can be best perceived as a more specific case privileging governance within Sarkar's larger theory. Certainly PROUT
the social movement, would gain from examining the implications
of a theoretical posture that is strongly critical of the liberal democratic discourse. And of course the liberal democratic perspective
would have to fundamentally rethink its site of politics when confronted with a Sarkar and the alternative episteme he inhabits.

Before we conclude this chapter on grand theory with Toynbee
and Sorokin, we will now make some minor points with respect to
Spengler who too has used Sarkar's notion of social classes. Galtung,
as well, who uses these social types will enter this end of the meal
discussion (as he has throughout).

Culture and Decline

Oswald Spengler (1880–1936) is useful to us for numerous reasons.
Like Sarkar and others, his history is contextualized by a spiritual
perspective of life. While he does not go so far as Eric Voegelin's
meta-search for Being in its self-interpretation, nor does he remain
solely with a history of power like Pareto and Mosca, rather Spengler
is consumed by culture. Cultures are the key units of history. "Cultures
are organisms, and world history is their collective biography" (Spengler,
1972, 104). His central metaphor is the life cycle—birth, growth,
aging and death. "Morphologically, the immense history of a . . . culture is the exact equivalent of the petty history of the individual
man, or of the animal, or of the tree, or the flower . . . In the destinies of the several Cultures that follow upon one another, is com-
pressed the whole content of human history" (104).

Borrowing from Goethe, Spengler raises the key problem of the
20th century as that of exploring "the inner structure of the organic
units through and in which world history fulfils itself, to separate
the morphologically necessary from the accidental, and, by seizing
the purpose of events, to ascertain the languages in which they speak"
(105).

Spengler's history then is certainly a far step removed from Comte.
Indeed he specifically rejects the positivistic notion of a science of
history based on causality. Rather, like Voegelin he uplifts the work
of Joachim of Flora and sympathetically presents his insights. And
like Voegelin, he locates the current problems of the West in the

misreading of Joachim's mystical reading, in the re-articulation of the trans-historical division of Father, Son and Holy Ghost into the historical language of scientific reasoning, of the Gnostics.

History, for Spengler, is not based on truth or falsity, but on levels of insights: superficial and deep. According to Spengler,

> We must not lose sight of the fact that at bottom the wish to write history *scientifically* involves a contradiction. True science reaches just as far as the notion of truth and falsity have validity. . . . But real historical vision belongs to the domain of significances, in which the crucial words are not 'correct' and 'erroneous,' but 'deep' and 'shallow.' . . . Nature is to be handled scientifically. History poetically (Widgery, 1961, 198).

This is similar to Sarkar and the Indian notion of truth. In this view, there are levels of truth—the seer can see the more profound levels of history and thus illumine the past so that it can teach the people of the present. For Sarkar, this teaching would be about the challenges that humans have faced and conquered and about the voices that have been silenced by the ruling classes.

Spengler furthers this notion of history as insight by dividing history into two types. The first is the Ptolemaic system of history that is primarily linear, causal and divides history into three phases: ancient, medieval, and modern. This history is Euro-centered and even when European philosophers moved out of the explanatory scientific model (Herder, Kant and Hegel), they remained within the threefold division. However, Spengler presents an alternative Copernican view. He writes,

> I see, in place of that empty figment of one linear history . . . the drama of *a number* of mighty Cultures, each springing with primitive strength from the soil of a mother-region to which it remains firmly bound through its whole life-cycle; each stamping its material, its mankind, in its own images; each having its own idea, its own passions, its own life, will and feeling, its own death. Here the Cultures, people, languages, truths, gods, landscapes bloom and age as the oaks and the stonepines, the blossoms, twigs and leaves (Widgery, 1961, 194).

But there is no aging of Humankind. This macro unit of analysis does not exist for Spengler. Spengler then asserts, again, countering Eurocentric thought (or any universalizing thought):

> Each Culture has its own new possibilities of self-expression which arise, ripen, decay and die to never return. There is *not* one sculpture, one painting, one mathematics, one physics, but many, each in its

deepest essence different from the others, each limited in duration and self-contained, just as species of plant has its peculiar blossoms or fruit, its special type of growth and decline (194).

Each culture in this sense is a separate person with its own equally valid view of the real. And there are many cultures each with its own pattern yet each following a general overall pattern—that of birth, growth, decay, and death. But for Sarkar, the unit is human civilization, not the various cultures in history. Sarkar only differentiates culture (and thus seeks to recover pre and non-modern cultures) as a political strategy to counter the homogenizing influences of the false culture of materialism. For Sarkar, plainly "the sum total of the different expression of human life is called culture. Human culture is one and indivisible" (Sarkar, 1987b, 8:2). Culture is simply human expression. His ideal is the unified existence of all cultures wherein each can add its own uniqueness thus creating a unity in diversity tension, or to use Sarkar like-prose, such that each culture is like a flower in a bouquet of universal love.

Once this stage is reached then death will certainly follow. Cultures begin not with struggle or unity as with Khaldun, but with the awakening of a great soul. Each culture has a prime characteristic symbol. The classical Greek culture is represented by the body, the Chinese culture by the tao and Western culture is represent by pure and limitless space (expansion). In addition, there are specific types of art, music, literature that reflect that culture. These are the works that define the formative and climax phases of the culture (Thompson, 1985), that capture its spirit. It is through art, the unconscious, the myths that create our dramas that we can understand history, not through a scientific objectification of history. In Spengler's words:

> All great creations and forms in religion, art, politics, social life, economy and science appear, fulfill themselves, and die down contemporaneously in all the cultures; the inner structure of one corresponds strictly with that of all the others; there is not a single phenomena of deep physiognomic importance in the record of one for which we could not find a counterpart in the record of every other, and this counterpart is to be found under a characteristic form and in a perfectly definite chronological position (Etzioni, 1973, 25).

Each culture than is vast system in which the parts relate and can only be understood by the larger pattern. Each culture then exists in its own cosmology. Culture understood in this way follows the ordering of the classic episteme, the Indian episteme, wherein the universe is symmetrically balanced: as above as below, as within as without. The person, the social and the cosmic exist can be understood as parts of the larger whole; when one dimension is perfectly understood, the whole reveals itself.

Like Sarkar who makes the difference between culture and materialism or pseudo culture, Spengler makes the distinction between culture and "civilization." For Spengler, culture is a unique creation of various cosmic forces which eventually over time degenerates into civilization, meaning city life dominated by the desire for money.

Spengler thus gives us stages for his scheme as well. The first is pre-culture, the second is culture which is divided into a early and late, and the third is civilization. In the pre-culture stage "there are no classes, no mass, no state, no politics" (Sorokin, 1966, 192). This is obviously Sarkar's early shudra phase and Marx's early communism. These pre-cultures are the basis from which cultures can develop. Why some develop and other do not, Spengler leaves to cosmic forces, in opposition to Toynbee who argues for the right mix of challenge and response. The development of culture is characterized by the emergence of two classes, the nobility (ksattriyas) and the priests (the vipras). Along with class development is the emergence of the city. However, over time, the culture passes into its late culture phase, wherein the idea of the state and national government are realized.

At this point the next class emerges, the bourgeois, or Sarkar's vaeshyan class. According to Sorokin in his interpretation of Spengler, "urban values replace agricultural ones. Money emerges victorious over landed property and values" (193). At this time also money and democracy are destroyed from within. At the beginning, democracy is controlled by the intellect, soon however, money buys votes. And in Spengler's words, "Through money, democracy becomes it own destroyer, after money has destroyed intellect" (196). Or in Sarkar's words, the vaeshyan destroys the vipran ideal of democracy. The balanced state, as Mosca writes, ends. No longer are the nobility, clergy and bourgeoisie in a unified state. At this stage of civilization, the fourth class, the mass, develops. Spengler does not relate this state, however, to pre-history, as Sarkar's cycle does.

The city develops into the megalopolis, thus size as Leopold Kohr has argued in his *The Overdeveloped Nations* becomes a critical variable for Spengler. With this size, there is a revolution and anarchy. Clearly, Sarkar's shudra's revolution. In Sorokin's interpretation, "just as in

the late period of culture, money becomes victorious over aristocratic
politics and values, so now the politics of rude force triumphs over
money and the money policies of the bourgeoisie" (194). Once power
is consolidated in a Caesar-like rule, a new religiosity develops. This
for Sarkar, is the next transition from the Ksattriyan era to the Vipra
era, although for Sarkar, religiosity can be expressed in other than
the conventional religious discourse (ideological). But the key point
is that it is the intellectual force that dominates. But for Spengler,
this is already the end; there is no cycle, simply the last breath of
a dying culture. Although, as with Khaldun, there is often a brilliant moment in which it appears that all is well, that is the culture
is in bloom, but indeed death is near. To Spengler this is the current phase of the West.

While the similarities with Sarkar's work are striking—the stages,
the spiritual emphasis, the alternative interpretive epistemology of
history, the life cycle—Sarkar does not use culture as his key variable. It is not culture that rises and falls. Moreover, no culture necessarily must die by itself. Cultures (and other units of association)
can be regenerated by spiritual forces, or can be vanquished by
external forces if they are weak in some major areas (a universal
social outlook, for example). And critically, Sarkar sees the Shudra
revolution not as a degeneracy of culture, but as a necessary event
to balance the social forces again, to end their oppression. But for
Spengler the mass phase is only indicative of a culture that has
passed on to its end phase. The earlier days of the agriculture, of
the city, of chivalry, of religious ideas, are over. Instead, the money
spirit has won over the culture, and now this money spirit is attacked
by rude force, first in the form of the masses, and second in the
form of Caesarism (Sarkar's subsequent centralization of power after
the Shudra revolution).

While cognizant of the decline of the West, Sarkar would argue
that Spengler's analysis is too simple. First, humanity is one and second, a spiritual transformation and a restructuring of the West along
spiritual cooperative lines would allow it to regenerate. Indeed, for
Galtung, the West has two dimensions. An ego that is expansionist
and sensate and alter-ego that is cooperative, partnership and distributive justice-based. As the ego expands, the alter-ego shrinks and
searches for other avenues of expression.

While Galtung has been a theoretical asset throughout this book,
we now gloss his theory of social types mainly to contrast with them

Mosca, Spengler and Sarkar. Johan Galtung (1986) too uses these four classes and asserts that they exist in all cosmologies, as representations of economic, ideological and military power. The assertion of this power is over the fourth class, the peasants, workers. However, Galtung adds a fifth class, which, in general, includes the untouchables, the pariah, the gypsies, and the foreigners (and even the environment). He then reads European history as the successive revolt of:

First, the aristocracy against the clergy (the Cromwell revolution); *Second*, the bourgeois against the aristocracy and the clergy (the French); *Third*, the peasants against the bourgeois, aristocrats and the clergy (the soviet revolution); and *Fourth*, the outsiders against the other four in the form of the Green movement.

Thus, the basic types (structures) are there, but Galtung adds a new category, the outcastes. For Sarkar, the last revolution for Sarkar is the sadvipra society, a transformative revolution of class itself.

Toynbee

Besides Spengler, the two most spectacular macro-thinkers of this last century have been Arnold Toynbee and Pitirim Sorokin. In his study on the rise and fall of capitalism and communism, Ravi Batra has provided an extensive and detailed comparison of Sarkar and Toynbee. Batra associates Toynbee's universal state with Sarkar's Ksattriyan era; Toynbee's universal church with Sarkar's Vipran era; Toynbee's challenge and response with Sarkar's physical and mental clash theories of change; and Toynbee's spiritual Christian vision of the future with Sarkar's own Tantric spiritual vision. The main difference between the two is in the units of analysis they use. Toynbee, along with Spengler and others, takes concrete historical civilizations or cultures as his unit (as an important and necessary reaction against the national histories of the time), while Sarkar searches for deeper patterns beyond person, nation, culture and civilization. In the end, Sarkar stays with the psycho-social mentalities of the Indian episteme, while Toynbee develops a theory of the rise and fall of all civilizations.

Along with the contributions of the authors touched upon in this section, Pitirim Sorokin stands out as one in who is similar to Sarkar.

Sarkar and Sorokin: Varna and Super Rhythm

In *Social and Cultural Dynamics* and *Sociological Theories of Today*, Sorokin comprehensively presents a critique of macro theories of sociology from ancients to modern theories, from class theory to functional theories. The main thrust of his critique is that theories have either been unclear as to their basic unit of analysis—civilization or culture, for example—or have taken one aspect of the real (the material) and upgraded it to an entire theory, as in Marxism. Previous writers, then, have not perceived the much larger and deeper pattern.

Besides Sorokin's masterful critique, is his own theory. In developing it, he first defines culture, then develops the various patterns of this culture, provides evidence of this rhythm in numerous areas—art, music, literature, government, epistemology, economy, family—explains why the pattern is the way it is, and then outlines his image of the future.

The similarities to Sarkar's work are numerous. However, Sorokin is far more detailed in applying his theory to world history than Sarkar or his students are, especially in the data-oriented methodology he employs. However, while Sorokin is outstanding at taxonomy and explaining why patterns rise and fall, he is weak at providing a theory that can be used to change the world. One cannot develop a movement based on Sorokin's work; although one can have a greater distance from the present and if one disapproves of the present stage, then one can eagerly await the next stage. Finally, Sorokin is nowhere as neat in the order of things as Sarkar (in the search for symmetry). The pattern does not always work; there are times when events change the pattern. Sorokin is less willing to claim that his basic types explain all reality, through all time.

Sorokin begins with the problem of the appropriate unit of study. Toynbee's unit of civilization or Spengler's unit of culture are too functional in their approach. Their units of analysis are not causally related. They are not unified systems. Sorokin would certainly make similar charges against Batra's use of civilizations in his effort to "prove" Sarkar's theory. Against Sarkar, little can be said since he does not clarify these categories in the language of social science, rather the definitions are based on notions of group mind, group thought-waves which become reflected in human expression, or culture. But varna is, as Sorokin would want, essentially causally integrated.

The starting point for Sorokin's analysis is the problem of culture.

> Is every culture an integrated whole, where no essential part is incidental but each is organically connected with the rest? Or is it a mere spatial congeries of cultural objects, values, traits, which have drifted fortuitously together and are united only by their spatial adjacency, just by the fact that they are thrown together, and by nothing more? (Sorokin, 170, 2).

This then is another restatement of the problem of order in history. For Sorokin, the starting definition of culture is simply the total of that which is "created or modified by the conscious or unconscious activity of two or more individuals interacting with one another or conditioning [their] behavior" (2). A sole human being is then not a culture. Culture is interaction and it can be at any level and not necessary high or low culture (Spengler's culture and civilization, for example).

Sorokin then develops a typology of the main ways of cultural organization. First is the Congerie or spatial or mechanical adjacency. This is ordering the world when there is no logical or causal connection between the elements of social reality. Second, is the indirect association through a common external factor. The example Sorokin gives is that of physical objects present in a certain geographical area. While this indirect association has greater unification than congeries, still there remains no functional or causal connection. The third area is causal or functional integration wherein the parts relate to the whole due to a purpose. The component of a computer on a floor is mere spatial adjacency, but assembled they have a causal connection. At a more complex level, Sorokin gives us the following definition.

> Any cultural synthesis is to be regarded as functional when, on the one hand, the elimination of one of its important elements perceptibly influences the rest of the synthesis in its functions (and usually in its structure); and when, on the other hand, the separate element, being transposed to a quite different combination, either cannot exist in it or has to undergo a profound modification to become a part of it (6).

Wall Street stock markets cannot be implanted in pre- or non-modern societies. The stock market is functionally related to a modern capitalist society. Most sociological theories, especially modern ones, articulate this level of analysis. But there is a deeper level of integration. This is the logico-meaningful integration of culture. This is where the parts are perfectly related to the whole. They are unified not by function but by logic. It is this level of analysis that best orders the universe. This goes beyond the search for patterns of uniformity found in the causal-functional approach.

> Different in nature, but similar in function, is the role of the logico-meaningful method of ordering chaos. Here, however, the ordering element is not uniformity of relationship between the fragmentary variables, but identity of meaning or logical coalescence. Hidden behind the empirically different, seemingly unrelated fragments of the cultural complex lies an identity of meaning, which brings them together into consistence styles, typical forms and significant patters. If, therefore, uniformity of relationship is the common denominator of causally united phenomena, in the logico-meaningful union it is identity of central meaning or idea (10).

While the causal method may be appropriate for the natural science, a humanistic interpretative method is needed for history. There is no cultural atom in music or art or any other division of culture. Rather, "it is the identity (or similarity) of central meaning, idea or mental bias that permeates all the logically related fragments" (10–11). Or as Sarkar would assert, it is the mental wave, the collective psychology, or the dominant perception of the real. For Galtung, this would be cosmology—the irreducible whole which defines the parts—for Foucault, it is the episteme, the way in which we knows the real and in which this knowing creates subjectivity, "we." What emerges from congeries is mere description; from causal-functional analysis are explanatory formulas; from the logico-meaning method, what emerges is the reason "which permeates all the components, gives sense and significance to each of them, and in this way makes cosmos of a chaos of un-integrated fragments" (14).

Sorokin continues the work of Comte emerging with a similar theological, metaphysical and positivistic division of the real, with the middle division a mixed one. For Sorokin, however, history is not linear, rather there is a rhythm—a pendulum pattern—to the cosmos, with history never ending. The first description of reality is super-sensory and the second is sensory with the in between a both-and type. What are the characteristics of this grand system?

First, every logico-meaningful culture is an integrated unity and second, any change in a given component affects other components and thus the system as a whole. Each system also has a certain degree of autonomy and a certain degree of independence from the external environment. Thus, there is autonomy as the system will reject certain external changes (which are not isomorphic to its central meaning structure) and inject other ones. And finally, "functions, change, and destiny of the system is determined not only and not so much by the external circumstances (except in the case of catastrophic accidents), but by the nature of the system itself and by the relationship between its parts" (18). Thus, there is structure and there is choice.

Sorokin devises his grand system by asking the simple question: What is the real? From this he adds the question what are the needs and ends to be satisfied, the extent to which these needs and ends are satisfied, and the various ways that satisfaction is achieved. The question of the natural of reality is answered as either the real is super-sensate or material or some version of both. Needs can be sensual or they can be spiritual or a mixed mental. There is also a hierarchy of needs to be satisfied. Finally, needs are satisfied by modifying one's milieu (the external, sensate approach), modifying one's self (internal approach), or some version of both.

Based on these questions, Sorokin deduces and induces that there are two types of cultures, the ideational and the sensate. Each answers the above questions differently.

> Each has its own mentality; its own system of truth and knowledge; its own philosophy and Weltanschauung; its own type of religion; its own form of art and literature; its own mores, laws, codes of conduct; its own predominant forms of social relationships; its own economic and political organization; and, finally, its own type of human personality, with a peculiar mentality and conduct (24).

But while these two models differ with each other, indeed they represent the basic philosophical tensions of Western philosophy (and to some extent Eastern as well), "within each culture all the values fit closely together, belong to one another logically, often functionally" (24).

For Sorokin then there are three answers to his basic question as to the nature of the real. The first results in the ideational system, the second in the sensate and the third in the mixed idealistic. Form the outset the relationship to Sarkar is obvious. The ideational is the vipran era. The sensate is the vaeshyan, and the mixed is the Ksattriyan (where both are present, the battle with the environment and the worship of the other world). The Shudra era is the short time in between eras and, in effect, is a transitional phase.

For Sorokin, in the ideational era,

> reality is perceived as non-sensate and nonmaterial, everlasting Being;
> (2) the needs and ends are mainly spiritual; (3) the extent of their sat-
> isfaction is the largest, and the level, highest; (4) the method of their
> fulfillment of realization is self-imposed minimization or elimination of
> most of the physical needs, and to the greatest possible extent (27).

Again an identical description of the Vipran era. But Sorokin distinguishes between two types of ideational culture. The first is "ascetic
ideationalism" where material needs are minimized and indeed the
world is seen as unreal. This is the classic Vedantic view. The second
is "active ideationalism" closer to the Christian concept where instead
of fleeing the world of illusion, the goal is to bring others to the
ideational real. There is thus a degree of structural societal reform,
but usually at the level of faith, not at the level of new technologies. The first is contraction-oriented, the second expansion-oriented.
While this second view is closer to Sarkar's, he would directly link
structural change with faith.

The Sensate mentality is defined as the following:

> It views reality as only that which is presented to the sense organs. It
> does not seek or believe in any super-sensory reality; at the most, in
> its diluted form, it assumes an agnostic attitude toward the entire world
> beyond the senses. The Sensate reality is thought of as a Becoming,
> Process, Change, Flux, Evolution, Progress, Transformation. Its needs
> and aims are mainly physical, and maximum satisfaction is ought of
> these ends. The method of realizing them is not that of a modification
> within the human individuals composing the culture, but of a modification
> or exploitation of the external world (27–28).

The sensate world is a near opposite of the ideational. Crucial for
Sarkar's theory is the above definition of dilution. For Sarkar, his
types are seen often as perfect, with the discourse of empirical facts
(as constituted by the dominant episteme) stretched to accommodate
the type, for example, in Batra's studies. However, learning from
Sorokin, we can posit that there can be a range or level of the vipra
mentality in a vipra era, and there can be range of leadership and
class styles as well. This is similar to Vico's soft laws, his humanistic
science.

As with the Ideational, Sorokin develops different types of Sensate
mentality. The first is the active one, fundamentally the assertive
ksattriyan civilization. It seeks to modify the external world through
its efficient reconstruction and though technology. For Sorokin, "the

great executives of history, the great conquerors, builders of empire are its incarnation" (28).

There is, as one might expect, a passive sensate mentality as well. In this mentality, the sensate world is the only representation of the real, but the world is not transformed through conquering or through technology, rather it is there to be enjoyed since death is near and human existence is short. Given Sarkar's spiritual perspective, this category is rejected as an ideal system.

Sorokin adds a third category, however. This is the "cynical sensate mentality" wherein any perspective is used to gain individual advantage. Values are readjusted to gain ends.

Unlike Sarkar—who does not mix his varna, but needs to—Sorokin admits that there are many possible combinations but these are not integrated except the mixed mentality. Sorokin uses the confusing term "idealistic" for this category, dualistic or mixed describes it better. Quantitatively it represents a more or less balanced unification of Ideational and Sensate, with however a predominance of Ideational elements. Qualitatively it synthesizes the premises of both types into one inwardly consistent and harmonious unity. In the Idealistic (dualistic, mixed), reality is many-sided, with the aspects of everlasting Being and ever-changing Becoming of the spiritual and the material. Its needs and ends are both spiritual and material, with the material, however, subordinated to the spiritual. The methods of their realization involve both the modification of self and the transformation of the external sensate world.

In this way, it is Ksattriyan, but also a variant of the vipran, and sums up Sarkar's project as well—a spiritual based model of the real that includes the material and ecological world, but has at its base the spiritual.

The last mentality is a version of the Mixed type. Sorokin calls this the "Pseudo-ideational Culture Mentality." Instead of beginning with the ideational, this construct starts with the sensate. Desires are minimized because of external variables. In general, this is the mentality that emerges when individuals are oppressed as prisoners, during times of catastrophe, or because of cruel regimes.

The brilliance of Sorokin is that he then manages to use this theory to catalog most of human history. Sarkar writing from Calcutta without research assistants, just marginalized revolutionary youth, instead of hiring Harvard graduate students, as Sorokin did, took an alternative approach. Sarkar created a spiritual and social organization to reconstruct the world in the mentality he prefers, the ideal mixed idealistic system.

Given his definition of culture—the interaction of two or more people—Sorokin uses these categories to locate leaders, groups, families, societies, civilizations and, if it were possible, aliens.

While Sarkar refers to the priestly class in general as the viprans, Sorokin does not always place them there. His model is too sophisticated. For example, in general they occupy the ascetic ideational category while liberation theology members occupy the active ideational. But during times of decay, the clergy often resorts to various sensate mentalities (the passive or the cynical).

Sorokin proceeds to develop a taxonomy of linear and cyclical patterns in history. He begins by dispelling the argument that there are unique processes, largely arguing that the process of generalization and language preclude the argument of uniqueness. Next he argues that while there are linear trends, they have elements of repeatability in them. More important is his notion of the existence of limits. After a period of movement in one direction, a limit is reached and there is a change in direction, a new stage sets is. Thus, progress as linear uni-directional movement is impossible. However, this does not mean that the cycle is essential either. Sorokin's world is open. Sarkar's too, for the universe is constantly impacted by the thought waves of Consciousness. However there are naturals that for human purposes can be considered laws. For Sorokin, "for history as a whole, since it is not finished as yet and since the future is unpredictable, we do not and cannot know whether there is any continuous and main trend and any terminal point to which Humankind is being led" (64). Finally, Sorokin argues that the direction and rhythm is regulated by the principle of *immanent change*, meaning that an organism, a socio-cultural process, changes based on its own logico-meaning structure.

Sorokin continues his work by classifying the fluctuations of the forms of religion, art forms, literature, music, painting, sculpture, literature, systems of truth and knowledge, scientific theories, ethics, family, social relationships, war, government, and internal disturbances. These categories he places within his overall framework. In addition, he finds other significant rhythms. For example, under government, he finds a logical rhythm between totalitarian and laissez faire societies. But the reasons do not always follow the pattern of his super rhythm. There are exceptions. The ascetic ideational culture will have little use of the state and government, and hence is easily conquered by outside forces or adopts a laissez faire system. The active ideational culture, however, is apt to have a strong government and social body, as in Sarkar's model. Vipran society is often as Sorokin states a religious government. The totalitarian state is a production of Sensate society with its need to expand and manage. It rises with Sensate culture and then declines with it.

In his section of Theocratic and Secular government again Sorokin finds a cycle, a pendulum. This fluctuation naturally correlates with the Ideational and Sensate.

> The concept of Ideational culture implies logically that if, no external circumstances hinder, the government and the intellectual, moral and social leadership (aristocracy) in such a culture must belong to the persons and groups that incarnate, or are supposed to incarnate, in themselves the Ideational values. Since the sensory-empirical values, whether wealth, physical might, sensory happiness, and the like, are only pseudo values to the Ideational mentality, the rich, the physically mighty, the capable organizers of the economic, political and other enterprises in such a society cannot be its recognized 'aristocracy,' its leaders, and its rulers, if they are not backed by the Ideational values, are not their upholders, or are not supported by the group that is thought to be the incarnation of these Ideational values par excellence (474).

Thus, power in the Ideational system must be located with the priests, shamans, or the wise persons, the elders.

Alternatively, "in the sensate culture, with its disbelief in Ideational reality and values, the leaders and rulers can be only those groups which are the bearers, the creators, the organizers, of the most important sensory values" (475). Thus, they must be people who organize expansion: territorial or economic, the military (or leaders of criminal gangs) or the wealthy or scientists who create new forms of technology. And in the mixed Idealistic society, we would expect to have a variation of both.

Sorokin does not only develop taxonomies, he also places them in a historical context. For Western civilization, for example, the fifth to thirteenth centuries were dominated by Idealism (Vipra). This has been followed by six hundred years of Sensate civilization, just as Wallerstein and other world system theorists write. Prior to the Ideational era there were various fluctuations of Ideational, Idealistic and Sensate. The rise of Rome was a type of Sensate era. Rome's decline began the theocratic Christian era. With the rise of the

Sensate world, government changed to rule of the wealthy and rule of the mighty—the money and war spirit.

The central key point for Sorokin is the rhythm, change. His metaphysics privilege change, not the status-quo. Trends do not continue in one way. They reverse. Thus, those that assert that the future will see increasing levels of one form of government, for example, democracy, will err. At the same time, the theories of the ancients, Plato, Ssu-Ma Ch'ien and others, who argue in a sequence also will err since there is no definite periodicity. In addition, the pattern of change is different in different cultures.

But there are patterns Sorokin continues to find in all areas of thought: he finds fluctuations in linear, cyclical, and mixed conceptions of cosmic, biological and socio-cultural processes. They fluctuate, for the culture fluctuates. Naturally, the Sensate system develops linear theory of life, of progress. During its decline, cyclical theories emerge. Most cyclical theories relate to ideational super systems since they base their theories on the biological, seasonal, life-cycle discourse. Finally, in mixed periods one might expect and one finds mixed, linear and cyclical theories. Thus, it is not surprising that Sarkar's is both, linear and cyclical. In recent history, Sorokin finds a significant increase in cyclical theories, one among many, of indicators, of the decline of the Sensate civilization.

We now further develop the theoretical assertions of Sorokin that Sarkar can most gain from in explicating his theory. There are three main contributions, each of which aids in understanding Sarkar's work or can be used along with it. The first, mentioned earlier, is the theory of immanent change. To come to this theory, Sorokin catalogs how we perceive change. First, there are external reasons. These are environmental theories and the positivist efforts to search for independent variables to explain various phenomena. The second view is dialectical or internal—things change because of their own nature. Sorokin takes a mixture of both, "the principle of immanent change of each socio-cultural system supported by the external principle, within certain conditions and limits" (634).

For him, insofar as all cultures act they change naturally. It would be far more difficult to explain why things do not change. Once the system begins to change, it must deal with its outputs, with its consequences. It must then change. Thus the external world causes change.

But there is internal change as well. Once a system emerges, then it develops its potential, it articulates what it already is. Its destiny is determined by itself, unless it is ended by external forces; however outside forces cannot change what it essentially is. By definition, the system is such. It is deterministic since it is expressing its own potential, but since it is its own potential, then in that sense, it is self-determining, and thus, free. Thus, it is totally determined and undetermined. How a culture unfolds, depends on the milieu and the type of cultural system it is. For Sarkar, an era must play itself out, once it emerges as a dominant mentality. However, how it unfolds itself is unknown, thus allowing the role of the sadvipras to change the system, or to re-actualize its direction. There is then a both/and and neither/or perspective toward structure and agency, external and internal change.

This is better understood by using the next two hypotheses of Sorokin. The first is the Principle of Limit. This is the idea that a system will change in time because of the first principle of immanent change; it will wear itself our, by modified or transformed. In addition, he uses the Aristotelian argument that all objects eventually reach their antithetical poles and thus must change the direction of movement. Hegel, too, is brought in with Sorokin arguing that since all reality has its negation (Ideational and Sensate) the opposite will eventually emerge thus changing the direction of the pattern. This is concluded by the argument that if a system did not have limits, it would change so much that it would no longer be the same system. It would be thus have to be defined differently. "The limits transgressed, the system disappears" (654). This is true for humans, cultural systems, and other forms. And although humans can adapt, they remain within certain boundaries, for example, they are not birds. There are thus only a certain number of economic organizations (hunters, gatherers, pastoral, agricultural, industrial, and so forth), political organizations (monarchy, republic, democracy and so forth), as with truth systems, ethical systems, law, science, types of societies (religious or secular, *Gemeinschaft* or *Gesellschaft*) and so forth. While Sorokin continues to refine this, more important to use, is the how of the super rhythm. Why only these three societies, and not more?

> Why in the course of the historical unfolding of the Greco-Roman and Western cultures has its super system twice repeated the triple

rhythm of the Ideational-Idealistic-Sensate phases, from the twelfth century B.C. to the end of the Middle Ages, and after the fifteenth century for the third time entered the Sensate phase, which is seemingly
declining at the present time (676).

The rhythm is there because of the principle of immanent change.
But why does it reoccur? Here Sorokin warns us this is true for integrated cultures that follow logical meaningful patterns, but the un-
integrated do not necessarily follow this pattern.

But why do integrated systems follow this pattern? His answer is
metaphysical and functional. For Sorokin, with regard to the meaning of the real there are only five solutions: Ideational, Sensate,
Idealistic, Skepticism, and Unknowable (knowable it its phenomenal
aspect, but unknowable in its transcendental aspect, if it has one).
The last two cannot serve to create an integrated culture. No culture
can maintain cohesion when the dominant worldview is not grounded
in the real; a grounding not possible if the attitude toward the real
is skeptical or unknowable at some level. Thus, the first three continue to repeat themselves through history. In Sorokin's words:

> Since there are only five main possibilities, two of which are negative
> and can hardly serve as a basis for a long-existing integrated culture,
> by virtue of the principle of limit and immanent change, three of these,
> and two others as subsystems, cannot help being repeated in the inte-
> grated cultures that continue to exist after the first run of all the three
> or five fundamental forms. Hence repetition of these forms; hence our
> super-rhythm in the history of the cultures studied (678).

But there is a deeper and more important reason. For Sorokin, logically, each one of these systems may be entirely true, entirely false,
or partially true and false. If one system was totally true (or perfect)
then it could exist forever, since it would be able to fulfill human
needs. The problem of existence would be resolved. If they were all
totally false, then none of them could have existed. However, historically they did exist for centuries meeting various needs, creating
new conditions. Thus, each system is partly true, partly false, partly
adequate and partly inadequate.

> Only because each of them contains a vital part does it give to its
> human bearers the possibility of an adaptation to their milieu—cos-
> mic, organic, the social; gives them a minimum of real experience to
> meet their needs and serves as a foundation for their social life and
> culture. But because each of the three systems has also an invalid
> part—error and fallacy side by side with truth—each of these systems

> leads its human bearers away from the reality, gives them pseudo knowledge instead of real knowledge, and hinders their adaptation and the satisfaction of their physiological, social and cultural needs (681).

Over time, one system becomes dominant and thus its false dimension increases while its truth dimension decreases. This is so because once it dominates it drives out the truth of the other systems as well. Thus, as with Sarkar, there are four classes that represent a part of the truth but not the whole truth; over time one varna dominates and becomes increasingly false. The varna does not over time represent the needs and desires and adaptation of the people. Eventually the system declines and the society (Ideational, Mixed or Sensate or Shudra, Ksattriya, Vipra, and Vaeshya) built upon them crashes down, and the next era begins. As with Sarkar, the new system then dominates and then it too follows the same path of exaggeration and since this new system now represents falsehood the next system of the real must come in its place. For Sarkar, each class represents one dimension of the complete mind as it has evolved. When one dominates, the other minds are suppressed, eventually leading to an imbalanced society. The next aspect of the complete mind asserts itself, and the cycle continues. The ideal system for Sarkar would be one wherein those with complete mind—knowledge of all the systems of the real through struggle and intuition—limit the time of each system. They do not allow the system to exaggerate for too long. However, unlike Mosca, Sarkar does not call for a balance of all the social forces, rather he calls for the harnessing of the best of each representation of mind, and attempts to move to the next cycle, once the falsity of the one view become oppressive and suppressive. And given that each way of thinking corresponds to an alternative polity, we would then not be surprised to see a fluctuation of polities as the ancients Greeks and as Sorokin have asserted.

For Sorokin, the order, however, is not eternal. Ideational, Idealistic, Sensate and then Ideational again is the pattern largely because Sensate civilization becomes so tragically false that only the discipline of the Ideational system can replace it. Following the heights of the ideational system, humans then slowly descend to a both and mixed level.

For Sorokin, we are at the end of the Sensate civilization with a spiritual ideational civilization to follow. Like Sarkar, he asserts ending his magnum opus, "If [an] apocalyptic catastrophe can be avoided, then the emerging creative forces will usher humanity into a new magnificent era of its history" (704). Ensuring that this next era will be magnificent is Sarkar's project. Sorokin's hope.

Sorokin and Sarkar have similar intellectual and personal projects. Sorokin's theory, indeed, adds a considerable deal to Sarkar's argument, as the theoretical explanation for Sorokin's theories of societal change are equally useful for Sarkar.

One main difference is that while Sarkar has a Shudra era, Sorokin does not. The Shudra era for Sorokin would be chaotic and unintegrated, thus not useful for his theory. It does not last long. But what Sorokin forgets is that chaos as a response as to the nature of the real is a possible answer. But, insofar as an integrated culture (Sorokin's aim and departure point) can not be maintained with such a society, it is not a category. But Sarkar, by keeping the Shudra era a historical category delivers an asset to workers and peasants; a deliverance impossible with Sorokin's model. Moreover, Sarkar shows that the end the Sensate era will not necessarily be a peaceful one, violence, chaotic and structured, is indeed a possibility.

Sorokin is useful to Sarkar because of his principle of immanent change, his principle of limits, his theory of the real and the false (the why and how of the super rhythm) and his departing point of epistemology as a categorization of society. Also useful is Sorokin's notion that the stages do not have to exactly fit (the soft laws). There are variations. Finally, Sorokin's categories of congeries, functionally related systems and logical meaningful related systems help explain Sarkar's notion of varna. All in all both projects are isomorphic, Sorokin is stronger theoretically and empirically while Sarkar is stronger in terms of his vision of the future and in terms of the actual application of his theory to the real world of suffering and bliss.

We finally come to the end of this section on macro-thinkers. Tea, appetizers, dinner and more dinner are over. While each thinker touches upon Sarkar's theory—the forces, the rise and fall, the stages—none have them have stated it quite the way Sarkar has, possibly because of the background that he emerges. Only an Indian living within the caste system could see the pattern. Only he could then universalize it. And perhaps because of the rigidity of caste, it is but natural that Sarkar would conclude that his model his space, time, and observer invariant. But Sarkar does give us exits; he does provide an alternative image of the future and an alternative episteme from which to construct objectivity and subjectivity.

With all these grand thinkers, the similarities are perhaps more obvious than the differences. All must deal with same issues of leadership, political economy, the problem of the absolute, the problem of laws, the problem of the cycle, and the problem of progress. Each one attempts to develop a construction that accurately captures the real, and, of course, each one focuses on issues that others forget. Ssu-Ma Ch'ien places virtue ahead of other categories. Chang looks at the rise and decline of the tao as government and learning become separated. Khaldun focuses on unity, the village/city distinction, and the rise and fall of dynasties. Vico develops an alternative science that includes the self-interpretation of humans. Comte notices the basic types of Theological, Metaphysical and Positive and places the Positive and the end of history. Hegel finds ways to speak of the spirit in history. Marx sees the dialectic operating in history and develops a vision of the future to end human suffering. Gramsci reminds us of the role of the ideological and the importance of organic intellectuals. Pareto and Mosca assert that power is always controlled by elites; both then social types to explain this phenomena. In addition, Mosca moves from the Greek and enlightenment model of governance and calls for a balance of social forces. Spengler's history is poetic not scientific. To him each culture has its own history. Western culture is now in the final stages of its life cycle. Toynbee traces the rise and fall of civilization and demonstrating the importance of challenge/response in civilizational growth. He also provides a theoretical scheme that explains empire and religion, while Sorokin develops a three-pronged social theory that examines mentalities. Sorokin also develops language to explain how change is internal and external to a system. He also explains how all systems will continually fluctuate. Foucault gives us epistemes and discontinuities in history. He also shows us the different ways in which the rational has been constructed. Voegelin provides us a history of how the ancient spiritual was secularized by the Gnostics. His level of history is that of Being itself. Galtung gives us the unit of cosmology and explains to us the revolutions of the modern period.

Moving from the level of grand theory, we now proceed to the critique of patterns and laws. We criticize Sarkar's theory of history, compare it with Marxian laws of dialectics, and finally place Sarkar's theory within a poststructural politicized interpretation of science and social theory.

CHAPTER SIX

SITUATING SARKAR'S LAWS

While in earlier chapters we laid the groundwork for the ways in which Sarkar can be understood, this chapter begins as its point of departure the actual knowledge claims of Sarkar and then proceeds to understand these claims, to contextualize and theorize. The central question for this chapter is: how to comprehend Sarkar's social cycle and his claim that the social cycle has an evolutionary basis and will continue through time and space, irrespective of observer.

Consistent with the epistemological emphasis we have taken, we place Sarkar's laws in the positivist-empirical approach, the interpretive-phenomenological approach and finally the poststructural approach. In the first approach, Sarkar's social laws are seen to fit historical reality better, proof of this assertion either comes from rigorous studies of world history or from quantitative studies of recent history. Sarkar's theories then must be operationalized and placed within the social science discourse. The weaknesses with this approach are that the problem of knowing is left unexamined, history is seen as factual and not interpretative, and the empirical is not placed in the context of epistemes. This view ultimately favors the Western, the temporal present, and male interpretations. However, intelligibility is clear, knowledge grows steadily, and there are obvious grounds of comparison; that is, a hierarchy of knowledge and progress is possible.

In the second view, Sarkar's laws must be understood in the cultural and historical context in which they are uttered. In this case, his laws are not problematic (as they are for the empirical) as in the Indian episteme laws are natural. Quantitative research is inappropriate since history includes humans and their self-interpretation. In addition, his laws must be understood within Sarkar's own criteria: do they inspire action? Do they aid in creating a new society? Do they allow voices previously silenced to be heard? Do they speak for all classes? And, does his theory lead to human welfare, *satya* and to *ananda*, bliss? The weakness with the interpretive-phenomenological view is that Sarkar appears to argue that his laws are universal and "true" irrespective of place, time, and observer, of interpretation. In addition, in this view truth becomes totally relativized leading to a philosophical position where any theory is as good as any theory— total pluralism.

The third, poststructural approach sees each theory as a regime, as a way of constructing the world. Theories exist in discourse, in ways of knowing which become dominant due to various reasons (technology, power, class, demographics, for example). Important is then how a theory delivers power to various groups and how power travels within and without a theory. Problems with this approach are that the grounds of comparison are in themselves impositions, that is, a local, peculiar will to power, to interpretation. There is no universal way to argue that structural violence is bad or good in this deconstructionist perspective, for example.

It is in the first approach that most efforts of understanding Sarkar have been located. While Ravi Batra (1978) and others have attempted to uphold Sarkar's theories (searching for empirical-historical proofs), sociologist Phil Carspecken (1990), alternatively has prepared a critique of Sarkar's social cycle. We review Carspecken's critique as it is thorough and typical of the type of critique Sarkar can expect from Western social sciences. At the same time we respond to this critique, not by rereading history or searching for additional data— not by entering the discourse Batra and Carspecken inhabit in their particular works, but by arguing that while Carspecken's critique is useful, it itself must be located within a discursive field. His critique is valid within the modern social science episteme, but less useful, insightful, within the alternative epistemological sites where we have placed Sarkar—the classical Indian episteme and, indeed, Sarkar's cosmological moves, his new boundaries. Finally, we privilege the poststructural perspective. In this approach, the key to valuing a theory is not only its predictive value (a good theory need not predict), nor only its ability to interpret the world (interpretation is based on the present epoch, our language frames our interpretation), but rather the view that theories are primarily assets delivered to various discourses, disciplines, and various constituted subjects. New theories thus reconstruct reality by creating new possibilities for practice and praxis.

In earlier chapters, we argued that Sarkar's laws of society can be understood as laws in much the same way that humans have two legs and arms—a given structure with little malleability. His law is an evolutionary principle justified as it is historical and thus, while not deterministic, it is certainly patterned. It does not violate agency, from the Indian view, since there are for any system only so many possible structures. For example, there is only a range of possible variations of a polity—democracy-aristocracy-monarchy. Similarly, and this is the key, there are only a few ways of interacting with the environment: either by being dominated by it, by dominating it through the body, dominating it through the mind, or dominating it by manipulating the environment itself (and of course living with nature in harmony, the neo-humanist solution Sarkar proposes). Given this structure and given these motivations, their order is explained, first, through the evolutionary discourse, and second, through the notion that in the second cycle, it is only the chaotic power of the workers that can overthrow the acquisitors (led by the intellectuals and warrior workers). However, as worker power is chaotic and un-disciplined, it is natural that the most powerful among the workers will take charge. Over time, as the warrior mentality pursues its own ends, it too expands and resorts to the control of the environment through the mind. This eventually leads to their own dissolution and the rise of intellectuals. Finally, the preoccupation of the intellectu-als with mind leads to the rise of the capitalists who reconstruct the environment as a marketable commodity. The capitalists take power and pursue their own class goals of increasing capital and reducing labor costs and exploiting the environment, until labor revolts (and now the environment as well) and the cycle continues. Each stage naturally emerges from the previous stage.

While the social cycle is an insightful macrohistory, as developed in the previous chapter, the theories of Khaldun, Marx, Sorokin and others add greatly to Sarkar's theoretical position. They assist in the development of the mechanisms of change and the role of the elites, for example.

But the site of macro grand theory is not where the critique of the social cycle lies. The current debate within PROUT publications and the theoretical ground with which the debate continues is within the empirical-applied level. The guiding question is: Are there his-torical laws and, indeed if there are, are there proofs of these? For Batra there are. Batra has taken Sarkar's quadra-divisional theory and applied it specifically to Indian, Western, Egyptian and Russian civilizations, arguing that these societies/civilizations have undergone not only one large cycle but many cycles. However, Sarkar appears to argue that most societies are in the final stages of capitalism, while a few have had their workers' revolution and have moved to warrior societies (and recently with the end of communism to vipran, parliamentary societies). Typically these are viewed as the Marxist nations: Cuba, Russia, China and Eastern block nations (which are continuing the cyclical process). Batra, however, has reinterpreted the case of Russia and argued that the socialist revolution was in fact a non-revolution as Russia was not in its capitalist era, rather it was in a long warrior era with power centralized with the Czar. The martial communist era will soon die out and a new ideology will replace it (obviously PROUT). What Batra does not explore is that perhaps Marxism can be seen as a vipra ideology and that Russia has reverted back to the warrior era and thus a new progressive communism is ahead. Of course, conversely given its emphasis on material satisfaction, it is problematic to assign Marxism an ideational or idealistic status: is it then sensate? Sarkar provides little help here.

In addition, Batra has classified many of the newly emerging nations as warrior. Thus, their polities are centralized not because of the larger world capitalist system (authoritarian state capitalism), but because they have moved from the shudra era to a warrior era.

In any case, Batra's conclusion is that Sarkar's theory has not only tremendous explanatory value (explain things better than previous macrohistorical theories, explain anomalies in Marxist theory—why various revolutions have not occurred, for instance) but predictive value as well (be able to accurately foretell the next evolution or revolution). Thus, he locates Sarkar's theory within the Occidental scientific method. For him, Sarkar's theory is more valid, reliable, and precise than other social change theories. Batra does not see the positivist effort as merely one method of knowledge that has now led to knowledge becoming identical with science as Jurgen Habermas (Giddens, 1982) has argued. Thus, Batra instead of making science contentious, argues that Sarkar's theory succeeds on the terms of science and social science itself. We argue that this is only one way to ascertain the truth of something, given the problematic nature of determining causality, proof, and the real, that is, the difficulty in determining the objective truth of anything. It is the most superficial sort of analysis, which holds in abeyance cultural and epistemic factors. For us, the empirical view is one discourse among many. It is nested in a particular paradigm, one might privilege it in a particular construction, but the gaining of agreement to that position has as much to do with the politics of knowledge and language than with the objective and independent basis of the reality discerned. The fact basis of the empirical must be contextualized in the social and ideological worldview of those who have interests in those facts.

For Batra, Sarkar gives a better understanding of social change, he explains more of the variance of the data. The data in this case is history itself, as conventionally recorded or believed and as understood in the Occidental model. For Batra, history is not so problematic, there is now finally someone with a complete mind to understand it, to lay it bare.

Marx, Science and Sarkar

Batra thus sees Sarkar's social cycle as scientific and presented within the scientific spirit. However, he sees science in the Western context, not as we have argued earlier that science means quite a different idea to the Indian, in any period of Indian history, even the present. Moreover, it is from the interpretive view that we can better understand Sarkar, we assert. For example, the similarities between Marx's view of science, history and truth and Sarkar's are useful. To begin with the empirical is constructed differently. Marx claimed that his knowledge was scientific as opposed to philosophical knowledge that was ideological. Marx's theory was not false, that is, bourgeois, but indeed a true reflection of real historical states. In Marx's words, "Where speculation ends—in real life—there real, positive science begins: the representation of the practical activity, of the practical process of development of men" (Parker, 1990, 25). It was not just socialism but scientific socialism; in Perry Anderson's words, "one governed by rationally controllable criteria for evidence and truth" (Parker, 1990, 27). Marx's point is that his theory is based on the practical and the historical not on the transcendental and metaphysical. Moreover, "philosophers have only interpreted the world, in various ways; the point is to change it" (Parker, 1990, 25).

Sarkar, too, is concerned with developing not just a spiritualism or a mere socialism but a progressive spiritual socialism based on intuitive science, not merely on Hindu dogmas that offer no logical reasons for its belief system. Sarkar's intuitive science is also scientific in that it can be argued against, it is not to be solely accepted as traditional Indian scriptural authority. He too places himself in opposition to philosophy by arguing that a true spirituality is an attempt to transform the harsh realities of the world. For Sarkar devotion to humanity, is devotion to the transcendental, for there are no greater realities then the cruelty of the world, a cruelty that must be destroyed in this era.

Like Marx who uses these prior metaphysical categories to make his own distinctions and thus exists within the metaphysical discourse of the period—for example, he uses Hegel's stages of world history with minor reinterpretation—Sarkar exists within the traditional spiritual discourse. In this discourse Consciousness is the a priori focus and the ground of existence, for example. As we argued earlier, Sarkar emerges from the classical Indian episteme. Thus, just as Marxism must absorb the field it hoped to transcend—philosophy— Sarkar must absorb the field he seeks to transcend, Indian metaphysics. For Marx, it is only "when capitalism is overthrown that sense perception can once again prove capable of providing true knowledge" (Parker, 1990, 35). For Sarkar, when through proper practices such as meditation, the deeper layers of the mind are attained, then the science of the world is easily perceived and the glaring inequity of history laid bare. One can then truly transform the world, a world where all can obtain the science of spirituality.

But as one might ask, can indeed Marxism be scientific in that since all knowledge is class knowledge and thus incomplete? Moreover, at another level of thought, if history is the contradiction between the relations and modes of production and history moves through material forces, how can Marxism explain its own non-material but ideational, ideological affect? The question is equally valid for Sarkar. If indeed a science is obtained by unifying with absolute being and if it is true that humans are embedded in the relative world of time, place and observer, then the gaze seen from the cosmos must become relativized when found in the mind of humans and spoken in the relative grammar and structure of time, place and person. How indeed can it be scientific (in the sense of objective, space, time, and observer invariant)?

And if the guru and disciple both become deaf and dumb in their inability to express—to speak and hear—this transcendental truth then why do we find Sarkar producing volumes of talks and books? Indeed, given India's transcendental intuitive perspective, why are there tracts and tracts, texts and texts, waiting for the eager student? This might be the tragedy of the mystic: the writing of the philosophy

betrays the philosophy itself. Phil Carspecken, for example, has argued
that Hegel's main error was to write "his philosophy out, the core
metaphor [that of the idea that cannot take any particular form but
is immanent in all forms] getting cruder as he did, the motivation
to write it out contradicting the motivation necessary to re-experience
this insight" (Carspecken, 1989, personal communication). Hegel initially may have truly understood the metaphor of God-talk, as he
did not hold to any one image of God, while Indian philosophy may
speak the language of metaphor but claims that the absolute is just
that, independent of our knowing, eternal and ultimately really real.

Again Sarkar would respond that he expresses himself in discourse
because of his larger project. His work is scientific and spiritual in
that it does not support any narrow interest but the interest of the
cosmos, the "good and happiness of all," not mere selfish interest.
Moreover, it is a better theory because it is more comprehensive
(thus echoing Max Weber's criteria for a better, good theory). It is
scientific not that it resides in the domain of positivist (prediction/
control) tradition, but scientific in the sense that (1) it is systematic;
(2) it is not based on authority (the Vedas or other texts); (3) open
to logical criticism, and, (4) not based on irrational sentimental, but
rather on rational intuition, meaning his theory comes from the spiritual and is translated into the intellectual.

As we developed earlier, the Indian episteme that Sarkar resides
in and of does not separate science, religion, and philosophy. For
Sarkar there can be an intuitive science and a material science: one
synthetic and the other analytic. The division in the Western episteme between the natural and social sciences has not occurred or
certainly not at the same level: there is no *verstehen* versus *erklaren*: no
physics versus psychology. The division between explanation and
understanding (Weber and Vico) did not occur in India, rather science, philosophy and religion often remain complimentary ways of
knowing the real. For Sarkar and other Indians, science is systematic, and empirically based (at least material science), that is, practical, while religion is authority and sentiment based (the higher forms
being *bhakti*, the lower emotionality and dogma), and philosophy is
intuition and reason based.

And again, it is not his authorship that is critical, but the ideology that reflects and touches the spiritual world—here ideology is
the subtle idea, not a false or particular worldview. New ideologies
result from the Idea that then becomes dialectically translated into

the material. Similarly, for Marx it was "to win a scientific victory for our party" (Parker, 1990, 41). Thus, both are scientific in that they are both universalistic speaking not to a particular group, but to Justice itself. Of course, Marx spoke for the proletariat, while Sarkar's ideal leader is not part of the cycle, neither proletariat nor bourgeois neither intellectual nor military, but extra-cyclical leadership is outside of the vortex of fame, power, money and lust.

The Empirical

In his dated but still valuable article, "Playing the Devil's Advocate", Phil Carspecken[1] is unconcerned with the above placing of science, philosophy and tradition. Rather he is committed to a position of science qua empirical social sciences. He has argued that there is no historical evidence for Sarkar's theory. From his view for PROUT to succeed it must meet the social sciences on their terms. There are anomalies, unexplained cycles, problematics in operationalizations, and in general theoretical weaknesses in Sarkar's work. He concludes that belief in the social cycle and PROUT is predicated on acceptance of Sarkar as one's spiritual teacher. The social theory is accepted on faith in Sarkar's infallibility not on any evidence of the social theory itself. Thus, his view is that no one can be impressed or convinced of this theory in academia or other spaces where faith in authority is made routinely contentious. In addition, Sarkar's theory is vague (are they classes, personality types, structures, ideal types?). Alternatively, it is bad metaphysics in that Sarkar believes there are laws to history that are generally unchangeable. As an empirical theory that explains long term processes in history it fails. Carspecken thus concludes that in effect it is but an ideology, a theory developed to justify a particular knowledge and power interest. This is evidenced by PROUT theorists continuous resort to

---

[1] Phil Carspecken sees that particular article, "Playing the Devil's Advocate," as an attempt to incite PROUTists to do better research instead of merely using Sarkar's works as a priori truths. He does not locate his own thinking in the positivist tradition, but has taken that position (and quite strongly) since PROUT research is presently abysmal as the level of empirical research (Personal Communication, February 1990). Unfortunately, Carspecken does not take the next necessary creative act and ask: how would he resolve the many problems he has raised?

citing Sarkar to prove a particular point. Equally noteworthy is their unwillingness to question Sarkar's theory, or only to criticize the theory when they have left the PROUT movement and only then not in terms of any historical claims, but in terms of Sarkar's position as guru. He is the authority.

For Carspecken even at the common sense level, there appear to be basic problems with Sarkar's work, for example, there appear to be more than four types of people. In defense of Sarkar, however, he does not classify people, rather he is concerned with abstract mentalities, ways of perceiving the real. However, given the symmetrical nature of Sarkar's universe—as per the classic Indian episteme—it is but natural that there exist correspondence of the four-fold structure at the level of the person *and* society. And at the level of the person, humans tend to fall into these categories, but there are deviations and inter-varna movement. In addition, Sarkar reminds us that these are not genetic qualities, but environmentally and spatially induced, they are not based on heredity or a theory of exclusion/inclusion, the classical model of purity based on the Aryan conquering of Dravidians. Sarkar sees it has a historical division of labor which became reified, closer to what Plato meant in his basic types: philosophers, soldiers and common men or in India, Brahmins, ksattriyas, shudras. It is a fundamental and deep human structure that takes different forms through history (the priest becoming the bureaucrat, the king's soldier becoming the State's soldier, the peasant becoming the industrial worker) and across culture. Thus the argument is that these categories are historical and empirically derived, over time they function as structures and as ideal types similar to Sheldrake's morphogenetic fields (which for Sarkar are embedded in cosmic mind and expressed via microvita). For Sheldrake, recent fields are easily malleable, while more ancient fields have become deep structures and thus collective habits and are fundamentally unchangeable. Thus, habits are laws but not in the sense of eternally unchanging, new behaviors can lead to changes in these fields of awareness, either immediately starting new patterns or changing the old pattern. Thus even with the context of laws, there is room for contingency.

As mentioned in the beginning of this chapter, for Sarkar, these operate under a condition of laws that are deep structures and not philosophically derived, that is, from the philosophizing of intellectuals (not from the *Vedas*, nor deduced), but rather they are laws because they are *historical, evolutionary,* and *empirical* (empirical in the sense of practical and inductive and intuitional). These mentalities have not developed because they serve Sarkar's particular knowledge interests, rather, as mentioned earlier, they developed in an evolutionary manner as a way to deal with the external environment. Evolutionary development for Sarkar results from physical clash, the battle with the environment, intellectual clash, the battle of ideas and ideologies and the attraction of the great, the emanations constantly emerging from the Supreme Spiritual Nucleus, the Macrocosmic entity, to use Sarkar's language. They are empirical in the sense that they can be observed in humans and observed in history. They become laws because they have existed historically. They will remain laws in that this basic evolutionary model continues to repeat itself; it has become a deep structure of humans. They are also laws in that Sarkar exists in a model of knowledge wherein the empirical world is real, the body is real, the natural world is real. Foremost in front of us is the pattern of the life cycle; birth, rise, plateau, decline, death and then the next cycle—this is the grand theory model used by Spengler, Toynbee, Sorokin and others. The mentalities in the cycle exhibit this function as well. The ancient Indians understood this cycle, but a particular class became dominant and used the model to maintain its own power and absorbed other classes irrespective of the dominant mentality of the individual or group at the bottom level. The social cycle became the caste system. An ideal type, historically and evolutionarily derived, became hereditary and a vehicle for domination by the Aryans of the Dravidians.

Will it then always be a law? Sarkar's notion of truth here is well worth mentioning. For him, it is not *rta* the facts of a particular situation, but *satya* that which is stated for the benefit of all. The goal of theory is to produce a state where humans can attain bliss. For Sarkar, these theories are made available at the level that they can be intelligible, they are not the absolute truth.

They will change in time and the humans of the future will reconstruct present theories, they might develop new mentalities and new bodies as well. But until the time when the human life cycle in itself is transformed—when evolution in itself is transformed and new selves are constructed—the social cycle will continue unabated. The obvious tension is with Sarkar's distinction between the Cosmic Entity which is eternal and infinite and the universe which is always changing (because of the emanations of the cosmic entity) and dependent

on space/time and person, that is, it is relative. Sarkar, unfortunately, does not clarify this tension. We are only left to assume that:

(1) he operates under an alternative episteme where this seeming
    contradiction/tension is tolerated;
(2) he operates under a different episteme, the Indian, where laws
    can be laws notwithstanding relativity, in the sense that they are
    analogies, or in the sense that they are models, or perhaps, simple
    fixations, points of departure, for a universe in flux;
(3) he sees the significance of his theory as educational, similar to
    the poststructural perspective where the value of a theory is in
    the asset that it gives to a particular economic class or mental
    class, or other;
(4) he considers the social cycle as a deep structure that for all prac-
    tical purposes is immutable, but that as humans move into space—
    as they become less grounded in the physical, as the shudra way
    of perceiving the world decreases—and as evolution moves to
    the psychic realm, an alternative structure may develop;
(5) he defines relativity not in the politics of real perspective of the
    poststructuralist, but to simply mean that reality changes over
    time and that humans cannot really see things as they are, but
    that there still remains a real to be discovered. That is, his view
    is closer to the a spiritual empiricist view than that of a radical
    deconstructionist Buddhist view, in that the world is to be *dis-
    covered* not *invented*, and;
(6) the Supreme Consciousness is changing the universe (through
    microvita and other emanations) at the microscopic and galactic
    level but not at the social level—the real than operates differently
    at different level, there is constant change *and* there is structure.

Of course, alternatively:

(1) one might argue that he does see it as a historical law and is
    wrong;
(2) is wrong that the theory is invariant for space and time and
    observer, but still is contributing an important insight—even bril-
    liant—to current macrohistory and macrosociology;
(3) is clearly ideological and thus partisan in its orientation;
(4) it is still unclear if he is wrong or correct given that there is a
    paucity of historical applied evidence or present quantitative
    empirical evidence to "test" his theories, that is, we must wait
    and see;

(5) aspects of it are indeed insightful and true (but not throughout all time and space) but the exact order of the changing of the elites is not true, Johan Galtung's position;

(6) one cannot determine if it is true or false given that it is so broad and thus is not a theory in the present definition of what constitutes sociological theory;

(7) it is useful in terms of political activity and in terms of recovering alternative ways of thinking, but no theory can be proved empirically anyway as theories exist in particular discourses or ways of knowing the world from which objects and subjects become constituted;

(8) it might be "true" or comprehensive from the viewpoint of Oriental or Indian traditions, but not so for the Occidental, which is linear in approach and empirical, "scientific" in proof, especially since it appears derived from an interpretation of Indian values, assumptions of the real, and Indian history, itself, and;

(9) it is true or useful for Indian history alone, the data from which the theory was derived.

However, the above attempt to search for alternative ways of composing the real in terms of the world as Sarkar sees it, Sarkar's subjective view, would not persuade present Occidental sociologists and those Indian and Oriental ones that have adopted Occidental cosmology. Nor would the alternative compositions of the Occidental view; they would certainly argue that it is not true. For them, the conventional Academy, the social cycle types are only descriptive not explanatory terms, they thus are not useful to psychology or other divisions of social science (too broad and little predictive value).

Irrespective of how we might interpret Sarkar, Carspecken argues that insofar as Sarkar treats his theory as a law of history and insofar as PROUT writers treat it as revealed truth with perfect empirical correspondence, then it should be criticized from the empirical view. Even in terms of social theory, argues Carspecken, *varna* is not a useful category. For example, within most social groups, class, education, income, and ethnicity are much better predictors of future social behavior. So too, with the working class. In terms of history, he also finds historical contradictions in the application of *varna*, such as the emerging French bourgeoisie which were more interested in prestige rather than wealth. One could counter by asking were they then indeed bourgeoisie, that is, Carspecken begins with Marxist language and then relates it to Sarkar's language. Vaeshyan is a different concept with prestige not necessarily that different from wealth accumulation, or alternatively one could argue that the desire for prestige was a precursor for the desire for wealth. Most likely, Sarkar would argue that Carspecken's analysis of the social cycle at too micro a level, a "nitpicking analysis" one might expect from an intellectual speaking from the positivist or from a critical philosophical level. Galtung's metaphor as tó the different levels of historical thinking is useful. Most history is written from the ground floor. At the ground floor level, sense observation is critical, the sizes and space between cars is equally significant (and critical for planning and policy research), but at the level that Sarkar is writing, one cannot see the cars or persons in them only structures and deep patterns are perceptible. Sarkar narrates a history from way above, yet with total concern for the history of the oppressed, the Subaltern project mentioned earlier.

But the contradiction is that Sarkar's theory is used to describe local behavior and thus must stand the tests of the empirical/predictive mode if it is to be accepted and create the civilizational revolution he hopes for. Our alternative view is that one should not use Sarkar's theory to describe local behavior or indeed nation-state behavior, rather it should be used as one tool among many to better understand social reality. But for Carspecken, the social cycle is not a useful category at the psychological level or at the sociological level of class analysis.

The social dynamics language of Sarkar's theory are additionally seen as weak in that the metaphor of the social cycle (or revolutionary movements and of short-lived counter-revolutionary movements) must be delineated into measurable and understandable terms. For Carspecken, to even begin to take Sarkar's theory seriously—at least in the minds of academicians and those, we would argue, interested in mid-range empirical theories where issues of validity, reliability and precision are central—the following questions must be asked.

(1) Is it a law, an empirical law? Is there proof for it? Can it be disproved? Sarkar's law counters current thinking that considers laws as operating under certain conditions and sees them as not provable (as David Hume has shown that causality cannot be proved as it may always be undermined, the sun may not go up one day). Thus, the universe is open and laws in this view are only long-term tendencies that change as other variables change.

(2) To prove that there is a law, one has to prove that there exists something called a society. This too is contentious. What is a society? How is different from civilizations? From Sorokin's congeries? From mentalities? From nations? Systems? Or does Sarkar speak of deductive-nomological laws established through observation and induction from which sub-laws can be derived.

(3) Does the social cycle really explain social change or does it only organize historical material according to these categories? Moreover, his categories of the dynamics of change are too broad as well. What does physical and mental clash mean? What does attraction to the Great mean?

(4) Why do some societies rotate prior to other societies: is it level of exploitation; is it rising expectations; is it class conflicts; is it new means of production; is it the relationship with the world system as a whole?

In general, Carspecken concludes that Sarkar's theory is:

(1) impossible to operationalize;
(2) definitions of the various explanatory categories are non-existent;
(3) the descriptions of the eras do not fit into generally agreed upon definitions of history;
(4) there are anomalies within Sarkar's texts themselves, that is, internal inconsistency;
(5) they have little or no predictive ability;
(6) they are stated in such general ways, that they are impossible to prove or disprove and thus again have little utility value, and;
(7) since the theory cannot be disproved, it cannot be legitimately considered a theory. Thus, the social cycle theory and PROUT itself lacks any rigorous analysis and can only be believed because one accepts the authority of Sarkar, not because of the merits of the theory itself. It is neither science nor philosophy but simply *gurudom* creating an alternative ideology.

In Search of Truth

While we do not argue that these questions are trivial—indeed they are crucially important and debate and research needs to be conducted to negotiate these questions—but for us they are too narrow and apolitical. For us, both conventional empirical research and an analysis of alternative sites of understanding are necessary. Carspecken, insightful as he is, does not take the more radical epistemological viewpoint that argues all positions are interest driven. Indeed all *are* ideological. For example, while Jurgen Habermas asserts that in the communication act there exists the possibility for universal interests, for truth, Foucault argues that there is no universal and that truth is power. Reality then becomes conventional, with truth becoming a will to knowledge. Thus, in this perspective:

> [W]hat makes a science a science, in short, whatever its subject matter, is not its degree of predictive success—prediction is only one important validating device and only one kind of use to which scientific theories are put [for example, the theory of evolution which accounts for the past but leaves the future to "what Monod has called 'chance and necessity'"] but the standards governing its structure and application (Shapiro, 1981, 96).

Habermas, however, attempts to reconcile the hermeneutic interpretative perspective and the positivist empirical perspective by positing an ideal speech situation that contains "not only the rational attainment of consensus" but also complete mutual understanding by participants and recognition of the authentic right of each to participate in the dialogue as an autonomous and equal partner (Giddens, 1982, 88).

This is in contrast to the articulation of Peirce "who argues that scientific truth concerns not [only] the relationship between an isolated observer and a subject matter, but a consensus arrived at through the discourse of many observers where that discourse is not constrained by anything other than the cannons of logical procedure and rational argumentation" (88). Thus, truth is possible but only under specific mutually democratic conditions, where each freely participates in the construction of the real. Foucault takes a much more epistemologically nihilistic position. According to Shapiro,

> For Foucault, truth is conventional, as it is for Habermas, but the conventions extend to the constitution of subjects as well as objects and object relations. There is no nonconventional arena exterior to discourse within which subjects can transcend convention and pursue universal interests (as in Habermas's ideal-speech situation) (Shapiro, 1981, 141).

Thus, within this perspective a history of science is possible, but not simply a history as Thomas Kuhn would write. For Kuhn, paradigms change because of anomalies that appear in the accumulation of knowledge. These anomalies then lead to new theories in the context of the rational assent of the relevant community (Shapiro, 1981, 147). But for Foucault "ruptures and transformations in knowledge systems" (148) emerge as "a result of changing interests within a society that locate persons in various roles and distribute authority and responsibility differently" (148). Paradigms do not change through rational assent but through changing political distributions of wealth, power, technology and meanings. Foucault's thus takes a much more politicized view of the history of knowledge. Suffice to say, this more politicized view of science makes problematic efforts to attack Sarkar's theory for not being appropriately scientific. The response from Sarkar may well be change your science or enter more complex politicized epistemological spaces.

But Carspecken does make some cogent suggestions in terms of the implications of Sarkar's theory which are useful to us in understanding and developing a critique of Sarkar. For example, he argues that *varna* is a hierarchical concept with potentially disastrous effects. This is asserted notwithstanding that Sarkar's whole theory is based on universalism, dignity for humans and mutual respect and equality and is written in response to the human disaster that is India in specific and the globe itself in general. Moreover, left untouched is Sarkar's own political battles with Hindu political movements, his refusal to work with any group which at any level supports caste (and the numerous attacks by Hindu groups on Sarkar's movements). To Hindus and others, Sarkar is an iconoclast. But Sarkar's motivations and his personal and movement politics are incidental because a hierarchical concept of class is compatible with various structures of inequity, thus his theory simply rewrites hierarchy on the body and mind of persons. It is from the very beginning seriously flawed and dangerous to the task of building a good society: liberty, fraternity and equality are doubtful results when one begins with *varna* as a central cosmological concept. The theory, by remaining with the traditional caste model although critical of it, has the potential to reinscribe (particular vertical notions of identity) it in the long run. Sarkar, however, would object arguing that he sees it as psychological class, not *varna* as caste. He has simply extended Marx's economic notion of class to a mental, social-psychological, level, an extension which as we have argued is entirely compatible with the Indian episteme given its privileging of mentalities as real.

Unfortunately as we have alluded to above, Carspecken speaks only from a position of empiricist sociology, and from a position which makes science interest free and a position which takes Sarkar's theory in the context of the Western project. He does not attempt to see it as part of the Indian episteme, as a rupture within the Indian episteme, or a response to British interests and Gandhism. Carspecken does not acknowledge its use value in revealing parts of society that previously were misunderstood; the notion of four classes instead of two, the inclusion of ideational-religious systems as part of power; the notion of the cycle and so forth. In this sense, he attempts to see a grand theory from the micro theory view and then finds it problematic that it is not specific enough or rigorous enough to meet the criteria of a micro theory.

In addition, the phenomenological question as to how Sarkar himself sees his theory is not attempted. In our view, Sarkar sees it in different ways. In his *Human Society*, his main effort is story-telling, in developing myth and archetypes: the warrior, the intellectual, the acquisitor and the worker. In addition, he is not dealing with empirical measurable eras, but with the nature of group mind. Finally, Sarkar's theory can thus be seen as an asset and a resource to various groups. To us this is the key.

Similarly, Michael Shapiro speaking of Marx's theory says it well. "Thus part of the *value* of the Marxist economic discourse is that political and economic relations meet within it" (Shapiro, 1981, 140). When Marx promoted the labor theory of value, he was delivering an asset to a class of people, not simply trying to build a "better" theory (in the traditional scientific sense). Foucault is explicit about this. "[F]rom the moment of its existence . . . [discourse] poses the question of power; [discourse is] an asset that is, by nature, the object of a struggle, a political struggle" (140).

Of course Marx had his own style and his own idea of theory within which his theory was to be judged. In this regard, an appropriate question for Sarkar would be: Does his theory follow his own stance as to what constitutes a good theory, that is, does it satisfy his own criteria: Is it based on induction? Does it educate the people? Does it help society's problems? Does it deal with physical, mental and spiritual worlds? Are those who put it to practice experienced and able to do so, that is, is there a social movement, a community to put the theory into practice? Is the theory useful not only for the particular moment of inception, but also for periods after it, that is, is it more than a thought experiment suitable for one environment but not for the next? Within these criteria, Sarkar's theory can be "judged" from the viewpoint of consistency to its own measures of what constitutes a good theory. But more important for Foucault and Shapiro is to understand how a theory functions in terms of the way it reconstitutes subjects and objects and the way that it revalues and promotes some interests while silencing others. Thus theory is removed from a knowledge site to a political site, power is laid bare, and inquiry made possible. This, of course, is Sarkar's goal to recast and reconstitute a new subject for the centuries ahead.

From the interpretive view—developed in the previous chapter on grand theory—Sarkar's theory can perhaps be better understood as an attempt to come to terms with deep structures and patterns, much in the way Marx has done, or Sorokin has done with his ideational, idealistic (dualistic) and sensate systems. Sarkar's work is an attempt to provide a guideline to history and a perspective on the future. That is, his theory should be seen from an interpretive view that seeks to enrich our understandings of the world, not argue for any one hegemonic understanding. To understand Sarkar we must be culturally sensitive to his context. Indeed, thinking about the Indian episteme, we would be far more surprised if there were no laws. The universe is orderly, symmetrical with many levels of reality. As there are physical laws, there *must* be social and spiritual laws. Precision with respect to understanding the real is far less important than telling stories about Reality while having tea in the early afternoon or monks around a fireplace describing their spiritual experiences.

And even from the empirical view, for PROUT supporters Sarkar's work certainly does provide additional explanatory power as well as predictive value, besides being comprehensive, and thus cannot be easily thrown away. It provides a better understanding of feudalism, of Brahmanism, and other idealistic, ideational systems, as Batra has tried to prove (we here would strongly prefer to use the word demonstrate, or suggest). It provides a better understanding of the Tibetan theocracy than the materialistic perspective, the liberal democratic tradition, the institutional perspective, developmentalist model, or the Marxist or neo-Marxist model. Tibet simply has remained in a Vipran era and has recently been vanquished by a Warrior polity. Eventually China will move to a Vipran era itself, but in the meantime Tibet will have to wait. Alternatively, as Tibet is doing, it can make alliances with the larger world vaeshyan community, hoping that will spur

China to action. Sarkar's theory provides useful, albeit still unrefined alternative structures in which to understand the structure of power and it provides an alternative perspective in which to see power: neither the material nor the analytic, nor the idealistic. Thus, as with most of science, it is not that Sarkar has little "empirical" validity, but that not enough research has been done.

Our view, however, is that what Carspecken complains about is not truly a problem with Sarkar but a problem with contemporary sociology and its move away from grand theory to micro/macro policy oriented data-building. For us, the empirical must be contextualized as what is presently considered data is merely the authoritative representations of a particular construction of the real (the liberal materialistic scientific worldview, Western cosmology). Data in our alternative view emerges from theory, from episteme. While Sarkar's works may not always correspond to present notions of the real, the problem may not lie with Sarkar; the problem could be with our reality constructions. Of course, the problem with this argument is that any theory is as good as any other theory since all criteria are local specific and no theory can then speak to any other theory— total relativization! What is needed is either a recourse to self-criteria (judging the theory in terms of its own criteria) or a grounding in temporarily chosen guide posts (Galtung's direct and structural violence, for example, or Maslow's hierarchy of human needs). For the poststructural, the grounding is the power implications of every view of the real.

Finally, this is not to say that endeavors to develop empirical indicators should not be attempted or his work should not be applied to individual societies or nations, but rather his theory should be seen in a different context. Moreover, Sarkar's theory should not be seen as a definitive end to all theory building. If we adopt the Indian model, there are five ways of knowing, four explicit and one implicit. Sarkar speaks from his intuitive, cosmic perspective wherein he provides a macro perspective of large deep patterns in world and Indian history. What in the Western context one would call prophecy (this word is not current in the Indian context since the spiritual is available to all, albeit situated in the enlightened ones and in either case prophecy is more pluralistic). This is then accepted by many as authority, yet at the same time Sarkar asks his students to develop the rational/applied basis for these theories, much as Batra has attempted to. In addition, these theories are not meant to stand alone. They work with other theoretical perspectives and can thus be made more rigorous, more analytic by, for example, using insights from other macrohistorians such as Khaldun, Marx, Sorokin and others, as we have attempted to do in the previous chapter. Finally, there still exists the possibility of developing empirical indicators for various aspects of the theory. What is given is an incredibly rich but vague story of the human condition, the larger interpretative meaning structure of what has happened and what will happen.

Let us recap the argument of the previous pages and attempt to find alternative placements for Sarkar's law of history. Is his law like Newton's law or Einstein's law, useful in explaining unexplained phenomena (giving a more complete picture of the world and predicting future observations), but eventually to be overthrown by a new theory? Is it then a social science law in the sense of operating under certain conditions (all things being equal) and in this sense of speaking of tendencies not determinations? Is it a law that assumes that the universe is fixed and unchanging? If so, does this contradict Sarkar's own assertion that Cosmic Consciousness is constantly emanating new spiritual, psychic and physico-psychic phenomena? Or by claiming that Sarkar's law is an empirical law in the sense of natural sciences, is this simply imposing a particular view of knowledge on to Sarkar's model since Sarkar may be speaking from an alternative view? Or is it rather that Sarkar's metaphysics is best understood from the interpretive model?

Indeed, Sarkar creates new structures while at the same time recovering old and ancient structures that have been hidden and put aside by current materialistic, imperialist, colonial, empiricist, nationalistic discourses. Shouldn't Sarkar's theory then be seen as a great exercise in story-telling that includes epistemology, metaphysics, ontology, sociology, politics and economics? Is it not an attempt to produce a new cosmology with its own social codes, a new cosmology that must speak to its Indian frame of thought yet at the same be intelligible to various Western discourses: liberal, Marxist or religious. In addition, to the myth-oriented story-telling perspective, cannot Sarkar's view be better understood from the poststructural perspective which assigns theories to resource grammars and sees them as effort to redistribute meanings, power and wealth. The question there is not one of predictability, but of revealing insights, of showing new meanings, of finding new configurations of exposing power, of analyzing the world—the question becomes how does Sarkar's enterprise add to or detract from present projects. This view ostensibly removes Sarkar from the authorship position placing meaning first in structure and then reader.

The critical view, however, is that Sarkar's theory is but ideological underpinning for his own power moves—to justify his spiritual society project. The task here becomes to expose the implications of his thought on various categories one privileges such as democracy, non-violence and so forth.

However, to evoke the critical view and then assert that Sarkar's theory is valueless because of its lack of theoretical rigor, or it is overly mystical metaphysics forgets, for example, the history of Marxist thought (as well as other systems). Marxism is certainly analytically useful not because its predictions were correct (they were not), not because it is universal (it is plainly European and indeed imperialist and Orientalistic in its language), not because of the success of so called communist nations (they have failed on their own terms and only theoretical moves such as by Wallerstein have saved the entire project by arguing that world egalitarian socialism has yet to emerge—one cannot be an island of socialism in a sea of capitalism). Rather Marxism is current because it broke with previous theory (German Idealism) and created a new discourse, because it developed a more insightful alternative model of conflict and social change, because it brought forth a class-oriented model of political economy, because it created new social movements, because Marx created a politics which spawned a range of new theories, including world systems, dependencia, imperialism. By and large, Marx created a new way of seeing the world that led to a new kind of praxis; the empirical (repeatability) verity of his theory was secondary. It is to explain the world and to see it in a new light that is the larger task. Of course, the key issue in assessing Marxism are its real world implications.

Similarly, our view is that to understand Sarkar one must see him in this type of light, at the universal but especially in light of Eastern cosmology. Of relevance are his attempts to develop an alternative political economy, an alternative social movement, an alternative theory of consciousness, an alternative rational for spiritual practices, alternative practices themselves, a new theory of history, an alternative model of knowledge, an alternative way of being, and knowing that indeed is Indian, but not Indian (and thus perhaps truly Indian).

The question then is what model should one use to understand Sarkar: the natural science, the social science, the interpretative, the mythological, or the poststructural. However, like Marxism, Sarkarian thought claims to include all these models in an inclusive model of thought. We prefer the poststructural and the interpretive and place the empirical within the larger text of the politics of knowledge and meaning, a layered complex approach.

Finally, is the perspective that the acceptance of a theory is not about modeling at all, but rather about power. A particular discourse becomes hegemonic because it has political resources behind it: remunerative, coercive and normative. Sarkar's discourse, as the Marxist, might become a significant way of seeing the world if it manages to either control State power, or amass ideological power. Here, power is truth and truth is power.

We have stayed at the general level so far. Now, again using Marx to understand Sarkar, we will attempt to better understand Sarkar's laws and their criticisms.

Dialectical Laws: Marx and Sarkar

Continuing our analogy of Marx's dialectical laws and Sarkar's dialectical *varna*, Harold McCarthy (1973) is instructive. He summarizes the basic critique of Marxist history.

> The dialectical analysis of history provided by historical materialism is either a great over-simplification and therefore theoretically false, or much too broad to be a significant tool in historical study; and in either case the emergence of a classless society organized in terms of a single world-view is not a logical necessity but at best a speculative prediction or prophecy which not only may be erroneous, but seems quite incompatible with what we know concerning human individuality and diversity with respect to human thought and desired action (McCarthy, 1973, 23).

As mentioned earlier, prophecy is one useful way to understand Sarkar, although it is a non-word in the Indian context. For the Western social scientist, the only site for Sarkar is prophecy. Continuing, in terms of epistemology:

> Indeed, since the Dialectical Materialist insists that most of the philosophical ideas of the past are erroneous, and therefore (at best) distorted reflections, he has no sound reason to exclude the possibility

that his own dialectical ideas are equally distorted, and hence equally
false to the nature of things. Sensations and ideas may reflect, but
reflections may also be distorted reflections (23).

The similarity is obvious, indeed, glaring. Of course, instead of false
we would change it to the level of the true, but still how can Sarkar
be sure that he too speaks from less than a totally unconditioned—
top of Brahma—level. Others, historically have thought the same,
and in retrospect, are now either perceived as false or simply one
truth among many. Dogmatism and authority may have clouded his
view as well. We cannot place him outside of history as well, irrespective of his location in the Shiva/Krishna cycle.

Thus, critically, Marxism can be but taken as a speculative philosophy, not a science, with Marx as the prophet, the "workers of
the world" as the chosen people. For Sarkar, however, there are no
chosen people, since his attempt is to stand outside of all the classes,
the only one chosen are the *sadvipras*, but their life is life of leadership as burden, responsibility and sacrifice. Sarkar does not stand
for any class, for all classes are historically and ontologically bound
to become oppressive (the law of *vidya* and *avidya*) and Sorokin's principle of limits. But Sarkar is clearly the prophet, PROUT is the
party, and at one level his students the chosen people. In this sense,
articulation of the social cycle as a science is absurd.

How then to understand laws? Let us quote again from McCarthy:

> The three Dialectical Laws are not revealed truths; they are not ratio-
> nally self-evident truths; if scientific laws, they are not true in the sense
> in which ordinary scientific laws are said to be true; if hypotheses,
> they are open to modification and even total rejection, which would
> mean the subversion of dialectical materialism; if pedagogical instru-
> ments, they are conventional only; if speculative principles, they can
> support a metaphysical interpretation but cannot mediate precise scientific
> description or historical prediction without serious error or distortion
> of scientific or historical fact. All in all, they seem to take the place
> of Divine Providence in Christian Theology, and are just as difficult
> to support on purely philosophical grounds; and to say that they sim-
> ply ARE correct reflections of objective reality is mere dogmatism (23).

Again the similarities with Sarkar's laws and their critique is glaring. And again the response to this type of criticism would be similar for both writers: Marx and Sarkar. While Marxism rejected
theism and thus developed a humanism, Sarkar rejects secularism
and caste and develops an alternative spiritual Neo-Humanism.

The Sarkarian response to the speculative problem of laws would, like the dialectical materialist, not make a pure distinction between speculative principles and scientific ones. Certainly, the Indian view as we have suggested redefines these words differently: these rigid dichotomies are not held. Conventional positivist science in itself can be critiqued for similar infractions. How can, for example, Newton's laws be empirically proved, there is no place where every body is isolated from other body, so as to judge his laws of motion. That is, scientific laws in themselves can be judged from the above criticisms, or even more critically from the Foucauldian perspective, who shows them to exist within certain knowledge boundaries. McCarthy's conclusion about the dialectical laws mirrors what we have suggested of Sarkar's laws:

> All in all, the Dialectical laws, though not scientific in a narrow sense, are not speculative in the sense of merely conjectural. They are not tautological and do have an important and crucial function with the context of both scientific and philosophic inquiry. They are indispensable guides to fruitful and significant inquiry (80).

Meaning: they help us see ourselves and our world differently. They point to places of silence that were previously unheard, shadows that lurked outside of our sight, and smells that went unnoticed. Sarkar's thought too fulfills these requirements within the Indian context and outside of it as well.

Equally relevant is McCarthy's commentary on the notion that the stages are overly simplistic. As we have suggested, Sarkar attempts to place them in an evolutionary model. It is like comparing Marx's theory to Darwin's, in that both are general, both are evolutionary, and both explain much, but leave a great deal unaccounted for. Like Marx, Sarkar looks for patterns, searches for order in a world, and attempts to generate claims as to fundamental reasons for change. Marx (according to McCarthy), "does not attempt to give us detailed case histories of specific societies but rather provides us with dynamic archetypes, of each of which there will inevitably be, historically speaking, a diversity of exemplifications" (84). The evolutionary model is appropriate—Sarkar titles his essays on the cycle as "The evolution of human society." Like Darwin's theory which in

> broad movement outlines, a movement from invertebrates to vertebrates and (within the sphere of vertebrates) from fish to amphibians to reptiles to birds and mammals and most recently to human beings,

is a theoretical model which does not as such fill in and automatically account for all details, but is, for all that, an indispensable tool for historico-biological investigation (84–85).

Sarkar is simply less rigorous then Marx and Engels in that his style is different. He does not speak as an intellectual, nor does he speak to intellectuals: it is not a politics of footnotes and theory-building, rather he speaks as a guru and relays his theory to his disciples. In his view, it is up to movement intellectuals—his Renaissance Artists and Writers Association—to translate his narrative for intellectual consumption, and to do so, dialectically and creatively (as Batra has tried to do).

One might also subject Sarkar's thinking to unfulfilled predictions of the future (in the future, it is still too young at present) as with Marx's predictions. But again this freezes the theory and indeed, from a Foucauldian position, centers the subject. However, insofar as theories speak subjects, then, we can distinguish between thought that is literal (these predictions must happen) and thought that is conditional, given the present state of knowledge (these predictions will *probably* occur). Sarkar, however, unlike Marx, is more apt to speak from what is commonly called vision or from the Western view, prophecy, since he speaks from a transcendental viewpoint, while scientists speak for an empiricist viewpoint (and bounded by the phrase, if all things remain equal, or if present trends continue); nonetheless, both make claims about future states. The non-occurrence of these claims in the Marxist case has simply lead to refinements; in the scientific case it has lead to new theories or to refinements again. We can expect the same in Sarkar's case.

Alternative Placements

Again, we return to our initial quest of situating Sarkar. There are numerous ways to criticize Sarkar's philosophical thought. A dominant perspective is methodological individualism as defined by Karl Popper: "All social phenomena, and especially the functioning of all social institutions, should always be understood as resulting from the decisions, actions, attitudes, etc. of human individuals . . . we would never be satisfied by an explanation in terms of so-called collectives" (Giddens, 1983, 95). This view would reject the view of cultural totalities or Sarkar's history of humanity, or the Marxian history of class and economic power; Sarkar speaks of non-existent societies, of humanity itself, while indeed it is only persons who exist (although in social situations which structure their choices) or one can move to a societal position of holism and agree that societies exist and indeed they follow certain patterns. Another position is to move beyond and place theory in cosmology (Galtung, 1981a). Here one looks not at persons or societies, but the deep structures that give meaning to both, that pattern society and individual. Cosmology is an irreducible concept and thus laws and agency must be understood in the context of the particular cosmology. Cosmological analysis is an attempt to sidestep the issue of what is primary: mind/body, structure/agency. It is an attempt to look at this cosmology and then understand it through a comparison with other cosmologies. Its weakness is that it does not answer the question of how the particular cosmology became so, for, indeed, this question would place it back in the position of paradox.

Examining Occidental cosmology, science (natural and social) is primary and is seen as knowledge itself. Alternatively, this division is not made in the Indian context; thus using one to criticize the others in the final analysis is a useless exercise—since every cosmology has its own criteria for the real. Critique of another cosmology is useful only if it aids in learning about one's own cosmology and the differences between both.

Unfortunately, this relativistic view does not aid in social analysis. The other choices are to examine internal consistencies or to structure a range of values (and explicitly declared as such) and then determine how the various theories stand to those. Again Galtung has done this in his various works. We have attempted this to some extent in the previous chapter.

So far we have used the poststructural view as a way to defend the various possible critiques of Sarkar's theory of social change. We have sought to understand his theory on his own terms, as an asset being delivered not to one class, but to all classes, especially those classes who are not in power—for they will have their day—and we have argued that to understand Sarkar we must place him in the Indian episteme. But a critique not developed so far is to argue that Sarkar and Indian thinking have not had the type of enlightenment that the Europeans had, that is, Indian thought remains backward since the transcendental has not be secularized and made scientific, that is, entered the modern era, or more radically, that Sarkar's theory remains as a modernist theory that reinscribes that which it is fighting against.

For example, Robert Brown in *The Nature of Social Laws* argues that in the classical era there were laws because the universe was controlled by God. God was then the divine legislator and as such, there must be laws for the society as there were for nature. It was incumbent upon men and women to find these laws to better appreciate His majesty. Accompanying these laws were moral laws. In fact, God would issue physical laws to the obedient Nature and to humans in the form of moral laws. Using current language, God was the divine legislator. "The existence of the Christian God ensured the presence of His plan, and the character of that God guaranteed the reliability of the plan's operation and hence the reliability of scientific predictions" (Brown, 1984, 12). This coincided with the center-periphery cosmological view of the Occident. The West was part of the privileged land, it was following the laws, the evolution, while those outside the West were in a pre-evolution stage, either behind or like nature to be used and exploited for the larger Christian project.

In this sense, it could be argued that Sarkar's laws are simply the laws of a religious era: India did not experience an enlightenment where the "irrationality" of the Church was overthrown by the "rationality" of the modern subject, the modern state, and modern reason, science itself. Kant, for example, broke with this classical worldview and made man the center of being. According to Richard Ashley, "Not beholden to classical epistemology, modern discourse since Kant has asserted its independence of the classical assumption that God had arranged a chain of being and arranged language in pre-established correspondence with it" (Ashley, 1989, 264)). The problem with this perspective of the Indian episteme and Sarkar's discourse is that the Indian god was not outside of the self. God is immanent in self *and* God is external. There is a unity of being that cuts through the familiar Western problematique. There was no Enlightenment like the Occidental Enlightenment because the problems were different. The enlightenment that did occur but it did not attempt to throw off the Indian spiritual worldview. Rather it was a Gandhian revival of the truth of the past along with an attack on British colonialism and its commodification, secularization, and linearization (attempting to transform Indian time to Western time) tendencies as well as an attack on the hierarchy of caste. It was influenced by the Marxist call for equality, but it was not an attack on the pre-modern episteme. Gandhi through and through was embedded in the spiritual logos of Indian thought. Gandhism also was a rejection of the modern world of the West: its scientism and its unquestioned faith in industrialism. Sarkar in one sense, although he takes great pains to distinguish himself from Gandhi, continues this Indian enlightenment. He attacks caste, attacks capitalism and communism, but accepts technology under spiritual control (and thus he is not particularly sensitive to the discourse of technology, the social messages encoded in Western technology) and in the context of self-reliance. Thus, the Indian enlightenment is about a nationalism becoming globalism, about the spiritualization and socialization of the science and technology fetishism of the West, and it is about the return of the cycle, the laws of history. The Indian era is an assertion that one cannot escape history, that power moves in cycles, and thus those in the center will one day fall, and those in the periphery will rise. But this modern era of India at least as Sarkar sees it, is not the creation of a sovereign voice of man: rather it is a neo-humanism in which man is part of a larger ecology.

Poststructuralism and Sarkar: Deconstruction and Vipra-Talk

Of course a much more serious examination than the attempt to place the Indian/Sarkar's view in the pre-modern discourse (arguing that it is pre-scientific and pre-rational since India did not have an enlightenment) is that of the poststructuralist which argues against the modern discourse. In a now classic essay titled "Living on Borderlines," Richard Ashley (1989), following Jacques Derrida, takes exception to logocentrism.

"This is the expectation that all interpretation and practice must secure recognition and power by appeal to some identical consciousness, principle of interpretation, or necessary subjectivity having at lest two *qualities*" (261). Two aspects of this are critical: first, there is a

> central interpretive orientation—a coherent sovereign voice, if you will—that supplies a unified rational meaning and direction to the interpretation of the spatial and temporal direction of history.... second, as a sovereign voice, this principle is itself regarded as a pure and originary presence—an unproblematic, extra-historical identity, in need of no critical accounting (261).

Thus, there is a voice that interprets history but does not take a
critical stance of itself: it does not explain where it stands and how
it has come to stand there. This voice then is outside of history yet
has a special vantage point of seeing history as it is. This is the writing of modern history. In addition, the logocentric perspective adopts
a narrative structure; one where the ambiguity of history is controlled
and order imposed. Stages are developed (Marx, Comte, Sorokin,
or Sarkar), ideal types are imposed. This narrative asserts itself

> by imposing a central ordering principle whose categories and stan-
> dards of interpretation are taken to express the essential and timeless
> truth integrating all of the historical times and places among which it
> discriminates. It constructs a story in which all time, all space, all
> difference, and all discontinuity are cast as part of a universal project
> in which the ordering principle is itself redeemed as necessarily, time-
> lessly, and universally true (264).

Now these are not simply excursions into grand theory, they are also
critiques of grand theory by those who stand on the side of science,
for they too believe that they are outside of history, they too believe
that they stand at a point of "interpretation that is taken to be fixed
and independent of the time it represents" (263).

Fundamentally, this practice of logocentrism is based on the sovereignty of "reasoning man" (264). This was the Enlightenment in
which man suddenly appeared, according to Foucault. The classical
assumption that "God had arranged a chain of being and arranged
language in pre-established correspondence with it" was thrown out
(264). Man became the maker of language, of history, and of meaning. Through reason man could achieve the age-old dream of total
knowledge and power. However at this point, as mentioned earlier,
modern European man and modern Indian man, separate. For the
Indian (at least the ancient episteme, the Islamic, and the modern
have features of the old, but have modifications as well) Man and
Brahman both exist. Both make the world in an evolutionary dialectic. *That is perhaps why, for Sarkar, the State will always exist*, unlike the
European man where the reasoning man makes a compact with the
State, with man "the source of truth and meaning, the [State] as
the site and resources that modern discourse reserves for the exercise of force, violence wherever history refuses to bow to man's reasons" (268). Modern man can only imagine the end of State only
at the end of time, when man has achieved total knowledge and

freedom, when history is subordinated to man's will, either as the victory of communism, the perfect marketplace, the ideal speech act, or the meeting of all needs. Contrast this with Sarkar's perspective where total knowledge is total individual enlightenment. The State continues to exist for it controls, manages and disciplines the various exploitive tendencies of the group self. There is no end of time except for the self: there is no perfect state: time will never stop for the group, there will always be periods of pause and movement: his goal of total knowledge is to reduce these downswings in a type of macro social engineering of cosmic proportions.

Ashley's perspective is applicable here as well, for it is the sovereign voice that is a source of truth outside of criticism. Sarkar reveals history, shows the desperate plight of workers, females, the environment, shows how each class becomes oppressive and yet, as he does this, he develops a voice of the way out, the alternative where the future lies, where freedom lies, the society where it is possible for this suffering to end. As Ashley writes:

> Even as modern discourse criticizes an ideology, a repressive culture, an order of domination, a ritual of state legitimization, or a pathology of social life—regarding it in some sense as imprisoning, false, or ill—modern discourse must invoke a sovereign subjectivity of man that is taken to be the ultimate origin of freedom, truth, or health. So it is with Marxism's appeal to a dialectical materialist proletarian consciousness, radical liberal's appeals to Christian humanism values, and Habermas' appeals to the universal pragmatics of the ideal speech situation (266).

All this is done by theorists who while critical of other theories from the past, create new voices from reason, unsuspecting that they reinscribe this logocentrism on their theory.

From a poststructuralist position, it does not matter that this is done only by reasoning "man," it could be believing "man," or the more complex Indian "man," or the process-oriented ideal of Buddhism—it is the offering of a solution bound in logocentrism. Yet there are similarities. For instance, the view of Jiddhu Krishnamurti presented in the introductory chapter: man and his search for a solution, a system, a way, is in itself the problem. Thus, "by following a method . . . a means through which to know myself, I shape my thinking, my activities, according to a pattern; but the following of a pattern is not the understanding of oneself" (Krishnamurti, 1967,

25). It is this search for a position, a method, this sovereignty of the subjectivity of man that is part of the problem of man. For the post-structuralist, what Krishnamurti is not sensitive to is that the problem is not in the system or the way, but the actual construction of the self. More sensitive was the Buddha who refused to locate the self in the eternal or merely in the material. The self was changing and not-changing.

But for Krishnamurti, there still remains a way out to knowledge, to the natural: it is the watching of the self, an attentive watching of the mind, from a position of non-method (non-self), simple attentiveness. If is this pursued by all or many, there then is hope of a new freedom. For Krishnamurti, it is not the creation of a new structure, but like the poststructuralist, it is a watching of all structures. For Sarkar, however, this remains a type of meditation, useful, helpful, but those in the streets still are homeless, intellectuals still purposeless, and theories still groundless. History, then, while some contemplate on what is real, is actually created by the powerful and the dominant. While the self of history can be escaped theoretically, it still remains at the level of the practical.

For Ashley, Sarkar's works, although unread by him, would be seen as another version of modern man imposing a paradigm of sovereignty on history. Modern reasoning man imposes a totalizing vision on history from a viewpoint that is claimed to be outside of history. History then becomes less unwieldy. For the modern European this point of view of history is reason or science; a point of view of truth wherein all can be seen. For Sarkar, the point of view is the suffering of humans: he can see history because he, himself, is outside of it, although Indian and part of Indian culture; as one who is outside of all the faculties of knowledge (here Indian man steps outside of pure reason)—reason, sense, authority, and intuition—but emerges because of the call of suffering. He is outside of history because history has called him to be so.

While for Western reasoning man, since he

> is the origin of universal truth and meaning, he can and must aspire fully to deny his finitude, to transcend historical limitations, and to achieve total knowledge; but since man is enmeshed in history, his very knowledge reveals him in his finitude, in the sheer facticity of the historical reality that bears down upon him, determines him and limits him in what he can here and now do and know (Ashley, 1989, 265).

For Sarkar, this is a false problem. Man correctly identified is infinite, falsely identified is finite. The problem of the sovereignty of man does not appear. System building creates the possibility for revolution throughout and the possibility for purpose and reflection, action and consciousness. But there is a familiarity between Sarkar's system and that of the moderns. There is a real that cannot be questioned, that is, outside of history, and is the source of truth, the vantage point from which all can be seen. For the mystic eventually speaks, and when he does, his assertions are believed to be outside the prevailing modes of knowing. For modern Western man it is reason, for Sarkar, it is the spiritual view. For Ashley, then, if he was to look at Sarkar, he would likely argue that Sarkar has a ground to stand on, sees history from a vantage outside of history, and although Sarkar remains in an alternative Indian episteme that falls neither in the reasoning episteme of the Modern period or the religious episteme of the classical period, he still posits a truth that is outside contention. Ashley's view is to create a non-place that is not a reaction to a particular structure or paradox and thus does not reinscribe a polarity (mind/body, violence/nonviolence, structure/agency, cyclical/linear), that does not call it what it is fighting against, but a place that is ungrounded, constantly shifting, that is neither asserting nor denying a specific place to reason, and history. Krishnamurti, too, attempts this, and situates this non-place in the ever attentive mind, always watching and watching this very watching.

Poststructural theory (like cosmological analysis) thus takes the position of undecidability when it comes to central issues in all modern historical analysis, the paradox is that all practices and actions of humans are dependent on structure *and* that all structures are created by the actions of humans. We highlight modern here, for alternatives to modern epistemes can and do include the actions of non-humans in the forms of extra-terrestrials, but more importantly in the forms of Spirit, God, Redeemer or other forms of intervention which at one moment solve the paradox, but on reflection (why does god act, do humans call the spirit, or does it ascend/descend by itself, that is, the relationship of the transcendent and the temporal) cause a deepening paradox. In the modern world, behavioralists take the position that actions are primary and grand theory writers privilege structure. Attempts at creating theories of structuration (Giddens, 1982) also decide on a primary and secondary although they attempt to include both. The poststructuralist stays detached from both points, for deciding on either creates a sovereign man, a grounded subjectivity that can then speak from outside of history, that can speak from a ground outside of politics, of time.

Thus, what Krishnamurti calls for in the understanding of the self, Ashley calls for in the understanding and creation of theory. But what Ashley does not examine is that this non-place can also be conceived as a reaction to the place of history; to the historical attempt to ever create a perfect place. While outside of the enlightenment project, it does privilege the particular epistemology of reason, forgetting that reason too is a particular point, a particular historical development in epistemology. Its theoretical stance too must be intelligible to the dominant ways of knowing if it wants to be heard, thus, even while it attempts to particularize and deconstruct the fixations of science and history, it too falls within a particular mode of knowing, for one, the intellectual project of the West. The question of what comes after postmodern politics also can be asked—will Ashley's poststructuralism be yet another attempt to create a politics of everything which will eventually lead to a new structure even while it attempts to remain outside of agency and structure.

Alternatively, the Indian view attempts to avoid becoming caught in a reification. There is history, but it can be for convenience; there is truth, but it has many levels of interpretation; only Brahman ultimately sees the truth and that truth indeed is inexpressible and inexplicable—the world of man is relative and it is a world in which other entities, beings, energies, other planetary life forms as well as plants and animals exist. Thus the sovereignty of modern man is questioned, for Consciousness itself can intervene. But again this poses the problem previously mentioned as to how (the vehicle) will Brahman act—through the state, structures, great individuals, (or Marx's workers, the capitalists and the divine marketplace)? Moreover, as Sarkar hints through his Shiva/Krishna cycle, this intervention too can become a structure. Thus, while the classic Indian episteme and Sarkar himself do not go as far as the poststructuralists in ungrounding history, in showing history to be an attempt to speak from a sovereign, nonpolitical place, in granting a space to history that is not concrete, however, by calling, by developing a history that is *itihasha* (history as education), they come close to what Roland Barthes call for in his "The Death of the Author". For Barthes the unity of the text, the unity of discourse lies not in its origin but in its destination, in the reader (Ashley, 1989, 258). In this death, the history imposed by the author is not critical, rather it is the history read by the reader that is central and primary. But again whether one author or a million readers, the value of the theory still lies in communicability of man.

Although there are many similarities between the poststructuralist effort and the Sarkar's (we have developed some in the earlier chapters: distancing, non-reification of the self, view on language, end of man perspective), from the viewpoint of the poststructuralist, Sarkarian thought remains a grand design. As Ashley states:

> The task of poststructuralist social theory is not to impose a general interpretation, a paradigm of the sovereignty of man, as a guide to the transformation of life on a global scale. In contrast to modern social theory, poststructuralism eschews grand designs, transcendental grounds, or universal projects of humankind. The critical task, instead, is to expose the historicity—the arbitrariness, the political content, and the dependence upon practice—of the limits that are imposed in history and inscribed in paradigm of the sovereignty of man (284).

It is thus a project to uncover politics and not speak from a voice outside of a politics of interpretation, history is never finished and never totally understood.

For Sarkar, however, the poststructuralist view is what one might expect from vipras, especially intellectuals speaking at the end of the capitalist era when old structures are declining and the chaos (physical and theoretical) of the workers' era is arriving. What they do is theorize. Even their anti-theory is but a theory, even their theory of imposition is but an interpretation of interpretation, a product of mind that has glimpsed the deeper layers of the mind, since it has seen the malleability of all, that the real changes are perception, *but* it has not expanded totally and thus has not experienced empathy with the toil and suffering that is the world today. Krishnamurti finally merely becomes an escapist, neither in bliss nor in revolution, merely calling for an understanding of mind. For Sarkar, this is not new. Merely, vipra-talk. Moreover, while their theories are on the margin, their lives are not: in the context of, say Calcutta, where concrete space to lie at night is problematic, where one knows the world through neither reason, intuition, authority, nor even senses (they have become blunt) but through hope and fear, then only theory, that inspires individuals to break out of the horror that is life, can be of any significance. Poststructuralism, is perhaps useful, to show how Calcutta has become so, how it is interpreted. The final question for him, however, is not the Western Modern question, nor is it the Indian one, but the specific Sarkarian discourse that we have developed; namely, *how can the self be spiritually realized, and how can the world as it is be materially transformed.*

While this might get a disappointing response from the empiricists, from those critical of Sarkar's laws of social change, from the poststructuralists, and others for either being unscientific, vague, humanistic, or modern, for Sarkar these are all responses from the present. His theory, while outside history, remains for a future to be. Perhaps, the Wallersteinian view places Sarkar best:

> A major function myths play is to mobilize people by their (the myths) promise and their optimism. Crushed by the realities of routine, we all hesitate to engage ourselves in political struggle. We fear wasted energy. We fear repression. We fear cutting ourselves off from family and friends. One of the most basic mechanisms that sustains the status quo is always this pervasive fear of the oppressed to break with routine. A revolutionary movement is precisely a movement that calls for a break with routine, that demands sacrifice in the present for a better world in the future. And because the sacrifice is real and immediate, while the better world is in the distance and uncertain, it is always difficult to organize. Myths are an essential element in the organizing process, and in sustaining the troops during the long political battle (Quoted in Abidi, 1989, 9–10).

But the paradox remains. As Nandy writes "yesterday's dissent is often today's establishment and, unless resisted, becomes tomorrow's terror" (Nandy, 1987, 13). But without utopian grand knowledge claims, theorists would not be able to mobilize activism; their efforts would be mere intellectual talk. The visions of Sarkar, of the prophets, of the Enlightenment are significant because of their grandness. Without their unproblematic representations of the real, of the natural, of the belief that their movements are guided by destiny, they would not have been able to sustain the myths needed for individual and social transformation. Thus the paradox. To change history, texts must stand outside of history, unfortunately it is this very placement that leads to terror. And yet theorists continue to develop grand visions of history and the future based on natural laws. The sovereignty of man remains.

Restating the above, the question that remains to be asked then is why not call a theory what it is: a myth, a way of seeing instead of the new truth, the new real? But would it then have potency? Would Marxism have potency without the promise of a classless society? Would capitalism have potency without the promise of the ideal magical marketplace, where hard work is perfectly rewarded? Would humanism be successful without the creation of the sovereignty of man and a hierarchy of needs? Can sustained transformation be possible without myth, with solely a will to transform, with solely a politicization of all, and a mythification of nothing? Is truth possible without lies?

We suggest that with regards to Sarkar's social cycle and his other theoretical assertions, the empirical/applied perspective is important, indeed, crucial in searching for contradictions, anomalies, deviations from conventional truth and historical data, these conventions change, but that solely placing the social cycle within the empirical perspective may tell us more about the context of the present modern episteme than about a fatal flaw in Sarkar's cycle (or spiral). The theory might get a better response and more insightful critique at a time when grand theory is more acceptable in the social sciences, when a good theory is not defined by its operational, predictive/control axis.

More important is the theory's ability to make voices heard that previously could not speak, to remove the future from the confines of history, the cycle, and to create the possibility for the spiral—an acceptance of structure, but a willingness to transform the suffering associated with the downswing of the cycle, and to find previous pockets of darkness and illuminate them, to pierce through silences. As mentioned earlier, for Galtung, Sarkar's laws can be seen as soft laws. They reveal probable pasts and futures not necessarily in perfect correspondence with reality but close enough to help us better understand history and recognize the likely futures ahead. Sarkar's theory gives us warnings of future exploitation. While we may not believe his forecasts, we should heed his warnings (Galtung, 1996; 1997).

Our own perspective is that while the empirical is useful for it too aids in the move from theory to data and back, the comparative is more useful as it places the real in the context of other similar efforts, thus allowing an interdiscursive, civilizational dialog, it is the poststructural perspective that is the most rewarding. There can thus be levels of reality (Inayatullah, 1998). At a basic level is the empirical, does the theory fit reality. At a deeper level, we take a historical evolutionary view of reality, seeing it as changing. Critical questions at this level are: how does the theory reveal limitations of current knowledge frames? What new insights does it give? At an even deeper level is the issue of worldview. What civilizational perspective is the theory derived from? The question is not proving a theory true or false but situating it. Does the theory develop within the boundaries of the cosmology it springs from? Does it challenge its own cosmological roots? At an even deeper level is the mythic discourse. At this level, at issue are the new meanings the theory gives, the story it transforms.

We thus see Sarkar's theory is seen as an asset, wherein Sarkar's works can be seen as a project to develop a new meaning system outside of, yet inclusive of *varna*, outside of the Indian tradition, yet emerging from it with its primary emphasis on the removal of human suffering and military, intellectual, economic, and mob exploitation. For ultimately, the asset that Sarkar is manufacturing is a new language, a new interpretation of the real, a new politics, economics, and culture. A new discourse. Perhaps a new cosmology. It is in this context that we read Sarkar's laws of change.

CHAPTER SEVEN

CONCLUSION: A NEW DISCOURSE, A NEW FUTURE

The previous chapters have been a dialog with Sarkar's thought. We have contextualized Sarkar's philosophy by placing it in a variety of habitats: the Indian episteme; the Indian construction of history; Chinese, Islamic, and Occidental approaches to macrohistory as exemplified by writers such as Ssu-Ma Ch'ien, Ibn Khaldun, Hegel, Vico, Mosca, Pareto, Spengler, and Sorokin, to mention a few; and finally, the various sites of the classical, modern and postmodern interpretation of structure, practice and laws.

Specifically we have presented and represented Sarkar's various theories. His theory of social change; the theory of collective psychology; the theory of the six spokes of civilization; the theory of sentiments; the theory of the rise and fall of dharma and the central role of the redeemer; and his theory of future leadership. We have also presented his theory of consciousness, the cycle of creation and its balanced physical, mental, and spiritual emphasis. Nested in this is Sarkar's theory of microvita that intends to reconstruct previous mind/body dichotomies. Also salient was Sarkar's alternative political-economy and his various social movements, even though we did not examine these in depth.

Clearly, the most impressive feature of Sarkar's work is its comprehensiveness: theory and strategies. His is no doubt an effort to create not only a new discourse but to rethink Indian thought in the context of the contributions of other civilizations. At the same time, while there were clear differences between the various macro-thinkers, they are remarkably isomorphic, similar especially in terms of the problems they face: for example, the role of consciousness, cyclical vs. spiral, and external vs. internal mechanisms. William Irwin Thompson is instructive when he talks about the four-fold structure found in these types of writers.

> The model of four seems to be a persistent one; it recalls the rule of four in the Indian caste system [which Sarkar reinterprets], Plato, Vico, Blake, Marx, Yeats, Jung and McLuhan. So many people look out at reality and come up with a four-part structure that one cannot help but think that it expresses the nature of reality and/or the Kantian

a priori pure categories of understanding. But whether the structure
exists in reality or is simply a projection of the categories of the human
mind is, of course, the traditionally unanswerable question of science
(Thompson, 1971, 78).

In our chapter on laws we examined this tension as to the nature
of the real and found ourselves favoring the cosmological and poststructural approach, asking what are the implications of any interpretation of the real, instead of searching for proofs, proofs that in
our mind will always remain contentious. With respect to Sarkar,
the real costs were best recognized by Homer: your excellence is
your fatal flaw, your greatness hobbles you (Thompson, 1976, 80).
In Sarkar's drive for comprehensiveness, has he indeed closed the
future? Said in other words by James P. Carse in his *Finite and Infinite
Games*, "The Renaissance, like all genuine cultural phenomena, was
not an effort to promote one or another vision. It was an effort to
find visions that promised still more vision" (Hedlund, 1989, 23). No
doubt Sarkar would object and argue that the essence of his project
is cultural diversity, the recovery of frames of meaning hidden and
distorted by capitalist pseudo-culture. Moreover, for Sarkar the spiritual revolution is the beginning of vision, not the end, it will allow
a vision that is no longer weighted down by the hunger of the world.
The comprehensiveness of his theory is there because of the tragedy
of what is today, because of the global civilizational crises facing
humanity, and because of the critical juncture that we stand at: the
spiritual model is the *only* defense and the *only* future.

Briefly summarizing, we started this journey by restating the comprehensiveness of Sarkar's work, specifically his contributions to various fields. We also placed Sarkar's own life within the discourse of
myth, leaving open the problem of mythification. The necessity of
this study was that other studies had simply attempted to apply his
thought to a given area: we, however, have attempted to understand
it in epistemic and comparative terms. We have come not only to
uphold the text, but to deconstruct it. This book has been in Indian
tradition of commentary. However, our way of seeing the real benefited
greatly from the poststructural Foucauldian view. This view is not
concerned with the predictive truth of a theory, nor only with a
phenomenological engagement, but rather asking what are the implications of the construct, its price so to speak; and how does the theory function in a politics of meaning schemata. This Foucauldian
method attempts to distance by historicizing and by comparing and
by whenever possible denaturalizing.

To begin this struggle, we placed Sarkar in the Indian episteme. He speaks to it, compares his thought with it and is derivative of it. However, at the same time he radically modifies it so as to reduce direct and structural violence *and* create the possibility for an economy strong on distribution and growth dimensions. Sarkar seeks to, like other philosophers, to reconcile the idealism-materialism, mind-body debate, settling for a layers of consciousness theory, wherein everything is real, while recognizing that truth has many dimensions to it, thus allowing for an open approach to the problem of philosophical diversity. Truth is real in different ways—the ultimate truth, however, is outside of discourse, unfathomable and inexpressible.

We furthered this discussion by placing Sarkar's theory of change within the context of Indian theories of history. His work is isomorphic—we should not be surprised that he has placed the division of economic, military, ideological, and worker power at the center of this theory—with Indian constructions of history. However, he has transcended the various nationalistic, idealistic, spiritual and Marxist theories and provided a new synthetic overlay. At the same time, he stays within the classic model of the rise and fall of truth, of dharma. But Sarkar also provides an alternative vision of the future that is cyclical, yet has a progressive intended dimension to it, largely similar to the avatar and the Marxist tradition, but extending far beyond them. Sarkar's theory manages to meld the rational with the mythic, the linear with the cyclical, the spiritual with the material, power with transcendence. It is both Indian and not Indian, and thus perhaps at a profound level, utterly consistent with the classic Indian episteme.

Sarkar's work also follows closely the range of other macro-thinkers: with Ssu-Ma Ch'ien and the rise and fall of virtue; with the spiritual perspective of Khaldun and the rise and fall of asabiya; with the humanistic science of Vico; with the macro-spiritual work of Voegelin; with the discontinuous theories of Foucault; with the elite theories of Mosca and Pareto; with the efforts of Spengler, Toynbee, Marx and Sorokin; with alternative notions of power by Gramsci. At the same time, aspects of his work can be found in distance places such as Comte. His prose though follows a Marxist revolutionary style. The theories of these other historians, while differing on some important issues, in fact, fit into Sarkar's history, making possible an effort to synthesize a new model of history that includes many of the variables of all these macro-thinkers. This study, however, has left that task for another day.

Finally, while Sarkar claims his theories are natural laws, we believe that by virtue of his epistemic boundaries, he intends this differently than those in the Western notion of law and science. Sarkar does not follow the split in the West between the sciences and humanities, of causal explanation and empathetic understanding. Rather, he remains within the unified discourse of Indian philosophy, wherein science means causality, universality and systematicity. Science is political (engaged in the construction of the real) in that it means that which expands the mind toward the infinite and which provides ways to economically and efficaciously reduce human suffering. The Buddha, among others, is a prime example of a scientist, merging intuition, with observational sense-experience, with deductive rationality. Sarkar, however, emphasizes an alternative way of knowing, that of bhakti, or devotional love. For Sarkar good science is good philosophy; a good philosophy creates a good person, that results in a good society, and conversely a good society leads to a good person which leads to a good philosophy and thereby good science.

Our preference has been to look at Sarkar's work as a new discourse, a new way of seeing the world from which we—in the next century—will find our subjectivity and objectivity framed by it. Sarkar's goal is to use theory to give a new asset to individuals who have had their spirituality as well as material conditions removed from themselves. He intends through theory and praxis to construct a new self that will radically alter the universe of the future.

To us, his theory, his life, the myths he has created are revolutionary and are both a promise to the future and, exactly because of their brilliance, comprehensiveness and all embracing nature, a danger to the closing of other ideologies and possibilities. Our task has simply been to grapple with the contours of his work, making sense of them and ourselves in the context of the various epistemes and theoretical structures that create the conditions in which we can, indeed, know. Our task has been that of understanding: through commentary, comparisons and critical analyses.

This task has been faced with a tension—the tension between upholding the truth of the text and searching for evidence, however constructed, to place it above others, and the critique of the text, the effort to deconstruct, expose, and lay bare the weaknesses of Sarkar's text. This tension, given our view on the openness of texts and the problematic nature of truth within discourse, is not resolved.

On one level we can boldly state that Sarkar's theory is more creative, inclusive, and holistic than other attempts by macro-thinkers throughout history. Within the Indian context, along with Gandhi, he stands out as the premiere thinker of this last century, if not the past few hundred years. In the global context he synthesizes philosophy, political-economy, and praxis with a level that goes beyond Marx. His work is elegant and manages to transcend the narrow Western conception of the real. He, for example, is not caught in the Western problem of understanding and explanation, structure and agency, although our prose has attempted to catch him there, perhaps mistakenly, but such is the problem of writing within a Western discourse. Sarkar's theory also manages to transcend the science-religion problems in terms of evolutionary theory. Moreover, while assertive in terms of its own outlook, by placing it in the Indian episteme it takes a gracious view on the problem of philosophical diversity. There are different levels of truth, and understanding—living in these must be a holistic venture that uses intuition, devotion, logic-reason, sense-perception, and authority. Moreover, his theory, while having a strong hierarchical dimension as might be expected within a spiritual discourse, still remains faithful to the weak. Sarkar, whatever his critique of democracy, remains a committed humanist, nay, neo-humanist, concerned with plants, animals *and* humans.

At the same time, the weaknesses of Sarkar are obvious and as mentioned earlier, derivative of his strengths. While some of these weaknesses can be theoretically and practically worked out, others are endemic to the cosmology he has created. As mentioned earlier, they include: the closure of visions; the centralization of power; the reification of caste; a view of the future that seeks to go beyond traditional limits of what is natural (humans to become gods); and, finally they include a more relaxed posture (as compared to Gandhism) toward the use of violence. Of course from the Liberal position Sarkar's work is simplistic and utter nonsense: it is religious, lacking in supporting evidence, dangerous to individual rights especially property rights, and anti-democratic. Sarkar's work from this view is merely a power move by a cult leader attempting to recover a world that democracy, capitalism and science have rightfully destroyed. From the Marxist view, Sarkar's work is flawed because it is spiritual and thus will eventually serve to further the capitalist hold on the masses. Even though Sarkar intends to balance the spiritual and material, by having an a priori spiritual base, his theory will ignore the material, the real conditions of human life. From the Islamic view, Sarkar's worldview amounts to nothing new. Islam too emerges from a discourse that is unified, spiritually and materially; it too has an alternative political-economy, it too has spiritual practices, believes in global fraternity, and it too sees communism and capitalism as the enemy. Islam, however, does not make the mistake of objectifying God in humans; humans are to worship God, not become God. In general, Sarkar's theory left in Bengal is fine, but made global and popular is dangerous. In any case, democracy or Marxism, or Islam or . . . will win out and Sarkar's work will be destined to the rubbish bin of History.

We, of course, while sensitive to the above criticisms do not take that view of Sarkar. For us, the true test of Sarkar's theory will not come from efforts such as ours, rather it will result as Sarkar would want from the harsh realities of everyday life, from the ability of Sarkar's PROUT to genuinely transform the material, mental, and spiritual conditions of the world which is ours—from an engagement with the constituted world.

Closing out a text is often accomplished by pointing to the future or by coming to a definitive understanding about a text. Our pointing to the future reaffirms our openness to the possible interpretations of the text of Sarkar. We left much undone. What is the framework from which he speaks about economics? What is his implicit model? Is it neo-classical, or some version of pre-classical, or a postmodern view of future economics? Does he position himself with the efforts to create a Buddhist spiritual economics or is his theory of ownership, resources, wants, and the individual and collective different? We have yet to place his thought in the field of leadership studies. How does the notion of sadvipra relate to the recent attempt to develop a science of leadership? We have also been clearly theory driven. There was little attempt to negotiate the world of applied theory, to handle the world of data, past, present or future. But far more seriously, we have not examined the linkages between the theory and the political movement—PROUT and his socio-spiritual movement, Ananda Marga. We have not attempted a dialog between texts of Sarkar's utterances and the text of those who are shaping the empirical world of tomorrow. We have not placed the movement in the context of other contending movements: the labor movement, the green movement, the Islamic movement, the indigenous people's movements, to mention a few.

On a more critical self-note, we have not managed to ascertain what indeed Sarkar means by his various assertions. Most importantly, his theory of sadvipra society stewarded by sadvipras—those of complete mind—has been undeveloped in the context of leadership theory. Are they like Issac Asimov's second foundation, hidden psychics watching the development of society and secretly maneuvering it? Or is Sarkar really speaking about a permanent revolution? If so, can one theoretical structure create such a permanent revolution? If Sarkar's cycles are indeed large super-cultural systems, and if a particular phase lasts hundreds of years, is it conceivable that this notion of leadership would still be available to conduct such a revolution? Can we design future leadership when that future is a not possible until many hundreds of years from now? The questions of a planned leadership based on a theory of social change are at best problematic. Concrete questions to Sarkar's assertions are numerous, leaving us once again to comment that his theory in this regard is best seen as an asset—as a revolutionary mythology that intends to provide a focus, a point of unity, so that individuals will sacrifice their immediate gratification of desires for a destined tomorrow. But while we have left much undone, we have neither proved nor disproved any hypothesis, our main goal has been accomplished: that of better understanding Sarkar through comparison and criticism. Our goal has been to ask questions, not to definitively nor authoritatively create the world.

Thus our understanding of Sarkar remains open even though we posit that his theoretical moves and his social movements will most likely be among the most significant in the coming century if not centuries. But understanding the "text" of Sarkar is not a finished affair. Even though he passed away in 1990, the text of the writer can still remain open (assuming we wish to privilege agency here). Others can comment, the text can always be interpreted anew, especially in the light of changing epistemes and human suffering and transcendence.

Beyond Discourse

While we have predicated this book on discourse, some words that challenge the framework we have used to understand Sarkar are necessary. For Sarkar, discursive analysis privileges the intellect, and reduces the spiritual, the transcendental to the relative, to a mere discourse. Sarkar, himself, argues for a spiritual knowledge interest, one that de-legitimizes rationalistic qua modernity modes of knowing as well as intellectual qua mind ways of knowing. Sarkar would thus agree that the discursive approach is a critically important perspective and that language does create the world. This is why he and other mystics such as those of the Zen Buddhist tradition emphasize ways of knowing other than the intellect. For Sarkar, therefore, the poststructuralist effort is an activity contained within the arena of mind, the task then becomes to transcend mind through activities such as meditation, or through koans. Here the practitioner is forced out of mind, the self then no longer is constituted in ego, but in itself, in unmediated, inexpressible consciousness. The subject-object duality does not exist, rather there is a state of the unity of consciousness. In his words:

> That which comes within the orbit of mind is but a relative truth, not an eternal truth and so it will come and go. Scriptures (texts) and mythologies are but stacks of bricks, they are only arranged in layers, carrying no significance or intrinsic value. So how can they describe the Transcendental Entity that is beyond the scope of the mental faculty. How then can this intuitive perspective be interpreted, which is beyond the compass of body, words and mind? Here both the teacher and disciple are helpless, because the subject—that is beyond the domain of any academic discourse and discussion—is simply inexplicable and inexpressible. Whatever said and discussed comes within the ambit of the mind and so it is a relative truth—true today and false tomorrow. That is why, the teacher becomes mute when he is asked to explain transcendental knowledge (the Buddha remained silent when asked if the Transcendental entity existed and equally silent when asked if it did not exist) and consequently the disciple, too, becomes deaf. So . . . in order to explain this profound mystery, there is no other alternative than to emulate the symbolic exchange of views between a deaf and a dumb person (Sarkar, 1976: 114–115).

The transcendental, then, is the realm of the prediscursive, a space that cannot be talked of, or listened too, for such an effort would evoke the discourses of the present, past, and future, that is, the discourses that transpire because of mind.

For Sarkar, ultimately one can say nothing about the ultimate nature of being, except that any effort to say anything would be embedded in mind, in language and structure (time, place and subject), in relativity. The problem of the relationship between the absolute and the relative then becomes the key and it is not resolvable, by mind, issue. For once we define this nature (of Being), then, we, for the poststructuralist, simply create new categories, hierarchies, that is, models of existence, or what is commonly called philosophy. This is unavoidable since after the silence and the muteness, we (the teacher and student) still must return to discourse and recreate the world once again. We enter a discursive space, a space embedded in meaning, in language, in historical identity.

The task for Sarkar then becomes of privileging a spiritual discourse as for him one's theoretical formulations become better in that they are created from a non-discursive space that is intuitive, intellect is placed within a larger epistemological framework. For Sarkar the nature of Being itself cannot be answered, since "the tongue cannot taste itself." However, through action commitments, spiritual practices, more of the real can be accessible to the spiritual aspirant. The result is ananda for the individual and the beginning of the creation of a neo-humanistic planetary civilization.

As we close the discourse we have created, it is important to remember that for Sarkar, consciousness "cannot be expressed in language" (personal communication, 1989) and his own life, as he has indicated, will remain mysterious. This said, we provide this closing quote: "A bright future awaits you—your future is glorious, your future is luminous, your future is effulgent . . . the future of humanity is strikingly resplendent" (Sarkar, 1981: 52, 214).

APPENDICES

Appendix Chapter 2   Locating Sarkar in the Indian Episteme

A. Classic Indian Episteme	B. Indian Intellectual Style	C. Hindu Cosmology and Sarkar					D. Sarkar and Indian Schools of Thought

A. Classic Indian Episteme

1. Reality has many Levels (Deep and Shallow).

2. Truth as *Satya* (welfare) and *Ananda* (Bliss) not *Rta* (the facts).

3. Atman-Brahman identical (within-without and as above as below).

4. Additive, all inclusive.

5. Centrality of *Karma* and *Dharma*.

6. Time and history cyclical.

7. Social reality is hierarchical (guru and eventually caste).

• Islamic impact on classic episteme was to include horizontal dimension (fraternity) and to include the notion of dramatic time.

• British impact was to quantify time, thus aiding in the breakdown of the cycle and leading to cultural and economic peripheralization.

B. Indian Intellectual Style

1. Intersubjectivity among Schools of Thought.

2. Overall Project that of Creating, Understanding, and Distributing Self.

3. Idealistic.

4. Brahmanical with Priest as Center.

5. Intuition, Reason, Senses, Authority and Devotion (*Bhakti*) All Equivalent Forms of Knowing.

6. Commentary on Past is Central. Little Criticism of the Entire Project (except *Carvaka*).

7. Philosophically inclusionary but politically exclusionary

• Intellectual discourse remains within the bureaucratic discourse in Modernity. Brahmin structure is still the key, but moved from Delhi to Oxford. Lineage is still central.

C. Hindu Cosmology and Sarkar

	Violence		Economic	
	Direct	Structural	Distribution	Growth
Hindu	Low *Ahimsa*	High Caste	Low	Low *Karma*
Sarkar	Medium Radical	Low Cooperative Socialism	High Basic needs	Medium Limits to accumulation

1. Sarkar allows for revolutionary activity but focuses on compassionate social service.

2. Growth is medium as there are physical limits to wealth accumulation, but technology is placed within cooperative socialist framework. Polity is centralized, economy is democratized. Global and local.

D. Sarkar and Indian Schools of Thought

Accepts – *Moksa* as goal of life, truth as *ananda*, time as cyclical, *varna* or basic mental structure, divine intervention, philosophy is ultimately therapy, symmetrical relationship between natural, social, and cosmic worlds, and multiple view of reality and ways of knowing.

Rejects:

• Monism (*Vedanta*) as its denies material world and leads to escapism and privileges Brahmins;

• dualism of *Sankhya* and *Nyaya* since reality is unified;

• *Carvaka* as it is materialistic and atheistic;

• *Yoga* since it denies inner devotion (love as a way of knowing the real);

• Jain non-violence since it leads to hypocrisy (intent is the key and struggle is the essence of life for Sarkar) traditions that locate spiritual in the technical or sacrificial discourse; and

• aspects of Buddhism (the privileging of sorrow, and schools of nothingness). The self exists although language reifies it. The Real, ultimately, cannot be expressed in language.

Appendix Chapter 3 Sarkar and the Indian Construction of History

Construction	Structure	Agency	Stages
Gita-Theistic	Cycle—rise and fall of Dharma Degeneration and regeneration of History	In times of crises, humans are instruments. Otherwise, they have limited will; Agency in Cosmos	Truth/False/Divine intervention/Truth/False
Prakash	Cycle Degeneration and regeneration of History	Humans and Consciousness as exhibited in political/social events (Spiritual/IR model)	Inertia/Awakening/Activity (Kali/Dwapara/Treta/Krta)
Aurobindo	Cycle	God in nation and great men and other Associations	Rise and fall of nation Neo-Hegelian
National	Linear Modernity and Progress	Nation-state	Backward to integrated modern
Marxist	Cycle-Economic stages	Class; History as ideological	Asiatic/Feudal/British/Peripheral/Socialist
Sub-altern	Language and Power	Workers/oppressed. History is a political asset	Deconstruction/Reconstruction
Traditional	Linear	Dynastic	Hindu/Muslim/British/Nation
Philosophical	Cumulative/Additive	Ideas/Philosophers	Vedas/Upanishads/Buddhism/Islam/Secularism/?
Sarkar	Cycle and Spiral	Collective mind *and* Humans except in crises, then Cosmic Taraka Brahma model; History as educational tool and as a political asset for the silenced	Shudra/Ksattriya/Vipra/Vaeshya/ Shudra—Sadvipra Society—Shudra/Ksattriya

Appendix Chapter 4   Characteristics of Sarkar's Historical Stages

Stage	Time	Polity	Gender	Power	Emotion	Expansion	Example	Religion
Shudra	Present	Anarchy/Pure Democracy	Cooperation to Matriarchy	Mass Labor/Decentralized	Fear	Population	Pre-historic	Animistic to Polytheism
Ksattrya	Past/Present	Monarchy/Dictatorship Highly centralized	Matriarchy to Patriarchy	Military Protective/Coercive	Lust	Territorial	Roman Empire Caliphate	Polytheism to Monotheism
Vipra	Past/Present/ Transcendental	Republic/ Theocracy	Strong Patriarchy	Normative/Spiritual/ Dogmatic	Cunning/ hypocrisy	Mind/Idea	Holy Roman Empire	Monotheism
Vaeshya	Future/Time Colonized	Democracy Decentralised	Vicious Patriarchy	Economic Inventive/monopolize	Greed	Resource	World capitalist system	Monotheism to material idolism

1. Cycle is evolutionary based on interaction with environment; *shudra* is dominated by environment; *ksattrya* physically dominates environment; *vipra* mentally dominates environment and *vaeshya* transforms environment into an economic resource.
2. Each stage emerges dialectically from the previous.
3. Characteristics of the previous stages continue in the next.
4. Each stage has cycles of exploitation and benevolence.
5. Exploitation has a whole is maximized in the final *Vaeshya* stage.
6. Shudra revolution or evolution then leads to next *Ksattriyan* era.
7. There are however reversals, counter-revolutions and counter-evolutions.
8. Cycle is endless since it is historical, evolutional and structural, but exploitation can be minimized through permanent intervention and revolution.
9. Stages should be seen as soft laws or through Vico's river metaphor, as story-telling, not as discrete blocks of time and space.

Appendix Chapter 5   Sarkar and Macrohistory

Writer	Structure	Key	Unit	Problem	Comments
Voeglin	Cycle	Rise and Fall of Truth	Being	Immanentization of the spiritual in the world and in history	End of history view (Comte, Marx, Smith, Hitler) misinterprets spiritual metaphor
Foucault	Disjunction	Construction of the Real	Episteme	How has truth been constructed?	Truth is historical and political, not transcendental
Polak	Cyclical	Image of the Future	Civilization	Rising societies have compelling vision of the future	Balance between the transcendental and humanistic utopian
Ssu-Ma Ch'ien	Cyclical	Rise and fall of Virtue	Civilization	Virtue can be restored through the application of Wisdom to government	Universe has a moral structure which sage can know. Dynasty begins with sage-king; ends with tyrant
Chang	Cyclical	Rise and fall of Tao	Tao	Learning and government must be unified or tao disintegrates	The Tao is the natural, the harmonious; it is noticed by watching the ordinary man not by devotion
Khaldun	Cycle	*Asabiya*, unity	Dynasty/ Civilization	Why do empires disintegrate? Is there a pattern to history?	With unity, families and dynasties rise; at the top, they lose unity and then decline
Vico	River	Degeneration of History from Ages of God, Hero, Men, to Barbarism	Nation	The human sciences are different from the natural sciences	Articulated soft laws; the centrality of interpretation in understanding history. Spiritual can change history
Comte	Linear	Progress—Theological to Metaphysical to Positive	Society	To develop a Science of society	End of the cycle and history. Progress and Modernity now possible
Hegel	Linear	Progress and spirit in the world; Germanic State the final stage of history	State/Spirit	How does Spirit manifest itself?	In the state true freedom is expressed; Unity and Difference

Marx	Spiral/Linear	Dialectics/means and relations of production	Societies	How to end oppression of workers and create a communist society	Theory delivered assets to a new group of people, yet Orientalist
Gramsci	Spiral	Cultural forces/hegemony	Societies	Central role of intellectuals in realizing new society	Expanded Marx to include non-material factors: the organic intellectual
Pareto	Oscillation	Circulation of Elites	Societies/Residues	How elites and power move in society? What is the best gov't?	Residues include innovators and consolidators
Mosca	Expansion/Contraction	Balance of social forces	Society/Power	Why are warriors not in control? What is ideal political system?	Uses social forces—money, priests, labor, soldiers—instead of legislative, executive, and judicial
Spengler	Cycle	Biological organism	Culture	Characteristics and life-cycle of each culture; from high culture to decline—how and why?	Cultures have personalities and follow the life-cycle; history is poetic expression, truth is deep and shallow not right or wrong
Galtung	Pendulum	Expansion/Contraction	Cosmology	Search for isomorphisms and deep structures within and between cosmologies. How to create peace?	Economic, ideological, military power imposed on people. Four classes with a fifth class outside of structure.
Toynbee	Cycle	Challenge-Response	Civilizations	Why do some civilizations rise and others fall? Is there a pattern?	Breakdown of universal state leads to universal church; spiritual vision of the future
Sorokin	Pendulum	Ideational/Idealistic/Sensate systems	Integrated Meaning	What is the real?	Sociological approach to grand theory and to explaining change
Sarkar	Cycle/Spiral	Shudra/Ksattriya/Vipra/Vaeshya/Shudra revolution/*Sadvipra*-led society	*Varna*	Develop a theory of history to increase collective welfare	Cycle has many levels—exploitation phases can be reduced but cycle will continue

Appendix Chapter 6   Situating Sarkar's Laws

Positivist-Empirical	Interpretive-Phenomenological	Poststructural
Social laws are true if they fit reality. Laws must be operationalized and tested in history.	Laws must be understood in the social and cultural context they are uttered. Laws must be understood by the criteria of the theory itself (phenomenological view).	Theories must be understood in empirical MISSING a political context, in a politics of the real.
Problematic nature of knowing is left unexamined; history is seen as factual, not interpretive and the empirical is not placed in a larger political philosophical context. But grounds of knowledge are clear and a hierarchy of knowledge and progress (and control) are possible.	Truth however is culturally revitalized and inquiry (political) is not possible—total epistemological pluralism.	A theory becomes dominant because of politics (and technology or class or the capturing of state power). Theories are then political assets which privilege particular interests. The question then is which interests does a particular theory support? And how? Grounds for comparison are however themselves impositions.
Sarkar's laws have no empirical validity. Laws followed due to authority of Sarkar. They neither predict nor explain.	Laws are natural and necessary given the nature of the Indian episteme—unity of physical, social and cosmic.	Like Marxism, laws are 'true' if they change the world; if they lead to fruitful enquiry; rethink old power relationships; deliver political assets to new interests.
Theory as politics reduces knowledge to mere politics.	Sarkar's laws internally consistent with good theory—they are based on induction, can transform the world and lead to *satya* and *ananda*.	Sarkar's theories are necessary myths which aid in the revolutionary struggle, in creating the possibility for a new tomorrow.
Sarkar's theory reinscribes caste and hierarchy.	Sarkar's theory enriches social theory by adding new variables, new insights (cycle, four structures, leadership).	Sarkar's theory is significant as it is a new discourse, a new way of knowing the real.
Sarkar's theory, in that it stands outside history can lead to terror—myths can become lies.	Sarkar's theory should be seen as outside of mere intellectual discourse, empirical or post-structural (sovereignty of man issue).	
Theory needs refinement or needs to be less ambitious in its claims, less dogmatic.		

GLOSSARY

Ananda:	Bliss, state of no-qualities. In its absolute sense, non-discursive.
Asabiya:	Unity, the fiber that binds (central to Khaldun).
Atman:	Essential self. Identical with the Supreme self.
Avatar:	God descends into the body of Man to bring about righteousness, dharma.
Avida:	Basic force that pulls mind outwards toward the material world; from Consciousness toward matter.
Bhakti:	Devotion or the constant state of love. A way of knowing or constructing the world.
Bodhisattva:	Person who stays in the world for the spiritual enlightenment of others. Primarily a Buddhist concept.
Brahma:	Consciousness or God.
Brahmachakra:	Cycle of Creation.
Brahman:	Consciousness or God. In Vedanta as the only Reality.
Carvaka:	School of Indian thought. Emphasizes that the material world is the end all of reality.
Chakras:	Psychic centers which control emotions. At the level of the body they are related to glandular system.
Citta:	Mental plate wherein the real is reflected in mind.
Dharma:	The way, inner nature or essential characteristic.
Dukha:	Sorrow, suffering.
Dvapara Yuga:	The copper age in the classic Indian model of time (shaking off sleep for Buddha Prakash).
Guru:	Spiritual perceptor. One who dispels darkness and ignorance leading disciples to bliss.
Gurukul:	Abode of the Guru.
Itihasa:	History that has educational value.
Itikatha:	History as a factual record of events.
Jhat:	Caste, hereditary division of social value.
Kali Yuga:	Iron age or the age of materialism (age of sleep for Buddha Prakash).
Karma:	Collection of samskaras. Also fulfilled actions. Also law of action and reaction. Also as action, a way of knowing the world.
Kosa:	Layers of the mind. There are five.
Krta Yuga:	Golden age (age of activity for Buddha Prakash).
Ksattriya:	One who dominates the environment through physical prowess. Warrior.
Ksattriya Era:	Centralized political era that follows Shudra era.
Lokas:	Layers of the body of Cosmic mind. Symmetrical with layers of the individual mind.

Mantra:	Sounds which ontologically represent the real. Used in meditation to liberate the ego and realize Consciousness.
Maya:	Force that creates the illusion of the material (according to Vedanta).
Mimamsa:	School of Indian thought. Focuses on rituals.
Moksa:	The final liberation when individual self realizes the Supreme self.
Nirguna Brahma:	Consciousness without attributes. Unexpressible.
Niyamas:	Moral precepts.
Nyaya:	School of Indian thought. Dualistic theism.
Paramatman:	Supreme soul.
Prakrti:	Nature or the creative force. A basic aspect of Consciousness along with the cognitive dimension.
Prama:	Balance. Dynamic balance at multiple levels. Between Nations (poor and rich); in theories and between self and Society.
Puranas:	Mythological stories.
Rajasik:	Active force, one force among three that create the universe.
Rta:	Truth as the facts (specifically in Sarkar's epistemology).
Sadhana:	Effort to realize goal, usually a spiritual goal.
Sadvipra:	One with complete and pure mind. For Sarkar, the needed spiritual leadership to transform the cycles of history into a progressive direction.
Saguna Brahma:	Consciousness with attributes, God.
Samadhi:	Blissful state when individual mind is absorbed in the cosmic mind or cosmic consciousness.
Sankhya:	School of Indian thought.
Samskaras:	Potential reaction of desires. Karma in its unactualized form.
Satguru:	Perfect guru; world teacher at the social level, ideal teacher at the individual level.
Sattva:	Pure, creative or sentient force. One force among three.
Satya:	Truth as human welfare.
Shudra:	One who is dominated by the environment. Worker. Also type of power, peoples' power.
Shudra Era:	Initial era of human development. Also era of chaos and of revolution.
Sutras:	Aphorisms. Just repeating them has spiritual benefits according to the classical Indian episteme.
Tamasik:	Crude force, one force among three.
Taraka Brahma:	The door between the Nirguna and Saguna Brahma. Used as a metaphor by Sarkar to arouse devotion.
Treta Yuga:	Silver era (rising for Prakash).
Varna:	Mental color, collective psychology, way of perceiving the world. Ideal type, paradigm or structure.

Vidya:	Basic force that pulls mind inwards toward the spiritual world, from matter to Consciousness.
Viksubdha Shudra:	Disgruntled intellectuals and warrior types who cannot pursue their nature because of capitalist exploitation. They bring on the shudra revolution.
Vijinana:	Intellectual way of knowing the world.
Vaeshya:	One who dominates the environment by transforming it into a commodity, a resource.
Vaeshya Era:	Capitalist era.
Vaisheskika:	School of Indian thought. Dualistic and atomistic.
Vedanta:	Dominant school of Indian thought. Associated with Shankaracharya. Its central idea: only Consciousness is real, the world is an illusion.
Vipra:	One who dominates environment through the intellect.
Vipra Era:	Era where political power is often in the hands of the priests. Religious era.
Yamas:	Moral precepts.
Yoga:	School of Indian thought. Enlightenment through spiritual practices.
Yugas:	Era, cosmic time.

BIBLIOGRAPHY

Abidi, Syed. "Social Change and the Politics of Religion in Pakistan." Honolulu, Doctoral Dissertation, University of Hawaii, Department of Political Science, 1988.

Amin, Shahid. "Gandhi as Mahatama." Ranajit Guha and Gayatri Chakravorty Spivak, eds. *Selected Subaltern Studies*. New York, Oxford University Press, 1988.

Ananda Marga, *Ananda Vaniis*. Bangkok, Ananda Marga Publications, 1982.

———, "Baba, the Child." *Crimson Dawn* (Vol. 5, No. 5, 1976).

Anandamurti, Shrii Shrii. *Ananda Sutrum*. Calcutta, Ananda Marga Publications, 1967.

———. *Ananda Vacanamrtam. Vol. 7*. trans. Vijayananda Avadhuta. Calcutta, Ananda Marga Publications, 1987.

———. *Baba's Grace*. Denver, Ananda Marga Publications, 1986.

———. *Namah Shivaya Shantaya*. Calcutta, Ananda Marga Publications, 1982.

———. *Namami Krsnasundaram*. trans. Vijayananda Avadhuta. Calcutta, Ananda Marga Publications, 1981.

———. *The Great Universe*. Denver, Ananda Marga Publications, 1973.

Anderson, Benedict. *Imagined Communities*. London, Verso, 1983.

Anderson, Tim. *Free Alister, Dunn and Anderson*. Sidney, Wild and Wolley, 1985.

———. *Free Alister, Dunn and Anderson*. Sidney, Wild and Wolley, 1985.

———. *The Liberation of Class: P.R. Sarkar's Theory of History and Class*. Calcutta, Proutist Universal Publications, 1985.

Ashby, Philip. *Modern Trends in Hinduism*. New York, Columbia University Press, 1974.

Ashley, Richard. "Living on Border Lines: Man, Poststructuralism, and War." James Der Derian and Michael Shapiro, eds. *International/Intertextual Relations*. Massachusetts, Lexington Books, 1989.

Aurobindo, Sri. "The Spirituality and Symmetric Character of Indian Culture." K. Satchidananda Murti, ed. *Readings in Indian History, Philospophy and Politics*. London. George Allen and Unwin, 1967.

———. "The Triune Reality." K. Satchidananda Murti, ed. *Readings in Indian History, Philosophy and Politics*. London. George Allen and Unwin, 1967.

Avadhuta, Kalyneshvarananda. "Anandamurti, known and unknown." *Bodhikalpa* (1986).

Avadhuta, Krtashivananda. *Social Progress: Prout and Dialectics*. Manila, Ananda Marga Publications, 1988.

Avadhuta, Rudreshananda. *Microvita: Cosmic Seeds of Life*. Berlin, Ananda Marga Publications, 1989.

Avadhuta, Sugatananda. "Sambhavani." *Prajina Bharatii* (Vol. 8, No. 1, 1985).

Avadhuta, Tadbhavananda and Kumar, Jayanta. *The New Wave*. Calcutta, Proutist Universal Publications, 1985.

Avadhutika, Anandamitra. *Beyond the Superconscious Mind*. Manila, Ananda Marga Publications, 1986.

———. *Tales of Torture*. Hong Kong, Ananda Marga Publications, 1981.

———. *The Spiritual Philosophy of Shrii Shrii Anandamurti*. Denver, Ananda Marga Publications, 1981.

Batra, Ravi. *Muslim Civilization and the Crisis in Iran*. Dallas, Venus Books, 1980.

———. *The Downfall of Capitalism and Communism*. London. Macmillan Press, 1978. Second Edition: Dallas, Venus Books, 1990.

————. *The Great Depression*. New York, Bantam Books, 1988.

Beckwith, Burnham. *Ideas About the Future*. Palo Alto, Burnham Beckwith, 1982.

Bender, Frederic, ed. *Karl Marx: The Essential Writings*. New York, Harper Torchbooks, 1972.

Bhattacharya, Sabyasachi and Thapar, Romila, eds. *Situating Indian History*. Delhi, Oxford University Press, 1986.

Boggs, Carl. *The Two Revolutions: Antonio Gramsci and the Dilemmas of Western Marxism*. Boston, South End Press, 1984.

Boulding, Elise. "Futuristics and the Imaging Capacity of the West." Magoroh Maruyama and James Dator, eds. *Human Futuristics*. Honolulu, Social Science Research Unit, University of Hawaii, 1971.

Bowes, Pratima. "What is Indian About Indian Philosophy?" S.S. Rama Rao Pappu and R. Puligandla, eds. *Indian Philosophy: Past and Future*. Delhi, Motilal Banarsidass, 1982.

Braudel, Fernand. *The Mediterranean and the Mediterranean World in the Age of Philip 11*, Vol. 1. London, Harper and Row, 1972.

Braudy, Leo. *The Frenzy of Renown: Fame and its History*. Oxford, Oxford University Press, 1986.

Brown, Irene. "Ibn Khaldun and African Reintegration." 1971 Universities Social Science Council Conference, Makerere, December 14–17.

Brown, Robert. *The Nature of Social Laws*. Oxford, Cambridge University Press, 1984.

Burns, James MacGregor. *Leadership*. New York, Harper and Row, 1978.

Campbell, Joseph. *The Hero With A Thousand Faces*. New Jersey, Princeton University Press, 1968.

————. *The Masks of God, Vol. IV*. New York, Penguin Books, 1968.

Captra, Fritjof. *The Turning Point* New York, Simon and Schuster, 1982.

Carspecken, Phil. "Sarkar's Social Cycle: Playing Devil's Advocate." Unpublished manuscript. Prout Institute, 1990.

————. "Social Action and Social Structure." *Cosmic Society* (Vol. 10, No. 2–3, 1987).

Chaix-Ruy, Jules. *The Superman: From Nietzche to Teilhard de Chardin*. trans. Marian Smyth-Kok. Notre Dame, University of Notre Dame Press, 1968.

Challiand, G. *Revolution in the Third World*. New York, Viking Press, 1977.

Chandler, Keith. "Modern Science and Vedic Science: An Introduction." *Modern Science and Vedic Science* (Vol. 1, No. 2, 1987).

Channakesavan, Sarasvati. *A Critical Study of Hinduism*. New Delhi, Asia Publishing House, 1974.

Collingwood, R.G. *The Idea of History*. Oxford, Oxford University Press, 1961.

Comte, Auguste. *Positive Philosophy*. trans. Harriet Martineau. London, Trubner, 1875.

————. "The Progress of Civilization through Three States." Amitai Etzioni and Eva Etzioni-Halevy, eds. *Social Change*. New York, Basic Books, 1973.

Copleston, Frederick. *A History of Philosophy* Vol. V11. London, Burns and Oates, 1963.

Coyle, Gary. *Progressive Socialism*. Calcutta, Proutist Universal Publications, 1984.

Daniel, E. Valentine. *Fluid Signs: Being a Person the Tamil Way*. Berkeley, University of California Press, 1984.

Daniel, Sheryl. "The Toolbox Approach of the Tamil to the Issues of Moral Responsibility and Human Destiny." Charles Keyes and E. Valentine Daniel, eds. *Karma*. Berkeley, University of California Press, 1983.

Dasgupta, Surendranath. *History of Indian Philosophy*. London, Cambridge University Press, 1969.

de Chardin, Teilhard. *The Future of Man*. trans. Norman Denny. New York, Harper and Row, 1964.

Der Derian, James and Shapiro, Michael, eds. *International/Intertextual Relations*. Massachusetts, Lexington Books, 1989.

Deutscher, Isaac, ed. *The Age of Permanent Revolution: A Trotsky Anthology*. New York, Dell, 1964.

Dhawan, Gopinath. *The Political Philosophy of Mahatma Ghandi*. Ahmedabad, Navajivan Publishing House, 1957.

Dirks, Nicholas. *The Hollow Crown*. Cambridge, Cambridge University Press, 1987.

Dumont, Louis. *Homo Hierarchicus*. Chicago, The University of Chicago Press, 1979.

Eisler, Riane. *Scared Pleasure: Sex, Myth, and the Politics of the Body*. San Francisco, HarperCollins, 1996.

———. *The Chalice and the Blade. Our History, Our Future*. San Francisco, Harper and Row, 1987.

Eliade, Mircia. *The Myth of the Eternal Return*. New Jersey, Princeton University Press, 1971.

Elgin, Duane. *Awakening Earth: Exploring the Evolution of Human Culture and Consciousness*. New York, William Morrow and Company, 1993.

———. *Promise Ahead: A Vision of Hope and Action for Humanity's Future*. New York, William Morrow and Company, 2000.

Elvin, Mark. *Pattern of the Chinese Past*. Stanford, Stanford University Press, 1973.

Esposito, Joseph. *The Transcendence of History*. Ohio, Ohio University Press, 1984.

Etzioni, Amitai and Halevey-Etzioini Eva, eds. *Social Change*. New York, Basic Books, 1973.

Faghirsadeh, Saleh. *Sociology of Sociology: In Search of Ibn Khaldun's Sociology*. Tehran, The Soroush Press, 1982.

Faj, Attala. "Vico's Basic Law of History in Finnegans Wake." David Verene, ed. *Vico and Joyce*. New York, State University of New York Press, 1987.

Ferguson, Marilyn. *The Aquarian Conspiracy*. Los Angeles, Tarcher, 1980.

Foucault, Michel. *Power/Knowledge*. Colin Gordon, ed. New York, New York, 1980a.

———. *The Archaeology of Knowledge and The Discourse on Language*. trans. A.M. Sheridan Smith. New York, Pantheon, 1972.

———. *The History of Sexuality*. trans. Robert Hurley. New York, Vintage Books, 1980b.

———. *The Foucault Reader*. Rabinow, Paul, ed. New York, Pantheon Books, 1984.

———. *The Order of Things: An Archaeology of the Human Sciences*. New York, Vintage Books, 1973.

Fox, Warwick. *Toward a Transpersonal Ecology: Developing New Foundations for Environmentalism*. New York, State University of New York Press, 1995.

Frank, Andre Gunder and Gills, Barry, eds. *The World System: Five Hundred Years or Five Thousand?* London, Routledge, 1996 (paperback).

Frank, Manuel and Frank, Fritzie. *Utopian Thought in the Western World*. Cambridge, The Belknap Press, 1979.

Fromm, Eric. *Marx's Concept of Man*. New York, Frederick Ungar Publishing, 1976.

Gadamer, Hans. *Truth and Method*. New York, Seabury Press, 1975.

Galtung, Johan. *Buddhism: A quest for Unity and Peace*. Honolulu. Dae Won Sa Buddhist Temple of Hawaii, 1988.

———. "How Universal Are the Human Rights?" Honolulu, Institute of Peace, 1989.

Galtung, Johan and Inayatullah, Sohail. *Macrohistory and Macrohistorians*. Westport, Ct., Praeger, 1997.

———. "On Alpha and Beta and their many Combinations," Tokyo, United Nations University, 1978a.

Galtung, Johan, Heiestad Tore and Rudeng, Eric. "On the Decline and Fall of Empires: The Roman Empire and Western Imperialism Compared." Papers. Oslo, University of Oslo, 1978b.

———. "On the Last 2500 Years in Western History: And Some Remarks on the Coming 500." Peter Burke, ed. *The New Cambridge Modern History*. Vol. 13, Companion Volume. London, Cambridge University Press, 1979.

Galtung, Johan. *Peace and Social Structure: Essays in Peace Research, Vol. 111.* Copenhagen, Christian Ejlers, 1978c.

———. "Religion as a Factor," Berlin, Wisserschaftskolleg zu Berline, 1983.

———. "Prabhat Rainjan Sarkar's Social cycles, World Unity and Peace". Speech delivered to Renaissance 2000 honoring Sarkar's 75th Anniversary, LA. October 19, 1996.

———. "Social Cosmology and the Concept of Peace," *Journal of Peace Research* (Vol. 18, No. 2, 1981a).

———. "Structure, Culture and Intellectual Style: An Essay Comparing Saxonic, Teutonic, Gallic and Nipponic Approaches." *Social Science Information* (Vol. 20, No. 6, 1981b).

Galtung, Johan and Nishimura, Fumiko. "Structure, Culture and Languages: An Essay Comparing the Indo-European, Chinese and Japanese Languages." *Social Science Information* (Vol. 22, No. 6, 1983).

Galtung, Johan. "The Green Movement: A Socio-Historical Exploration." *International Sociology* (Vol. 1, No. 1, 1986).

———. *The True Worlds.* New York, The Free Press, 1979a.

———. "Western Civilization: Anatomy and Pathology." *Alternatives* (Vol. 7, 1981a).

———. "Western Civilization in the Contraction Mode." Tokyo, United Nations University, 1979b.

Galt, Anthony and Smith, Larry. *Models and the Study of Social Change.* New York, John Wiley and Sons, 1976.

Ganguly, Tapash. "Blissful Self-Support." *The Week* (17 September 1989).

Garrison, Omar. *Tantra: The Yoga of Sex.* New York, The Julian Press, 1983.

Gasset, Jose Ortega Y. *The Revolt of the Masses.* Notre Dame, University of Notre Dame Press, 1985.

Geyl, Pieter, Toynbee, Arnold and Sorokin, Pitirim. *The Pattern of the Past: Can We Determine It?* New York, Greenwood Press, 1968.

Giddens, Anthony. *Central Problems in Social Theory.* Berkeley, University of California press, 1979.

———. *Profiles and Critiques in Social Theory.* Berkeley, University of California Press, 1982.

Gillespie, Michael Allen. *Hegel, Heidegger, and the Ground of History.* Chicago, University of Chicago Press, 1984. Gilman, Robert. "Peace and the Warrior." *In Context* (No. 20. 1989).

Goodman, Lenn. "Ibn Khaldun and Thucydides." *Journal of American Oriental Society* (Vol. 92, No. 2, 1972).

Greenberg, Edward. *Understanding Modern Government.* New York, John Wiley and Sons, 1979.

Guha, Ranajit and Spivak, Gayatri Chakravorty. *Selected Subaltern Studies.* New York, Oxford University Press, 1988.

Hansen, Marsha. "Antonio Gramsci: Hegemony and the Materialist Conception of History." Johan Galtung and Sohail Inayatullah, eds. *Macrohistory and Macrohistorians.* New York, Praeger, 1997, 128–131.

Haragovind, Acharya. "Sweet Side Lights." *The Advent* (Vol. 2, No. 4, 1978).

Harmon, Willis. *Global Mind Change.* Indiana, Knowledge Systems, 1988.

Hatley, Shaman and Inayatullah, Sohail. "Karma Samnyasa: Sarkar's reconceptualization of Indian ascetism," in K. Ishwaran, ed., *Ascetic culture: renunciation and worldly engagement* (Leiden, Brill, 1999, Vol. 73, International Studies in Sociology and Social Anthropology), 139–152.

Hawking, Stephen. *A Brief History of Time.* New York, Bantam Books, 1988.

Hedlund, Christopher. "The Pursuit of Possibilities—The 1990's and the Uranus-Neptune Conjuction." *Magical Blend* (Issue 23, 1989).

Hegel, George Wilhelm Friedrich. *Philosophy of History.* trans. J. Sibree. London, George Bell and Sons, 1888.

Heilbroner, Robert. *The Worldly Philosophers: The Great Economic Thinkers*. London, Allen Lane, 1969.

Hofstadder, Richard. *Social Darwinianism in American Thought*. New York, Brazilla, 1959.

Hook, Sidney. *The Hero in History*. New York, John Day, 1943.

Hughes, Stuart. "Gaetano Mosca and the Political Lessons of History." James Meisal. ed. *Pareto and Mosca*. New Jersey, Prentice-Hall, 1965.

Inayatullah, Sohail. "Causal Layered Analysis: Poststructuralism as Method," *Futures* (Vol. 30, No. 8, October, 1998), 815–830.

———. "Marxism and Prout." Minnesota, Renaissance Universal Institute, 1981.

———. "An Interview With Johan Galtung." *PROUT Journal* (Vol. 4, No. 1, 1989), 16–20.

———. "PROUT in the Context of Alternative Futures." *Cosmic Society* (Vol. 11, No. 17, 1988).

———. "Rethinking Science: P.R. Sarkar's Reconstruction of Science and Society," *International Foundation for Development Alternatives Dossier* (No. 81, April/June 1991), 5–16.

———. "Sarkar's Spiritual-Dialectics." *Futures* (Vol. 20, No. 1, 1988), 54–66.

———. *Situating Sarkar: Tantra, Macrohistory and Alternative Futures*. Maleny, Australia and Ananda Nagar, India, Gurukul Publications, 1999.

——— and Fitzgerald, Jennifer, eds. *Transcending Boundaries: P.R. Sarkar's Theories of Individual and Social Transformation*. Maleny, Australia and Ananda Nagar, India, 1999.

Inden, Ronald. "Orientalist Constructions of India." *Modern Asian Studies* (Vol. 20, No. 3, 1986).

Jaynes, Julian. *The Origin of Consciousness in the Breakdown of the Bicameral Mind*. Boston, Houghton Mifflin, 1982.

Joseph, Earl. "Anticipatory Sciences Research: shape of alternative futures," Futurics (Vol. 3, No. 1, 1979).

Keyes, Charles and Daniel, E. Valentine, eds. *Karma*. Berkeley, University of California Press, 1983.

Khaldun, Ibn. *The Muqaddimah*. trans. Franz Rosenthal. N.J. Dawood, ed. New Jersey, Princeton University Press, 1967.

Kinsley, David. *Hinduism*. New Jersey, Prentice-Hall, 1982.

Kohr, Leopold. *The Overdeveloped Nations*. New York, Schocken Books, 1978.

Kosambi, D.D. "A Marxist Interpretation of Indian History." K. Satchidananda Murti, ed. *Readings in Indian History, Politics and Philosophy*. London, George Allen and Unwin, 1967.

Kothari, Rajni. *Caste In Indian Politics*. New Delhi, Orient Longman, 1970.

Krishnamurti, Jiddhu. *Commentaries on Living*. Illinois, Theosophical Publishing House, 1967.

———. *The Penguin Krishnamurti Reader*. Mary Lutyens, ed. Middlesex, Penguin, 1966.

Kumar, Anil, ed. "When the Attempt to Burn Baba Alive Failed." *New Crimson Dawn*. (Vol. 13, Nos. 1–2, 1984).

Laszlo, Irwin. "Footnotes to a History of the Future." *Futures* (Vol. 20, No. 5, 1988).

Logan, Ron. "Developing Our Ideological Rationality." Palo Alto, Prout Institute, 1989.

———. "Rupert Sheldrake's Theory of Formative Causation." *Cosmic Society* (Vol. 11, No. 17, 1988).

Loye, David. *The Spinx and the Rainbow*. Boulder, Shamballa, 1983.

Mahdi, Muhsin. *Ibn Khaldun's Philosophy of History*. London. George Allen and Unwin, 1957.

Majumdar, R.C. "History in Ancient India." K. Satchidananda Murti, ed. *Readings in Indian History, Politics and Philosophy*. London, George Allen and Unwin, 1967.

Manicas, Peter. *A History and Philosophy of the Social Sciences*. Oxford, Basic Blackwell, 1987.

Mantreshvarananda, Avadhuta. "Lest We Forget." *Cosmic Society* (Vol. 12, No. 8–9, 1989).

Manuel, Frank and Manuel, Fritizie. *Utopian Thought in the Western World*. Cambridge, Belknap Press, 1979.

Marx, Karl and Engels, Frederick. *Manifesto of the Communist Party*. Peking, Foreign Languages Press, 1975.

Marx, Karl. *Capital*. Robert Hutchins, ed. Great Books of the Western World. London, Encyclopaedia Brittanica, 1952.

Masini, Eleonora, ed. *Visions of Desirable Societies*. Oxford, Pergamon Press, 1983.

Mazzola, Lars. *Right Side Up*. New York, Baltar Enterprises, 1981.

McCarthy, Harold. "An Outline of Philosophy." Honolulu, Department of Philosophy, University of Hawaii, 1973.

McKnight, Stephan. ed. *Eric Voegelin's Search for Order in History*. Baton Rouge, Louisiana State University Press, 1978.

Meisel, James, ed. *Pareto and Mosca*. New Jersey, Prentice-Hall, 1965.

Minerbi, Daniela. "Vilfredo Pareto." Johan Galtung, Sohail Inayatullah et al, eds. *Macrohistory and Macrohistorians*. Wesport, Ct. Praeger, 1997.

Mohanty, J.N. "Indian Philosophy Between Tradition and Modernity." S.S. Rama Rao Pappu and R. Pligandla, eds. *Indian Philosophy: Past and Future*. Delhi, Motilal Banarsidass, 1982.

Moore, Charles, ed. *The Indian Mind*. Honolulu, University of Hawaii Press, 1967.

Mosca, Gaetano. *The Ruling Class*. trans. Hannah Kahn. intro. Arthur Livingston. New York, McGraw-Hill, 1939.

———, "The Varying Structure of the Ruling Class." Amitai Etzioni and Eva Etzioni-Halevy, eds. *Social Change*. New York, Basic Books, 1973.

Munshi, K.M. "A Nationalist Interpretation of Indian History." K. Satchidananda Murti, ed. *Readings in Indian History, Politics and Philosophy*. London, George Allen and Unwin, 1967.

Murti, K. Satchidananda. "History: A Theist's View." K. Satchidananda Murti, ed. *Readings in Indian History, Politics and Philosophy*. London, George Allen and Unwin, 1967.

Nakamura, Hajime. *Ways of Thinking of Eastern Peoples*. Honolulu, University of Hawaii Press, 1964.

Nandy, Ashis. "Shamans, Savages and the Wilderness: On the Audibility of Dissent and the Future of Civilizations." *Alternatives* (Vol. 14, No. 3, 1989).

———. *The Intimate Enemy*. Delhi, Oxford University Press, 1983.

———. *Traditions, Tyranny and Utopias*. New Delhi, Oxford University Press, 1987.

Naseef, Abdullah, ed. *Today's Problems, Tomorrow's Solutions: Future Structure of Muslim Societies*. London, Mansell, 1988.

Nehru, Jawaharlal. "History: A Scientific Humanist's View." K. Satchidananda Murti, ed. *Readings in Indian History, Politics and Philosophy*. London, George Allen and Unwin, 1967.

Nietzsche, Friedrich. *A Nietzsche Reader*. trans. R.J. Hollingdale. Middlesex, Penguin Books, 1987.

———. *The Birth of Tragedy and The Genealogy of Morals*. trans. Francis Golfing. New York, Doubleday Anchor, 1956.

Nivison, David. *The Life and Thought of Chang Hsueh-Cheng*. Stanford, Stanford University Press, 1966.

Organ, Troy Wilson. *Western Approaches to Eastern Philosophy*. Ohio, Ohio University press, 1975.

Panikkar, K.M. "A Critical Historian's Interpretation of Indian History." K. Satchidananda Murti, ed. *Readings in Indian History, Politics and Philosophy*. London, George Allen and Unwin, 1967.

Pappu, S.S. Rama Rao and Puligandla, R., eds. *Indian Philosophy: Past and Future.* Delhi, Motilal Banarsidass, 1982.

Paprocki, Charles. "Proutist Methodology." Washington D.C., Proutist Universal Publications, 1978.

Pareto, Vilfredo. Sociological Writings. intro. S.E. Finer. trans. Derick Mirfin. New York, Praeger, 1966.

————. *The Rise and Fall of the Elites.* Intro. Hans Zetterburg. New Jersey, The Bedminster Press, 1968.

————. "The Circulation of Elites." Amitai Etzioni and Eva Etzioni-Halevy, eds. *Social Change.* New York, Basic Books, 1973.

Parker, Andrew. "Re-Marx: Deconstructive Readings in Marxist Theory and Criticism." Rhetoric of the Human Sciences Series, University of Wisconsin, 1990.

Perkings, Robert, ed. *History and System: Hegel's Philosophy of History.* Albany, State University of New York Press, 1984.

Perry, Marvin. *Arnold Toynbee and the Crisis of the West.* Washington, University Press of America, 1982.

Polak, Fred. *The Image of the Future.* trans. Elise Boulding. San Francisco, Jossey-Bass, 1973.

Polan, A.J. *Lenin and the End of Politics.* Berkeley, University of California, 1984.

Popper, Karl. *The Poverty of Historicism.* New York, Basic Books, 1957.

Prakash, Buddha. "The Hindu Philosophy of History." *Journal of the History of Ideas* (Vol. 16, No. 4, 1958).

Prasad, Hari Shankar, ed. *Time in Indian Philosophy: A Collection of Essays.* Delhi, Shri Satguru Publications and India Books Centre, 1992.

Rabinow, Paul and Sullivan, William. *Interpretive Social Science: A Reader.* Berkeley, University of California Press, 1979.

Radhakrishnan, S. "History: An Idealist's View." K. Satchidananda Murti, ed. *Readings in Indian History, Politics and Philosophy.* London, George Allen and Unwin, 1967.

————. *History of Philosophy: Eastern and Western.* London, George Allen and Unwin, 1952.

Raja, C. Kunhan. *Some Fundamental Problems in Indian Philosophy.* Delhi, Motilal Banarsidass, 1974.

Raju, P.T. *The Philosophical Traditions of India.* London, George Allen and Unwin, 1971.

Reddy, V. Narayan. "Futurism and Indian Philosophy." S.S. Rama Rao Pappu and R. Puligandla, eds. *Indian Philosophy: Past and Future.* Delhi, Motilal Banarsidass, 1982.

Rieter, Jeff. "The Trial." *Crimson Dawn* (Vol. 5. No. 9, 1976).

Roy, Ramashray, Walker, R.B.J., and Ashley, Richard. "Dialogue: Towards a Critical Social Theory of International Politics." *Alternatives* (Vol. 13, No. 1, 1988).

Rudhyar, Dane. *Astrological Timing.* New York, Harper and Row, 1969.

Sabine, George and Thorson, Thomas. *A History of Political Theory.* Illinois, Dryden Press, 1973.

Said, Edward. *Orientalism.* New York, Vintage Books, 1979.

Sardar, Ziauddin. "Against the Common Man." *Muslim World Book Review* (Vol. 9, No. 2, 1988a).

————. *Islamic Futures.* London, Mansell Publishing, 1985.

————. "Reformist Ideas and Muslim Intellectuals." Abdullah Naseef, ed. *Today's Problems, Tomorrow's Solutions: Future Structure of Muslim Societies.* London, Mansell, 1988b.

Sarkar, Prabhat Rainjan. *A Few Problems Solved.* Vols. 1–7. trans. Vijayananda Avadhuta. Calcutta, Ananda Marga Publications, 1987a.

————. "DMC Discourse." *Ananda Parviira* (October 1989).

———. *Idea and Ideology.* Calcutta, Ananda Marga, 1978a.

———. *Light Comes.* Anandamitra Avadhuta and Vijayananda Avadjuta, eds. Calcutta, Ananda Marga Publications, 1986.

———. *PROUT in a Nutshell.* Vols. 1–16. trans. Vijayananda Avadhuta. Calcutta, Ananda Marga Publications, 1987b.

———. *Subhista Samgraha.* Calcutta, Ananda Marga Publications, 1975.

———. *Supreme Expression.* Vol. 1–2. Netherlands, Nirvikalpa Press, 1978b.

———. *The Human Society.* Vol. 2. Calcutta, Ananda Marga Publications, 1967.

———. *The Liberation of Intellect—Neo Humanism.* Calcutta, Ananda Marga Publications, 1983.

———. *The Thoughts of P.R. Sarkar.* Anandamitra Avadhuta and Viyayananda Avadhuta, eds. Calcutta, Ananda Marga Publications, 1986.

———. *Universal Humanism.* Tim Anderson and Gary Coyle, eds. Sidney, Proutist Universal Publications, 1982.

Schneider, Vimala. *The Politics of Prejudice.* Denver, Ananda Marga Publications, 1983.

Shapiro, Michael, ed. *Language and Politics.* New York, New York University Press, 1984.

———. *Language and Political Understanding.* New Haven, Yale University Press. 1981.

———. *The Politics of Representation.* Madison, The University of Wisconsin Press, 1988.

———. "Interpretation and Political Understanding." in *Occasional Papers in Political Science.* (Honolulu, University of Hawaii, Vol. 1, No. 1, 1980).

———. "Literary Production as a Politicizing Practice." Michael Shapiro, ed. *Language and Politics.* New York, New York University, 1984.

———. "Politicizing Ulysses: Rationalist, Critical and Genealogical Commentaries." Department of Political Science, University of Hawaii. (January, 1988). Published in Shapiro, Michael, *Reading the Postmodern Polity: Political Theory as Textual Practice.* Minneapolis, University of Minnesota Press, 1992, 18–36.

———. "Textualizing Global Politics." James Der Derian and Michael Shapiro, eds. *International/Intertextual Relations.* Massachusetts, Lexington Books, 1989.

———. "Weighing Anchor: Postmodern Journeys from the Life World." 19th Annual Northeastern Political Science Association. (November 12, 1987). Published in Shapiro, Michael, *Reading the Postmodern Polity: Political Theory as Textual Practice.* Minneapolis, University of Minnesota Press, 1992, 37–53.

Sheldrake, Rupert. *A New Science of Life: The Hypothesis of Formative Causation.* Los Angeles, Jeremy P. Tarcher, 1981.

Shetler, Brian. "Hegel's Philosophy of History." Research paper. Honolulu, University of Hawaii, 1990. Published as: Shetler, Brian, "George Wilhelm Friedrich Hegel: Dialectics and the World Spirit," in Galtung, Johan and Inayatullah, Sohail, eds. *Macrohistory and Macrohistorians.* Westport, Ct. Praeger, 1997.

Sorokin, Pitirim. *Social and Cultural Dynamics.* Boston, Porter Sargent, 1970.

———. *Sociological Theories of Today.* New York, Harper and Row, 1966.

Spencer, Herbert. "The Evolution of Societies." Amitai Etzioni and Eva Etzioni-Halevy, eds. *Social Change.* New York, Basic Books, 1973.

Spengler, Oswald. *The Decline of the West.* trans. Charles Atkinson. New York, Alfred Knopp, 1972.

———. "The Interpretation of the Historical Process." Gregory Alban Widgery, ed. *Interpretations of History: Confucious to Toynbee.* London, Allen and Unwin. 1961.

Stalin, Joseph. *Dialectical and Historical Materialism.* New York, International Publishers, 1970.

Suzuki, Daisetz T. An Introduction to Zen Buddhism. New York, Gover Press, 1964.

Szacki, Jerzy. *History of Sociological Thought.* Connecticut, Greenwood Press, 1979.

Tarde, Gabriel. *The Laws of Imitation*. trans. Elsie Parsons. New York, Henry Holt and Company, 1903.

Thapar, Romila. *A History of India* Baltimore, Penguin Books, 1966.

———. "Society and Historical Consciousness: The Ithasa-Purana Tradition." Sabyasachi, Bhattacharya and Romila Thapar, eds. *Situating Indian History*. Delhi, Oxford University Press, 1986.

The New Encyclopaedia Britannica—Micropaedia. 15th edition, 1988. s.v. "Ibn Khaldun."

Thompson, William Irwin. *At the Edge of History*. New York, Harper and Row, 1971.

———. *Darkness and Scattered Light*. New York, Anchor Books, 1978.

———. *Evil and World Order*. New York, Harper and Row, 1976.

———. *Pacific Shift*. San Francisco, Sierra Club Books, 1985.

Timasheff, N.S. *Sociological Theory: Its Nature and Growth*. New York, Random House, 1965.

Tomovic, Vladislav, ed. *Definitions in Sociology*. Ontario, Dilton Publications, 1979.

Towsey, Michael. *Eternal Dance of Macrocosm*. Copenhagen, Proutist Publications, 1986.

———. "Some Thoughts on the Social Cycle." *Cosmic Society* (Vol. 11, No. 13, 1988).

Toynbee, Arnold. *A Study of History*. London, Oxford University Press, 1972.

Varma, Vishwanath, Prasad. *Studies in Hindu Political Thought and its Metaphysical Foundations*. Delhi, Motilal Banarsidass, 1974.

———. *The Political Philosophy of Sri Aurobindo*. New York, Asia Publishing House, 1960.

Veblen, Thorstein. *The Theory of the Leisure Class*. New York, Modern Library, 1934.

Verene, Donald, ed. *Vico and Joyce*. New York, State University of New York Press, 1987.

Vico, Giambattista. *The New Science of Giambattista Vico*. trans. Thomas Goddard Bergin and Max Harold Fisch. Ithaca, Cornell University Press, 1970.

Voegelin, Eric. *The New Science of Politics*. Chicago, University of Chicago Press, 1987.

Wagar, Warren W. "Profile of a Futurist: Arnold J. Toynbee and the Coming World Civilization." *Futures Research Quarterly* (Vol. 2, No. 3, 1986).

Walker, Barbara. *The Crone*. New York, Harper and Row, 1985.

Wallerstein, Immanuel. *Historical Capitalism*. London, Verso, 1983.

———. *The Politics of the World Economy: the States, the Movements and the Civilizations*. London, Cambridge University Press, 1984.

———. "Kondratieff Up or Kondratieff Down?" *Review* (Vol. 2, No. 4, 1979).

———. "The Capitalist World-economy: Middle-run Prospects." *Alternatives* (Vol. 14, No. 3, 1989).

———. "World System and Civilization," *Development: Seeds of Change* (Vol. 1–2, 1986).

Walsh, W.W. *Philosophy of History*. New York, Harper and Row, 1960.

Watson, Burton. *Ssu-Ma Ch'ien: Grand Historian of China*. New York, Columbia University Press, 1958.

Weber, Max. "The Role of Ideas in History." Amitai Etzioni and Eva Etzioni-Halevy, eds. *Social Change*. New York, Basic Books, 1973.

———. "The Routinization of Charisma." Amitai Etzioni and Eva Etzioni-Halevy, eds. *Social Change*. New York, Basic Books, 1973.

Weinless, Michael. "The Samhita of Sets: Maharishi's Vedic Science and the Foundations of Mathematics." *Modern Science and Vedic Science* (Vol. 1, No. 1, 1987).

Welch, Sharon. *Communities of Resistance and Solidarity: A Feminist Theology of Liberation*. New York, Orbis Books, 1985.

Widgery, Alban Gregory. *Interpretations of History: Confucius to Toynbee*. London, Allen and Unwin, 1961.

Wilber, Ken. *Sex, Ecology, Spirituality: The Spirit of Evolution.* Boston, Shambhala, 1995.
———, *The Marriage of Sense and Soul: Integrating Science and Religion.* New York, Random House, 1998.
Xie, Chang with Inayatullah, Sohail. "Ssu-Ma Ch'ien: The Cycles of Virtue." Johan Galtung, Sohail Inayatullah et al. *Macrohistory and Macrohistorians.* Westport, Ct., Praeger, 1997.
Zimmerman, Michael. "We Need New Myths," *In Context* (No. 20, 1989).

ABOUT THE AUTHOR

Author and editor of a dozen books on a variety of subjects, including Macrohistory, the Futures of the University, Futures Studies, and Communication Studies, Sohail Inayatullah holds a number of academic positions. He is Professor, Tamkang University, Taiwan; Adjunct Professor, University of the Sunshine Coast; Visiting Academic, Queensland University of Technology, Australia and Professor, the University of Action Learning. Inayatullah is fellow of the World Futures Studies Federation and the World Academy of Art and Science. He is co-editor of the *Journal of Futures Studies* and Associate Editor of *New Renaissance*. He lives in Mooloolaba, Australia and grew up in Lahore, Pakistan; Bloomington and New York, USA; Geneva Switzerland; Kuala Lumpur, Malaysia; and Honolulu, Hawaii (website: www.metafuture.org).

INDEX

Abidi, Syed: 320
the Absolute: 234
adharma: 60
Advaita Vedanta: 38
agency: 18
ahimsa: 73, 74
Aitareya-Brahmana: 101
Allah: 201
America: as land of the future according to Hegel, 236; revolution, 230
Amin, Shahid: 50
Amra Bengali: 26
analysis: types of, 289
Ananda: 39, 43, 48, 51; definition of, 341
Ananda Gaorii Avadhutika: 10
Ananda Marga: 328; naming of, 39; origins of, 18; publications, 1; The Path of Bliss, 18; underground operations, 19; Universal Relief Team, 22
Anandamitra Avadhutika: 74
Anandamurti, Shri Shri (Sarkar, P.R.): 57, 152, 9
Ananda Sutram: 53, 55
Anderson, Benedict: and imagined community, 215
Anderson, Perry: 290
Anderson, Tim: 19
Anderson, Walter Truett: *To Govern Evolution*, 240-1
anima: 52
Annamaya Kosa: 61, 62
anomie: 27
antaryamitva: 52
anti-globalization: 25
apathy: 27
Aristotle: definition of God, 234
A'ropita: 74
Arjuna: 14, 42
artist: the role of, 83
the Aryans: 133, 137, 216, 294
asabiya: 207-9; definition of, 341; relation to unity, identity and legitimacy, 209; *see also* Khaldun
Ashley, Richard: 312, 315-6, 318; "Living on Borderlines", 313;

non-place, 317; poststructuralism, 318
Asimov, Isaac: 329
Ataturk, Mustafa Kemal: 103
Atimanasa kosa: 60, 61
atman: 40, 42, 51, 72, 89, 98, 109; definition of, 341
Attraction to the Great: critique of, 299; *see also* Sarkar
Aurobindo, Sri: 25, 35, 55, 104, 106, 144; and God, 108; and the Gita model of history, 106, 110; and the Godsent leader, 110; and the Superman, 112; and Yogocracy, 112; division of ignorance and knowledge, 109; theory of the rise and decline of nations, 111
author: 48-50; postmodern, 48; the role of, 36
authority: 47
avatar: 52, 59, 62, 85; definition of, 341
avidya: 64; definition of, 341; *see also vidya*

Baba stories: 15
barbarism: 222
Barthes, Roland: "The Death of the Author", 318
Batra, Ravi: 44, 114, 192, 214, 218, 287; on Marx, 243; on Sarkar, 82; interpretation of Indian history, 115; interpretation of Sarkar's macrohistory, 96; *The Downfall of Capitalism and Communism*, 149
Beckett, Samuel: 45
Beckwith, Burnham: 228
Bedouin: 33, 190, 203, 206, 214
Being: 3, 17, 53, 54, 85, 106; Absolute, 87; and Sarkar's cosmology, 88; Supreme, 107
Bender, Frederic: 248
Bengali language: 6
Bhagavad Gita: 14, 36, 42
bhakti: 13, 38, 45, 47, 48, 53, 55, 90, 96, 110, 292 definition of, 341
Bhudan movement: 23, 159
Bjonnes, Roar: 7

INTERNATIONAL COMPARATIVE SOCIAL STUDIES

ISSN 1568-4474

1. H.T. Wilson, *Bureaucratic Representation*. Civil Servants and the Future of Capitalist Democracies. 2001. ISBN 90 04 12194 3
2. J. Rath, *Western Europe and its Islam*. 2001. ISBN 90 04 12192 7
3. S. Inayatullah, *Understanding Sarkar*. The Indian Episteme, Macrohistory and Transformative Knowledge. 2002. ISBN 90 04 12193 5